"BELOVED FRIEND"

The Story of Tchaikowsky and Nadejda von Meck

PETER ILYICH TCHAIKOWSKY

"BELOVED FRIEND"

The Story of Tchaikowsky

AND

Nadejda von Meck

BY CATHERINE DRINKER BOWEN

AND

BARBARA VON MECK

NEW YORK · DOVER PUBLICATIONS · 1946

PREFACE

After the death of Tchaikowsky and Nadejda von Meck, their correspondence was by common consent given to Nadejda's favorite grandson, Vladimir von Meck, often mentioned in the letters as Volichka. Barbara von Meck, co-author of this book, is Vladimir's widow. Modeste Tchaikowsky's biography of his famous brother, published in Russian in 1900 and later translated into English by Rosa Newmarch, contained perhaps a fourth of Tchaikowsky's letters to Nadejda von Meck. From these all revelations of intimacy had been cut, and not one letter from Nadejda included.

During the revolution of 1917, all von Meck property was seized, and with it, the correspondence. Barbara von Meck, who with her husband left Russia in 1923 to make her home in New York, heard nothing of the correspondence until the autumn of 1935, when she acquired two volumes published in Russian by the Academie Press (Soviet Government), which included the first six years of the correspondence, entire.

It is from these volumes, therefore, that we have worked. Barbara von Meck, whose knowledge of English is limited, made literal translations of the letters and gave them to me for arrangement and presentation, together with her notes and recollections of the persons and places involved. It became immediately obvious that no further effort of translation could endow these letters with a literary quality they never possessed. Profuse and repetitious as they were, the extremely interesting content had to be dug for, spaded from a mass of detail, of exclamation and nervous ecstasy which, when it reached its fifth consecutive epistolatory page, lost for history the emphasis it may have contained for its writers. Therefore I have permitted the material to fall, very often, into narrative rather than epistolatory form. All direct quotations are, of course, authentic; and for the narrative text, I have added nothing that was not already there.

C. D. B.

The authors desire here to convey their thanks to Elizabeth Sturgis, who first suggested this book be prepared, and to Frances Woodward Curtis, for her valuable editorial help.

B. V. M.
C. D. B.

CONTENTS

CONTENTS

ILLUSTRATIONS

NADEJDA VON MECK

THE TCHAIKOWSKY BROTHERS
ANATOL, NICHOLAS, HIPPOLYTE, PETER, MODESTE

TCHAIKOWSKY AND HIS WIFE

VLADIMIR VON MECK
NADEJDA'S ELDEST SON

PRELUDE

Admiration for Tchaikowsky's music is a matter of personal bias rather than cold intellectual judgment. If you like Romanticism, if your heart beats in tune to Rousseau, Heine, Chopin, Dickens, Tennyson, Kipling—if you do not feel uncomfortable at the display of the true heart upon the sleeve, if your own heart renews its strength through tears and confession rather than through reticence and swift constriction—then you love Tchaikowsky!

This is not to say that Tchaikowsky's music will not bear critical analysis. It will. Tchaikowsky was a great composer; but, you like him or you do not. He was pre-eminently of his time, his century and his country. This, be it remembered, was the Russia of Imperialism, of Romanticism; Tchaikowsky and Nadejda von Meck were the very soul of it. Patriotism and poetry walked hand in hand; the Goddess of Reason, but recently enthroned in revolutionary France, had from Russia been admired—but she failed utterly to win a Russian crown. Here, even the princes of anarchy searched out life with hopeful rich curiosity, convinced that a world might be made anew. This was the century of Russia's artistic renaissance. By the time Tchaikowsky reached forty, his country was in dangerous confusion, internationally and domestically—but this chaos carried no artistic disillusionment. Artistic convictions were strong; artistic ideals were something to fight for, to champion. And everyone had time to talk, endlessly, till sunrise, concerning death and life and love and the exciting sudden flowering of a great rich country.

This was a world filled with bitterest social injustice—even Tchaikowsky and Nadejda von Meck, to whom their Tsar was a beloved father, deplored the current social evils. But its very extravagance made this a world wildly picturesque, a soil in which it seemed nat-

ural that art should flourish. In Petersburg, the musical Nationalists—
Balakirev, Moussorgsky, Borodin, Rimsky-Korsakov—were breaking
free of operatic tradition and going back to the people for their
strength; in Germany "Wagnerism" was richly triumphant; in
France, Claude Debussy was about to burst the ancient shackles of
tonality. Everywhere, musical progress roared on, exciting, contro-
versial, carrying its especial banners high.

Tchaikowsky ignored all this. He founded no school, he inaugurated no musical cult. In his head and heart were melody, his only
care was to write that melody down. Although his use of harmony
and his orchestration were daring for his day, Tchaikowsky's spirit,
musically and emotionally, was deeply conservative; he belonged
with Chopin and the Italians far more than with Debussy. He was
indeed, the apotheosis, the culmination—almost the last stand—of the
Romantic Movement in music.

And the Romantic Movement, of late, has lost its reputation.
Among intellectuals it is the fashion to deride Romanticism. As for
Peter Tchaikowsky—say these clever talkers—his music is like the
measles. You catch it once, probably in late adolescence, and then
you are done with it. His music often sounds—say they—better than
it is; the world is long since weary of Peter Ilyich Tchaikowsky.

When I began to write this book, I wanted to refresh my memory
of Tchaikowsky's music; the above well-worn statements imbued me
with a momentary panic. With the musical world clamoring for all-
Bach concerts, all-Wagner or pre-Schubert or post-Shostakovich—
would I ever hear Tchaikowsky's music? A glance at the newspaper
reassured me. Evidently, popular definition of symphonic music dif-
fered radically from the dictum of my intellectual friends. Concert
page and radio page were peppered with Tchaikowsky's name; I
had to run to keep up with the Fourth, Fifth and Sixth Symphonies,
the *Romeo and Juliet Overtures, Francesca, Hamlet*—even the operas.
At free concerts especially, the name of Tchaikowsky was sure to be
on the program.

And then began for me a curious experience, one which I believe
any reader of Tchaikowsky's letters will also undergo. I had always

known Tchaikowsky's music; I had heard it said that his symphonies were his autobiography, so personal, so highly individualized that with every measure the composer signed his name as it were, and drew a self-portrait. Listening to these slamming cymbals, these violins soaring to abandon, this plaintive woodwind, I pictured a bearded, throbbing Slav, slim, pale with an unhealthy, Chopinesque pallor—a man foreign to us of the Western hemisphere. I loved his music, but I was not sorry the man himself was safely in another world

Then I read Tchaikowsky's letters and knew how completely I had been mistaken. Why, this was no mad Kalmuck! This was Uncle Petia, coming smiling home to his sister's door, laden with presents for his nieces and nephews. This was the man who whenever he had ten roubles considered himself too rich and gave away five; this was the man whom everyone adored because he was so much fun to be with, yet who was so shy he fled society like a person with a hidden leprosy. One couldn't find a friendlier man than this. . . .

And now I went to Tchaikowsky concerts, with Uncle Petia in my mind, and I looked fearfully at my neighbor. All my life, henceforth, hearing this man's music, I shall look fearfully at my neighbor. What if my neighbor does not like the music written by this friendly, fervent creature, this polite and generous man who suffered and even in suffering, knew how to laugh at himself? I look at my neighbor and often enough, embarrassment seizes me, because often enough I do not like this music myself. It is overloaded, it bangs and whispers, it seems suddenly to have lost all direction. . . . But wait now!—I tell my neighbor, wordlessly. It will soon pick up. Tchaikowsky was an honest artist and honesty cannot remain long in disguise. . . . Sure enough, in a moment comes the tune, a real tune, an honest tune, rhythmic, strong, born rather of earth than heaven—sweeping down upon us, sweeping us away with it. . . . He could fall far, this man, but how high, how gloriously high he could rise!

In truth this music is personal, in truth it expresses its creator—one side of him—the dark side. This music is a casting out of the demon, an exorcism by the magic art of expression. Modeste Tchaikowsky was a shrewd psychologist when he said those words about his brother's last symphonies. And indeed Peter Tchaikowsky had something to hide, had a dark spirit to cast forth and a valid reason for his shyness. Modeste had it also; what it was, the two reveal in their letters. Just now, when the music is playing, that dark spirit is very evident. It is almost as though Peter Ilyich were in the room. We know his face well, now: the blazing blue eyes, the broad brow, the expression serious, intense. He would be up in the balcony where he could not be seen, and he would be desperately shy and gloomily sure his symphony would not be understood. He would slip out, and no one would have seen him.—Oh, play well, musicians! Roar, tympani, big bass fiddles! Shout, brasses! This is not music of the soul, ethereal, other-worldly. This is not Palestrina, it is not Mozart, gay, urbane, precise. This is music of the earth, with all the heat and tides of earth. Crash, cymbals! . . . "They say my symphony is noisy," wrote Peter Ilyich from England. "Yes, it *is* noisy."

And so is life, noisy. If ever there was a living man, a man above all else human, a sinner, struggling, sweating, trembling in the ecstasy of too-sensitive nerves—forever worrying, forever repenting, filled with a furious remorse that required but one sleep to turn again to impulse and more trouble—that man was Peter Ilyich. Therefore, my neighbor, do not be ashamed of your emotion. "Weep!"—Peter Ilyich would say. "Weep well, brother, and let your conscience rest."

Peter was a sinner—but his sins were all against himself. That is why his gloomy, violent music is no refutation of his kindly nature, and it is this paradox which the letters reconcile for us. Over-sensitive, over-shy, weak of will and overwhelmingly, frighteningly strong of emotion, Peter shunned the concert hall where his music was to be performed, shunned his friends and even the people who knew and loved him best. Again and again, in his letters to Nadejda von Meck, he confessed his social incapacity, his "pathological shyness," as he called it. Yet because of this reiteration of shyness and because of the constant spectacle in the letters of a man fleeing human society, let no reader be led to picture Peter Ilyich as unattractive physically, awkward in manners, or disagreeable to meet. Perversely enough, he was the very antithesis of these things: his trouble was over-attractiveness.

over-amiability; his only social incapacity lay in a ludicrous inability to say no. Everybody liked him, everybody sought him out, and as his fame increased, attempted incognito became impossible.

Many have born witness to his charm; Rimsky-Korsakov in his memoirs says Tchaikowsky was "sympathetic and pleasing to talk to, one who knew how to be simple of manner and always speak with evident sincerity and heartiness. A man of the world in the best sense of the word, always animating the company he was in." A few years before his death, Tchaikowsky came to New York to conduct his music. Thirty years later Walter Damrosch, who had brought him there, said of him: "In all my many years of experience I have never met a great composer so gentle, so modest—almost diffident. We all loved him from the first moment—my wife and I, the chorus, the orchestra, the employees of the hotel where he lived, and of course the public." Madame Ella Eichenwald,* who sang the role of Tatiana in the first professionally staged performance of *Onegin* and who, Moscow born and bred, knew Tchaikowsky all his life, has testified that Tchaikowsky's personal charm was uncanny. "Everyone fell in love with him, women and men and children and grandmothers. A train of people used to follow him around Moscow." Asked to explain his charm, to describe any mannerism of Tchaikowsky's that she could remember—any characteristic gesture or way of bearing himself— Madame Eichenwald raised both hands helplessly and smiled. "He had no mannerisms. Not one affectation . . . I have rehearsed under many directors. Rimsky-Korsakov would roar out upon the stage and frighten us all to death. But Tchaikowsky! He would speak to us like sisters, like children, and then in a little while someone would ask, 'Where is Tchaikowsky? The rehearsal is nearly over and he has told us nothing.' And they would find him in a corner somewhere, just watching. He would say everything had been wonderful. This used to annoy Nicholas Rubinstein very much . . . Mannerisms? Tchaikowsky? He was the simplest man that ever lived."

Rameau, that wise and bold musician, once said of himself, "From

* Living now in New York City.

day to day my taste improves. But I have lost all my genius." Peter Tchaikowsky's musical taste improved very little during his fifty-three years—but he never lost his genius. A life founded on raw nerves and abnormal sexual instincts contains all the elements of tragedy, but it is impossible to brand as tragic a life of ever-increasing artistic achievement. To the day of his death Tchaikowsky grew in artistic stature and knew it—and knew also who it was that for thirteen critical years supplied unfailing nourishment for his growth; Tchaikowsky's gratitude to Nadejda von Meck was never a burden to him but a joy.

C. D .B.

"BELOVED FRIEND"

The Story of Tchaikowsky and
Nadejda von Meck

1

Rubinstein plays for the Widow von Meck

Nicholas Rubinstein, his fur hat at a careful angle, the skirts of his fur coat striking against his short legs, walked down the steps of his Conservatory and turned northward along snow-lined, dimly-lighted Moscow streets. This was December, 1876, and northward lived, on the Boulevard Rojdestvensky, the richest woman in town—the respected, musical widow of the late equally respected, energetic knight, Karl George Otto von Meck.

Fortunate, thought Rubinstein, that the widow was musical! His Conservatory was ten years old now, but it could not have lived a decade without help—substantial help—from the Boulevard Rojdestvensky. Nadejda Philaretovna had never failed him, the more remarkable in that she was such an unapproachable person. Especially since her husband's death a year ago, she had declared her intention of living as a recluse for the rest of her life; as far as Rubinstein knew, he was the only man the widow received in her house. . . . Rubinstein smiled, pressing more tightly under his arm his ever-present portfolio of music; this time it contained a composition of one of his young professors at the Conservatory. Pray the Lord the widow would like this piano transcription of the *Tempest Fantasia*. Peter Ilyich Tchaikowsky, its composer, was all of thirty-seven—only five years younger than Rubinstein himself; but unfortunately Peter Ilyich had not the Rubinstein fingers for picking up money; he was as poor as he was talented.

Rubinstein turned a corner; somebody waved a greeting and he waved back; the man could not go two steps in Moscow without bowing; he knew everybody and everybody knew him. His step was unhurried, almost languid, but even the casual observer could discern purpose behind it. There was purpose behind everything this man did, and the world was beginning to recognize it. Was his languor a

pose, his friends sometimes asked each other; was he assuming aristocratic weariness and boredom, or did his languor derive from the fact
that the man never took time to sleep? Last night, for instance, he had
not gone to bed at all; he had been at the English Club, playing cards
—and had come off far from badly. Nevertheless he had arrived at
the Conservatory this morning on the tick of nine and taught all day,
but if he was tired he would never admit it. Nobody had ever seen
Rubinstein tired, nobody had seen him rest and nobody would until they saw him in his coffin; the stupendous energy, the nervous
force of his piano playing seemed to extend to every activity of his
day, and the same could be said of his famous elder brother, Anton.

Men of magic, these Rubinsteins! Anton up in Petersburg, undeniably the first pianist of Europe—the aging Liszt was his only
rival—had founded the Petersburg Conservatory, the first music
school to exist in Russia, and had thereby revolutionized the status of
all Russian musicians. Until then, a musician in Russia had been an
ill-paid member of a third-rate theatre orchestra (there were no first-
rate orchestras) a liveried servant fiddling in a nobleman's band while
the nobleman ate his caviar; or he had been the nobleman himself
who could, as an amateur, afford the time-consuming hobby of writing never-to-be-heard operas. Sometimes the operas were good and
very good, but because written in Russian around Russian themes,
they were at the time, absolutely unacceptable. To the Russian public
of the early nineteenth century, music meant opera and opera meant
Italian prima donnas; by the 1850's even the Italian opera had been
abandoned, and in polite circles of Petersburg and Moscow, Offenbach reigned supreme.

What place for a Rubinstein in such a society? In his *Autobiography,* Anton tells the incident that first inspired him to define the status
of a musician in Russian society. Everyone in Russia was at that time
required to go to confessional once in three years. Rubinstein (both of
whose parents had been baptized Christians) presented himself at
the Kazan Cathedral in Petersburg, confessed, and walked over to

the table to have his name enrolled in the books. The deacon, writes Rubinstein, began his inquiries:

"'Your name, rank and vocation?'
'Rubinstein, artist,' I said.
'Are you employed in the theatre?'
'No.'
'Then perhaps you give lessons in some school?'
'I do not,' I replied.
"The deacon appeared surprised, but no more so than I. We both remained silent.
'I am a musician, an artist,' I repeated.
'Yes, I understand, but are you in the government service?'
'I told you I was not.'
'Who are you then? How shall we describe you?'
"For several minutes the questioning went on. I know not how it would have ended had it not occurred to the deacon to say—
'May I ask your father's profession?'
'A merchant of the second guild.'
'No, then, we understand!' exclaimed the deacon, greatly relieved. 'You are the son of a merchant of the second guild, and as such we shall inscribe your name.'
"These questions and the careful definition of my social position left an indelible impress upon my mind. Evidently the name and estate of a musician, universally acknowledged in other lands, had in Russia no clearly defined meaning. Who was Glinka after all? A landowner, a nobleman in the government of Smolensk? Serov? An official in the Post Office Department. . . . In fact, all who had to do with music, whether as performers or composers, were either noblemen, government officials, attachés of the theatre, or pedagogues in public or private schools, etc. Was it possible that a man who had adopted music for his profession had no recognized position in Russia as a musician pure and simple?"

Anton determined to found an institution in which a musician might win the degree of Bachelor of Music, a title similar to that bestowed by the Petersburg Academy of Fine Arts upon painters, sculptors and architects. The Grand Duchess Helena Pavlovna, ever-kind goddess of the arts, approved the scheme, lent her house, gave her enthusiasm and, what was more, her money . . . ("Ah, money," wrote Anton, "that nerve of every artistic enterprise!")

Thus the Petersburg Conservatory was founded, and Peter Tchaikowsky, a young man of twenty, was one of its first pupils.

The school grew fast, too fast for Anton's taste. The Academy of Fine Arts possessed the privilege of military exemption for its students, and when the Grand Duchess procured a like privilege for the new Music School, young men with not a spark of talent flocked to Anton's door for enrollment. The place became a music factory and Anton was disgusted. He called his younger brother, then a student at the Moscow University, a night's journey to the south. "Nicholas," said Anton, "there is more than one city in Russia. Open a music school in Moscow, and mind you do not repeat my mistakes."

So with cool, characteristic audacity the brothers divided Russia between them. Free Artist, the title read upon the graduation diploma of their students. Free Artist, professional musician—synonymous terms, new and so very significant! Having battled for these titles with all the spirit of crusaders, the Rubinsteins emerged from the fight with every trace of timidity gone—autocrats, indeed, of musical Russia. They bore victory proudly; in appearance Anton had the head of a lion, within him the spirit of lion-into-fox. And in spirit his brother Nicholas resembled him. Handsome creatures the two of them, charming, audacious, unscrupulous. Anton, shaking his brown mane over the piano keys, Nicholas, cool, elegant, arranging his coat tails upon the piano stool—a very fury of talent lay within these two, a magnetism, a surety that brought all Europe to their feet. And Europe of the day needed skillful persuasion to accord any honor whatever —artistic, political or intellectual—to any son of the Russian bear. Savages, these Russians, dressed in bearskins, eaters of tallow candles —so the word went round in Paris, Vienna, Berlin. The Rubinsteins heard it and laughed, going softly, easily, implacably about their business.

Nicholas went easily now, through the Moscow streets to knock upon the door of the widow von Meck; against the snow his steps were noiseless. Brother Anton, thought Nicholas, would approve this mission; it was Anton who had sent Peter Tchaikowsky down from Petersburg ten years ago as a candidate for the professorship of musical theory in the new Moscow music school. Trust Anton to know a musician; Nicholas himself was a stern judge of men, but never so scornfully intolerant of mediocrity as his brother. . . .

Dogs barked through the cold dusk; on winter afternoons the dark comes early to Moscow. . . . Dogs barked, chimes from a hundred church steeples boomed beneath the cheerful jingle of troika bells. Horses' hooves were muffled on the snow that, for months to come, would mute all sound. And by this winter-quiet and by these bells and barkings a Muscovite, though blinded, knew himself at home. This was Imperial, Orthodox Russia, every house had its watch dog which sat at the gate before the courtyard; Sharik, Drujok or Sultan, they would descend from owner to owner when the house changed hands. This was Moscow, where one lived in the house one's grandfather lived in, and was served by the sons of one's father's servants. . . .

Not that Nicholas Rubinstein had had servants born in his house. Far from it. Nor was he a Muscovite by right of birth; he belonged neither to the rich and respected Moscow merchant class nor to the aristocracy whose quarter of the city he was at the moment traversing. He belonged nowhere, Nicholas Grigorievich; although born to the Christian religion he was a Jew, essentially homeless. A Jew and a Free Artist, this man, but he loved Moscow none the less, with its pleasant Bohemian artistic life, and felt himself rightfully a part of it. He often told his friends he could never endure to live in that stiff Petersburg atmosphere with his brother Anton. Everybody in apartments instead of big comfortable houses, fog over the streets from November till May, and from Tsar to cab driver, social lines drawn in bands of steel! Here in Moscow everything was different; winter was clear and cold and the snow was beautiful; night and day the streets were gay with sleighbells. Social circles over-lapped here, formed into groups by some mutual interest such as politics or art. In Moscow's famous restaurants—*Praga, The Hermitage, The Yar,* every night friends pledged each other and drank deep, while gypsy orchestras played and sang. . . . A toast to the new symphony, or the new play or the new picture! . . . Drinking was an art in Moscow of the seventies. So was eating, but then Moscow made an art of

everything and, drunk or sober, took its arts seriously. To the Muscovite of that day, a first performance was a vital question; he and his
neighbor would quarrel to the death over a symphony or a picture.
But there was one cause that could resolve any feud, unite on occasion
every social circle—the honor and glory of one's own beloved city
against the snobbish and fancied superiority of the Petersburgers.
Also, Moscow spoke, literally, one language—professor at the University and cabman in the street—the old Russian, without foreign words,
not diluted with affected gallicisms like the bastard Petersburg
tongue. . . .

Rubinstein spoke it now, in greeting to the old porter at Nadejda
von Meck's gate. As he crossed her courtyard the bell still jangled
from his vigorous pull, but old Sultan soon ceased his barking. This
was a visitor well known to the household. A liveried servant opened
the door, a footman seized his hat and coat—but they did not seize
the Rubinstein portfolio. That remained under his arm as Rubinstein
made his way to the drawing-room. And from front door to drawing-
room was no unimpressive journey. The great hall was dark, lighted
only by one small oil lamp; the long drawing-room was dim too and
a footman went ahead to light more lamps. In one corner was Nadejda's small pianino; the big Steinway was at the far end of the room
and Rubinstein made his way toward it through a forest of gilded
chairs, brocaded sofas, bronze cupids prancing upon little tables.
Heavy velvet curtains were drawn against the city night; on the walls
painted Venuses reclined in gilded frames; a bronze Mercury supported a mantel clock that, even as Rubinstein entered, told the hour
of five in polite, controlled Parisian accents.

Indeed, all the furniture was from Paris, made to the widow's order
as was the lapis-encrusted table upon which Rubinstein placed his
portfolio. By its side was a handsome red morocco writing case,
stamped in gold with the widow's initials; and stamped above the
initials with a large gold fleur-de-lys. The Rubinstein eye, lighting
upon this emblem, showed a sardonic gleam. The von Mecks had a
right to the lily; their coat-of-arms contained it; if the effect was a
shade too royal—never mind. The widow did as she pleased and the

lily was everywhere visible; on embroidered sofa cushions, on table covers and linen, and bravely stamped upon the very notepaper that had given Rubinstein permission to come here this afternoon.

And none of this escaped the clear and merciless Rubinstein eye— that eye which is the privilege and the curse of the man who is born an Outsider.

Nadejda von Meck, descending the stairs in a rustle of stiff black silk, was well aware that her visitor had not come this afternoon without a purpose—and Rubinstein knew she was aware of it. These two understood one another, but this did not mean they trusted one another. Too well each knew the world and the hardness of the world. Unlike Rubinstein, Nadejda had been born to wealth and social position—but she was not born to the wealth that supports it. There had been a time when the young wife fed her growing family upon twenty kopeks a day. She was therefore in a sense as self-made as Rubinstein, and her pride, her imperiousness, had fed upon the same fierce necessity, the same restless refusal to remain underdog.

Despots, the two of them, equal as sparring partners. Only one thing could put the widow off her guard: Music! This was a woman painfully reserved yet deeply, passionately musical in the Russian manner that loses itself completely in sound. Music acted upon her with physical force—made her ill, made her well—caused her to tremble from head to foot until she could not stand. But only certain kinds of music. . . . Rubinstein went to the piano. Would his purpose succeed, he wondered? Would the widow be pleased by *The Tempest,* and help his pupil?—(How Rubinstein loved to gamble!)

Without apology Nadejda moved swiftly away; Rubinstein knew her habit of listening to music from the adjoining room, alone and in darkness. . . . The magic fingers touched the keys—

There was a moment's silence after the music ceased, before a rustle and sweep of silk announced the widow's entrance. One hand was against her breast, her eyes as she faced the light were shining, her color high. Rubinstein looked at her, and knew that the day was won. Nevertheless he chose carefully his answers to her eager questioning. Who wrote this music that had color beyond all symphony she had ever heard, and that beyond all symphony seemed so strangely personal to her? It militated nothing against Peter Tchaikowsky for Nadejda to learn that he was a gentleman—not born nor bred to the ranks of professional musicianship. Nadejda had always shown scant sympathy for the jealousies and intrigues of Moscow musical life. Peter Ilyich, Rubinstein told her, was a Petersburger, a graduate of the School of Laws; his father was a government inspector of mines. As a boy, Peter had great love for music and learned to play the piano, but he showed no unusual talent. Even in young manhood his essential quality had not appeared; he was a dilettante in law as well as in art; idle, indeed, to the point of frivolity. He had been twenty-two before, influenced by a musical friend, he entered Anton Rubinstein's newly opened Petersburg Music School. But, once introduced to music, he had seized upon it with an extraordinary grip; he was like a man starving who learns for the first time the name of bread. Counterpoint was bread; musical theory, composition were bread to a young man who until now had thought music meant salon pieces to be played on the piano at evening parties. His progress had been amazing; a year after his enrollment as student at the Conservatory, Peter Ilyich resigned his post at the Ministry of Justice and resolved to become a musician.

A daring step for a young man with no private income! But Anton Rubinstein believed in him; Nadejda von Meck did not need to be reminded that to any young musician, a word from Anton Rubinstein was like a word from God. For the ensuing four years Peter had kept himself alive somehow without asking aid from his father; after all, Ilya Tchaikowsky had bought his son one career—the law—and there remained three younger brothers to educate. Peter found piano pupils, Anton Rubinstein gave him a small post at the Conservatory. But

Peter's struggle with poverty had been acute, many times he almost surrendered and returned to the safety of a government law position; once he nearly accepted a post as inspector of meat.

All this, Nicholas Rubinstein told the widow as the two faced each other in her drawing-room on the Boulevard Rojdestvensky. Of course, he added, Tchaikowsky's situation had been easier since he came to Moscow; he, Nicholas Grigorievitch, had seen to it that the young man had a roof over his head and enough to eat. If Rubinstein did not add that he had more than once given Peter Ilyich the clothes off his own back—a dress-coat for parties, a dozen shirts, a new frock-coat from the tailor's—he did not add either that the Conservatory had worked this young man cruelly. Long, grinding hours of teaching musical theory, day after day for ten years; for himself Rubinstein could weather such a life, varied as it was by triumphant concert tours —but unlike Peter Ilyich, Rubinstein was not torn from within, day and night, by a desperate urge to create music of his own. . . .

No need, of course, to confess all this to the widow; Rubinstein chose his words well. He told her of the young man's spirit and talent, and of how these things had triumphed over the inconvenience of his birth. It had been by no means easy to induce the directors of the Moscow Conservatory to accept as professor of musical theory a young man—a gentleman at that—with only two years' conservatory training. What was a mere two years, compared with the youth-long grind of most serious musicians? Also, the Petersburg School of Laws was admittedly a gentleman's school, and what snob, what amateur, ever had under his skin the makings of a serious musician? (Neither of the Rubinsteins ever consented to admit the Petersburg Five *—all of whom had salaried government positions—to what they considered the ranks of serious musicianship.)

Himself a graduate of the Moscow University, Nicholas Rubinstein took a broader view of these matters than his brother Anton, whose life since infancy had been that of a musical prodigy—music and nothing but music. . . . Nevertheless, the fact of being a gentleman

* The Nationalist Circle, Balakirev, Cui, Borodin, Moussorgsky and Rimsky-Korsakov.

had its drawbacks—did the wicked Rubinstein eyebrow lift as he said it? Peter Ilyich was a worker and a musician, but he was not a pusher; infernally proud and infernally shy, he would go in rags rather than ask for charity. Would Nadejda Philaretovna, who had helped so many musicians, care to give the author of *The Tempest* a musical commission—something he could work for and feel that he had earned?

Rubinstein ceased speaking; the widow was on her feet, her dark eyes eager, alight with a glow which those who saw it never failed to remark. . . . She shook her head gently, and smiled. "Nicholas Grigorievitch," she said, "I am immensely interested in all you have told me about this young man. But you need not have argued so eloquently in his behalf. His music spoke, before you."

2

Nadejda Philaretovna Frolowsky von Meck

RUBINSTEIN had asked for little. Had he known all that was eventually to be given, had he for a moment suspected the sacrifice this introduction would one day cost his beloved Conservatory, he would have flung *The Tempest* into Nadejda's porcelain stove rather than let her hear it. For it was Tchaikowsky's *music* with which the widow fell in love and continued in love; let there be no mistake about that. "For several days after hearing your *Tempest*," she wrote Tchaikowsky, "I was in a delirium from which I could not emerge." She never met the man who wrote *The Tempest*, never spoke with him face to face, but for the rest of her life she had only to hear his music to be thrown into all the transports of love.

We do not know what music she first commissioned Tchaikowsky to write that winter of 1876—but we know her reaction to it. Her brief note of acknowledgment is conventional enough in phraseology, but one senses beneath its single paragraph a very volcano of emotion. There is nothing extravagant upon this crested page, nor in her next note to him; why then, was the widow so fearful lest Tchaikowsky would laugh? Her very trepidation shows plainly what she would have liked to write, and how carefully, how thriftily she guided a pen that longed to betray her to a stranger.

Nadejda Philaretovna to Peter Ilyich

Moscow, Dec. 30, 1876

"Gracious Sir, Peter Ilyich:

"Permit me to express sincere thanks for the speedy execution of my commission. To tell you into what ecstasies your composition sent me would be unnecessary and unfitting, because you are accustomed to the compliments and homage of those much better qualified to speak than a creature so musically insignificant as I. It would only make you smile. I have experienced so precious a delight that I could

29

not bear to have anyone find it ridiculous, so I shall content myself with asking you to believe absolutely that your music makes my life easier and pleasanter to live."

The composer's reply:

Moscow, Dec. 30, 1876

"Gracious Lady, Nadejda Philaretovna,

"I am sincerely grateful for the kind and flattering words that you were good enough to write me. To a musician, with all the disappointments and failures that obstruct his path, it is a comfort to know there is a small minority of people like yourself who truly and warmly love our art."

Several months later Peter Ilyich received and executed another commission, and the widow wrote him again:

Moscow, Feb. 27, 1877

"Gracious Sir, Peter Ilyich,

"Truly I do not know how to thank you for your kind indulgence of my impatience. If it were not for my deep sympathy toward you, I should fear that you would spoil me. My great appreciation of your kindness prevents any such reaction.

"I should like very much to tell you at length of my fancies and thoughts about you, but I fear to take your time, of which you have so little to spare. Let me say only that my feeling for you is a thing of the spirit and very dear to me. So, if you will, Peter Ilyich, call me erratic, perhaps even crazy, but do not laugh—it could be funny if it were not so sincere and real."

Peter Ilyich to Nadejda Philaretovna

Moscow, Feb. 28, 1877

"Gracious Lady, Nadejda Philaretovna,

"Permit me to thank you for the generous recompense, too lavish for such a little work.

"Why did you hesitate to tell me all your thoughts? I assure you I should have been most interested and pleased, as I in turn feel deeply sympathetic toward you. These are not mere words. Perhaps I know you better than you imagine.

"If, some happy day, you will do me the honor of writing me what you have so far withheld, I shall be very grateful. In any case, thank you from my heart for the sympathy that I very, very much appreciate."

Tell me all your thoughts . . . perhaps I know you better than you imagine. . . . Had the widow followed her heart, she would have seized her pen then and there and told her thoughts. But she was a wise woman as well as an ardent one, and she waited three weeks before she permitted herself to answer. A bitter school had taught her the dangers of impulsive action; it was not without reason that she had lately decided upon the life of a recluse. Persons at the same time autocratic and impulsive, dare not expose themselves continually to the world. . . .

Nadejda waited three weeks, and then told Peter Ilyich what she had longed to tell him. But before displaying a document so extravagant and so spontaneous, it would seem kinder to examine its author further, that we may know from what stem sprang this strange life that lived itself out in such a maze of contradiction—that ran suddenly from the world to the shelter of domestic walls, preserving behind these walls, the imperious urge of its own individuality—a life that at the end was to turn from bravery and free-thinking, to abject fear and the defeated, tortured conscience of invalidism.

Nadejda Philaretovna was born in 1831. Her father, Philaret Vasilievitch Frolowsky, was a landed gentleman and a district judge; her mother Anastasia, born Potemkin, was descended from a cousin of that Prince of the Tauride, Gregory Potemkin, famous lover of Catherine the Great.

Like mother, like daughter: Nadejda's mother is described as a woman of great force; her father, according to Barbara von Meck, was a "quiet man who played the violin." The domestic picture is not difficult to reconstruct, but if it was the maternal line—the Potemkin inheritance—that gave almost masculine power to Nadejda Philaretovna, the quiet father gave her something of even more importance to this particular history—a love of music. As a little girl she would listen for hours while her father played his violin; when she and her sister grew older the parts were reversed, Philaret loved to listen while his daughters played duets upon the pianoforte—new and wonderful instrument imported from Germany, and so much more powerful than the harpsichord of his youth! Did the quiet Philaret, taking out his fiddle, sigh sometimes when his forceful elder daughter accompanied him upon this loud instrument of percussion?

But when at seventeen the daughter married Karl George Otto von Meck, the unequal domestic scene was not re-enacted. Quietness was not a distinguishing characteristic of the tribe von Meck. Proud Teutonic knights of Riga, they were accustomed to command. After her husband's death, Nadejda often expressed herself concerning the institution of marriage; she left no doubt that to her it was a necessary but highly distasteful business. "It is a pity," she once wrote Tchaikowsky, "that one cannot cultivate human beings artificially, like fishes; people would not then need to marry, and it would be a great relief."

But there was nothing artificial about the reproductive capacities of Nadejda and Karl George Otto; twelve children blessed the household von Meck. As antidote for super-forceful wives, what more effective treatment could be devised?

Six sons and six daughters—Nadejda did everything with style. And she was far from being daunted by child-bearing and child-rearing; here was a wife who found time for more than that, much more. Tchaikowsky's was not the only career this woman saved. One crucial day, early in their married life, Karl George, talented, powerful visionary that he was, stood hesitant between the paths of safety and adventure. The risk was great; poverty was plainly ahead and black uncertainty; Karl George went where his wife directed; it was the way of adventure and it was the way of triumph. Let Nadejda tell her own story as she told it later in a letter to Tchaikowsky:

"I have not always been rich,"—she wrote—"The greater part of my life I was poor, very poor indeed. My husband was an engineer in the Government Service, with a salary of 1500 roubles a year—which was all we had to live on, with five children and my husband's family on our hands. Not a brilliant prospect, as you see! I was wet-nurse, governess and dressmaker to my children and valet to my husband; the housekeeping was entirely in my hands; naturally there was plenty of work, but I did not mind that. It was another matter which made life unbearable. Do you know, Peter Ilyich, what it is to be in the Government Service? Do you know how, in that case, a man must forget that he is a reasonable being, possessed of will-power and honorable instincts, and must become a puppet, an automaton? It was this I found so intolerable that finally I implored my husband to send in his resignation. To his remark that if he did so we should starve, I replied that we could work and that we should not die of hunger. When at last he yielded to my desires, we were reduced to living upon twenty kopeks a day for everything. It was hard, but I never regretted for a moment what had been done."

"My husband's family on our hands." To this estate were the knights of Riga fallen! Every Russian history mentions the Teutonic knights, Germans who ventured north and conquered the Baltic provinces many centuries before Nadejda Philaretovna was born. Karl George Otto was the eldest son of the most ancient branch of the family von Meck, knights of Riga. A luxurious life ate up his father's patrimony; the estate Zunzel, which had been in the family for centuries, had to be sold. Karl George was a very small boy when his father died, and he was a small boy without a penny. The nobility of Riga, true to their caste, paid for his education, but when he had finished college and wanted further education, it needed another, more inward nobility to carry him on. The School of Engineering was in Petersburg, one hundred miles to the east; Karl George had no money for the fare. But he was a knight of Riga, and he had spirit, and he walked to Petersburg.

When his engineering education was completed he was given a position near Smolensk. There he met Nadejda Philaretovna, and Nadejda, eager, at seventeen, to fly the nest, eager—according to her nature—for life—married this northerner. They moved from place to place as the husband's work demanded. Nadejda bore a new child in five new towns before she persuaded her man to abandon the hopeless routine of Government Service. His engineering talent was more than talent, it was vision. His map of Russia, with all the railroads of the future traced upon it according to his judgment and imagination, is even today the pride and treasure of the Kazan Railroad. It existed, at least, at the beginning of the Revolution and the workmen were very proud of it. They would point with their fingers: "You see? As he planned, so has it been built."

Nadejda soon found that with all his talent, her husband was anything but a business man. He was utterly unable to forecast an estimate of work and therefore to bargain a contract. On his first engineering venture he lost every cent of his savings and his wife's dowry besides. This was too much for Nadejda Philaretovna. True daughter of her mother, she seized the reins of government; from then on she managed the business part of her husband's work, leaving him free for engineering designs and projects. With her help he built a railroad from Moscow to Riazan; his sons Vladimir and Nicholas in turn extended it across the Volga to Kazan and eventually still further eastward to the Ural Mountains.

Karl George died in his fifties; he left his wife a large fortune, two railroads and twelve children, the eldest of whom, Vladimir, was twenty-four. One of the roads, the widow sold, the other—the Moscow-Riazan—Vladimir managed with her.

This was her favorite son, her darling, and Vladimir deserved the title. Such a woman could choose as favorite son none other than a creature of sparkle, of vitality and style, with a force of personality equal to her own. Her relationship with this son was to influence not only her own life but Tchaikowsky's. It is well therefore to pause for a closer acquaintance with Vladimir, with his wife and son Vladimir II—the "Volichka" so affectionately mentioned in Nadejda's letters. . . .

Karl George's eldest son was as talented as the father, although Vladimir's gifts followed social and executive lines, rather than engineering or map-making. This was the only private railroad in Russia, and Vladimir managed it paternally. In love with his railroad, he knew every man on it from the humblest watchman up, remembered their names and the names of their wives and children, and on his tours of inspection, enchanted everybody by asking after them. This was a time and a land where loyalty between employer and employee was not a thing to be ashamed of—the workmen adored Vladimir. He had the dramatic quality possessed by all persons of great charm; what he did, he did with style. His mother, as shy as she was proud, could never, for instance, have equalled his manner of dealing with the arrogant house of Rothschild.

The railroad needed a big loan, and in the Europe of 1870 a big loan was synonymous with the name of Rothschild. Vladimir went to Paris to get the money, and with him went one—just one—book-keeper from the railroad. The Paris House of Rothschild was ex-tremely snobbish; it dealt not with individuals, but with govern-ments, and it dealt through secretaries. But this being the son of that von Meck who had built and owned a railroad, the banker decided to make exception and grant him an interview. The evening before the day fixed for the audience, Rothschild sent a messenger round to ask how many secretaries Mr. von Meck had brought with him.

Vladimir asked the messenger why he wanted to know, and the man replied that Mr. Rothschild wished to prepare chairs for the audience.

"How many secretaries has Mr. Rothschild?" Vladimir asked.

"Six."

Vladimir did not hesitate. "I have twelve," he said.

Next morning the son of Nadejda Philaretovna walked into the office of the House of Rothschild. He was dressed faultlessly in morn-ing coat and striped trousers, and he was not alone. Behind him walked his bookkeeper and eleven faithful friends, perfect secretaries, who stood or sat as occasion demanded.

And if this man knew how to uphold his authority abroad, against a Rothschild—he carried the banner even higher at home. His man-ner of living was as lavish as his nature. He knew how to spend money, did Vladimir; he had never lived, as had his parents, upon ten cents a day. Tablecloths to serve a hundred and forty—Barbara von Meck, who inherited them, says they were well-worn from use. He had the first electricity in Moscow, which meant a generator in the house, and an electrician to run it. He had also a very young, very black-eyed wife who could spend money as lavishly as he. When her son Vla-dimir II was born his mother was only sixteeen; to her the baby was but another toy. Fortunately, the baby's grandmother, Nadejda **von** Meck, adored her new grandson. His young mother would leave Volichka in Grandmamma's great gloomy house and run joyfully to Paris for new gowns. Already she was known as the best-dressed woman in Moscow; she never wore the same dress twice and during a particularly important evening would sometimes go upstairs and change.

But Paris dresses cost money, then as now. The young mother would come home to Russia with ten full trunks and an empty purse; then she would sit down and write to her mother-in-law: "Pay my bills, or give me back my son!"

The bills were always paid.

Her husband's country estate was near Borodino Field, where Napoleon was defeated in 1812. The Province made Vladimir Marshal of the Nobility, the Tsar made him Gentleman of his Court. Up to Petersburg went Vladimir and presented himself in full dress according to custom: the Palace lackeys reached out a hundred hands. Presentation tips never amounted to more than fifty roubles, but this time eyes gleamed, white silk calves trembled—between throne room and carriage door Vladimir had scattered five thousand roubles.

Such was Nadejda's eldest and favorite son, a man possessing a social audacity to equal her own almost pathological shyness—but a man whose inward spirit was no stronger, no more autocratic than her own. Had Nadejda but possessed, along with her desperate inward determination, a social elasticity equal to her son's, this story—Tchaikowsky's story—might have had a happier ending.

When Karl George died, his widow did not drift for a day; characteristically, she sat down and mapped her course. Now that wifedom was to make no further social demands upon her, she could indulge her shyness—the furious, uncontrollable shyness of a spirit desperately ambitious. Shielded by a widow's mourning, she kept to her house for the rest of her life, seeing no one but her children. This was, however, no harsh retreat, the widow had as many houses as she had children. Besides her house in Moscow, she owned a huge country estate—Brailov, in the Ukraine, and villas on the French Riviera or wherever she chose to spend the winter season. Since young woman-hood she had been subject to colds, by the time Tchaikowsky appeared she was threatened with tuberculosis. She was, therefore, continually on the move, a homesick fugitive from the long terrible winters of her native land. Emotional by nature, subject to alternate fits of exaltation and depression, there is little doubt that incipient tuberculosis, with its frequent colds and racking three-day headaches, exhausted her and deepened her tendency to depression.

When she became acquainted with Tchaikowsky in 1876, an army of people lived in the widow's house; seven of her twelve children were still at home, one had died in infancy. Her married daughter, Countess Bennigsen, often visited her, as did Vladimir—Volichka was not born until 1877. Nadejda was a Muscovite as all her father's family had been, and she loved her city as Tchaikowsky learned to love it.

Nicholas Rubinstein was in truth the one exception to the widow's rule of personal invisibility; she went nowhere except to concerts, where she sat alone in the balcony, preserving her incognito as far as possible. This shyness was to prove a great bond between herself and Tchaikowsky; he could understand it because he was so shy himself —although his avoidance of people sprang from a different—and far healthier source. The two often confessed the crazy things they had done to avoid people, the wild flights they had made from visitors . . . "I can challenge you," Nadeja once wrote Tchaikowsky, "as to which of us has more stories about our shyness. I am positive I shall win, first because I am older than you, and second, because I have severed relations with the world so completely that I never speak to people in hotels and shops; everywhere I go, I pretend not to understand the language. Once in Russia—and in our own native tongue—somebody asked me right out if I was Madame von Meck, and I said, No, I was not, there must be some mistake."

Nadejda's shyness cannot be explained wholly by her illness and frequent nervous fatigue. One is tempted to see another reason. She liked to have her own way; indeed, liked is too feeble a word. She *required* her own way, and surrounded herself only with those who would give it to her. She ruled her childrens' lives in every detail; as they grew up she arranged their marriages, bought houses for them and furniture for the houses; they were not always grateful. She consented to know her daughters-in-law and sons-in-law—but not their respective families. When she invited her married children to visit her, it was a command—and it was obeyed.

An army of servants surrounded this matriarchy; lackeys, footmen, estate stewards. English governesses for her children, German and French tutors—and above all, music teachers. The more she repudiated an ungrateful world, the more feverishly the widow desired music. She always had a musician living in the house to teach her children, or, when the children were away at school, to play duets with her. The list is long, from Danilchenko the Moscow cellist to Claude Debussy himself who came to her from Paris ("My Bussyk," she called him in her letters; "My little Parisian"). Her daughter Julia married one of these musicians, the Polish violinist Vladislav Pahulsky who worshipped Tchaikowsky and acted so often as messenger between the two.

We have, thus far, the picture of a woman intense and dominating; let no reader be led into the error of thinking her masculine. She was anything but masculine; her very quality of decisiveness had in it something captious—arbitrarily feminine. She was tall and low-voiced; she moved slowly, with poise and grace—the Russian word "swimmingly" has no English equivalent. Her dark eyes were thoughtful, quick to kindle; her grand-daughter-in-law, Barbara, describes these eyes as the center and soul of Nadejda Philaretovna's personality. Her dark hair was long and abundant; every morning her maid Lucretia combed and brushed it—part of the important ritual of preparing her mistress for the day. No trespassers were allowed in her room until the hair-brushing and facial massage were done—none, that is, until Vladimir II * came into her life. Volichka loved to watch the massaging machine, and his grandmamma loved to watch

---

* Vladimir II, affectionately known as Volichka, was the little boy who would some day, with his wife Barbara, inherit the letters between his grandmother and Tchaikowsky.

Volichka. One cannot but admire the eloquence of Russian diminutives. Ludmilla, youngest von Meck daughter, was called Milochka; Nicholas was Kolia, Vladimir I was Volodia, Vladimir II was Volichka. Tchaikowsky's brother Anatol was Tolia, Modeste was Modia, Alexandra was Sasha. The reader had best devise his own system for recognizing these nicknames; most of them are based on the last syllable of the original name.

After the hair-dressing and massage were accomplished, Lucretia, who had been with her mistress for many years, would take up her position outside the apartment door in a large armchair, a table beside her. There she would knit, a sentry in bonnet, huge white apron, and shawl. No one could pass unsummoned, not even the mistress' own children—excepting again, the two Vladimirs. Like all despots, Nadejda was shameless in her partiality. Behind this guarded door Nadejda von Meck sat in flowing peignoir and wrote her letters. Her sitting-room, was furnished lavishly, in the French style, and every inch of wall and tables was covered with framed photographs of her family. Over the writing table hung a portrait of Louis of Bavaria, one of Nadejda's correspondents. Nadejda had ordered the portrait from Kaulbach and had paid for it, Louis had graciously consented to pose, and with a magnificent royal disregard for the ridiculous, had chosen the white cloak of Lohengrin.

Periodically, Nadejda von Meck inspected her house. It was a tour; her eldest servants accompanied her from cellar to roof, and from cellar to roof the household trembled. This was a woman who was never idle; idleness for matrons was not the prevailing fashion, also, idleness was contrary to the habit of her own former active life and to her nature. String was saved for her to untangle and wind, books were bought so that she might cut the pages. She purchased quantities of wool which she would wind into balls and send to her daughter, Countess Bennigsen. And while she did these things, Julia would read to her. Julia had been *summoned* to read to her, and Julia loved to obey her mother's command. Of Julia, her third and favorite daughter, Nadejda Philaretovna demanded everything—and got it.

But a tyrant is lonely. There were many to obey Nadejda von

Meck, few to love her. Julia loved her, Volichka her grandson was to love her—to the credit of both Julia and Volichka: love for a tyrant in whose house one lives requires both gentleness and strength. But Volichka was as yet unborn. The widow needed, craved, the love of an equal; so passionate a nature can be satisfied with nothing less. More than an equal; Nadejda wanted a god to worship. Karl George had been her equal, she had made a great man of him, and in the process, had somehow lost her God. She was an atheist; this in itself was not unusual in aristrocratic Russia of the 1870's. Nadejda's atheism and her independence of God and society, so repeatedly professed in her letters to Tchaikowsky, are worth remark as a key to understanding what happened later. Such fury of independence is not always an attribute of the healthy being; genuine independence does not need so much protesting. She liked to call herself a "realist"; Tchaikowsky was nearer the point when he translated her realism as "idealism." Nadejda was a romantic idealist, with all the romanticist's desperate need of a god. The time was to come when this woman would call upon heaven and cringe before man, when a truly pathologic remorse would cause her to break with all that was dearest to her. But just now, and for the ensuing thirteen years, she called upon no one and nothing but Peter Ilyich Tchaikowsky and the music he evoked.

For Nadejda, in that winter of 1876, circumstance was ripe for this new friendship. Her husband was dead, she had money—a very large amount—and busy though she was with household and financial affairs, her Russian nature always had time to ponder on the needs of self and soul. She was a tyrant—but was ever woman tyrant who did not long to enslave herself to a man?

3

Peter Ilyich and the Tchaikowsky family

I𝐅, for Nadejda von Meck, the time was ripe for this new friendship, on Tchaikowsky's side the need was no less urgent. In adult life, a deep new relationship is seldom founded upon anything less than need; neither of these people had time or inclination to look about arbitrarily for friends. Life for Tchaikowsky had reached a crisis, and Tchaikowsky was not the man to seize crisis by the horns and wrestle it into submission. Rather, he was one to let himself be carried along by fate, submitting with a helpless patience very trying to the beholder; the worse things got, the more paralyzed Peter became; he would sit with tortured eyes, waiting for the foe to forget him. . . .

Yet—and for this reason the man's name became history—behind all this passivity, this almost feminine endurance, lay a smoldering fire of nervous strength that wanted only the hand of a friend to touch it to life. And in this most difficult year of Peter's life, the saving hand was to be Nadejda von Meck's.

On that December afternoon of 1876, Rubinstein had told Nadejda von Meck that Peter Ilyich was a gentleman, not born nor bred to the intrigues of a professional musical life. The Tchaikowskys were indeed gentility, but gentility by virtue of talent, education and bearing rather than birth. The name Tchaikowsky is met often in Russia; in Poland it is as common as Smith. Those who bore it were wage earners living the uneventful, routinized life of government officials. None lived upon income, none but the one we know possessed genius. Let Peter Ilyich tell his own genealogy as he wrote it to Nadejda von Meck not long after their correspondence began:

"I shall answer your question about my family. I warn you that the description of my dear ones will be an uninterrupted paean of praise, but let me assure you, my sweet friend, nothing is exaggerated in the eulogies that I shall squander on my relatives. The head of my family is my father, an old man of eighty-three. He was for many years a mining engineer, and also for a long time ran the Kamo-Votkin factory in the province of Viatka, where I was born. In 1848 he was retired and lived on the income from the small capital that he had accumulated after many years of service. In 1857 he put that sum in the hands of an adventuress who promised him mountains of gold, and lost all of it that very year, irrevocably. In 1858 he again started to work and was for four years director of the Technological Institute. In 1862 he retired and now lives on a pension in Petersburg.

"My mother died in 1854 from cholera. She was a fine, clever woman and loved her children passionately. In 1865 my father married for the third time. My step-mother, a half-educated but very intelligent and extremely kind woman, succeeded in inspiring us all with a sincere respect for her tender, unselfish devotion to her old husband. We all, I mean my sister and brothers, are devoted to her. My father, once a very clever engineer, has become childish. He is still very alert and healthy in body, but feeble in mind. Only his old love for his children is left, and the angelic kindness that always distinguished him but which is now especially touching. It can truly be said that he cannot hurt a fly. All other activities of his brain and soul have become quite childish. He nearly lost his memory after the dangerous illness he had last year. I have four brothers. The eldest, Nicholas, works on the railroad and lives in Kharkov. He is married but childless. After him I come; after me my brother Hippolyte, who lives in Odessa, married and also childless. Then come those whom you know of, the twins, Anatol and Modeste."

The three younger brothers were popular in society, Hippolyte especially, loved pomp and ceremony; as a boy he was playmate of the Grand Dukes and when he grew up, carried his Admiral's uniform and decorations with much style and satisfaction to himself and the beholders. He had a talent for laying corner stones; at parades he was magnificent, and family weddings would have been incomplete without him. He enjoyed immensely being brother to the famous Peter Ilyich. Alexandra Tchaikowsky, Peter's beloved sister, married a Davydoff, one of the oldest and most distinguished families of the Russian nobility. As for Peter himself, he cared not a pin for the social ladder, past or present; let one of his brothers discover a Tchaikowsky coat-of-arms or raise the family artificially to gentility, and ridicule descended swiftly upon them.

In his biography of Peter Ilyich, Modeste Tchaikowsky lets it be understood that there were no musicians among the family ancestry. He admits that their mother and their aunt and uncles had good voices and liked to sing "romances." (The German *lieder* had not yet become familiar as an art form in Russia.) There was a cathedral Protodeacon in the maternal ancestry, but Modeste in his record chose to ignore him—and with a reason. In the Russian Church, prayers are never said but intoned; therefore, especially in the big city churches, priests with rich bass voices were coveted; the country was scoured for them, and when found they were fought over by church and stage. This Tchaikowsky great-grandfather was cathedral Protodeacon in Petersburg itself, a position that to Western minds would seem to carry the very pomp and dignity so desirable upon armorial quarterings.

Not so, however, in Russia. There the clergy had no social standing; they were a class in themselves, disliking the nobility and looked down upon, as a class, in return; to Western eyes it seems strange to read of Russian noblemen who boasted they had "no Jewish or clerical blood." It will readily be seen therefore why Modeste, who was never the man to make a parade of social insecurity, did not stress the Protodeacon in the family geneology.

Peter Ilyich, on the other hand, would not have cared had his maternal grandfather been a Tartar or a red Indian. He wasted no time brooding over the bourgeois stamp of his ancestry. "There are a number of Poles bearing my name," he confessed to Nadejda von Meck. "I myself am probably of Polish descent, though I don't know positively who my ancestors were. I know only that my grandfather was a physician and lived in the province of Viatka, and then my geneological tree becomes lost in darkness. Perhaps Mr. Victor Tchaikowsky and the other fellow bearing the same name as I, who every day advertises in the Moscow News a corn plaster he has invented—are distant relatives of mine."

It is to be doubted if Modeste would have made a like lighthearted admission. Modeste was to be his brother's Boswell—without Boswell's genius. One cannot read memoirs of Russia's musical and literary life of the late nineteenth century without meeting Modeste's name; he was well known in intellectual circles; Barbara von Meck, who knew Modeste, says he had the Tchaikowsky charm. "Every man has his shadow and Tchaikowsky's shadow was his brother Modeste. One cannot name the composer without remembering his brother. Modeste was a demi-genius."

A shadow and a demi-genius—poor Modeste! Even as a shadow his outlines wavered badly; let James Boswell be witness that it requires more than demi-genius to be a first-class shadow. Modeste published a three-volume biography of his brother and for the information contained therein, the world is grateful. But Modeste wrote too soon; writing, he looked about him and saw a living face at every window. Not dismissable faces either; these were prominent people. Modeste shuddered; who now would receive him if he recorded what he knew? Besides, he loved his brother deeply and what better way to prove one's love than by guarding the secrets of the beloved? Also, Modeste never understood Nadejda Philaretovna; he was always rather jealous of the relationship between the two and refused to recognize the intensity of their mutual attachment. How could Petia be so dependent emotionally upon a woman? Modeste did not scruple to change and color his brother's motives to what he considered his brother's advantage.

Nevertheless there was something engaging about Modeste Tchaikowsky. He was shy, and like all shy people was overly aware of awkward social situations; through sheer intensity he would do the wrong thing and become horribly embarrassed. Afterward he would ease the sting by making a story of it, and Modeste could tell a story well. He liked evening parties, but preferably in the company of intimate friends; many of his relatives he did not even know. His twin Anatol, on the other hand, knew everybody and enjoyed his famous relatives. This was hard for Modeste because the twins looked so much alike; somebody was forever mistaking him for Anatol and reproaching him for ignoring them on the street. One day at the theatre Modeste decided the lady sitting next him was an aunt—the one, surely, that Anatol had so often mentioned. He must speak to her, she would be greatly offended otherwise. Modeste waited, he twitched in his seat, he leaned forward. "Auntie! How do you do! I am not Anatol, I am Modeste." The lady turned, gave him one look of horror and fled from the theatre.

Modeste is always described as "cultured"; there is no doubt he possessed a sensitive appreciation of literature and art.

"It is remarkable," Peter Ilyich wrote Nadejda, "that I, a musician by instinct, fitted for nothing but music, should be born into a family absolutely lacking in all feeling for music. Both my younger brothers understand music very well because they grew up in my company and through me came into contact with music and musicians. They both love music passionately. Modeste, though quite lacking in any talent for it, has nevertheless developed a wonderfully delicate musical understanding. He plays the piano and is ready to play the whole day long, he loves music so, but still he plays badly and cannot sing at all. The other members of my family do not even like music."

So little did they like music that they were often hard put to it to recognize their famous relative's compositions when played. Hippolyte in particular, when listening to his brother's music would look sad and close his eyes. "Petia!"—he would sigh. The von Mecks were sure that if Hippolyte had not been warned beforehand he would have had no idea the music was Petia's. . . .

Petia himself had little to say of Hippolyte in his letters, but he never tired of singing the praises of the twins.

"Without exaggeration," he told Nadejda, "one can say that these two young men are, by virtue of their moral and spiritual qualities, very pleasant persons. I am bound to them by a mutual friendship that is rare even between brothers. They are much younger than I— by ten years; when my mother died, they were only four. My sister was in the Institute. Our eldest brother, a good man but not very gentle, could not take the place of an affectionate and loving mother. Certainly I was no mother, but from the first moment of their bereavement I wanted to be to them what a mother is, because experience has taught me what an indelible imprint a mother's tenderness and caress can leave on the soul of a child. And from that time, between them and me such a bond has grown that I love them more than myself and am ready to make any sacrifice for them, and they are boundlessly devoted to me. They were educated in the School of Laws. Anatol is working and doing well. He is now an assistant attorney in Petersburg. Modeste is very richly talented by nature, but without definite inclination to any special occupation. He has not been very successful; being more interested in books, pictures, music, than in reports. We were all troubled about his future when suddenly a mutual friend had the brilliant idea of recommending him to a certain Conradi who was looking for a tutor for his only son who is deaf and dumb. The matter was arranged, and Modeste soon proved himself a perfect teacher. He spent a year abroad, studying the method of educating deaf and dumb children, and now he is wholeheartedly devoted to his work.

"Although I have two sisters, the eldest (by my father's first marriage) is much older than I—she lives in the Ural Mountains, and I know her only slightly. As to my own real sister (Alexandra Davydoff) I have written you about her. She is an irreproachable and wonderful woman in every sense of the word."

Before Nadejda von Meck came into his life, this sister's estate at Kamenka, near Kiev, was the only real home Tchaikowsky knew. Even without Tchaikowsky, Kamenka is part of Russian history; high tragedy was enacted there, and heroism. Yet when Peter Ilyich knew Kamenka, there was no longer tragedy in its mild monotonous landscape, only peace and the comfortable humdrum of Alexandra Davydoff's busy domestic household.

And Peter Ilyich needed peace; only in quiet surroundings could he do the work that was life itself to him. Living in Moscow with Nicholas Rubinstein was anything but peaceful. Rubinstein thrived upon noise and bustle and much business; during this first year of the Conservatory's life all classes were held in Rubinstein's house. Peter Ilyich was twenty-six when he went, in 1866, to Moscow.

"I have a little room next to Rubinstein's bedroom," he wrote his young twin brothers at their Petersburg school, "and truly I am afraid of disturbing him at night with the scratching of my pen, for only a small partition divides our rooms. I am terribly busy. I sit at home, scarcely ever going out, and Rubinstein who is always rushing about, can't marvel enough at my industry. I have hardly met anyone new as yet except Kashkin, an excellent musician and friend of Laroche's.

I have some very low moments, but an insatiable thirst for work consoles me. I have nearly finished orchestrating the overture I worked on last summer and to my horror it is shaping much too long. I have promised it to Rubinstein for a first performance here, then I shall send it to Petersburg.

"Yesterday while getting ready for bed I thought about you both; I imagined all the horrors of the first night after the holidays, with Modka's head under the bedclothes to hide his tears. How I longed to comfort him, poor child!—Modka, I bid you in all seriousness—not because I like to be pompous—to study, study and study. Choose your friends among the decent fellows, not with that crazy I——. I fear you will lag behind in your class and become one of the blacklisted. I am not anxious about Tolia and so give him no advice; I know he is studious. Sweet Tolka, conquer your laziness as a letter writer and send me a line. You, Modia, I know will write. A kiss for you both."

The letter is characteristic both in its playful tenderness and its solemn advice against that sin of indolence which had beset Tchaikowsky himself in his school days—until, indeed, he had begun, five years previously, to study music as a career. That first winter away from home (1866) was hard for Peter Ilyich; he was a man who needed roots. To the end of his life, removal from one place to another plunged him into panic. After a month in Moscow he wrote his sister, Alexandra Davydoff:

"Little by little I am becoming accustomed to Moscow, although sometimes I am sadly lonely. To my great surprise my classes are going very successfully; my timidity has completely disappeared and gradually I am beginning to look like a real professor. My low spirits also are disappearing, yet Moscow is still a strange town and it will be a long time before I can face without horror the fact that I shall stay here for years if not forever."

During the winter months, Tchaikowsky over-worked himself; besides teaching twenty-six hours a week, he was writing his first symphony, *Winter Day Dreams,* and by spring he experienced his first serious attack of those nervous symptoms which later were to be his constant companions. Insomnia was one of them, intestinal cramps and throbbing in his head; he often referred to these discomforts as his "apoplectic symptoms." At the end of April he wrote his brother Anatol:

"My nerves are completely out of order. Reasons: (1) The symphony which does not sound right. (2) Rubinstein and Tarnovsky having noticed that I am easily startled, tease me all day long by devising different manner of shocks for me. (3) The persistent conviction that I shall die soon, before I even have time to finish the symphony. I look forward to summer and Kamenka as to the Promised Land. Yesterday I gave up drinking vodka, wine and strong tea. I hate mankind in general and with pleasure would retire to a thinly populated desert. I have bought my ticket on the diligence for May tenth."

But the diligence went to Kamenka without him. He worked night and day but composition did not come easily: lack of experience meant lack of facility. His nervous symptoms became more and more alarming; real hallucinations, a constant, heavy, nameless fear. Too young to know that this kind of suffering cannot be vanquished by working hard at one's business in life, Peter Ilyich struggled on, ashamed of his symptoms, ashamed also to confess them: Nicholas Rubinstein, with nerves of steel-and-rubber, was hardly the confidant for a homesick young man who wanted badly to tell someone that his head was going to fall off, and would people think it funny if he kept his hand under his chin to hold it on?

By the end of June, 1866, Peter was ripe for a serious nervous breakdown and had it; the doctor said he narrowly escaped madness. For the first time, but not by any means for the last, Peter Ilyich was ordered to "rest, and stop writing music."

4

Tchaikowsky's music before he was introduced to Nadejda von Meck

Rest, and stop writing music." Futile command! Then and later, doctors and friends might as well have told Peter Ilyich to stop breathing for a while, and rest his lungs. Composing was not something controllable, it was like a man's heartbeat; it went on and on, no matter what one was doing with the rest of one's body. Whether taking off one's boots for bed, walking in the country with a friend, or waiting in a railway station—round in one's head went the tunes, old tunes remembered from a country childhood when peasants sang in the fields, new tunes never heard before—developing, interweaving, crying to be put upon paper that their creator might forget for a while their insistent voices. In his letters, Tchaikowsky refers again and again to his persistent need to compose:—"Like a bear in his cave I feed upon my own substance—my compositions, that never cease turning in my head." "I am of no use, except for music . . ." "I must hurry, hurry; I am afraid I shall die with all my music in me" . . . "To compose is for me a kind of musical shriving of the soul" . . .

In a word, music—"work"—he called it, was this man's salvation—music alone saved him for manhood and for self-respect—and he knew it in spite of the world and the world's advice. Your mediocre man is careless of salvation, lets it drift by unrecognized—but it is the part of genius to salute the angel no matter what her disguise, welcome her and cherish her to the exclusion of all worldly visitations. . . .

In the autumn of 1866, rested by his vacation, Tchaikowsky returned to the Conservatory, his first symphony, *Winter Day Dreams*, under his arm. He had sent it to Petersburg during the summer for the criticism of his one-time music masters, Anton Rubinstein and Zaremba, the counterpoint teacher, but to Tchaikowsky's great disappointment the two rejected it on behalf of the Musical Society. They were, indeed, harsh and unsympathetic toward the music, suggested changes which Tchaikowsky made against his will, nor did he like the changes when made. Even as altered, the Petersburg Musical Society consented to perform only the two middle movements of the symphony. These met with a cold reception, and the whole episode embittered Tchaikowsky toward Petersburg and all his former musical associates there, turning his heart toward Moscow, his future home.

All that winter he worked upon his new opera, *The Voyevoda,* and in the early spring both the symphony and the dances from the opera were performed in Moscow. The symphony, *Winter Day Dreams,* from which Tchaikowsky had erased the alterations, was presented in its original form with huge success; the composer was called out; he appeared upon the stage, spectators said, looking definitely untidy, and made an awkward bow. As to the *Voyevoda* dances, Tchaikowsky conducted the orchestra himself, his first experience with the baton—and his last for ten years, owing to the agony he suffered from shyness. Beforehand, to his friend Kashkin, Peter expressed himself as being perfectly calm—not in the least nervous—but from the instant he found himself on the stage, he was a lost creature. Mind fled and with it all sense and sensation save the old conviction that his head would fall off. With one hand Peter Ilyich held firmly onto his chin, while the other hand waved the stick feebly, giving all the leads at the wrong moment to the wrong instruments. Fortunately, the players were well trained, and disregarding the baton entirely, came through quite well.

The concert was important in Tchaikowsky's career because an incident connected with it brought him into contact for the first time with the Petersburg Nationalists, the talented and revolutionary Five: Balakirev, Cui, Moussorgsky, Borodin, Rimsky-Korsakov and their friend and ally, the critic Stassov. The Five had broken—they said— with musical tradition; they believed music could be composed better by inspiration than by rule, that a composer learned by composing, not by working out counterpoint problems. Moussorgsky was the fiercest rebel of them all, and in truth his genius was great enough to justify him had he said music should be written standing on one's head. Borodin also, the chemistry professor, writing his gorgeous tone poems while his test tubes were boiling, could well afford to laugh at rules. As to Rimsky-Korsakov, the other great talent of the Five, the world already knows—and Tchaikowsky's letters will retell—who it was that seduced him from rebellion to the slow and thorny path of traditional musical study.

The Five wished to create Russian music, for Russians, in the Russian language. No French words in their songs, no Italian libretti for their operas! The fount at which they drank was the deep well of Russian folk-song; fiercely they disclaimed all "foreign" influence, the French, the German, and more particularly the Italian operatic tradition to which Russian music had been enslaved for the past fifty years. Glinka was of course their forerunner, Dargomisky their immediate inspiration. The Five were especially scornful of Bach. "The old man is beginning to grind flour," Stassov would say when he heard one of the huge five-voiced fugues begin to roll up its giant momentum.

The Rubinsteins were of course regarded by the Five as hopelessly passé; not only did the Rubinsteins teach their pupils by the old despised conservatory régime, but more sinister still, the two of them laughed frankly at nationalism and would as soon write an opera around an Italian libretto as a Russian one. Trust a Jew to be an eclectic, said the Five; trust a Jew (even Christian-born) to laugh at nationalism and insist with a shrug of the shoulders, that beauty was beauty anywhere, anyhow—

And Tchaikowsky was as bad as a Rubinstein, if not worse—so thought the Five. Was he not a pupil of both Rubinsteins, first Anton and then Nicholas? Dangerous conservatives, all three, teaching music by rote in their "music factories," as the Five dubbed the Petersburg and Moscow Conservatories. And the suspicion was mutual; to Tchaikowsky the Five were not only dangerous radicals, they were dilettantes who toyed with a serious art, repudiating the hard preliminary study necessary to musical composition, repudiating Tchaikowsky's musical heroes, above all, his god, Mozart. But Tchaikowsky knew none of the Five personally, that is, until 1868 when his own *Voyevoda* dances were played in Moscow on the same concert program with Rimsky-Korsakov's *Serbian Fantasy*. A review of the concert appeared afterward in *The Entr'acte*. Tchaikowsky's music was highly praised while Rimsky-Korsakov's work was dismissed as "lifeless and colorless." During rehearsals, Tchaikowsky had learned to respect not only Rimsky-Korsakov's music but the composer himself; consequently he wrote a fiery reply to *The Entr'acte* which created a sensation both in Moscow and Petersburg and brought the Five from hostility to immediate friendship. At Easter when Tchaikowsky went up to Petersburg to visit his father, he was received with much cordiality by the Invincible Band, as the Five called themselves, and although neither Tchaikowsky nor the Five (excepting Rimsky-Korsakov) ever compromised concerning their respective musical philosophies, from this time onward their personal relationship remained cordial. During the next five years, three of Tchaikowsky's best compositions were dedicated to members of the Band. The symphonic poem *Fatum* and the *Romeo and Juliet* overture to Balakirev, who had suggested the latter as a subject—and to Stassov the symphonic fantasia which plays such a large part in our history, *The Tempest*.

During the winter of 1868-69 Tchaikowsky had what he liked to refer to as a "love affair" with the singer, Désirée Artôt, who came to Moscow for a few weeks with an Italian opera company. Peter wrote glowing letters to his brothers about this goddess, and then quite suddenly found himself engaged to marry her. He seems to have floated into the entanglement quite lightheartedly—and floated out again long before there was danger of complete submersion. From first to last the affair was shaped by events rather than by Tchaikowsky himself. This was characteristic of the man. He had heard Artôt sing and admired her intensely as an artist; later he met her at a musical party. "She expressed surprise," he wrote his father, "that I had not called. I promised to do so, but I should never have gone (because of my shyness with new acquaintances) if Anton Rubinstein, in passing through Moscow, had not dragged me there. Since then I have had numerous invitations from her and drifted into the habit of going to her house every day."

Tchaikowsky's friends, he went on to tell his father, tried their best to prevent a marriage. Nicholas Rubinstein especially, advanced arguments which Ilya Tchaikowsky countered in a return letter to his son:

December 29, 1868

"You ask my advice, dear Petya, upon the most important decision of your life. Truly, my friend, marriage is not a step to take heedlessly; it is a gambler's risk, it is the hazard of the brave. As a father I rejoice; Désirée is surely worthy because my son Peter loves her, and my son Peter is a man of taste and talent who would naturally select a wife with like qualities. The two years difference in your ages means nothing.

"You are both artists, both make capital from your talents, but she has already won money and fame, whereas you are only beginning, and God knows if you will go as far as she. Friends and sympathizers fear that your career will be sacrificed to this marriage; I disagree. You who for your talent's sake gave up a career in the Government Service surely will not, at the first momentary disappointment, cease being an artist. What musician but is unhappy at the start? Pride makes it bitter for you to depend financially on your wife—but if you both work you will forget this jealousy. Go your way and let her go hers, but let neither of you give up your vocation until you have saved enough money to say, 'This is ours, this is our mutual victory.'

"Let us analyze these words: 'As husband to a famous singer you will be a piteous slave, following her over Europe, fattening on her money and becoming too lazy to work on your own behalf.'—But if you love each other sincerely, maturely, this is a nonsensical picture. Happy marriage is based on mutual respect; you would never ask your wife to be your servant, nor will she demand lackey's service from you. As for travelling with her, that is your duty; but can you not compose on the road, seizing every opportunity to have your compositions performed abroad? With such a companion, your talent should grow rather than diminish. Suppose your mutual passion cools, leaving only 'wounded vanity, melancholy and ruin.' Why should this be? I lived with your mother twenty-one years, and all that time I loved her as ardently as a youth, respecting and venerating her as a saint. You resemble your mother; if your beloved has your mother's qualities, all these fears are vain.

"Artists have no country; they belong to the world. Surely you know this. What difference where you live; live where living is profitable. Even if your wife should have a long operatic contract in Moscow or Petersburg, it would not mean you need carry the train of her gown onto the stage. . . . No, my friend; be a servant, but an independent servant, so that when your wife sings your songs, the applause will belong to both of you.

"I question only one thing: Are you both quite sure of your love? 'To marry is not to cross a field'; would it not be wise to try your love —not, for heaven's sake, by jealousy, but by time? Wait a little longer and then decide, having asked God's help. Meanwhile describe your loved one to me truly, my darling."

Tchaikowsky had barely time to digest this affectionate advice when the question was taken out of his hands: in Warsaw, whither she had gone to sing, Artôt, without a word of warning to anyone, married a Polish baritone. Tchaikowsky was far from heartbroken. His opera, *Voyevoda,* was under rehearsal in Moscow; he had not time to think about a broken heart. When he saw Artôt a year later singing in the theatre he was, according to Kashkin who sat next him, deeply moved. "When the singer came on the stage Peter Ilyich put his opera glasses to his eyes and kept them there till the end of the performance, although it is doubtful how much he could see, because the tears ran unheeded down his cheeks."

This, however, was small proof of grief. Tears came easily to Tchaikowsky; they were a tribute he often paid to good music. Twenty years later, he met the lady again in Berlin at a dinner. "Whom should I sit next to but Artôt," he wrote his brother. "She was in evening dress, and fat as a bubble. We were friends instantly, as though the past had never been. I was inexpressibly glad to see her and found her as fascinating as ever."

So much for Désirée Artôt, a lady who in all probability knew when she was well out of a bad bargain. Peter Tchaikowsky was not the material of which husbands are made. For ten years after she jilted him Tchaikowsky was, happily, to be free of ladies until that dreadful spring when Antonina Miliukoff, lovesick and determined, would appear upon a horizon already fraught with storm. . . .

Artôt jilted him that winter of '68; his opera *Voyevoda* was a failure;

the libretto was insipid; Tchaikowsky had managed to cut from it every scene that might have proved good musical material. All his life he was to choose unfortunate subjects for his operas; his sense of the theatre was by no means his strong point. *Voyevoda* was a failure, so was the symphonic poem *Fatum* which followed it. Tchaikowsky tore up the score of *Fatum* and plunged into a new work, the three-act opera, *Undine*. *Undine* was finished in seven months but was never performed in full. Tchaikowsky destroyed this score also, except for an aria and a wedding march which he used in later compositions. None of these failures seemed to depress the composer unduly, and so it was all his life; by the time one work was ready for performance he was always engrossed in a new composition; buoyed up by faith in the new work, he sailed over the head of failure, merely pausing to remark that he had been chagrined, yes—but what a lot he was learning!

Even the *Romeo and Juliet Overture-Fantasia* for orchestra, written in 1869 and now considered one of Tchaikowsky's finest works and the beginning of his career as an important composer, when performed in Moscow early in 1870, attracted no notice at all. Nicholas Rubinstein conducted; the players must have been very clumsy indeed to conceal the power and the poetry of this composition. Perhaps the composer knew his music was good, for a few weeks after the performance he wrote his brother Modeste:

March 26, 1870
"I congratulate you on leaving school. Thinking over my life since my graduation from the School of Laws, I see with some pleasure that the time has not been lost. I wish the same for you. . . ."

During the next five years, Tchaikowsky's life was not especially remarkable. He taught, he wrote music, he travelled, he enlarged slowly but steadily both his fame and his personal circle of friends. After *Romeo and Juliet* his next big work was an opera, *The Oprichnik*, which had its first performance at Kiev in 1874, and was a success in spite of the fact that the Censor—that figure so devastating to the Russian Imperial Theatre—forbade the *Oprichnik's* hero, Ivan the

Terrible, to appear upon the stage. The opera has since found oblivion.

During the four weeks before Christmas, 1869, Tchaikowsky wrote his first opus of original songs—Opus 6. One of these, *Nur wer die Sehnsucht Kennt,* is the best known of the 117 songs he was destined to publish. The First String Quartet, in D major, was written soon afterward. It contains the famous *Andante Cantabile* that has wrung tears from so many listeners, a tune that, lovely as it is, has become tiresomely representative of the name of Tchaikowsky; like Handel's *Largo,* the world sometimes forgets its composer wrote anything else. The famous *Andante* is based on a folk-song Tchaikowsky heard at his sister's estate in Kamenka. He was in his room working on the orchestration of *Undine* when a gardener outside his window sang the song through to Russian words:

That summer of 1870 Tchaikowsky wrote his *Manual of Harmony,* for use in his courses at the Conservatory. The book is thorough and concise, abounding in those musical illustrations for which Tchaikowsky was famous as a teacher. Scanning it, one is faintly surprised that Peter Ilyich could have written anything at the same time so complete and coldly impersonal. Many a great composer of the 1870's and '80's struggled through this merciless little book, among them Rimsky-Korsakov who in his memoirs has confessed the hard work Tchaikowsky's counterpoint exercises cost him.

The Second Symphony, in C minor, was written in 1872 (later drastically revised). This year also saw the completion of music to Ostrovsky's poem, *The Snow Maiden.* Tchaikowsky himself did not think much of this; it has since been totally eclipsed by Rimsky-Korsakov's ballet music for the same story. *The Tempest* was begun that year and finished in the summer of 1873. Then came the Second String Quar-

t‑t, in F major, and an opera, *Vakoula the Smith*. (This opera was re-
modelled in 1885; produced in America in 1922 as *Oxana's Caprice*, it
was pronounced by the critics "extremely humorous, delightful and
fantastic.") Numerous songs and piano pieces followed the composition of the opera, and in 1874 Tchaikowsky composed one of his major
works, the brilliant B Flat Minor Piano Concerto. The principal
theme of the first movement of this concerto was also heard at Kamenka; Tchaikowsky wrote Nadejda von Meck that he first heard
it sung by blind beggars at the village fair, in this form:

As soon as it was written, the composer took the concerto to Nicholas Rubinstein for criticism. Four years later, Tchaikowsky wrote an
account of the episode to Nadejda:

To Nadejda von Meck

San Remo, January 21, 1878

"In December, 1874, I wrote a piano concerto. As I am not a pianist,
I needed a virtuoso's opinion as to what was technically impractical,
difficult, unplayable, and so on. I needed a serious but friendly critic,
but only for the pianistic aspect of my composition. Rubinstein is not
only the first pianist of Moscow, but is truly a perfect pianist; knowing
he would be deeply offended if he thought I had ignored him, I asked
him to listen to the concerto and give me an opinion on the piano part,
although some inner voice protested against my selecting him as
judge. It was Christmas Eve of 1874. We were both invited to a
Christmas tree that evening at Albrecht's, and Nicholas Gr. suggested
that we go to one of the class-rooms at the Conservatory beforehand.
And so we did. I arrived with my manuscript, and after me Nic. Gr.
with Hubert. Have you any idea, my friend, what the latter is like?
He is very kind and clever, completely lacking in independence, very
talkative, needing a whole preface to say yes or no, incapable of expressing an opinion in a simple way, always backing the one who at
the moment expresses himself bravely and decisively. I hasten to add
that it is because of lack of character, not servility.

"I played the first movement. Not a word, not a remark. If you only knew how disappointing, how unbearable it is when a man offers his friend a dish of his work, and the other eats and remains silent! Well, say something—scold, in a friendly way, but for God's sake, one sympathetic word, even if uncomplimentary! While Rubinstein prepared his thunder, Hubert waited for the situation to clarify so he would know which way to jump. The point was that I did not want a verdict on artistic merits, but advice as to piano technic. Rubinstein's eloquent silence had great significance. As much as to say— 'My friend, can I speak of details when the thing as a whole disgusts me?' I armed myself with patience, and played it through to the end. Again silence. I stood up and said 'Well?' Then from the lips of N. G. R. poured a torrent of words, first quiet, then more and more the tone of Jupiter, master of the thunder-bolts. It appeared that my concerto is worthless, impossible to play, the themes have been used before, are clumsy and awkward beyond possibility of correction; as a composition it is poor, I stole this from here and that from there, there are only two or three pages that can be salvaged, and the rest must be thrown away or changed completely! 'For example, that— well, what is that?' (And he plays the place indicated, exaggerating it.) 'And that? Is it possible!' and so on. I cannot convey the tone in which it was all spoken. An outsider, dropping into the room, would have thought me a madman, without talent, ignorant, a worthless writer who had come to annoy a famous musician with his rubbish. Noticing that I was obstinately silent, amazed, and shocked that a man who had written a great deal already, and who is teaching the course of free composition in the Conservatory, should be subjected to such a reprimand, to such a humiliating sentence, without appeal—a sentence such as one should not pronounce even on a pupil of little ability without first looking through his work with care—Hubert started to explain N. G. R.'s opinions, not differing from him, only softening what His Excellency expressed so unceremoniously.

"I was not only astonished but offended by the performance. I am no longer a boy, trying his strength in composition—I no longer need lessons, especially lessons expressed so sharply and in such a hostile manner. I need, and will always need, friendly criticism, but this was nothing like friendly criticism. It was a decisive, blanket condemnation, expressed in such a manner as to touch me in a sensitive spot. I walked out of the room without a word and went upstairs. I was speechless with excitement and fury. Rubinstein appeared soon after, and seeing my disturbed state of mind, called me to another room. There he repeated that my concerto was impossible, and, having pointed out many places needing radical change, told me that if I would alter the concerto according to his wishes by a certain date, he would do me the honor of performing it at his concert.* 'I won't change a single note,' I replied, 'and will print it exactly as it is now.' And so I did.

"This is the incident that caused Rubinstein to look on me as a *frondeur,* a secret enemy. He has grown colder toward me since then, though it has not prevented him from repeating on all occasions that he is terribly fond of me and ready to do anything for me."

This letter, written four years after the event, is very little exaggerated, and quite true in essence. As long as Tchaikowsky remained subservient, Nicholas Rubinstein looked upon him with greatest affection, but from the beginning, both Rubinstein brothers maintained an inexplicable, two-sided attitude toward Tchaikowsky. They recognized in him a great musician, yet they could not bring themselves to accept his music the first time they heard it; extreme caution characterized all their criticisms, often enough they never retracted this original harshness. Anton especially, while urging Tchaikowsky from the very beginning to embrace a musical career, greeted his successive compositions with scorn, or ignored them. Nevertheless, Peter Ilyich always returned for another beating from his old masters, always hastened with his compositions to the Rubinstein arena. In truth, Peter adored Anton, venerating him as something musically superhuman; as for Nicholas Rubinstein, he continued all his life to help Peter and to turn nasty whenever he thought Peter was acting independently of him or making a success without him. At such times Nicholas would be inexcusably perverse and harsh in his judgments of Tchaikowsky's compositions. After these bouts Peter found it an enormous comfort to take his bruised ego to Nadejda von Meck; her faith and her indignation proved balm and nourishment for any wound. . . .

As to the B Flat Minor Piano Concerto, after Rubinstein's condemnation Tchaikowsky scratched the word Rubinstein from the

---

* Rubinstein later played this concerto all over Europe, and with greatest success. This and the violin concerto remain the most popular of Tchaikowsky's works for solo instrument.

dedication and replaced it with the name of the famous German pianist and conductor, Hans von Bülow. Bülow had for some time
been an admirer of Tchaikowsky and was pleased with the compliment; he became more than ever a champion of Tchaikowsky's
music in Europe. But Rubinstein's strictures must have had more
eventual influence than von Bülow's praise, for fifteen years later
Tchaikowsky revised the piano part completely, and the concerto,
"that duel between piano and orchestra," became once and for all
one of the most popular of virtuoso piano concerti.

By the time the B Flat Minor Piano Concerto was written, Tchaikowsky had already effected somewhat of a separation from Nicholas
Rubinstein; that is to say, he no longer lived in Rubinstein's house.
Rubinstein had been married, earlier in life, but his wife had proved
unsympathetic toward his professional musical life; especially, she
had objected to concert tours. The spectacle of a wife—or anyone
else—trying to keep a Rubinstein off the concert stage, must have
been an interesting sight, not devoid of drama. Anyway, Rubinstein
left her, but he could not bear to live alone. Tchaikowsky came to his
house in 1886 and stayed six years, and for Tchaikowsky it was not
an easy situation. He was forced to adapt his daily schedule strictly
to his host's—and the two kept entirely different hours. Unable to
endure the noise of Rubinstein's pianoforte classes, Peter Ilyich used
to take his music paper to a nearby student café in the mornings,
and write there amid the empty tables. When he first came to Moscow, Rubinstein's rooftree had been a welcome shelter. As Peter
acquired more money he tried several times to leave Rubinstein and
set up independent quarters, but Rubinstein would have none of it.
Six years passed before a friend appeared who was willing to substitute as a Rubinstein guest. Tchaikowsky moved into a tiny three-
room flat and for the first time in his thirty-two years, found himself
alone and master of his days.

He was pleased as a child with his little establishment, set up his
sofa and his three chairs and hung his two pictures on the wall—one
was a portrait of Anton Rubinstein, the other—quite fortuitously—
the Dauphin. He engaged a servant, Michael Sofronov, brother of

that Alexis who was to share his later travels, and there the composer lived very happily. In the autumn he moved to a more commodious flat: what most men would call a necessary standard of comfort was always luxury to Tchaikowsky.

By this time he was earning 3000 roubles a year; 2000 roubles from his salary at the Conservatory and the sale of his published works, 500 from his newspaper and magazine articles. This latter work had begun with his defending Rimsky-Korsakov in the *Entr'acte* in 1868. Many of Tchaikowsky's critical articles have been preserved and published in English, but they are not to be compared in value or interest with his creative musical output. To write words was a burden to Tchaikowsky and he did it only when in need of money. In a letter to Modeste, written just after the completion of the B Flat Minor Concerto, the composer describes his difficulties with both kinds of composition, literary and musical. That winter he had written a great many newspaper articles on music.

To Modeste Tchaikowsky

Moscow, January 6, 1875

"Your newspaper article about the Kiev opera pleases me greatly. You complain that writing is hard and that one must ponder over every phrase. But how can you believe that anything completes itself without work and effort? Sometimes I sit for hours biting my pen, wondering how to begin my article. I feel sure it will be badly done, and then afterward people praise it and say it reads easily and fluently. Remember the trouble Zaremba's counterpoint exercises gave me, remember that summer of '66 at Miatleff's house when my nerves got so upset because my symphony would not work out as I wished. Even now I pace my room, bite my nails and smoke huge numbers of cigarettes before I can invent the main theme of my composition.

"Sometimes, on the contrary, the music writes itself with marvelous ease; ideas struggle and tumble over one another. All depends on one's mood, one's state of mind. But even lacking the right mood, one must force oneself to work. Otherwise, nothing will be accomplished."

Between this letter and the year that elapsed before Nadejda von Meck gave him her first musical commission, Tchaikowsky wrote his Serenade in B minor for violin with orchestral accompaniment, and his ballet, *The Swan Lake*—neither work showing the power or charm of the B Flat Minor Piano Concerto. The Second String Quartet, in F major, dedicated to the Grand Duke Constantine, had already been written and played; it is not to be compared with the melodious First Quartet nor the Third and last of Tchaikowsky's string quartets, written early in 1875. This is the E flat minor Quartet with the brilliant and popular *Scherzo*. As an admirer—really an adorer—of Mozart, Tchaikowsky liked string quartet music and often said so. His genius of course was pre-eminently orchestral, the fury of his emotions needed the sweep of many instruments; nevertheless no one can study his last quartet without a sense that the composer had a sound feeling for this difficult creative medium. It is a great pity that he ceased, after only a third attempt, to develop it.

During this same year, 1875, Tchaikowsky wrote *The Seasons,* twelve pieces for piano. They are utterly unimportant and Tchaikowsky knew it. He wrote them on commission for a Petersburg musical journal, tearing one off every month and then forgetting about it until his servant, under orders to do so, appeared next month and asked mildly, "Peter Ilyich, isn't it time to mail that package to town?" By mailtime the package was always ready.

Early in 1876, Tchaikowsky wrote the now almost notorious *Marche Slav* for orchestra, letting himself go in his most purple manner and earning for himself those Tchaikovskian adjectives that will forever cling to his name. And then came from his pen a piece of music deserving very different adjectives, a piece mature and masterly, the symphonic fantasia for orchestra, *Francesca da Rimini.* Tchaikowsky could not have chosen a subject more suited to his musical and emotional temperament; together with the *Overture-Fantasia Romeo and Juliet, Francesca* deserves a place by the side of his last three symphonies. With no resort to musical trickery, no bells ringing or horses' hooves galloping, the composer here achieves the very perfection of the romantic ideal of program music. Solely through the medium of musical sound, a familiar story is retold in all its color and poetry and strangely enough, becomes to the listener more real than if actors walked the stage before his eye, beating the breast or drawing the duellistic blade.

Thus Tchaikowsky's life moved on. Petersburg heard *The Tempest* without enthusiasm except in the camp of the Five, who reported upon it most favorably. Saint-Saëns came to Moscow to play some of his own music, and he and Tchaikowsky became instant friends. Peter Ilyich and Modeste went to Paris and heard *Carmen* for the first time, and so carried away was Peter by the music that his brother became quite embarrassed. "Bizet died three months later," wrote Modeste, "and his death seemed to exaggerate my brother's almost unhealthy passion for this opera."

Other events of the year were the successful performance of the Third Symphony in Petersburg and of the Third String Quartet E flat minor in Moscow. Exhausted by his winter, Tchaikowsky went abroad again for the water cure, and thence to Bayreuth. Here he was surprised to find himself received as a distinguished visitor. "It appears," he wrote home, "that I am not so unknown in Western Europe as I had thought." Consequently his days in Bayreuth were one long confusion of hospitality. "After the final note of the *Gotterdämmerung*," the letter finished—"I felt as if freed from poison. Perhaps the *Nibelungen* is in truth a great creation, but surely no music was ever so tediously longdrawn."

Such then, was the Peter Tchaikowsky to whom Nadejda von Meck, in the winter of 1876, gave a musical commission. Small wonder that the widow, accustomed in the Muscovite manner to accord honor to art, addressed Peter Ilyich with respect and even some timidity; already he was a far from inconsiderable figure in the musical world. But, forging steadily ahead musically, in other directions Tchaikowsky was for the moment blocked, halted completely; he needed emotional support as badly as he needed money. And the widow, whose active personal life had come to a standstill and who lived now only in the lives of her children (a program totally inadequate to her nature), needed Tchaikowsky as greatly as he needed her.

5

Peter's pension. The Fourth Symphony
and Eugene Onegin begun

DECEMBER—January—February—and between Peter Ilyich and Nadejda von Meck four letters have passed. Peter wrote the last one, a short note, but friendly enough to break down all the widow's reserves—or nearly all. A sensitive creature, this Tchaikowsky; already he has felt Nadejda's reserve and tells her frankly that with him, she need not be on the defensive. Why, he asks, does she fear he will laugh if she tells him all her thoughts? "I feel deeply sympathetic towards you," he writes. "These are not mere words" . . .

Nadejda's reply is in essence, touching; the difficulty is that Nadejda's letters are apt to be as long-winded as they are sincere, her emotions as unskillfully rendered as they are intensely felt. It was fortunate that from the beginning, Tchaikowsky saw nothing ludicrous in the widow's extravagantly ornamental style; he seemed to take for granted this flowery superabundance and to extract from it that strong essence which she was so eager to give. Also, it is interesting to remark, in this third letter she wrote Tchaikowsky, that already Nadejda sensed the strange fact that between herself and this man, physical presence and the spoken word would never be necessary; wise woman that she was, did she sense further that physical intimacy would be impossible, and the very hint of it would send Tchaikowsky flying in horror?

Nadejda Philaretovna to Peter Ilyich

Moscow, March 19, 1877
Monday

"Gracious Sir, Peter Ilyich,

"Your kind answer to my letter gave me an intenser pleasure than I have experienced for a long time. But you know human nature—the more one receives, the more one wants. I have promised you not to become spoiled, but now begin to doubt my own strength, for I dare ask you a great favor, a favor which will seem perhaps strangely unconventional.

"A person who lives, like me, the life of a recluse, naturally grows to feel that what people call conventions, social laws, decency—are but sounds without meaning. I do not know your opinion about this, Peter Ilyich, but from what I have heard, I believe that you, less than anyone, will hold it against me if I am mistaken. Say frankly 'No,' if you wish, without explanation— Give me your photograph. I have two now, but I want one from you. I want to search your face for the thoughts and feelings that inspired you while writing music that sweeps one into a world of emotion, hope and insatiable yearning. How much joy and sadness is in your music—sadness that one does not wish to relinquish. In it man feels his highest powers, his greatest hopes, and a happiness that reality cannot grant. The first of your compositions I ever heard was *The Tempest*. It is impossible to describe the impression it made upon me. For several days I was as one in a delirium from which I could not emerge."

The widow's critical acumen, ordinarily alert for any symptom of insincerity, any display of musical fireworks unauthorized by the innate musical idea of the piece, was apt, where Tchaikowsky's music was concerned, to be dulled by adoration. *The Tempest,* the second of Tchaikowsky's three overture-fantasias for full orchestra, was not up to the mark of *Romeo and Juliet* and *Francesca da Rimini.* On the other hand it was a vivid piece of musical tone painting, original for its day and definitely branded with that Tchaikovskian mark which would always bring Nadejda to her feet. Nadejda never pretended to be a musical critic, and indeed she was to be something far more valuable to Tchaikowsky—a person who upon first hearing, invariably understood and sympathized with the emotional content of his work.

"Let me confess," her letter continued, "that I am incapable of separating the musician from the man; and in him, servant of such a great art, more than in other people, I look for these human qualities I revere. My ideal man is a musician, but only when character equals talent does he make a deep and true impression. If, on the contrary, in the musician there is no man, the better his compositions musically, the more he seems to me a living lie, a hypocrite, an exploiter of simple people. I think of a Musician-Man as one of the greatest creations of nature. Even after many mistakes and disappointments, I cannot change my opinion. That is why I feel such intense interest in musicians, and why I immediately wanted to know, after my first great joy in hearing your music, what the man was like who created such a thing. I began looking for opportunities to know more about you, never permitting means of such news to escape me. I listened to general opinion, personal opinion, to any chance remark, and I can tell you that often enough, what others criticized made me very enthusiastic— Everyone to his taste! Recently in a chance conversation I heard one of your opinions quoted that excited me very much; it was so like me that it made you very near and dear. I think that, more than contact, similarity of opinion and feeling brings people together; two persons can thus be close though very far. I am interested in everything about you; I should like at all times to know where you are and approximately what you are doing. From all I have observed or heard about you, favorable and unfavorable, a great sense of fellow-feeling and enthusiasm has grown. I am happy that in you, musician and man unite so beautifully, so harmoniously, that one can give oneself to the full charm of your music; it expresses fineness and truth. You have not written for the crowd but to express your own feelings and ideas. I am happy that my ideal can now be realized, that I need not abandon it and that, on the contrary, it grows more precious and dearer. If only you knew what I feel, listening to your music, and how grateful I am for those feelings!

"There was a time when I wanted to meet you. Now, the more I am charmed, the more I fear meeting. I could not talk to you. If somewhere, accidentally, we should come face to face, I could not look upon you as a stranger—I should give you my hand, but only to press yours wordlessly. At present I prefer to think about you at a distance, to hear you in your music and in it to feel with you. It is too bad that I have not yet heard your *Francesca da Rimini*. Impatiently I await the time of its publication for piano.

"Forgive me, Peter Ilyich, for saying all this—you do not need it— but do not regret giving to one who is drawing near the end of her life, who is indeed practically dead, the opportunity to feel alive, for a moment, in such a beautiful way.

"I have one more favor to ask, Peter Ilyich, that may seem odd. I don't know how people feel about such things, so please feel free to refuse without ceremony. It is this: in your *Oprichnik* there is a passage that drives me distracted. Oh, what music! One could give one's life for it. I should like to die hearing it. So, from these themes, Peter

Ilyich, make me if possible, a *Marche Funèbre*. I enclose the opera with the parts marked that I should like to have in the march. If you can, I beg you to arrange it for four hands. If you find my request inconvenient, refuse. I shall be disappointed but not offended. But if you consent to do it, please, Peter Ilyich, do not try to do it quickly, for it is a favor to which I have no right and I am ashamed to take this advantage. Allow me to print the transcriptions you did for me. Shall I have them done at Jurgenson's or at Bessel's? And finally, Peter Ilyich, permit me in writing you to drop such formalities as 'Gracious Sir' . . . Truly they do not come naturally to me. And in your letters to me, please do the same. Surely you will not refuse?

"Cordially,

"N. von Meck

"P. S. Do not forget my first request."

Nadejda Philaretovna to Peter Ilyich

Moscow, March 30, 1877

"Thank you, thank you, without end, Peter Ilyich, for the photograph, for your sweet picture. It made me very, very happy, made my world glow and my heart light and warm. May life be always as beautiful for you as it was for me at that moment. I rejoiced to see you, and also that you had granted my wish, for I must confess that I was beginning to be afraid, not knowing how you had received my request. In your letter, so dear to me, only one thing worried me, and that was your explanation of my fear of meeting you. You think I am afraid of not finding the unity of Man and Musician of which I dreamed. But in you I have already found it! Before I was sure of this, I might indeed, as you say, have feared that you could not personify my ideal in all its attributes, that you could not be the recompense for all my disappointments, mistakes and disillusionments. Yet now, had I happiness in my two hands, I should give it to you. My fear of meeting you has now quite another reason behind it, quite another feeling.

"Permit me, Peter Ilyich, to send you my photograph. I am fond of this picture, first, because I am not alone in it and second, because it is the work of one of my daughters. I do not send it expecting to give you pleasure, but because I want to try to express my deep feeling for you. I know you will understand that, and also a mother's pride.

"Your *Marche*,* Peter Ilyich, is so beautiful that it lifts me, as I had hoped, into that mood of blissful madness in which one can forget all that is bitter and offensive in the world. It is impossible to describe

* The *Marche Funèbre*, never published, was lost.

the chaos that reigns in my head and heart when I hear it. A shiver runs through my nerves—I want to sob, to die, I long for another life, but not the life that others believe in and look forward to, a life that is different, intangible, indescribable. Life, death, happiness, pain, all merge. I soar above the earth, my temples throb, my heart beats wildly; mist darkens my eyes and I hear only the enchantment of that beautiful music. One loses the outer world, feeling only the beauty within, and dreads awakening. *Dieu,* how great is the man that can impart such moments to another soul! How I wish I could enter into your soul when you listen, for instance, to *Francesca,* or one of the others. Oh, what a joy *Francesca* is! What better portrays the horror of hell and the charms of love, and all the emotions that belong to the rarer levels of feeling! How can Wagner, with his realism, compare with you? He profanes the art, though unhappily he has great talent. God be with him. It is lucky we are not Germans or we should have to admire him. Now, we can say with impunity, 'Thank God, we have no Wagner, but have Peter Ilyich.'

"Your promise to give me another photograph pleased me enormously, and please forgive me if some day I remind you of it. I understand and sympathize with your dislike of having them taken. Since you have decided to have it done, however, please pose so that your eyes look straight at one, as I dislike pictures that turn from me.

"Excuse me, Peter Ilyich, for writing such long letters. As you always find something to say in music, so I always have something to say when I write to you—and yet I leave much unsaid. Thank you again, many times, and remember sometimes your,

"Cordially devoted,
"Nadejda von Meck

"P. S. Forgive me, Peter Ilyich, for delaying until today to write. Yesterday one of my children, a seven-year-old boy, had an operation on his eye. You will understand, surely, that I could not write, especially as the chloroform, which I had hoped would relieve him from pain, had no effect. They gave him so much that his pulse stopped. He did not lose consciousness, however, nor the sensation of pain, so the poor child suffered a good deal.

"My comrade in the photograph is my youngest, my five-year-old daughter Ludmilla, or Milochka, as she is called in the family. Permit me to introduce this person and ask you to love her. She knows that, among the royalties, I like the King of Bavaria, and remembers seeing him when we were in Bayreuth. She has just asked me to whom I am writing, and on my answering that I am writing to you because I like you very much, she asked me, '*et pourquoi est-ce que tu n'écris pas au Roi de Bavière?'* Similarity of feeling suggested this question to her. I want to present this person to you."

Having made such a beginning, from now on the two showered one another with a very prodigality of photographs. Nadejda was never satisfied with her Tchaikowsky gallery; again and again she asked for new pictures; desiring not only photographs of Peter Ilyich but of his sister, his twin brothers and all the Davydoff family, father, mother and grandmother. The photographs of Tchaikowsky's pretty Davydoff nieces she had done over in color in the prevailing rather horrifying fashion and professed herself immensely pleased with the result. In return she sent numerous pictures of herself, taken with various of her children. The two derived enormous satisfaction, even some little excitement, from this exchange—especially Nadejda. Their accompanying comments and explanations of photographic features reached a length and profuseness impossible of quotation.

Nadejda Philaretovna to Peter Ilyich

Moscow, May 12, 1877

"How lonely I was, not hearing from you, Peter Ilyich, and how happy now that I have heard! Had I the right, I should ask your permission to write you at any time I wish—by so doing I would always know where you were, especially in the summer, when I have no other news of you. Your letters are not only a pleasure, but truly good for me. So, dear Peter Ilyich, even though I have no claim on you, if you will say 'yes' to this desire of my heart, you will make me unspeakably happy.

"Yesterday I returned from Petersburg. I am unlucky—again I missed your *Vakoula,* for they did not give it. I shall have to recompense myself somehow, so I ask you, Peter Ilyich, be good enough to write me a composition that might express, and be called *Reproach* (for violin and piano). I have a short composition by Kohne, called *Le Reproche,* also for violin and piano. I like it, but it does not say what I want, and also seems to be about some one person. My *Reproach* must be impersonal. It can depict Nature, or Fate, to me, but not to anyone else. It must be the expression of unbearable weariness of spirit, like the French phrase: *Je n'en peux plus.* In it must be the broken heart, faith trampled on, hurt pride, lost happiness, all, all that is dear and sweet to man and that is mercilessly taken from him. If you ever have lost what you loved and held dear, you will understand that feeling. In this *Reproach* must be heard the longing of unhappiness, the surrender to despair, the impotence of the soul, and, if you think proper, death. It is possible in music to find the solace that life does not give for the asking. Oh, yes, in the *Reproach* must be heard too these memories of happiness of which one has been robbed. Nothing can portray such a spiritual mood so well as music, and no one could understand it better than you. And so I bravely hand over to you my feelings, my idea, my desire, and I am sure that this time I surrender my dearest possession into the right hands.

"I cannot write briefly to you. I have so much to say! It is because I feel so near you in spirit that I have this impulse to open my soul to you. I know you will judge not from the ordinary point of view, but from your own. Your standards and ideals are rooted in musical earth, but thank God, they have not grown in a stereotyped musical environment, which is the reason they are so honorable and high. These are not mere words and compliments, but are a small expression of the feeling and enthusiasm you arouse in me.

"*Au revoir,* I don't want to say 'Good-bye,' because I don't want this letter to end.

"Devotedly yours (devoted from my soul)
"Nadejda von Meck"

Peter Ilyich was not the man to balk at a commission; he was a professional artist and he could write to order. But *The Reproach* was too much for him. *He* had not lost what he held dear; let Karl George Von Meck rest in peace. Peter Ilyich had written one funeral march and did not, apparently, feel like writing another:—

Moscow, May 13, 1877

"Dear Nadejda Philaretovna,

"As always, I shall be very glad to fulfill your request, and to put into my composition as nearly as possible what you want to hear. But I shall have to ask you to wait longer this time than you had to wait for the other compositions. I am very busy just now and don't know if I can find a moment and the appropriate mood. I will write you in detail one of these days. *Au revoir,* my dear Nadejda Philaretovna."

Tchaikowsky must have sent this by the bearer of Nadejda's letter and then gone back to his desk and writtten another long one; anyway, they are both dated May 13th. The long letter he kept until he saw how Nadejda received his refusal of her commission. She received it with graciousness; womanlike, she decided his nerves were upset:

"I am sending you, Peter Ilyich, the book of Kohne's *Études Characteristiques,* in which you will find *Le Reproche.* Judging by what you write me and what I already know, I think, Peter Ilyich, it would be wiser to postpone the work I asked for until summer, when the Conservatory examinations are over and you are quite free.

"And now I want you to do another, less important work for me—arrange your first quartet for the piano, four hands. I do want this very much.

"I hope you will answer both my letters, and permit me to remind you of your promise to send me your latest photograph. I feel that your nerves may suffer from the Conservatory examinations. God grant they will not be disturbed too much, so that during the summer you may regain abundant health."

"Truly devotedly yours,
"N. von Meck"

Tchaikowsky replied instantly:

"Dear N. Ph.

"Yesterday I wrote you a letter which this morning I decided not to send. But your letter of today definitely convinced me that I was right in the reasons on which I based mine of yesterday. I am sending it, then, and if it seems tactless, please excuse and forgive.

"Yours devotedly,
"P.T.

"P. S. The arrangement of the quartet for four hands is already in the printing press."

Peter Ilyich gave the portentous letter to Nadejda's messenger and then, like many a man who has launched a letter—sat down and worried about what he had written. Actually, he had asked Nadejda von Meck for 3000 roubles—a request flagrant enough to make a man less sensitive than Peter Ilyich pace his room while awaiting an answer.

On the face of it, a request for 3000 roubles was, to say the least, surprising, coming from a gentleman whom Nicholas Rubinstein had described as too proud to ask for charity. The sum exactly equalled Tchaikowsky's current income; $1500 a year was, in those days, sufficient for a man who cared nothing for luxury; why then had the composer need to ask for more? Simply because, as regards money, Peter was and would always be, utterly without sense. The possession of ten dollars was to him riches and security; when in 1866 his salary—his total income—had been raised to $600, he wrote home to his brothers that he had "money enough and to spare." Whenever there was money in his pocket, Tchaikowsky was extremely pleased and said so, but he instantly spent it or, more likely, gave it away; when it was gone he was surprised, as though suddenly in the midst of sunshine, rain had begun to fall. Toward the end of his life he earned enough, from his operas and published writings, to be more than comfortably off, but he never seemed to have money in reserve. Once a friend asked him where he was in the habit of investing his capital. Tchaikowsky was astonished at the question; how would anyone invest capital except in buying what one wanted for oneself and one's friends? He burst out laughing; in fact, this was such a funny idea that Peter could scarcely speak for laughing. "I'll tell you where I made my last investment of capital," he said. "In the Kokorev Hotel where I stayed in Moscow. Where my next investment will be, I can't say until I know my itinerary!"

His friends used to remonstrate with him, but never on the score of personal extravagance; not only did Tchaikowsky live simply, but he never talked about luxury or seemed interested in it; to him luxury was defined not as physical comfort but as solitude. His friends' reproaches concerned his reckless, helpless generosity. Peter could not refuse even the well-lined palm when it was extended. One of his greatest pleasures was to walk in the country, but by the time he had a country place of his own, even his daily walks had been ruined by his habit of giving coppers to the peasant children. One day he promised two close friends who were staying with him— Kashkin and Taneyeff his pupil—that he would give up this habit; if the children gathered, he would evade or ignore them. The three started out; Tchaikowsky's hour for walking was known to every child in the neighborhood; he knew they would be waiting for him outside the grounds of his estate. The three friends had to cross a bridge on the road to Klin; here Tchaikowsky left the other two and slipped down to the river bank, hiding under some bushes so the children would think his friends were walking without him, and would go away. It was all useless; the children knew their man and had posted spies; by the time Tchaikowsky emerged, boys were massed upon the bridge waiting for him. Kashkin and Taneyeff came along just as the mob, shrieking with laughter, bore off the booty. Peter Ilyich blushed, and said he had given the children scarcely anything, but nobody believed him. He had called it a mere nothing that other day when he had dispensed fourteen shillings, besides borrowing all his friends had and giving that away too.

During his whole life, Peter Ilyich gave away about half his income—but there was one thing he never gave away, and that was his musical integrity. Nowhere is this better illustrated than in this first of financial letters between him and Nadejda von Meck. The letter that the widow opened in her bedroom on the Boulevard Rojdestvensky on that cold spring morning of 1877 was daring, but never servile—and above all, it was honest:

Moscow, May 13, 1877

"Dear Nadejda Philaretovna,

"In spite of the most emphatic denials on the part of our mutual friend,* I have reason to believe that I owe to his friendly scheming the letter I received from you this morning"—(commissioning Peter Ilyich to write music for *The Reproach*)—"Your former musical order had already given me the idea that you were guided by two motives; first, you really wanted one or another of my compositions; second, you wished to help me. The too-generous payment with which you rewarded my little work convinced me of it. This time I am quite sure that you are guided by the second reason only. That is why, reading your letter, in which I glimpsed between the lines your tact and kindness, your touching sympathy for me, I felt an uncontrollable distaste for beginning the work and hurried in my brief answer to put off the fulfillment of my promise. In my relationship with you, I do

* This was Kotek, a young harmony pupil of Tchaikowsky's who for some time had been coming regularly to Nadejda's house in the capacity of violinist; he adored Tchaikowsky and was always ready to sing his praises and relate to the widow those details of the composer's life that she was avid to hear.

not want any of that falsity and insincerity which would inevitably appear if I should not wait and listen for the inner voice and inspiration which are necessary to create what you wish. Should I not wait, I would hurry to create something, send the 'something' to you and get from you undeserved payment. In which case you could not help feeling that I was willing to dash off all sorts of musical works, the result of which would be little hundred-rouble papers. Would it not then occur to you that if you were poor, I should refuse your requests?

"This is a delicate matter; every time I receive an envelope from you, money falls out. It is assumed that an artist is never humiliated by receiving remuneration for his work. But in creative work such as you now demand, there must be a certain mood, so-called inspiration, which is not always at one's disposal. I do not wish to be artistically dishonest for the sake of improving my circumstances, and by taking advantage of my technical skill, give you false metal for true. Yet I am in great need of the despised metal! It would take long to explain how and why a man, earning enough for more than a comfortable living, has managed to get so into debt that it often poisons his life and paralyzes his inclination to work. Just now, when the time before leaving for the summer is short, and when, before going, I must find means for returning, I have involved myself in a most disagreeable financial difficulty, from which I cannot extricate myself without help.

"For that help I have decided to ask you. You are the only person in the world from whom I am not ashamed to ask money. First, you are kind and generous. Second, you are wealthy. What I should like to do is to put all my debts in the hands of one generous creditor, and with his help, free myself from the clutches of the money-lenders. If you would be good enough to consent to *lend* me enough for this, I should be immensely grateful. The sum of my debts is large—approximately 3000 roubles. I could repay in three ways: first, by making for you musical arrangements and transcriptions such as I have already made for you; second, by giving you the royalties that I get from the Directory for my operas; third, by paying part of my monthly salary. As to the first—you can ask me for that type of work at any time, without any fear of inconveniencing me. The experience of many years has taught me that these arrangements such as you have already ordered, cost me little effort; so if for twenty years you should ask me to do one every day, I should not think it equal in value to the help for which I am asking you.

"Quite another thing—about that composition, *The Reproach*. The necessary mental attitude is not always possible. For instance, I am now busy with the symphony I started this winter (No. 4) which I want very much to dedicate to you, because I think you will find in it an echo of your innermost feelings and thoughts. Any other composition at this moment would be difficult—I mean work that needs the creative mood. Secondly, I am in an anxious, nervous and irritated frame of mind just now, very bad for composing, so that even the symphony progresses very slowly.

"It will pain me very much if my request seems tactless to you. One reason I decided to make it was that, once for all, it would exclude from our relationship the element of money, very embarrassing when it has to come up so often. I think that without it our friendship would be easier and more sincere. A correspondence in which every letter means payment and the reception of money, cannot be absolutely frank. Anyway, I am sure that this letter will not alter your opinion of my honesty. In case it displeases you, please forgive me. I am very nervous and upset these days, and tomorrow I shall probably regret having sent it.

> "Very sincerely yours,
> "P. Tch.

"P. S. Positively I shall write *The Reproach,* but when I cannot say. When I decide my summer plans, I will write you. Please send me the Kohne piece."

Nothing could have pleased Nadejda more than such an appeal. Instantly she replied:

"Thank you sincerely, Peter Ilyich, and with all my heart, for the confidence and friendliness you have shown in addressing me on such a matter. What I appreciate especially is that you have come straight to me and I beg you always to do so as to a close friend who loves you sincerely and deeply. As to paying me back, please, Peter Ilyich, do not worry. I myself will find ways for that.

"You have not yet answered me concerning my writing whenever I want to hear from you—which means that I want to write you from inner impulse rather than upon business. However dilute their religion may have become, the devout need saints and prophets. I need you, the pure prophet of my greatly beloved art. So, if you have no reason to say no, Peter Ilyich, save my sinless musical soul for earthly musical happiness—beautiful though not eternal—by allowing me to correspond with you. For this, some Lord Apostle will forgive you one sin.

"As to your dedicating your symphony to me, you are the only person from whom such an honor would be pleasing and valued.

"Sincerely, devoted with all my soul
"I am your friend,
"N. v.M.

"P. S. The man whom I usually send to you is not at home and I must send this by a Frenchman. That is why the address is in French."

Peter Ilyich wrote two replies on the same day; in the first one he did not address the lady by name. Perhaps he feared the straying eye of a pupil.

To Nadejda Philaretovna

Moscow, May 15, 1877

"I am in my class at the Conservatory, and that is why it is impossible to answer at greater length, and to thank you properly. You have helped me very, very much, dear N. Ph. Thanks to you, I am going to live a peaceful life, and it will surely have a good effect on my musical work.

"Today or tomorrow I shall write you further.

"Devotedly and gratefully yours,
"P.T."

May 15, 1877, Moscow

"Dear N. Ph.

"I have lived through one of the most difficult days of my life. I was ashamed. At the bottom of my heart, I knew that you would take my letter as you did. I knew it was not right to ask favors from a person like you, who would not know how to refuse. I reproached myself for exploiting your kindness, generosity, and delicacy. Vainly I invented all sorts of excuses for myself—an inner voice continued to reiterate my guilt. But your letter today is full of such sincere friendship, such warm wishes for my welfare, that the consciousness of having demeaned myself by asking for material help, no longer detracts one iota from the simple fact of my gratitude. Fear that it might be otherwise has been really painful. The kind and friendly tone of your sweet letter has persuaded me that I have done exactly the right thing.

"So I am doubly grateful. Not only have you rendered me invaluable service, but you have known how to defend me from the inner pricks of conscience. I know I express myself badly. Even the sincerest gratitude can impose a heavy yoke. In order not to impose that yoke, when granting such immense material gifts as you have granted, one must possess infinite tact and delicacy.

"You ask if I would find it agreeable to have you write me any time you feel inclined. Please, dear Nadejda Philaretovna, never doubt this. Correspondence with you can never be other than a pleasure; to discuss music with you is a joy. I have told you already of my deep feeling of sympathy toward you.

"This summer I plan to work very hard and to take a cure. Last year I drank the waters at Vichy, and found them very good for me physically. But unfortunately, I became so depressed there that the doctor advised me to leave before finishing the cure, at the same time urging me to renew the treatments this year. Probably toward the end of the summer, I shall go to Essentuki in the Caucasus where the waters are much the same as at Vichy. Until then, I plan to stay at my sister's. I want to start the opera, but first I must finish the symphony I am writing now, the dedication of which you have accepted. The first three parts are already sketched out. I have started the finale, but for the last few days I have not been disposed to work, so am postponing it till summer.

"I will write the piece you desire, after the style of *Le Reproche*. But I shall not hide from you the fact that this composition does not appeal to me. One can, however, often do better work feeling this way, and I hope to finish it up in neater style than Kohne. Please do not take this as an insinuation against your artistic taste. Sometimes, in music, one is drawn to something that is impossible of any critical analysis or pinning down. For instance, I cannot listen to the *Nightingale* of Alizhieff without tears!!! And authorities agree in calling it a sublime vulgarity.

"Once more I thank you, kind N. Ph. Remember that you have helped me out of a very, very bad situation, and I shall never forget the delicacy with which you gave such great help. Before you leave Moscow I hope you will write once more and give me your summer address. I shall be glad to keep up an active correspondence with you.

"Cordially yours,
"P.T."

Nadejda replied happily. She was going soon, she said, to her estate in the Ukraine. She wished Peter Ilyich could share beloved Brailov with her. She was worried to think of him in the Caucasus. "I am afraid of war. And if there is no danger from a regular war, there is always danger of a descent of the 'children of the Turk.'

Please be careful. In August, if there is no war with Austria, I shall go abroad—where, I have not decided."

Summer vacations in Imperial Russia assumed, it would seem, more than domestic proportions; before taking one's family to the country, one looked up the international situation in the newspapers. . . . Peter Ilyich answered immediately; the letter dated May 27, 1877, was to be his last for more than a month. There was good reason for the delay: The happiness, health, etcetera, at the end, has a hollow valedictory sound, and well it might: the "something" that bothered him so much was Antonina Miliukoff, who, innocent but determined young woman that she was, would very shortly play a part in this man's life far too sinister to be referred to merely as a bother.

Peter Ilyich to Nadejda Philaretovna

Moscow, June 8, 1877

"Thank you for your sweet, kind and friendly letter, dear Nadejda Philaretovna. It meant much to me, especially because before it came, my conscience had begun to torture me again for fear I had taken advantage of your wonderful kindness and generosity. Well, let us say no more about that. Know only, N. Ph., that my gratitude to you will never end; always I shall remember how much I owe to you.

"The examinations are nearly over. I am very tired of them and also of other worries connected with my departure. Then there is something else that bothers me greatly. I can't write to you at present about it, but surely in my next letter I shall be able to explain what the matter is and how it will end. It was great good fortune that material worries did not confuse my spirit or I should have fallen ill. On Sunday I am going to the country place of K. S. Shilovsky, a very agreeable man who with his equally agreeable wife and family lives on his estate near the New Jerusalem Monastery. I shall have a house and a piano at my disposal; I want to start steady work on the opera. Shilovsky, under my supervision, is doing the libretto which is taken from the poem of Pushkin, *Eugene Onegin*. Isn't this a brave idea? The few people to whom I have spoken about writing such an opera were first astonished and then enthusiastic. The opera will certainly not contain much action but the setting should be interesting. What poetry it contains! For instance, the scene of Tatiana and the nurse.

If only I can find the peace that is so needed for composition, I feel
that Pushkin's text will inspire me.

"I have finished the symphony—I mean the outline. Toward the
latter part of the summer, I shall orchestrate it. I have heard, N. Ph.,
that you never before consented to have a composition dedicated to
you; I am very grateful that in my case you made an exception. But
if you do not wish to have your name on the symphony, we can omit
it. Let you and me alone know to whom the symphony is dedicated.
Please decide as you wish. The arrangements printed by Jurgenson
will certainly be sold to my advantage in spite of the fact that we have
not decided the details. He has made a mistake in putting on the front
page 'property of the editor,' but it was done through carelessness.
Thank you a thousand times for that present also.

"I wish you happiness, health and all good fortune, kind Nadejda
Philaretovna.

"Yours,
"Peter Tch."

6

Plans for marriage

Peter Ilyich was thirty-seven when he wrote to Nadejda, complaining that "something" was bothering him. He was thirty-seven, he was an established musician making 3000 roubles a year. High time for something of the kind to bother him. High time, indeed, for him to take a wife and settle down.

So thought, at any rate, Peter's father, the respectable old Ilya, thrice married himself and securely pensioned, now, for his long service as a government engineer. Families always desire their members to marry; it increases the tribal prestige, it induces steadiness; a bachelor is a flighty fellow at best. Now that Petia was thirty-seven and a professor of music, the frivolity of his youthful days had, it is true, disappeared, but it had been replaced by what Ilya considered an almost unnatural nervous intensity.

Ilya did not know what lay at the bottom of that nervous intensity and frequent distressing hypochondria of his son's. Peter's sister knew it and so did one or two friends; artistic circles in Moscow suspected it. Peter had a dark secret to hide, and the urgent necessity for this concealment was to him a source of unremitting torment. For a man whose outstanding characteristic was sincerity in all personal relationships, such a secret was enough to cause more than hypochondria; it might well have caused—and would soon be on the brink of causing—madness.

Peter Ilyich was a homosexual. This fact has hitherto been strangely ignored or covered up by his biographers; we exhume it, not to rattle the old bones of scandal but because it was in truth the very structure and architecture of the man's personality. Had Tchaikowsky been possessed of lesser genius his abnormality might well have been his whole existence and we should never have heard of him; had he been a man of less self-control we should have heard of him in a blaze of

80

notoriety. His brother Modeste was a homosexual and also the nephew Bob Davydoff, Tchaikowsky's heir, who killed himself. All others of this large family were normal, and except for the paternal grandfather's "fits"—which may or may not have been epileptic—there is no ancestral history of degeneracy, disease or genius. Nothing, in short, exists to tell us whether the frequent homosexual trait was congenital with the Tchaikowskys, or if it developed environmentally. Only Tchaikowsky's attitude toward his affliction—for so he considered it—inclines one to the belief that homosexuality, like genius and hypochondria, was forced upon him by nature rather than chosen as a way of life.

Not until Peter Ilyich planned to marry, did he give posterity any overt proof of this dark secret which he never named outright but referred to in his letters always as *The*. Proof is lacking, not by accident but by design; Tchaikowsky's friends and family destroyed every bit of evidence they could lay hands on, and because the man did not live notoriously, he and his brother Modeste managed to cheat posterity of much gossip. And they had a right to such deception. For our part, we see no purpose to be gained in exposing every word that has filtered down to us concerning Peter's abnormality; we do not desire to record the names of his inamorata nor any incidents connected with these affairs. The facts are not of nearly so much interest as are the inferences to be drawn from the facts. What concerns us here is Peter's psychologic and spiritual reaction to his trouble, his own view of it, its enormous and poignant influence upon his character and indirectly, upon his music.

Here then was Peter, the second Tchaikowsky son, already past his thirty-seventh birthday and still, to his old father's distress, a bachelor. A restless, dissatisfied bachelor at that, only too prone to be defeated by his own strange nervous intensity. Peter himself recognized the havoc wrought upon his physique by his "nerves"; as definitely as any twentieth century psychiatrist, he attributed most of his physical ailments—his "heart cramps," his persistent intestinal indigestion—to disorganized nerves. A later century would have called his difficulties emotional, but whatever the name for them, old Ilya thought they could be cured by a wife. His two daughters were already safely provided with husbands; of his sons, Nicholas the eldest, and Hippolyte the naval lieutenant, were married and settled down—but the three others, Petia and the twins who were now twenty-seven, seemed to be further from marriage the older they grew. True, Anatol, the second twin, was always in love, always sighing after some girl too rich or too high-born for him, but neither Modia nor Petia—except for that short-lived Artôt episode ten years ago—ever seemed to mention the name of woman. Ilya Tchaikowsky was eighty-three when son Peter announced that he was to be married, and at eighty-three the news, wrote the old man to his son, made him ready to jump for joy.

But Peter did not tell his father about his marriage until ten days before it occurred in July, 1877; long before this—in August, 1876, he had mentioned it to Modeste. This letter to Modeste is the first written news we have of Tchaikowsky's "intentions"; obviously, he looked upon marriage as a major operation, painful but necessary.

"I have now," he wrote, "to pass through a critical moment in my life. By-and-by I will write you about it more fully; meanwhile I must just tell you that I have decided to get married. This is irrevocable . . ."

Tchaikowsky said his life had reached a crisis; this was true, as it had been true in 1862 when he decided to give up his government position and embrace a musical career. In both cases the crisis was within him; it was emotional and, far from being brought on by outward event, was rather the forerunner of event, the inspiration for action. In the first case Tchaikowsky's action was right because it followed his nature and his genius; but concerning the second crisis, the second time Tchaikowsky felt his life in chains and tried to escape—we shall see how disastrously he suffered by his choice of an "escape" which recklessly denied his own nature.

During the four years beginning in 1872 when he left Rubinstein and set up housekeeping for himself, Tchaikowsky had been growing more and more dissatisfied with his Moscow life. He was popular in society, he had many friends, but essentially he was lonely. He longed for some close tie, some intimacy that would extend to every detail of his daily life; again and again he expressed this wish and this unhappiness in letters to his brothers. In January, 1875 he wrote Anatol from Moscow:

"I can't stand holidays. On week days I work at fixed hours and everything goes like a machine; on holidays the pen falls from my hand and I long for someone near and dear to whom I might confide all my troubles; and truly, here in Moscow there is no one I can call a real friend. I am not intimate with the Conservatory people and their wives. If I had money I should like very much to be in Petersburg. I am very very lonely, and only persistent work keeps me from desperate depression. Unfortunately there is in me a timidity, an immoderate shyness and distrust of people that seem to increase. Can you imagine that lately I have thought seriously of the monastic life? Don't think I feel badly physically. I am quite well, sleep well, eat even better; merely I have let myself drift into sentimentality."

The monastic life! If, instead of Antonina Miliukoff, a persuasive Trappist Father had appeared, perhaps Tchaikowsky would have plunged into a monastery instead of into matrimony. Like many a man of intense emotions and weak will, desperate measures in a crisis appealed to him more than patience, control or steady going. In March, two months after the above letter, he wrote Anatol again:

March 9

"Fate, the Mocker, has arranged it so that for the past ten years all whom I love most in the world are far from me. I am extremely lonely in Moscow, not from lack of company but from lack of my dear ones. Perhaps you have already observed that my friendship with Rubinstein and the other Conservatory people is based only on the fact that we work in the same place. I have no one to whom I can pour out my soul. Perhaps this is partly my fault. I do not make friends easily. Anyhow while I was suffering from attacks of hypochondria, the lack of intimate friends was very hard. Nearly all winter I was constantly unhappy, sometimes to the very edge of despair; I longed for death. With the coming of spring these attacks have ceased, but I know that every winter they will return, stronger than ever. There fore I have decided to keep away from Moscow all next year. Where I shall go I don't yet know, but I must have a change of place and surroundings."

Tchaikowsky seemed convinced that his hypochondria was due to loneliness; later events point to another cause. Indeed, the entire testimony of his life proves that solitude held no terrors for this man, provided he could write music. Wandering in Europe by himself, living quite alone in the country, he was happy as long as he was composing. But let any outward event, any person or circumstance, interfere with his hours of work or with his creative flow, and he was instantly black with melancholy. In the four years prior to his marriage, his creative powers were approaching their zenith; the voices in his head were becoming more powerful, more insistent—and his Conservatory duties gave him little or no time to listen to the voices. Always his own music must wait upon his pupils—those idiots into whose heads he must, day after day, pound the elementary rules of musical theory. He disliked teaching and felt himself—erroneously—to be a poor teacher. As a matter of fact he was the most valuable man the Conservatory had; his pupils adored him. Not only was he extremely conscientious in his teaching, but he was especially well-equipped to teach theory because of his remarkable musical memory. At his finger-tips he always had a wealth of pianistic illustration for whatever musical form he wished to expound.

Nevertheless Tchaikowsky's nature was far too sensitive to rebound, in the Rubinstein manner, from the daily assault of a roomful of pupils. Knowing himself exhausted and rendered unfit for composition, Tchaikowsky was, very naturally, torn within himself. In proportion as he became conscious of his creative powers, he resented a world that seemed to conspire against the realization of those powers.

But why he should have thought marriage a solution is one of those perversities to which genius seems especially prone. The less a human being knows of marriage, the more likely he is to look upon it as a panacea. "Marry and settle down," a man's friends tell him. "Then life will be safe for you." It reminds one of the advice given so often to bewildered young wives: "Have a baby, and all your troubles will disappear."

Troubles seldom disappear by doubling. . . . It was unfortunate that Peter Ilyich did not possess some of Modeste's mildness, but that is like wishing the thunder would accomplish its business silently. Not without reason did posterity coin that purple adjective, *Tchaikovskian*. When Peter was gloomy he was gloomier than anybody before or since, and knew it. The fact that afterward he could laugh at his own Tchaikovskianism, did not render it less genuinely painful at the time. It was no wonder that he chose Modeste as his first confidant concerning marriage. Modeste was a homosexual too, but his natural mildness saved him from any such violent measure as marriage: fate does not require extreme penance from a nature incapable of extreme remorse.

And now we come to the second reason for Tchaikowsky's marriage: the first was his belief that marriage would stabilize his life so that he could do better work. The second reason does not make nearly such pretty reading—the man lived in mortal terror lest his homosexuality should be discovered by the world. This was a time and a place, be it remembered, that gave no quarter to this kind of sinner; a decent citizen would step off the sidewalk in passing rather than be contaminated by touching the garment of a homosexual. Peter Ilyich lived in continual terror, stalked forever by a horrid phantom—and a like shadow pursued his beloved brother Modeste. Neither of them, as we have said, ever named it on paper, always they referred to it as *The*. Anatol, Modeste's twin, knew of it too, but Anatol was a normal man and could never fully understand; Anatol had nothing to fear. No wonder Peter Ilyich clung to Modeste; with each other, these two could drop the rigid and exhausting mask they were forced to present to a world of normal men. When the brothers parted even for a month, they wept and were not ashamed of weeping.

Three weeks after writing Modeste that first excited but rather vague announcement of his matrimonial plans, Peter Ilyich wrote more fully:

.

To Modeste Ilyich

Moscow, September 22, 1876

"I have been thinking much, these days, about myself and my future. The result of all these thoughts is that dating from today, I shall
make a serious effort to marry, legally, anybody. I am aware that my
inclinations are the greatest and most unconquerable obstacle to happiness; I must fight my nature with all my strength. . . . I shall do
everything possible to marry this year, and if I am not brave enough
for that, at any rate I shall conquer my old habits for once and all."

September 29, 1876

"I am not inclined to hurry in this matter. You can be sure that if
I really tie myself to a woman, I shall do it with great prudence."

October 4, 1876

"There are people who do not despise me for my vices only because
they began loving me before they suspected I was only a man with a
lost reputation. Among them, for instance, is Alexandra" (Peter's
sister). "I know that she guesses everything and forgives everything.
So it is with many of those I respect and care for most. Is it not a bitter
thing to be pitied and forgiven when, truly, I am in no way guilty? So
it has been a hundred times, and will be a hundred times more. In
a word, I should like to marry, or by some known liaison with a
woman, shut the mouths of all despicable gossips, for whose opinion
I do not care a bit, but who can hurt people close to me.

"Fulfillment of my plans is not as near as you think. I am so confirmed in my habits and tastes that to throw them away as one would
an old glove, is impossible. And then I have far from an iron
will. . . ."

Almost on the same day he wrote Anatol:

"Tolia, I live to see you again. I am bothered because I fear that in
Moscow I was not thoughtful of you and did not let you see the real
depth of my love for you. If you noticed this, realize (surely you know
it already) that if I did not treat you kindly it was not because I did
not love you, but because I was annoyed with myself. When I am
annoyed with myself it always looks as if I were angry with others. I
was annoyed with myself because I felt I had lied when I told you I
had decided to make a thorough change in my life. Truly I have not
made this decision at all! I only have it in view, though seriously;
I wait for something to force me into action. Meanwhile I must ad-

mit that my cozy little apartment, my solitary evenings, the peace and quiet of my life has for me an especial charm. When I think that I must give it up—and to marry one must give it up—'the frost pricks my skin. . . .' "

To Alexandra Davydoff, the sister, he mentioned in the letter of October 4th, Tchaikowsky wrote under date of October 6th:

"Please, my angel, don't worry about my getting married. First, I don't expect to take such a step soon, certainly not within the school year. During these months I only want to look around and prepare for matrimony, which for many reasons would be a very good thing for me."

This was October. The winter was busy, and matrimonial plans, which so far had fixed upon no particular lady, were for a while in abeyance. Only now and again when captured by severe melancholy, did the idea of a wife recur to Tchaikowsky. It will be of value therefore, to follow him briefly through the winter and see what were the events that preceded his final decision to marry.

Late in November his opera *Vakoula* had its first performance in Moscow—characterized by the composer as a "brilliant failure." "I alone am to blame," he wrote Taneyeff. "*Vakoula* is not good opera style—it has neither movement nor breadth." In Vienna, Tchaikowsky's symphonic overture, *Romeo and Juliet,* was played and, as he himself recorded, "triumphantly hissed." But in Western Europe of the time, hisses were by no means a criterion of musical value. Russian music was not regarded seriously; how could a savage Tartar write sensible music? It required some courage on the part of a conductor to include in his program music written by savages. In Paris the popular conductor, Pasdeloup, attempted the overture, but his orchestra played it so badly—according to Tchaikowsky's faithful friend Taneyeff, who was there—that the intrinsic quality of the music was by no means evident. Tchaikowsky tried in vain to raise funds to have it played properly by Colonne's famous Paris orchestra—that same orchestra which was to be Nadejda von Meck's vehicle for hearing Tchaikowsky's music.

Just before the Christmas holidays—at about the time Nadejda was writing to thank him for executing her first musical commission—Tchaikowsky became acquainted with Leo Tolstoi. Tchaikowsky had always admired Tolstoi's writings and characteristically, whom he admired, Peter Ilyich adored. He regarded Tolstoi as a demigod, and said so. On his side, Tolstoi had heard Tchaikowsky's music and expressed a desire to meet him; so Nicholas Rubinstein arranged a musical evening at the Conservatory during Tolstoi's Moscow visit. Included in the program was the *Andante* from Tchaikowsky's D major String Quartet. "In all my life as a musician," wrote Peter in his diary, "I don't believe I was ever so flattered and touched as when Leo Tolstoi, sitting by my side, listening to the *Andante* of my first quartet, started to cry."

When Tolstoi returned to Yasnaya Polyana, he wrote Tchaikowsky as follows:

"I send you, dear Peter Ilyich, the songs. You will make of them a wonderful treasure, but for God's sake, arrange them after the Mozart-Haydn style, not the artificial Beethoven-Berlioz style that tries only for effect. How much I left unsaid to you! There was not time for all I had to say; I was simply having a good time. That last day in Moscow will remain a cherished memory. I never had such precious reward for my literary labors as on that wonderful evening. How charming Rubinstein is; thank him again for me. I liked him so much, and those other priests of the highest art in the world who sat with us around the board—they left with me such a pure and serious impression. All that was so kindly done for me in the round room I cannot remember without a shiver of emotion. Tell me which of the men in the quartet do not own my works and would care to read them. I should like to send them each a book.

"As yet I have not looked over your things, but shall. Whether or no you desire my opinion I shall write it frankly, because I already have learned to admire your talent. Good-bye, I press your hand.

"Yours,

"L. Tolstoi"

To this Tchaikowsky replied:

"Count —— I thank you sincerely for the songs. I must tell you frankly that they have been taken down by an inexperienced hand and therefore retain no more than traces of their original beauty. The chief defect is that they have been artificially forced into conventional rhythm. Only the Russian choral dances have regularly accented rhythm; the Bylini (legends) have nothing in common with the choral dances. Also, most of the songs have been forced into the key of D major, unsuitable for the true Russian folksong, which nearly always has an indefinite tonality, more like the ancient church modes. The songs you sent cannot be treated systematically, that is, they can never be made into a published collection of folksongs. That would require the most authentic research, an exact transcription of the original songs as sung by the people. This would be a very difficult task, demanding the most refined musical sensitivity and profound historical knowledge; except for Balakirev and perhaps Orokunin, I know of no one who could do justice to the work. But your songs are symphonic material—very good material, and I shall certainly make use of them some day.

"How glad I am that the evening at the Conservatory remains a pleasant memory with you! Our quartetists played as never before. Which proves that one pair of ears, if they belong to an artist as great as yourself, can inspire musicians more than a thousand ordinary pairs. You are one of those authors beloved for themselves as well as for their work. As for me, I cannot tell you how happy and proud I was that my music could touch and charm you.

"Fitzhagen cannot read Russian, but all the other quartetists know your work. I know they would be very grateful if you gave each of them one of your books. For myself, I should like best to have *The Cossacks,* if not now, then next time you are in Moscow—a day I shall look forward to with much impatience. If you send your photograph to Rubinstein, do not forget me too."

In a letter to Modeste, Peter Ilyich, evidently feeling very gay, mentioned the Tolstoi episode as one brother to another:—

"Gracious Sir, Modeste Ilyich:

"I don't know if you still remember me. I am your brother, a professor at the Moscow Conservatory who has written some music; operas, symphonies, overtures, etc. There was a time when you honored me with your personal attention; last year we even took a trip abroad that left a lasting and agreeable memory in my heart. Afterward you often wrote me charming letters; all of which now seems an impossible, beautiful dream. But I am not like you. Although I am tired and it is midnight, I sit down to write you, to congratulate you on the New Year and to wish you happiness. Greet your sweet

Nicolenka for me" (Modeste's deaf and dumb pupil). "Is he in good
spirits, and does he remember me? My holidays have been dull and
much too idle; I wanted to work but they would not let me.

"Before the holidays, brother mine, I met Count Tolstoi the writer
and liked him very much; since then I have had a kind and much
cherished letter from him. And brother of mine, when he heard my
first quartet he shed tears at the *Andante* and I am very proud of it.
So, my brother, you had better not forget me because I am, sweet
brother, a very important bird. Farewell then, little one.

"Your furious brother,
"Peter"

The friendship with Tolstoi went, however, no further; it ceased
indeed, with some abruptness. In his biography of Peter, Modeste
Tchaikowsky blames this upon his brother's constitutional shyness;
Peter felt uneasy in the presence of so great a man. An extract from
Tchaikowsky's diary, written ten years later, confirms this, and with
an extremely significant addition. The trouble was more than shyness; Peter had reason to dread the probe of a great man's eye; he
was quite convinced that anyone who could write so inspired a book
as *War and Peace,* had only to clap eyes on Peter Ilyich Tchaikowsky
to know him for the outcast he was.

"When I met Tolstoi," wrote Peter Ilyich, "I was possessed by fear
and a feeling of uneasiness. It seemed to me that this great searcher
of hearts could pierce at a glance every secret of my heart, that before
him a man could not hide the nastiness that lurks in the lowest depth
of every soul, nor could a man put the best side upon it. I told myself that if Tolstoi proved kind (which he surely would) then purposely, like a physician with his scalpel, he would delicately probe my
wound, seeing instantly the sorest spots and avoiding them—and
this very avoidance would prove that nothing was hidden. Or, lacking compassion, he would lay his finger on the very center of pain.
I was terribly afraid of these two things. Neither occurred. He who
in writing is so astute, so great a searcher of hearts, in conversation
proved simple, sincere, wholehearted, making no parade of the om-
niscience I had feared. He did not regard me at all as a subject for
dissection, he simply wanted to chat about music, which interested

him at the time. Meanwhile he seemed to enjoy depreciating Beethoven, frankly doubting his genius. That is a trait unbecoming to a great man. To abuse and deliberately refuse honor to a genius who has been recognized by all the world, is an indulgence practised, as a rule, only by small souls."

During January and February of this year—1877—Tchaikowsky seemed in high spirits. His symphonic fantasia, *Francesca da Rimini,* was beautifully performed under the baton of Nicholas Rubinstein in Moscow, and met with heart-warming success. Tchaikowsky began to sketch out his Fourth Symphony—the one he had proposed to dedicate to Nadejda von Meck. All seemed merry and normal enough—and then suddenly, for no reason except perhaps, the fatigue attendant upon the end of a long winter—Tchaikowsky walked into blackness. Suddenly, life was not worth living. To his friend Klimenko he wrote under date of May 8th:

"Since last we met I am very much changed—especially mentally. Not a kopek's worth of fun and gayety is left in me. Life is terribly empty, tedious and tawdry. My mind turns toward matrimony or indeed any other steady bond. The only thing that has not changed is my love for composing. If the conditions of my life were different, if my desire to create were not balked at every step—for instance by the Conservatory teaching which every year I find more irksome— I might write something really decent. But alas! I am chained to the Conservatory."

Why Peter should have connected the taking of a wife with the irksomeness of his Conservatory duties is impossible to understand, but it was so; for some time past he had not mentioned one problem without the other. . . . Once more the leaven of an ancient formula was at work: "Take a wife, young man! Settle down, and all your troubles will cease."

Fallow soil this—a young man, lonely, overworked, depressed, in search of a remedy for life. Ground prepared—and onto it, surrounded with all the persuasive panoply of spring, walked Antonina Miliukoff, young, pretty, good-natured, and madly in love with Peter Ilyich.

7

Two women and one man

Iᴛ is May, 1877, and along the streets of Moscow the trees show a young, delicious green. The schools are busy with examinations, the big houses are beginning to close; servants stand on ladders to give city window-panes their summer whitewash; it is time to go to one's country home. The air is filled with apple blossoms; in the long evenings all the world drives to Petrovsky Park or Sokolniki to hear the nightingales sing—the rich in their carriages behind prancing horses, the shopkeepers in their open cabs. But prince and shopkeeper share a blissful knowledge, a bit of news that causes them to laugh, to greet one another, to sing. Winter is over! The great oppression of the long cold is lifted. To a Russian, spring is more than spring; it is resurrection. It is a sign from on high that God has not forgotten his promise to man. . . .

Poor Antonina Miliukoff! We do not know where she first saw Tchaikowsky, but we know that from first sight she was violently in love. Perhaps she saw him at the Conservatory, perhaps at a concert—by this time Tchaikowsky was one of the prides of Moscow. If he was not yet famous, he was on the verge of fame. Antonina, ten years his junior, was utterly obscure both as to background and talent. The Miliukovs were not, as a family, attractive people; they were lower middle class, with none of the sturdiness of the class just below them nor the imagination of the class just above. They were, in short, haphazard and commonplace—the last persons for a Tchaikowsky to choose as life companions.

Antonina was pretty, she looked, according to Peter Ilyich himself, twenty-three rather than her real age of twenty-eight. She was blonde, with a pleasing figure and a beautiful, clear complexion. The testimony of those who knew her leaves no doubt that at the time Tchaikowsky became acquainted with her, Antonina was an attractive person—and this same testimony leaves no doubt also that she was temperamentally as impossible as a woman could be. Those who saw her a fifth and sixth time testified that while her appearance at first deceived the beholder, in the end it made her stupidity only the more irritating; she was decidedly subnormal in intelligence. Her persistent delusion that the world of men was in love with her, was a symptom of something far more sinister than stupidity. In the first letter we have that she wrote Tchaikowsky, this tendency is evident, although as yet it is only a tendency, and would be in no way remarkable did we not know to what appalling proportions the tendency was to grow. Antonina Miliukoff ended her days in an insane asylum. It is only fair to Tchaikowsky to state this now, at the beginning, and to state also that Tchaikowsky was not responsible for her loss of sanity. She suffered great unhappiness at his hands, nor is his treatment of her easy to condone. But with or without Tchaikowsky, hers was a nature that could never have achieved happiness; she proved that she could not live with anyone, husband or lover or her own family. Her type of insanity is well known to psychiatry: a sexual delusionary madness that can develop without provocation.

From the beginning, Antonina showed herself irresponsible and capricious beyond the normal actions of a woman of twenty-eight. She did not seem to know the difference between a lie and the truth, nor did she seem able to recognize this as a fault in herself. It was this characteristic more than any other that made her so difficult. She did not plan her lies nor defend them afterward; she lied like a child, incautiously and stupidly, often without provocation. There was no harm in Antonina and no meanness; beyond a natural resentment at humiliation, there was no desire to hurt her enemies. A woman who, writing a letter to the man she loves, drops blood upon the page from nails bitten to the quick, is a woman to be pitied. But we must be careful, in pitying her, not to cherish a corresponding resentment for the man who received the letters. Let us remember that Antonina bit her nails to the quick habitually, letters or no letters, and that this is not a normal trait, and let us remember also that although Tchaikowsky failed most lamentably in his relationship with her, almost anybody would have failed. It is not nearly so easy to be magnanimous concerning the capriciousness of a crazy person when one does not know the person is crazy; toward such hopelessly entangled, senseless behavior as Antonina's, the natural reaction is extreme irritation—and Tchaikowsky showed it.

The first letter we have from Antonina to Peter Ilyich is dated May 16, 1877. Unfortunately for historical justice, all his letters to her were destroyed. When she wrote this letter, Antonina had seen Peter, had written to him and had a reply, but the two had not met except in the company of other people.

Antonina Miliukoff to Peter Ilyich

Moscow, May 16, 1877

"I see it is time for me to make myself over, as you yourself suggested in your first letter. Now that I don't see you, I console myself with the idea that we are in the same city. In a month, perhaps even sooner, you will be sure to leave town, and heaven knows when I shall see you, as I don't expect to stay in Moscow. But wherever I go, I shan't be able to forget you or stop loving you. What I like in you I shall not find in anyone else—in short, I don't want to look at any man but you. And yet a week ago I had to listen to the declaration of a man who has been in love with me almost since school days, and has been faithful to me for five years. It was hard to listen to him, and I realized then that it cannot be easy for you to read my letters, not having anything encouraging to answer me, and with all the good will in the world, not being able to show more than absolute indifference. For a whole week I was in agony, Peter Ilyich, not knowing whether or not to write you. I see that my letters begin to annoy you.

"But is it possible you may drop the correspondence before meeting me even once? No, I am sure you won't be so cruel! God knows, perhaps you think me a fickle, infatuated girl, and because of that don't trust my letters? How can I prove that what I say is true? Surely in such matters one cannot lie. After your last letter I loved you twice as much, and your faults mean absolutely nothing to me.

"Perhaps if you were perfect I should have remained quite indifferent to you. I am dying with unhappiness and sorrow because I want so terribly to see you, to sit and talk with you, yet I fear that at first I should not be able to say one word. There is no fault that could make me stop loving you. It is not the love of a moment but a feeling that has been growing for a long time. I simply cannot, and will not, destroy this feeling now."

There is no question that this was an affecting letter; the frank fierce avowal of a girl helplessly in love, is always affecting. Even now, after fifty years, one feels sorry for Antonina. How much more affected then—and how much more fatally affected!—must Peter Ilyich have been when he read it. And how natural and indeed, flattering he must have thought the girl's statement about the suitor she had had to turn away. Impossible for Peter to see in that simple statement the future hint of madness, of a delusion that was to inspire a hundred such little stories—whether or not this particular one was true. Impossible, indeed, for anyone to have divined it, and this very impossibility, this innocence of Peter's in the face of oncoming, implacable fate is, from the vantage point of history, an awful thing to watch.

Antonina wrote again only two days later; reading her mention of his "frankness," how one longs to know what Peter Ilyich had said! Had he told the girl what he was to reiterate so often—that he might return her love by affection, but that she must never expect more than affection?

Antonina to Peter Ilyich

May 18, 1877

"I sent you a letter today, by messenger, and was much surprised to find that you are not in Moscow, which made me more unhappy. I sat at home the whole day, wandering from one corner to another like a half-mad person, thinking only of the moment when I may see you. I shall be ready to throw myself on your neck, to kiss you—but what right have I to that? You would think me bold. You were frank with me and I owe you a like frankness, but I must add that it would be very unfortunate if you should misinterpret this confession of my feelings. I can assure you that I am a girl of good reputation. I have nothing to hide from you. My first kiss will be for you and for nobody else in the world. Good-bye, my dear. Don't try to disillusion me about yourself, because you will only waste your time. I cannot live without

you and so, perhaps I shall soon make an end of myself. Let me look
at you and kiss you so I may carry that kiss into the other world.
                              "Good-bye,
                                      "Eternally yours, ——"

"Don't try to disillusion me about yourself," said Antonina. Peter
Ilyich never indulged in mock humility or coyness; he knew his
worth and he knew his weakness; there is not much doubt about what
he was trying to tell Antonina. Certainly, he was frank about it before
he married her. But such confession could not be put to paper—even
with one's brother one must be careful to refer to one's shame by
hieroglyphic. And how much more foolhardy, if one confessed *The*
under signature to a stranger! Peter Ilyich was by nature an impulsive
man; he showed no caution about money, about the formation of new
friendships, or indeed about anything save this one matter—and even
here, the necessity for secrecy and dissimulation caused him great misery. The genuine homosexual is never ashamed of his homosexuality,
but if he be an honest man—and Peter Ilyich was an honest man—he
is bitterly ashamed of the disguise he must wear and the lies he must
tell. As to the suicide threat in Antonina's letter, it was the most effective move the girl could have made. Peter Ilyich, who knew so
little of women, took it quite seriously. If his sister Alexandra Davydoff, whom he knew and loved so well, had said she was going
to kill herself, why sure enough—reasoned Peter—she would have
been found in the river next morning! It was a bad business all
round, this Antonina affair, and how on earth had it developed so
rapidly? True, he had told Modia and Tolia he was planning to
marry, but heaven knows, he had had nothing specific in mind in
the way of a wife. Bachelors are always saying they have decided
to marry. On the other hand, his father wanted him to settle down,
and here was this girl, ready to kill herself for love of him. How
easily, with what few words, he could turn her misery to joy!

Thus Peter Ilyich, to himself. Easy-going, always eager to see
everybody happy, always sliding round corners to avoid fights—
righteous or no though the quarrel might be—loving solitude, yet

finding his rooms continuously filled with friends because he had not the courage to refuse a hand upon the knocker. Why, one wonders, could the man not see that this woman, once admitted, would be a guest more terrifying than any he had entertained?

Peter Ilyich met the girl as her letter requested; he listened to what she had to say but refused to call on her in her rooms. She wrote him again at the end of the month:

Antonina to Peter Ilyich

June 7, 1877

"Let me know ahead, please, when you will come to see me, because Tuesdays, Thursdays, and Saturdays I am not in Moscow. Now that I cannot see you, I look at your picture, but Panoff has made you so terrible that I am indignant for you. Here I have finished my letter and still I do not know what to do with myself, I am so crazy with unhappiness. I hope you enjoy your stay in the country.

"It is three days since I wrote my letter, but I kept it until today, understanding you are not yet in Moscow. Once more, I implore you, come to me. If you knew how I suffered, surely you would have mercy and grant my desire. Having only one room at my disposal I shall have to apologize for such an uncomfortable way of receiving you—but I trust you will not think less of me because of it. It was my own wish to work and be independent. Tomorrow, Thursday, I must go to Hovrino, by the Nicholas Railroad, and I shall look for you all day Friday.

"I kiss and embrace you ardently, ardently.
"A.M."

And on the very same day that Antonina wrote this letter, another lady sat down to write Peter Ilyich. A very different lady, with a royal emblem upon her writing paper, a footman to carry her message across the city, maids to guard her door from interruption—but a lonely lady for all that, and one quite as much in need of companionship as Antonina Miliukoff. Perhaps more in need, because Antonina, in spite of her avowals, needed not only Peter Ilyich but the world of men. Antonina was young and her heart opened easily. Whereas Nadejda von Meck's heart, at forty-five, fiercely and furiously though it could love, was stifled under years of social training and restraint, under that constriction and that pride she called shyness—

How long—wrote Nadejda—how very long since news had come of Peter Ilyich! Nevertheless she must write anyway, to congratulate him on his approaching name-day. She wished him the health, joy and happiness that she knew he deserved; she would drink his health and her heart would be with him. . . . She had been target-shooting—went on the widow conversationally—but she had not hit center very often. . . . About the Fourth Symphony now in process of composition and Peter's request that he might dedicate it to her—she had never given such permission before, and even this time she could not say yes until she asked one question:

"Do you, Peter Ilyich, consider me your friend? Because of my under-standing of you and boundless desire for your good, I have reason to call myself your friend. But as you have never called me by that name, I do not know whether you recognize or consider me so. If you can say yes to that question, I should be most pleased if you would dedicate the symphony to your 'Friend,' without mentioning the name. If you cannot do so, forget, Peter Ilyich, what I have said, and be sure my feeling for you will not change one iota. I shall await news from you with impatience."

The widow had a long time to wait. All through June, no word came. Nadejda was at her southern estate, Brailov, in the Ukraine, before she had her answer. And what she read in it was indeed news—"For God's sake, dear Nadejda Philaretovna," Tchaikowsky wrote from Moscow on the third of July, "forgive me for not writ-ing before. Briefly, here is the story of what has lately happened to me.

"In the latter part of May, to my own great surprise, I became en-gaged to be married. This is how it happened . . ."

"The story of what has happened to me" . . . Not, be it observed, the story of what he himself had done, but passively, of what had happened to him. Patently, Peter Ilyich had no easy time writing this letter. From day to day he had put it off; before breaking the news

to Nadejda, he broke it to his brothers, his sister Alexandra Davydoff
and his father. He wrote them all on July 5th, and with his wedding
day fixed for July 18th, he knew well enough that nobody would
have time to advise him or come to his wedding. Then, on July 15th
—only three days before the fatal step was taken—he wound himself up to the task of confessing to Nadejda—for between these two
an intimacy had been established that could declare the inclusion
of another woman by no lesser ceremony than confession.

Here is the letter, entire:

Moscow, July 15, 1877

"For God's sake, dear Nadejda Philaretovna, forgive me for not
writing before. Briefly, here is the story of what has lately happened
to me.

"In the latter part of May, to my own great surprise, I became engaged to be married. This is how it happened. Some time ago I received a letter from a girl whom I knew and had met. From it, I
learned that she had honored me with her love for a long time. It was
written so sincerely and warmly that I was led to do what in such
cases I had always carefully avoided—to answer. Although my answer
did not give any hope that the feeling could be mutual, the correspondence started. I will not tell you in detail about it, but the result
was that I consented to go to see her. Why did I? I now feel as if Fate
had drawn me to that girl. When I met her I again explained to her
that I felt no more than sympathy and gratitude for her love. And
when I left I began to think over all the giddiness of my behavior. If
I did not care for her, if I did not want to encourage her, why then
did I go to see her, and how will it all end?

"From her next letter I found that if I should suddenly discontinue
all relations with her after having gone so far, I would make her most
unhappy and drive her to a tragic end. So I had a difficult alternative
—to save my freedom at the price of the girl's ruin (ruin is not an
empty word—she really loves me to distraction)—or to marry. I could
not do otherwise than choose the latter. One thing that helped me to
a decision was the fact that my eighty-two year old father and all my
relatives live in the hope of having me marry. So one fine evening, I
went to my future wife, told her frankly that I did not love her, but
that I would be a devoted and grateful friend, described my character
in detail, my irritability, my variable temperament, unsociability, and
finally my circumstances. Then I asked her if she would be my wife.

The answer, of course, was 'yes.' I have no words for the feelings I experienced during the days following that evening; it can only be imagined. Having lived thirty-seven years with an antipathy for marriage, it is hard to be goaded by circumstance to the role of a fiancé completely indifferent to his bride. It means altering one's whole life, thinking of the welfare of the person to whom one is united. All this, for an egotistical bachelor, is not easy.

"In order to think it over and adjust my mind to such a future, I decided to go to the country for a month, according to my original plan. The quiet country life, surrounded by pleasant people and beautiful nature, had a beneficial influence. I decided that I could not avoid my destiny and that Fate itself had decreed my meeting with this girl. Also, I know from experience that very often in life, what frightens and appalls results in good, while on the contrary, the very happiness we have longed for and worked for, disappoints us. Let what is to be, be.

"Now let me tell you a little about my future wife. Her name is Antonina Ivanovna Miliukoff. She is twenty-eight. She is rather attractive. Her reputation is irreproachable. To be independent and free, she supports herself. She has a loving mother. She is quite poor, educated not above the average (she was educated in the Elisabeth Institute) and seems to be very kind, capable of giving herself without reservations.

"One of these days, we shall be married. What the future holds I do not know. I doubt if I shall be able to take the cure, as I must think about arranging a home for us.

"In June I wrote the main part of the opera *Eugene Onegin*. I should have written much more had I not been so disturbed in spirit. I do not regret the choice of subject. I cannot understand why, Nadejda Philaretovna, loving music so intensely you do not appreciate Pushkin, who by the power of his genius very often breaks out of the narrow sphere of poetry into the infinite space of music. His words are more than mere words. Over and above his literal meaning, the verse itself possesses something that pierces to the depths of one's soul. And that something is Music. Also I cannot understand how anyone so sensitive to music can be a champion of Pisareff, who argued that to love music is as stupid as to love salted cucumbers, and who held that Beethoven is on a par with the cook of Dusso. Forgive my defending Pushkin and attacking Pisareff and his opinions so bitterly, but I admire the first as deeply as I despise the other for his contempt for my art. It is a pity we do not agree in this.

"You ask whether I call you friend. But how can you doubt it? Have you not read again and again between the lines of my letter how deeply I care for your friendship, and that my tenderness for you is very true and warm? How I should like to prove sometime, not by word but by deed, all the strength of my gratitude and sincere love for you! Alas, I have only one way, my music. Well, in that way, I am always ready to serve you; so why don't you write about the work you wanted me to do? If I cannot always satisfy your wishes as to the composition of one or another piece, because I cannot always be in the mood that is needed for composition, I can always do any other type of musical work. I even urge you, order such things from me as often as possible so that I can, little by little, pay my debt to you.

"I shall write on the symphony, 'Dedicated to My Friend,' as you have desired.

"And so good-bye, my dear, good, sweet friend. Pray that I shall not break under the approaching change in my life. God knows I am filled with the best intentions regarding my future help-mate, and if we are unhappy, it will not be my fault. My conscience is clear. Though I am marrying without love, I do it because circumstance would permit no other course. I giddily accepted the first declaration of love she sent me; I should not have answered her; but once I had encouraged her love by responding and visiting her, I had to do as I did. Anyway, I repeat, my conscience is clear. I have not lied or pretended. I have told her what she can expect from me and on what she must not count. Please do not tell anybody what has led to the marriage. Except you, nobody knows.

"Yours,
"P.T.

"P.S. Please give Milochka * a very tender kiss."

It was two years before Nadejda Philaretovna told Peter Ilyich what his "news" had really done to her; her confession is to be found in a later letter in this volume. But there is hardly a woman living who need turn to any page or chapter to know what Nadejda felt at that moment. . . .

On that summer day in Brailov when Nadejda received her letter, she sat down instantly and replied—and she wrote like a lady and a sportsman. Also, she wrote like a woman; observe her neat way of showing that she, as well as Peter Ilyich, could discuss other

---

* Nadejda's youngest child, a little girl of five.

subjects than marriage. Cautiously but clearly she leaves open a double road for future correspondence—it can be personal, or it can confine itself to Pushkin and music:

"With all my heart"—(how this opening phrase must have reassured Peter Ilyich, and how little he deserved reassurance!)—"I congratulate you, my dear friend, on the new step, a step that is always a gamble. In your case it rejoices me, because it would be a sin for a man with so golden a heart, so delicate a capacity for feeling, to bury such treasures. You have given happiness to someone and so you will be happy yourself, and in all justice, who should be happy if not you, the giver of such great joy to others? In this you have acted with the honor and delicacy that is always yours. You are good, Peter Ilyich, and certainly you will be happy.

"I cannot find words to express how deeply and sincerely grateful I am for the confidence and frankness shown in your letter. They are precious to me as happiness itself. Be sure, Peter Ilyich, that I appreciate your trust, and can be silent when necessary.

"I was very glad you were a little cross with me regarding Pushkin and Pisareff, because in it I see proof of friendship. But if I do not agree with Pisareff about music, there is a great deal in which I sympathize with him. In Pushkin I love, like you, the music of his verse, but my liking is entirely objective.

"With all my heart I thank you for the dedication—the symphony will always be a light to my life.

"I am sure, my dear, good friend, that in your new life, or under any circumstances, you will not forget that you have in me a deeply loyal friend, and will, regardless of all the fabrications and errors of public opinion, always see in me a soul that is devoted and true to you. You will write me everything, everything about yourself, frankly? Indeed, my dear Peter Ilyich, nothing that concerns you will ever be a bother to me.

"I shall hope to hear in your next letter that you are satisfied with the new life and that you are happy. May Heaven send you every good thing.

"From my heart, I press your hand. Do not forget one-devoted-with-all-her soul,

"N.v.M."

Thus Nadejda, to her "friend." . . . Not everyone would have accepted that symphony dedication, after what had happened. Not everyone would have called it a sun, a future beacon to her life. . . . Remember, this was no casual woman, casually bred. This was a gentlewoman; behind her, generations of women who had learned restraint, generations of ladies who did not cry when they were hurt.

8

Marriage. A growing breach and a growing friendship

Q<small>UITE</small> different in tone from his confession to Nadejda were the letters Tchaikowsky sent his brothers and father concerning his marriage. These were rather in the nature of announcement, the mood calm and affectionate. Peter Ilyich was in the country when he wrote them—the first sentence would seem to indicate that Anatol had a keen nose for trouble.

To Anatol

Glebovo, July 5, 1877

"Dear Tolia,

"You guessed rightly that I was hiding something from you, but you were wrong as to what the 'something' was. At the end of May something happened that I planned to keep for some time from all my near and dear ones, so that you should not be anxious for fear I was acting unwisely. I wanted to finish the matter entirely and then make full confession. I am going to be married. At the end of May I became engaged, planned to marry early in July and announce it to you all afterward. But your letter has changed my mind. First, knowing I shall see you, it would be hard to invent a whole drama of lies to explain why I can't go with you to Kamenka. Second, it would be wrong to marry without Father's blessing. Give him the enclosed letter. Please don't worry about me. I have given the matter much consideration and I take this important step quite calmly; you will believe this when I tell you that with marriage so near, I could write two-thirds of my opera." (*Eugene Onegin.*)

"The girl I am marrying is no longer very young, but quite honest and possessing one great attraction—she is in love with me. She is quite poor. Her name is Antonina Ivanovna Miliukoff. So I not only announce my future marriage but invite you to it. You and Kotek will be the only witnesses. Ask Father to be sure not to tell anyone, and the same to you. I myself will write Sasha" (Tchaikowsky's sister Alexandra Davydoff) "and the other brothers."

Once more, Tchaikowsky banishes what he has done somehow—somewhere—outside of himself. Something has happened, he writes Anatol, as though he himself had sat passively watching. As to his working hard and sketching out a new opera, this was a usual state with Peter before he took an important active step, good or bad. It would seem that the emotional turmoil necessary to propel his external life forward, was equally effective inwardly: emotional suspense was for Peter a state of balance as well as tension. Only when action occurred did the scales tip—and tip horridly—and Tchaikowsky's world went sliding into chaos.

The letters between son and father are cheerful and easy—the last untroubled words that Peter Ilyich will put to paper for many a long day. Except for his solicitude lest his father be shocked by the suddenness of his news, Peter writes like a little boy who, before leaving the house for a party, comes to show himself to his parents, all dressed in his party clothes:

To Ilya Tchaikowsky

Glebovo, July 5, 1877

"My very dear Father,

"Your son Peter has decided to marry; he asks you now to bless him on the threshold of a new life. My future wife is poor, but a pleasant, worthy young girl who loves me devotedly. Dear Father, you know that at my age a man does not marry without forethought, so do not be anxious on my behalf. I am sure my future wife will add greatly to my peace and happiness. . . . Keep well, my darling, and answer me at once. I kiss your hands."

Ilya Tchaikowsky's reply

Pavlovsk, July 9, 1877

"My sweet Son Peter,

"Tolia gave me the letter in which you ask my blessing upon your marriage. It made me so happy I crossed myself and jumped for joy. The Lord be praised, and His blessing be upon you! I don't doubt that your intended deserves the same blessing that your old father of eighty-three and all his family bestow upon you; not only your father but all who know you. Is this not true, my dear Antonina Ivanovna? From now on, permit me to call you my beloved, heaven-sent daughter, and to bid you love your chosen bridegroom, for indeed he deserves your love. Tell me the day and hour of your wedding. I will come myself—(may I?)—to bless you, and for the purpose I will bring the ikon with which you were blessed by your own godmother, Aunt Nadejda Timothevna, a kind and clever woman."

Poor Ilya Tchaikowsky! Not even the ikon of Aunt Nadejda— kind and clever though she may have been—could bring blessing to this union. Anatol knew it and rushed to Moscow—but he was too late; he could do no more than stand by and try to conceal real grief as he saw his brother plunging into a situation he knew would be disastrous. One other person witnessed the ceremony; Kotek the violinist, Tchaikowsky's young pupil who in the beginning had acted as go-between for Tchaikowsky and Nadejda von Meck. That same evening Anatol saw the bride and groom off to Petersburg for a week's "honeymoon." The wheels of the train were scarcely in motion before the bridegroom was assailed with a thou-sand misgivings, a thousand inner questionings. . . . Marriage! . . . He was married; he had rushed into a serious, lifelong relationship with no more consideration than one would give to the acceptance of a dinner invitation. What he had believed to be thoughtful considera-tion had in reality been nothing more than a childish anticipation of something new. All his life he had suffered from a wound, his real motive in marrying, he knew now, had been to cure this wound. Would it prove true, what the world said about a woman's healing power?

Two days after his marriage, Tchaikowsky wrote the first of those frightened letters to his brothers that were to continue for two months, wavering sometimes between fear and a temporary hope-fulness, but rising always toward the dark climax of September.

To Anatol

"I should lie to you if I said I was already quite happy, quite ac-customed to my new position. After such a terrible day as the eight-eenth of July, after that ghastly spiritual torture, one cannot recover quickly. I suffered intensely to see how you were afflicted for me, yet you were responsible for the fact that I fought so bravely with my agony. When the train started I was ready to scream; sobs choked me. But I had to entertain my wife with conversation as far as Klin to earn the right to lie in the dark in my own armchair, alone with myself. My only consolation was that my wife did not understand or realize my ill-concealed unhappiness. She has looked quite happy and satisfied all along. *Elle n'est pas difficile.* She consents to everything and is satisfied with everything. We have had conversations that have made our mutual relationship clear. She consents absolutely to everything and will never raise any objections. She needs only to fondle and take care of me. I have kept my full freedom. . . . I have so arranged matters that when my wife and I once become used to one another, she will not really bother me. I don't deceive myself. She is very limited, but even this is good. A clever woman would scare me. With this one I stand so high and dominate her to such an extent that I feel no fear of her."

There is no doubt that Peter Ilyich was trying hard, was "doing his best." During these first days, the kindly dispositions of both bride and groom served to conceal the true state of affairs. In spite of his nervousness, Peter had always been an easy-natured man— alas, too easy!—and it was impossible for him not to answer smile for smile. As for Antonina, she was both good-natured and extremely stupid. There is small doubt but that she disbelieved entirely her husband's declaration of his homosexuality and considered that to win him over would be only a matter of time and proximity. Where, after all, was the man that could resist her? She would bide her hour, she could well afford to; had she and her husband not a life-time in which to make love? Meanwhile she would accord Peter Ilyich all the respect he deserved and that she truly felt for him. Was he not a great musician, a genius, and she but an ignorant girl?

Peter Ilyich to Modeste

July 20, 1877

"My wife has one great quality—she blindly obeys me in everything, she is easy to get on with, content with everything, and asks only the happiness of being my support and consolation. To say that I love her I cannot as yet, but already I feel that I will love her when we grow used to one another."

To Anatol

July 23, 1877

"Truly I am going through a hard time. Yet I feel that little by little I am becoming used to my new position. It would be quite insufferable and inexcusable if I should mislead my wife in any way, but I told her long ago that she could expect only my brotherly love. Physically she has become absolutely repulsive to me. . . ."

At the end of this first week of marriage, the pair returned to Moscow. Peter hurried to the Conservatory and found there what he hoped to find—a letter from Nadejda von Meck. It was in answer to his of July 15th wherein he had announced his impending marriage. Nadejda's letter, we will remember, had spelled reassurance with the first words: "With all my heart, I congratulate you on the new step . . ."

And now we come to a difficult task; Tchaikowsky's reply is not grateful reading for a biographer who is fond of his subject. Barely had Peter Ilyich read Nadejda's friendly words when he sat down and asked her for money. We cannot excuse Peter Ilyich, we can only sit by helplessly while before our eyes a man goes to pieces morally, emotionally, and last of all, mentally.

Peter Ilyich to Nadejda von Meck

Moscow, July 27, 1877

"Yesterday I came to Moscow and found your letter at the Conservatory, dear Nadejda Philaretovna. In my present excited state of nerves, your friendly words and warm sympathy were very helpful.

"Nadejda Philaretovna! Strange and crass though it appears, I must again ask you for material help. This is what has happened: Out of the sum you know of, there was enough left to go to the Caucasus and live quietly during the summer without worrying about expense. On the scene comes my marriage. All that money went for the wedding and for the expenses connected with it. I did not worry, because my wife had inherited from her father a stretch of forest land in the district of Klin, worth approximately four thousand roubles. Just before the wedding, she decided to sell it and had every reason to think a sale had been arranged; indeed, she had been assured it would go through. We planned to use the money for our living in Moscow before leasing an apartment, for the furnishing of our future home, and afterward for my trip to Essentuki. As often happens with impractical people—she was misled, the forest was not sold. So we are badly in need of ready funds. We have nothing to live on, we can't take an apartment, I can't go to Essentuki. And yet I need to go away, far away, to be alone, to rest, to think things over, to be treated, and lastly, to work. I desperately need rest from the excitement I have been through. Because of all this, I must ask you to augment my debt by one more thousand. I make no further apology.

"It is hard for me to write you this; I do so because only you can give me a helping hand, only you will not consider my request troublesome or misread my motives, only you can save me from an intensely disagreeable situation. Tomorrow or the day after I go with my wife to meet her mother, who lives in the country. We shall stay about five days and then return to Moscow. I don't know what will happen after that. I know ahead that you will again help me. If I am not mistaken, you are a person who does not know how to refuse. Nadejda Philaretovna, let me postpone the story of all I have lived through these last days until I write again. I am so nervously upset that I cannot speak of it calmly or in detail; moreover, I do not yet well understand what is happening to me. I can't decide whether I am happy or not. I am sure of only one thing—I cannot work. It is a sign of an excited, abnormal state.

"Good-bye, my dear sweet friend. Whatever happens to me, the thought of you helps me, quiets me. Your friendship will always be the joy of my life.

"Loving you truly,
"P.T."

A real test, this, of a woman's love and generosity; a burning test. First, the man around whom her life has begun to revolve, marries a woman he has never thought it necessary to speak of until the day before his wedding; next, he writes asking for money. One thing to send money to a beloved friend who is alone, another to put money into the hands of a beloved friend's wife—and that Nadejda already hated the wife, we know from her later confession.

Money—how it can poison a relationship! But Nadejda refused to let it poison this one; her perfect trust in Tchaikowsky's honesty was, from first to last, amazing. She was a very rich woman, and the really rich are seldom careless of what is theirs; they have long since paid for their wealth with the price of their innocence. They have eaten of that tree which tells them that an inch given to the poor is a mile of inroad taken; bitter to them is the conviction that, given a chance, their beneficiaries will "take advantage" of them. And they are more than apt to be right. . . .

"Crass though it be, I must again ask you for material help". . . . How bitterly might the widow have refused this help, and how disastrous her refusal would have been to Tchaikowsky! The world of music lovers owes a debt to Nadejda von Meck for the brief note she wrote Peter Ilyich from Brailov in July, 1877, and for the accompanying fact of money—the first of those *lettres chargées* that were to grace the composer's mail so often. "Go to the Caucasus," she wrote, "and go quickly." Nadejda knew she need not add, *Go alone*. There is small doubt also, that she was not sorry to be the instrument of his going "alone"! . . . "Think of me sometimes," she continued. "Enjoy nature, be quiet and happy. I hope your next letter will explain more fully, and that from it I shall know all, all."

What a strong weapon is patience, for womankind! Had Nadejda demanded to know all—and surely, she had a right so to demand —she might never have progressed another inch with this difficult creature. But from Peter Ilyich the widow did not, then or ever, demand; she merely "hoped," and her hope was rewarded.

"Thanks, Nadejda Philaretovna," replied Peter Ilyich. "Thanks!" His brief reply is one long gasp of fear and tension; one feels it written in the very act of fleeing, of escape, the writer casting a terrified glance now and again over his shoulder. His pursuers—Antonina, and all the world that sympathizes with Antonina—will it catch him up before this last hour is over and he shall be gone from Moscow?

"Thanks, Nadejda Philaretovna, thanks! I am afraid to say anything that would look like a formality, so I add nothing to that word. I am leaving" (Moscow) "in an hour. I shall stop for some hours in Kiev for the special purpose of writing you a long letter and pouring out my soul to you. If I emerge from this struggle victorious, it will be due to you and you alone. A few days more and I swear I should have gone mad. Good-bye, my dearest friend, my Providence. In three days you will have my letter with the details.

"P.T."

And in three days she had it:

Kiev, August 9, 1877

"Nadejda Philaretovna, here, briefly is the story of all I have lived through since the eighteenth of July, the day of my marriage.

"I wrote you that I married, not because affection urged me, but because of a chain of circumstances inexplicable to me, which forced a hard alternative. I had either to jilt an honest girl, whose love I had carelessly encouraged, or marry. I chose the latter. At first I thought surely that I would fall in love with a girl who was so sincerely devoted to me; also, I knew that my marriage was fulfilling the dreams of my old father and others close and dear to me. The instant the ceremony was over and I found myself alone with my wife, realizing that our fate was henceforth to live inseparable and together, I knew suddenly that I felt for her not even simple friendship, but that she was abhorrent to me in the full sense of the word. There came to me the conviction that I, or rather the best and perhaps only good part of the being that is I—music—had perished forever. My future life seemed mere vegetable existence—a dreary, unbearable comedy.

"My wife is in no way guilty. She did not ask for marriage. To make her feel, therefore, that I do not like her, that I look on her as an insupportable nuisance, would be cruel and mean. All that is left is to pretend. But to pretend all one's life is the height of torture. How could I ever work? I felt desperate, especially as there was no one to turn to for support and encouragement. I wished terribly to die. Death seemed the only way—but death by my own hand was out of the question. I care deeply for some of my family, my sister, my two youngest brothers, and my father. I know that to decide on suicide and carry it through, would be to deal them a death blow. There are many other people, dear friends, whose love ties me to life. And then, I have the weakness (if one can call it a weakness) to love life, love my work, love my future success. I have not yet said all I have to say, all I want to say before the time comes to migrate to Eternity. Death does not come to me of her own accord. I shall not and cannot go to her, so what remains?

"I told my wife that I shall travel through August for my health.

which is truly impaired and needs radical treatment. No sooner had I said it than my trip began to take on the aspect of freedom from prison—though temporary; the very thought that the day of departure was not far away, gave me strength to endure. After a week in Petersburg, we returned to Moscow. There we found ourselves without funds, as a certain Kudriavseff who had promised to sell her forest, had duped her. So began a new series of anxieties and tortures. An uncomfortable lodging, the necessity of arranging a new home, the impossibility of so doing without money, all chance of getting away cut off for the same reason, worry, and a stupid, idle life in Moscow (I had no impulse to work and our living quarters were very uncomfortable), without friends, without a moment's rest from it all. I don't understand why I did not go mad.

"Then I had to visit my wife's mother. Here my torments increased. I have an antipathy for the mother and the whole *entourage* of the family I have entered. Their ideas are narrow, their opinions wild, they are all at swords' points. My wife (perhaps it is unjust) hourly became more abhorrent to me. It is hard to describe, Nadejda Philaretovna, the spiritual agonies I experienced. Before going to the country, in a desperate effort to find a way out of the terrible situation and longing to get away, I applied to someone well-known to you, a sweet and dear friend, living at present at Brailov. The thought that she would help me, the certainty that she would free me from these awful bonds of sorrow and madness, bore me up. But would my letter reach her? The idea that the letter might go astray tortured me. We returned to Moscow.

"That terrible life dragged on for some days. I had two consolations, first, I drank a good deal of wine which made me dizzy and gave me some moments of forgetfulness, and secondly, talks with Kotek cheered me. He is the only person except you that knows all I am writing now. He is a good man in the real sense of the word. It is a fact that sorrows do not come singly. I received news of the sudden death of one of my closest friends, Adamoff. We were in school together, started our service together, and regardless of the fact that our paths lay apart, were close friends until his death. He had every good fortune in life; perfect health, a very good official position, money in his wife's name and a completely happy family life—then suddenly, death. It quite broke me up.

"At last, one happy evening, a letter came from Brailov . . . I began to feel more cheered. The intervening days were occupied in preparations for departure and arrangements for future lodgings, and on Tuesday, at 1 P. M., I left. I don't know what the next step will be, but I feel as if I had waked from a terrible, painful nightmare, or rather from a long illness. Like a convalescent from fever, I am still very weak. It is difficult to think consecutively. It was very hard to write even this letter. But what a sensation of sweet rest, what a drunken feeling of freedom and solitude!

"If my knowledge of the way I am constituted does not deceive me, it is very possible that, after resting and calming my nerves, returning to Moscow and the routine of occupation, I shall look upon my wife quite differently. Truly, she has many qualities that can make for my future happiness. She sincerely likes me and does not desire anything more than my peace and happiness. I pity her.

"I am staying in Kiev for a day. Tomorrow I go to my sister, and from there to the Caucasus. Forgive the incoherence and inconsecutiveness of this letter, Nadejda Philaretovna. My nerves, my whole spirit, are so tired I can hardly put two thoughts together. Yet, exhausted though my spirit may be, it is not so broken that it cannot glow with the most unbounded and profound gratitude to the hundred-times-dear-friend-without-price that is saving me. Nadejda Philaretovna, if God gives me strength to live through the horrible present, I will prove to you that this friend has not helped me in vain. I have not said one tenth of what I want to say. My heart is full. It wants to pour itself out in music. Who knows, perhaps I shall leave after me something truly worthy of the fame of a first class artist! I have the audacity to hope so. Nadejda Philaretovna, I bless you for all you have done for me. Good-bye, my best, my dearest, sweet friend.

"P.T.

"P.S. I shall await a letter in Essentuki with impatience."

Tchaikowsky did not go to Essentuki; he had "the waters" brought to him. His next letter is from Kamenka, his sister Alexandra Davydoff's country home, where he was to pass six blessed weeks without a wife. Whatever may seem false in the above letter—such as Tchaikowsky's intimation that he was trapped into marriage by concern for a girl's broken heart—one thing rings true throughout. He loved life, loved his work, loved his future success. And the three were, for Tchaikowsky, synonymous; the awful mistake of his marriage was to prove this to him irrevocably. He had made the gesture of trying to live as other men live, he had taken a wife, tried to shape his life about a central intimacy, a personal responsibility: what, as a result, was happening to him?

He did not know as yet, he could not define this fear and this *malaise;* after two weeks of marriage Peter knew only that he was vastly bewildered and vastly distressed. Perhaps rest and the shelter of his sister's household would enable him to order his thoughts once more and take stock of what his life was to be. Here at Kiev as he paused to write Nadejda, he knew that already a great gain had been made; twenty-four railroad hours away from his wife, and he felt once more the blessed urge to write music, the inspiration that alone spelled manhood and self-respect.

But it was fickle in its visitations, this urge to create music. Arrived in Kamenka, finding himself surrounded by people who had known him since his youth, the tension of desperation relaxed and with it, for a little time, musical inspiration. "Nadejda Philaretovna," wrote the composer—

"I have been here four days, surrounded by the closest and dearest of my relatives, which means not only my sister and her family but my two favorite brothers" (the twins). "The doctor, my sister and both brothers have persuaded me to take the Essentuki waters here. They fear that in Essentuki (a very dull place) my depression will come back and destroy all benefit from the treatments. To stay with them is so agreeable that I could not resist consenting.

"If I should say that I have returned to normal, I should lie. Only time can cure me, and I don't doubt that recovery will come little by little. But those around me are balm to my soul. I am tranquil and begin to be able to look on the future without fear. I regret one thing—I cannot yet work. Work frightens and terrifies me. And yet just that is the greatest cure for my sickness of spirit. I shall hope for a return of the desire to work."

The letter goes on to ask whether Nadejda has received his long letter from Kiev, and soars suddenly into a paragraph concerning the soul—Nadejda's soul in particular—a dithyramb which for want of better qualification we can only describe as Russian.

"Dieu!" cries Tchaikowsky, "what kind, beautiful souls live on this earth! Meeting such people as you on the thorny road of life,

one grows to feel that humanity is not as selfish and wicked as the pessimists say. There are wonderful exceptions sometimes; among a million others, if such a one as you appears, it is enough to save a man from despair. I know I express myself badly and stupidly. But I am sure you will not read empty phrases where I want to express the deepest and sincerest love for you.

"Good-bye, my dear friend . . . Good-bye. Yours until death,

"Devotedly,

"P.T."

There is no doubt now of what was happening to Peter. In despair of his relationship with Antonina, he was turning to another woman, a being as far removed from Antonina, in character and position, as woman could be. And he was not proceeding cautiously, but with all the impulsive violence of his personality. Antonina was of the earth earthy; Antonina was a presence, Antonina was some nine-odd stone of flesh and blood that spoke with a warm young voice, that reached continual greedy hands. . . .

This man had never wanted a wife; he had wanted, in company with all homosexuals, a mother, someone at the same time intimate and remote whom he could worship and who would in turn worship him—always at a safe distance. And who, among womankind, could fill the role so beautifully, so convincingly, as Nadejda von Meck? Had she not, in almost the first letters she wrote him, declared him her ideal, and in the same breath had said she did not wish to meet him or to speak with him in the flesh?

Not that Peter Ilyich sat down, there in Kamenka, and thought this out. He was too sick to think things out, and anyway, in his emotional relationships with other people, it was this man's misfortune never to think things out, but to plunge blindly into disaster or peace, whichever chanced to present itself in human form. . . . Here in Kamenka were happy people, normal people, living in peace with one another. Alexandra Davydoff was a perfect wife to the good Leo who worked so hard as a landlord, who worried so over his beet crops and his sugar factory. How sweet the sound of children's voices from garden and nursery, and how gracious, over all this household, the old grandmother Davydoff's presence as benediction! . . . Antonina, for all her sensuality and parade of womanly nature, did not care for children and had said as much. How, in the future, could he ever introduce Antonina—or any Miliukoff—into this house of peace and utmost refinement? How could he, indeed, introduce Antonina into any department of his life?

Nadejda von Meck, on the other hand, would be adored by this household. Everything about her would fit—her bearing, her intelligence; and was she not a lover of children? Mother to twelve—a glorious woman, this, one who had faced life as Peter himself knew he could never face it—and yet a being of refinement, possessing a reserve that would never trespass upon a man's weakness, never lay finger upon a man's sore and sensitive soul. . . . How much did she know, Nadejda von Meck? Rumor had been busy in Moscow concerning over-emotional friendships at the Conservatory; often enough it had come scorchingly back to Peter's ears. And could Nadejda, a woman of the world and moreover, a woman intensely curious about everything concerning himself—have escaped hearing this slander? Well, if she knew, she had apparently put it behind her or, like Alexandra, she had forgiven. One thing he was sure of: Nadejda would never challenge him concerning this matter, and she would never hint. She was honest, she was frank, she had said she hated the roundabout methods of conventional relationship. . . . Oh, how could he tell this woman, how could he express to her what, at this most terrible moment of his life, her friendship meant to him? "Yours until death," wrote Peter at the end of his letter—and meant it, and rejoiced that he meant it.

And on her side, Nadejda had cause for rejoicing. She had asked for this man's complete confidence and she knew now, that she had won it. She wrote from Brailov that she had received his letter from Kiev, and that she was relieved because he had not gone to the Caucasus; nobody could ever tell how far that ancient enemy, the Turk, would venture. Also, her dear friend was now among people who not only *cared* for him, but *understood* him. . . . (How shrewdly and how blandly a Madame von Meck could dispose of an Antonina Miliukoff!)

"Thank you deeply, my best of friends," the letter continued, "for telling me all that has happened. How I suffered for you, how I pitied you when I read that letter, I can never say. Several times, tears filled my eyes. . . . What would I not give for your happiness! But I hope as you do, that after some rest, some time passed among people with whom you have so much in common (if you only knew how I am drawn toward them!), you will regain your strength, and find things not so bad as you thought. I am not an optimist—I do not lay false colors upon the bad things in life—but I find there are conditions to which one must *se résigner,* or, more exactly, in Russian, at which one must wave one's hand, make peace with, and grow accustomed to. Truly, resignation is stupid, but what can one do? One cannot torture oneself by constant fighting. I must honestly admit that although this theory is the result of experience, yet it remains only a theory, because with my mental and physical constitution, it is impossible to put it into practice. Only for your peace, for your happiness am I willing to preach what I do not live up to. From my heart, I implore heaven to give you joy again, pray that all your past unhappiness may be but payment for future good, because no good thing can be had for nothing.

"You have understood my moods, you would like to make my life gayer—already you are making it easier. Your music, your letters, give me moments when I can forget all the trials, all the misfortunes that everyone must have, no matter how fortunately placed in the world. You are the only person who gives me such profound, such great happiness; I am infinitely grateful, and only hope that what inspires it will not end or change, because such a loss would be unendurable.

"I have not written you at Essentuki because I thought you could not yet be there. In a week I am going abroad for a month and a half; directly from here to Vienna, then Munich, Milan, Florence, Rome, Naples. My daughter and I are very fond of Italy.

"There is great military activity here. I have a hospital of two hundred beds on my estate; we are all busy sewing linen for the wounded. Today the Hussars of Grodno are passing through; they are already having to use the regiments of the guard. My son-in-law and sons took wine to the soldiers for a treat.

"Good-bye, my sweet, dear, unforgettable one. Write me at Brailov some words about yourself.

"N. v. Meck"

It was wise of Nadejda to counsel patience: "resignation," she called it, yet she was honest when she confessed that her nature would not permit her to practice what she preached. At forty-five the widow von Meck, insisting vociferously that she was an old woman whose life was done, had enough fire in her for ten, and was possessed of a thousand devils of restlessness that would never leave her until breath itself was gone. Tchaikowsky's reply showed much improvement of spirit; he was again at work upon the Fourth Symphony, hereafter referred to, in writing Nadejda, as "your symphony," or "our symphony."

Kamenka, August 23, 1877

"Dear Nadejda Philaretovna:

"Your letter just came, and I send you a few hasty words to Brailov. Tomorrow I will write at greater length to Vienna."

"I feel very much more at peace. The pleasant society, the quiet and tranquillity, together with the water cure that I started last Saturday, have made me over. I must confess that I showed terrible cowardice in my trials and a complete absence of strength. I am ashamed that I let myself go to such an extent and gave way to that sinister nervous excitement. Please forgive me for disturbing and alarming you. I am sure I shall emerge from this situation a victor. I must fight this feeling of alienation toward my wife, and learn to give her good qualities the appreciation they deserve. There is no doubt that she has them.

"I have so far recovered as to work a little on your symphony. One of my brothers—the twins—whose opinion I greatly respect, liked the part I played to him. The orchestration of the first movement will take a good deal of effort. It is very complicated and long, but is, I think the best movement. The other three are very simple and will be great fun to orchestrate: The *Scherzo* will demonstrate a new instrumental effect from which I hope much. First, only the strings play, *pizzicato;* in the *Trio,* the wood-winds enter for a solo passage; they are replaced by a group of brasses also playing alone; at the end of the *Scherzo,* all three groups call to one another in short

phrases. I think it will be an interesting musical effect. I hope you
will like it. That is the most important thing of all.

"Good-bye, best of friends,

"Your

"P.T."

Tchaikowsky had mentioned his fatherly love for the twins, Anatol
and Modeste, ten years his junior. What he says is borne out by his
treatment of them. He had indeed watched over them as children;
in this man was a great capacity for tenderness; children—and dogs
—loved him instantly and spontaneously, the way he loved them.
To the young Davydoffs, Uncle Petia was not only a heaven-sent
Saint Nicholas who from time to time arrived with pockets filled
with adorable presents, he was their guide and mainstay even when
they were grown. Tchaikowsky's life at the moment is moving too
rapidly for us to stay and draw a picture of him at Kamenka as
Uncle Petia; during these days of self-condemnation and nervous
distress, no doubt the kind Alexandra was more thoughtful than ever
toward the wayward and talented brother. The girls were always
after him, especially Tatiana the eldest was forever beseeching
him to play waltzes that she might dance. When he had no music
at hand, the girls would order him gayly to write some, and he would
always comply. "Uncle Petia cannot say no, Mother; he is too *good*
to say no. . . ."

It was true enough that Petia could not say no. . . . Alexandra
must have sighed, for she loved her brother. But she was not so
sure now, about the *goodness*. Petia had said yes once too often, with
this girl, this Antonina. He had done wrong, grievously wrong, and
others beside himself would suffer for it. . . . But thank God his
nerves seemed to have improved, here at home; she had feared for
his sanity, those first few days. The spirit was utterly out of him;
he had gone about dragging his feet in a way almost furtive—
he who was wont to move so quickly. And his eyes had looked so
queer. Petia was a handsome man, and his flashing blue eyes were
his best feature; when they went dead, all distinction was gone,

somehow, from him. . . . But since he had begun to work again, these last few days, the life had come back to his face and after a morning with his new symphony he would actually run from his room to the garden, shouting to the children with his old gayety. . . .

"Our symphony," Tchaikowsky wrote Nadejda, "is advancing a little." And forthwith he went on to mention the "new instrumental effect" of the *Scherzo,* from which he "hoped much." That his hopes were not too high, every conductor who likes to play Tchaikowsky will testify; the effect is tense and brilliant. So brilliant, in fact, that ambitious conductors are tempted to take the movement too fast, and sacrifice melody to show off their orchestral control.

Nadejda found this letter in Vienna, on her way to Italy; her impatience to have it in her hands had made the forty-three hours in the local train between Brailov and Vienna, interminable. She was of course delighted that Peter Ilyich was working, and pleased to have him call the symphony "ours." "I like *pizzicato* very much," she wrote. "It runs like an electric current through all my nerves." But, if the symphony was so nearly finished, what next? "How," asked this indefatigable woman, "is your opera coming along, Peter Ilyich?"—(*Eugene Onegin*) "How far have you gone with it?"

This was characteristic of Nadejda. From first to last, Tchaikow-sky's music was not an excuse for this relationship, it was the basis and foundation stone on which the whole matter rested, and the widow never let Tchaikowsky forget it. To her, his music *was* Peter Ilyich, if his music prospered, *he* prospered; this man's music was his growth, the kernel his life fed upon; if she sent him money, it was to feed this life that she knew was so well, so very well, worth nourishment.

The rest of Nadejda's letter is concerned with the details of her journey. She always travelled with a retinue—one or two personal maids from Russia, a butler and lackey, three governesses and a tutor for the four young children, and usually a musician to play duets with her. Julia, of course, travelled with her mother, and this time as usual, Julia stepped into the void left by two French govern-esses who had to be dismissed *en route* for which Nadejda described as "erratic behaviour." "Julia teaches and looks after the younger children," Nadejda wrote—

"She runs the household, serves as my secretary, thinks of and does everything, and all as if she enjoyed it. She loves me to the point of self-sacrifice, but never caresses me . . .

"Forgive me, Peter Ilyich, for waxing so enthusiastic. Does it annoy you? But please don't think I exaggerate. Believe me, however much I love a person, I am never blind. I can admire the qualities of someone outside the family—like you for instance—as I can those close to me. It is so good to talk to you about what I hold dear! Good-bye, my dear, sweet friend. Don't forget me, because always, everywhere and with all my heart, I am your devoted friend,

"Nadejda von Meck"

Tchaikowsky's reply was gloomy. He had been a month in Kamenka; it was high time for him to go. Had he known what in truth awaited him, he would have dreaded Moscow with something more than the nostalgia he felt now. . . . His letter is, however, concerned mostly with Nadejda's question about his opera. It is plain that at Kamenka Peter Ilyich had buried himself in Pushkin and Pushkin's *Eugene Onegin*. And this was peculiarly fitting, because Pushkin was one of the traditions of Kamenka; as a friend of Vasili Davydoff (the Decembrist) Pushkin had often visited Kamenka. In the grand days of Kamenka—fifty-odd years ago—the grotto above the west garden had been used as a banquet hall. Alexander Davydoff had it built as a cool place to eat his Lucullan suppers in summer; while he and his friends feasted, an orchestra of servants sat on the roof and played. . . . Now all this grandeur was vanished; Leo Davydoff, conscientious gentleman-farmer that he was, had no use for feasting or grottoes. But Tchaikowsky loved the grotto; dreaming in its shade on warm summer afternoons he saw the creatures of Pushkin's glorious verses pass across the grotto's mouth. . . . Striding through the sunlight—to sweet and melancholy music—Onegin, that arch-swaggerer. And clinging to his arm—lovely, young and tragic—Tatiana, with a song upon her lips . . .

Indeed, it was in the grotto that old Elizabeth Davydoff, Siberianborn during her father's exile, bred in the old régime, sat through the whole night with Peter Ilyich, beseeching him not to do the sacrilege he had planned with Tatiana, not to have her leave her husband and run off to illicit, joyful love with Onegin. In his verses, Pushkin had not let her run off. Sitting bolt upright, a frail tiny figure in her old-fashioned grey gown and pelisse, Elizabeth implored. . . . And as the sun rose, Tchaikowsky agreed against sacrilege, so that the generations of opera-goers may sigh over the melancholy triumph of Tatiana's sinful love denied.

But grottoes and delicious old Davydoff ladies could no longer have part in Tchaikowsky's life and he knew it. Something was awaiting him in Moscow, something of his own shaping which had small relation to innocence.

To Nadejda von Meck

Kamenka, Sept. 11, 1877

"I am writing in a gloomy state of mind, dear Nadejda Philaretovna. The fields are bare and it is time for me to go. My wife writes that our apartment will soon be ready. It will be hard for me to leave. But anyhow I shall go from here a healthy man, with strength to fight my fate. I know there will be hard moments, but then habit will assert itself, which as Pushkin says, 'is given to us from above in place of happiness.' For instance, I became accustomed to my duties at the Conservatory, that in anticipation had loomed as the direst misfortune.

"You ask about my opera—it progressed very little here, but I have orchestrated the first scene of the first act. Now that the primary enthusiasm has gone and I can look on it impartially, I think it is condemned to failure and indifference from the public. The story is simple, there are no stage effects, the music has no splendor or brilliance. Nevertheless it is possible that some of the elect, listening to this music, may be moved to the emotion that moved me when writing it. I am not trying to say that my music is so beautiful; merely, I know it is not within reach of the vulgar. In a word, I am unable to write for the express purpose of pleasing either the crowd or the elect. I think one must, in writing, submit to one's instinctive bent, without thought of pleasing one camp or the other. I began *Onegin* without any particular purpose, but the way it has developed, the opera will not be interesting theatrically. So those for whom the first condition of opera is dramatic action will not be satisfied, but those who can see in an opera the musical interpretation of simple human feeling, far removed from the theatrical and dramatic, can (I hope) be satisfied with mine. In short, it is written sincerely, and on that I rest my hopes.*

"If I have been mistaken in choosing my subject, if my opera is not included in the repertory, it won't hurt me at all. Last winter I had several interesting conversations with the writer, Count L. N. Tolstoi, that revealed much to me. He convinced me that the artist who works not from inner inspiration but with careful calculation of effect, who forces his talent with the idea of pleasing the public, is not quite an artist, his works will not endure, his success will be ephemeral. I am quite convinced of the truth of this.

"Thank you for the dear letter from Vienna. What a charming person your daughter Julia is! I am glad you have such a devoted soul near you. Good-bye, my sweet friend.

"Your
"P.T."

Tchaikowsky did not leave Kamenka until September 11th, but history possesses only one more letter written from there. Perhaps, with Moscow and Antonina drawing ever nearer, he feared to write Nadejda; even when writing to Anatol, he tried to reassure himself as to the horror that awaited him by referring to it with such light words as "indifference" and "annoyance":

To Anatol, in Petersburg:

Kamenka, September 23
"Only when thinking of a loved one far removed can a man realize the full strength of his love. Tolia! I love you terrifically. But oh, how little I love Antonina Ivanovna Tchaikowsky! With what deep indifference does that lady inspire me! How little does the prospect of meeting her cheer me! Yet she does not frighten me—she is simply an annoyance."

Nothing, here, about *Onegin;* no mention of music, no eager words concerning *pizzicato* or Tatiana's lyrical soliloquy. It will be some time, indeed, before we see Peter Ilyich once more as we love to see him, in that guise that was his best self, his only real

---

* His hopes were not too high. The simple lyricism of *Onegin* still enchants audiences the world over.

self—the guise of an honest workman. He is leaving Kamenka and his friends, he is about to enter that particular hell which Fate reserves for persons of enormous emotionality, enormous sensitivity, and weak will—the hell of terror and remorse over crazy, futile actions for which the subject well knows he has no one to blame but himself.

And while we follow Peter into this place of darkness, while we watch him sliding ever deeper down this blind declivity, let us, in all mercy, bear in mind not only what the man *was* during those weeks, but what he wanted to be—and was to become. Let us remember his answer to the effusive lady who once insisted that he define for her his goal in life, his "ideal." Peter Ilyich replied soberly, but he did not keep the lady waiting. "My ideal," he said, "is to become a good composer." *

* From *Tchaikowsky, His Life and Works*, by Rosa Newmarch. Grant Richards 1899.

9

Disaster

ANTONINA does not frighten me . . . She is simply an annoyance . . ." *She does not frighten me—I am not afraid—not afraid—
not afraid—*

The train wheels, carrying Peter Ilyich from Kamenka to Moscow,
chant a refrain. Brave words, these, but ominously persistent. Peter
turns unhappy eyes to the car window and the autumn landscape
rolling by. How familiar these country fields around Kamenka—
unwalled and unhedged, the black Ukrainian soil steamy now with
the autumn rains. The straw-thatched village huts are whitewashed,
the churches are white too, with roofs painted green. Not a beautiful landscape, yet how Peter loves it! Every undistinguished square
foot of it. . . .

And at the end of this journey, what awaits? Will Antonina be
at the station? Petia! she will cry. Her voice is sharp, with a na-
sal quality, insistent, penetrating. Not the girl's fault, of course, that
she lacks all evidences of culture. . . . Will she stand there on the
long platform, her fresh face seeking him through the carriage window, her hands reaching. . . .

Ah, those hands! Reaching, always reaching—greedy, inescapable.
. . . She will turn her face up. . . . And she will have a right to
expect a response, this woman, wife of Peter Ilyich Tchaikowsky.
All the world knows or will know, when the news of the marriage
spreads—all the world will know of Antonina's right to a bridegroom's greeting. . . .

Antonina was at the station, as Peter testified next day in a letter
to Anatol. And why, indeed, would she not be there? She had
waited six weeks alone, without her bridegroom; she had been very
busy, preparing the little home. She had found a flat on an unpretentious street not far from the Conservatory, and had furnished it

prettily with what money she could lay hands on. In fact, Antonina had run considerably into debt over it, but she felt confident that would all straighten out soon. Her agent would be sure to sell that Klin forest some day, or else Petia would write another opera and they would all be rich.

Thank God, this interminable visit of Peter's to Kamenka was ended. Why, wondered Peter's wife, could Peter not have taken her with him? Did he, perhaps, consider her not good enough for his fine relatives? Davydoff—the name was familiar, not only to high society and court circles, it was a part of Russian history. More than once, Peter had told proudly of how the old grandmother Davydoff, widow of the Decembrist, still wore on her wrist the iron bracelet made from the links of her husband's prison chain. Antonina was tired of hearing about it. Well, glory or no glory, Madame Davydoff was nothing but a wrinkled, helpless old woman now. . . .

And I, thinks Antonina Ivanovna Tchaikowsky, putting on her hat to go to meet her husband's train, and casting a last look round the neat home she has created—I am not old and wrinkled, I am young and desirable, and I would wear ten iron bracelets for Petia—if he would let me. Foolish creature, how shy he is! Even with his own wife. Well, she could soon cure him of that. Surely, love begets love. A woman like herself, whom so many men—so very many—had desired. . . . Antonina, smiling into the mirror, gave a last pat to her blonde hair. Then she picked up her gloves, stepped out the door, locked it, put the key in her purse and went to meet her husband.

Peter Ilyich to his brother Anatol, the day after Peter's arrival in Moscow

Moscow, September 24, 1877

"My wife came to meet me . . . I know you are wondering how I feel now. Tolia! Don't ask me—I am frightened—that is all I shall say. I was too happy in Kamenka, maybe that is why the contrast seems so sharp . . ."

Upon his arrival in Moscow, Peter found a brief note from Nadejda Philaretovna, in which—strangely enough, she did not mention

Peter's troubles, but expressed herself as lost in profound depression, a pessimism that seemed to have no foundation, no source and no ending. The creation of man—wrote the widow—this life that ends in death and a handful of dust—is it not a grim and hideous joke perpetuated by someone upon us helpless victims here upon earth—?

Thus Nadejda, from the depths of her Russian nature. Peter Ilyich responded in kind—but with one essential difference. The widow's gloom had neither object nor reason, it was a kind of oriental resignation, a black shrug of the shoulder, a turning away from life. Peter Ilyich, on the contrary, has the devil at hand, here, over his shoulder. And Peter will not turn to the devil and face him down. Peter does not desire to fight the good fight. He desires but one thing, and his face is turned toward it—Flight! Escape! "To run away, somewhere —how—when—?"

Twice, on that morning after his first night alone with Antonina in the new home, Peter sat down and wrote Nadejda:

To Nadejda Philaretovna

Moscow, Sept. 24, 1877
9 A. M.

"Yesterday I arrived in Moscow and found your letter from Lago di Como, dear Nadejda Philaretovna. Your profound and poignant unhappiness is at one with my own spiritual condition since I left Kamenka, and which today is hopelessly low—beyond words or any describing. Truly, death is man's greatest blessing, and I pray for it with all my soul. To describe my feelings, it is enough to say that my only desire is for the chance to run away somewhere. But how and where? It is impossible, impossible, impossible!

"Forgive me for not restraining this confession of misery when you have enough troubles of your own.

"I haven't been to the Conservatory as yet. My classes start today. As to our new home, my wife has done everything possible to please me. The apartment is comfortable and nicely arranged; everything is clean, new and attractive. And yet I look upon it all with hatred and resentment."

Same day, 11 o'clock
"Two hours ago I decided I could not send you those lines. Now I have reconsidered. I want to write you; I cannot leave you with-

out an answer and I cannot write you anything but the truth. Very probably, the black mood will soon pass. I realize that difficult moments lie before me—I foresaw them and armed myself to meet them. But I was weaker than I thought. God, how hard and bitter life is, and what a price one pays for the few happy moments! When I sat down to write this letter, I wanted to help you with your own distress. I wanted very much to console you but all I can do is tell you of my great sympathy. Nadejda Philaretovna, look for solace and reconciliation with life through the contemplation of nature. The privilege of wealth is that it gives one the opportunity to run away from people and to be alone with nature, which in Italy is finer and more lavish than anywhere.

"I have orchestrated the first movement of the symphony. Now, after a few days devoted to adjusting myself to the new life, I hope to work. When I feel a necessity for work (the first sign of mental recovery) I shall begin orchestration of the opera or the last movement of the symphony, depending upon which I think more urgent. In any case the symphony will be finished before winter.

"Good-bye, dear Nadejda Philaretovna,

"Your unchanging and deeply devoted friend,

"P.T."

For the ensuing two weeks, from September 24th to October 6th, Tchaikowsky stayed with his wife. He attended his classes at the Conservatory and during the first week even went a little into society. Kashkin, the close friend whose brief memoirs constitute the only record we have of these two weeks, testifies that upon returning to Moscow from his own vacation, he was invited to Jurgenson's house to dine—Jurgenson was Tchaikowsky's publisher—and there he was astonished to meet Peter Ilyich—*and his bride!* The news was out at last, and Kashkin was not the only Muscovite to be astonished. Peter Tchaikowsky, the foremost musician in Moscow—after Nicholas Rubinstein—married suddenly, and to a nobody? To a little person without a name, with no talents to redeem her, no nothing beyond a pleasing figure and pretty face! When had Peter Ilyich ever bothered with pretty faces! As a teacher he was notorious for his disregard of female wiles; it was a standing joke of the Conservatory that here was one teacher no pretty face could cozen into praise or leniency. On the contrary, indeed—well, that other rumor then, must have been unfounded. All those ugly stories about "love affairs and worse than love affairs at the Conservatory" must have been sheer slander. Anyway, Peter Ilyich had accomplished one thing by this marriage, be this girl princess or peasant, by his alliance with her, slander was quashed forever. . . .

And while Moscow was gossiping over Tchaikowsky's marriage, shrugging shoulders, perhaps, and smiling a bit—in Venice Nadejda von Meck was organizing her cumbrous household for the return trip to Russia. The gloom and despair of her last letter may have been due to the cold she had contracted in Naples; these repeated colds were a serious matter for a woman threatened with tuberculosis. But whatever the cause of her despair, she found Tchaikowsky's reply more than adequate. And with this letter of his from Moscow urging Nadejda to find recuperation for her spirit in communication with nature, their positions were for the moment reversed. Tchaikowsky became cheerer and adviser, Nadejda, the lost soul seeking help. In her reply is to be found a remark she will reiterate often— "My life is nearly over." At forty-five, still handsome and vital, Nadejda quite genuinely considered herself an old woman, ready for chimney corner and lace cap. No doubt the spirit of the times was responsible for this; the 1870's would have frowned upon a mother of eleven who dared admit such lust-for-living as lay within the widow's capacity. Nadejda was a grandmother, and a grandmother's bosom should be adorned on the outside by a lace fichu and on the inside, by a heart purely maternal.

It was late in October when Nadejda wrote from Venice. How she would like, she said, to follow Peter Ilyich's advice—run away from the world and live with Nature—but he has overlooked the fact that escape requires more than money. Freedom cannot be bought at a price. Eleven children drag her back to Russia, to the cold she hates. "I draw near my end" (Nadejda had sixteen years ahead of her) "but my life has nothing to give the world, whereas you, dear friend, deserve consideration." And Nadejda goes on to tell Peter Ilyich what she never tires of telling him—of his great worth to herself and to the world. All her concern for him is selfish.

she says; he alone, prophet of the art she worships, can make her life happy. If he will permit her to send him away somewhere to rest, all the gratitude will be on her side.

"I must scold you, Peter Ilyich, for saying you ought not to write me everything that worries you. Why not? You know how devotedly I love you, how much your friendship means. If you don't want to hurt me, write me everything, everything about yourself. As to my own unhappiness, it is of little importance to me, and you must not let it burden you.

"I plan to be in Moscow not later than the 15th. The journey fatigues me terribly; we shall not be able to take it in easy stages because I must hurry to Russia.

"If you want to cheer me with a letter, Peter Ilyich, write me please, to my house on the Rojdestvensky Boulevard."

It was unfortunate that three weeks elapsed before Peter Ilyich received this letter. For if ever man needed cheer, needed the prop of a woman's love and understanding, that man was Tchaikowsky —although it is to be doubted if even Nadejda could quickly have repaired the psychological damage of two weeks in the little flat with Antonina. It was such a small place, the flat—intimate. "Cozy," was the word people used to describe it. There was no escape from this tiny place, from the strong, all-pervading femininity of Antonina. Tchaikowsky's piano was set up in a corner of the sitting-room, and during those first days he tried to work, so he told Kashkin. Tried in vain.

But the evenings! With Antonina always at hand, laughing, chattering, gossiping. How inane, this woman's chatter, and how ceaseless, nerve-tearing, the harsh flatness of her voice. And she was so *close* to him, there in the little room! Why could she not sit apart —so—against the other wall? Beads of sweat stood on Tchaikowsky's brow. . . . But if he got up and walked away, she would question him . . . Where are you going, Petia? Petia, do you want anything. . . ? She would follow him to another room; behind him he felt the horror of her reaching hands and knew with ill-concealed

shudder this physical presence that he afterward described—and described repeatedly—as "unbearable torment."

But Peter did not describe it now. At least he wrote no letter, and if his diary gave him any relief of expression, we shall never know because those pages were burned. Something of what he suffered during those two weeks we know through Kashkin, in whom Tchaikowsky afterward confided. When on these evenings, the tension engendered by Antonina's presence rose within him to the frightening point, Tchaikowsky would go quickly from the room and the house, and wander for hours through the Moscow streets. His old hysterical symptoms crowded upon him tenfold; capricious, utterly senseless. He thought his head would fall off, or he would begin screaming and never stop; his breath would be cut off and he would suffocate. . . . Whatever nameless, senseless terror pursued the man, relief came only in escape from Antonina's presence. He did not dare, he told Kashkin afterward, to drop in upon friends for a chat or a game of cards; he feared their questions. . . . *"But where is Antonina on this fine evening? Peter Ilyich, where is the little bride? Surely you have not left her sitting alone? How strange your face, Peter Ilyich!"*

For the same reason, Tchaikowsky dared not go to the theatre. Hour after hour, he wandered aimlessly about the dark streets, the less frequented byways of the city, a lonely, skulking figure in great coat and round fur hat. Head bowed, shoulders hunched, the step now slow and dragging, now rapid, terrified. . . . How often, in former years, against the shame of *The*, Peter had bolstered himself with the artist's excuse: "But if I refuse this duty laid upon me, if I refuse a son, I am not refusing the act of creation. My music is my creation. To posterity I shall leave a progeny far greater than any generation of flesh and blood . . ."

But tonight this reasoning fails because for a week now, music has failed, and to Peter Ilyich a week without musical inspiration is a year, an eternity. The night streets are empty, the autumn wind is harsh against his lips. He is broken, and he knows it. Madness threatens—what else are these phantoms but madness? Oh, let me die—prays Peter to the dark Moscow sky. Let me die quickly, before the final shame overtakes me. Before I am a maniac, babbling my inmost secret to the world. Babbling of *The*. . . .

On one such night, Tchaikowsky, almost delirious, found his way to a lonely place on the banks of the Moscow River and under cover of darkness, waded into the water up to his waist. It was almost October, a hint of snow was in the air and the slow waters of the river were icy. Peter stood there as long as he could bear the intense cold; the water was not deep enough to drown a man, but perhaps, reasoned Peter, sobbing, muttering to himself—perhaps a man might catch pneumonia and die without the final obloquy of suicide? Battering his way home through empty streets, his icy clothes heavy against his legs, Peter, sobered for the moment by his act, knew well that tonight he had not played the part of a hero: a half-suicide is always a subject for ridicule, open to the suspicion of self-dramatization and self-pity, not desperate enough in his grief to deserve even the forgiveness accorded a suicide.

So when he got home, Peter told Antonina he had joined a fishing expedition and fallen into the water, and except for Kashkin, no one ever heard the truth. Even Nadejda never learned of that foolish and ineffective gesture. But what he had done frightened Tchaikowsky still further; he knew himself scarcely sane now; only a thread held him from utter irresponsibility. And when that thread should snap, when once he slipped into that black labyrinth, there would be, he knew, no return. . . . And most horrible of all was this irrational and dangerous hatred for Antonina that he felt growing within him. After all, the girl was blameless. Tonight, for instance, when he came in she had run to him, exclaiming over his wet clothes. She had knelt to help him off with his boots and the most horrible, ghastly impulse had come over him. He wanted to lift his foot and smash the girl in the face; he wanted to reach down and take that white neck in his hands and twist it until the breath was gone from it. . . . He had thrust his hands behind him and groaned aloud, and Antonina had looked up, startled. . . .

On the morning of October 6th, Tchaikowsky appeared at the Conservatory, records Kashkin, looking "strangely agitated. He said he had been summoned to St. Petersburg by Napravnik" (the orchestral conductor), "and took hasty leave of his colleagues." What really happened was that Peter Ilyich had written Anatol to telegraph him in Napravnik's name to come to Petersburg, and Anatol had complied. It is not unlikely Anatol had been expecting something of the kind.

But Anatol was not prepared for what he saw early next morning. Hurrying through the gate of the Nicholas Station and along the cold platform, he searched for his brother's face and quick familiar figure among the travellers descending from the Moscow train— all of them a little pale, perhaps, and dishevelled from a night of travel. One white face he saw that might be his brother's, but Anatol turned quickly from it. That huddled figure standing by the train steps was too old, too haggard and helpless for Petia. . . .

Anatol drew nearer, and looked again. He spoke his brother's name and a pair of frightful eyes were lifted to his—

Somehow, Anatol got his brother into a cab and to the nearest hotel, where after a dreadful nervous attack, the manifestations of which Anatol never disclosed, Peter became unconscious and remained so for forty-eight hours. The doctor feared for his life, and as soon as the patient became conscious and the crisis was passed, told Anatol that the only chance for his brother's recovery lay in a "complete change of life and scene." Complete change of life and scene meant, of course, complete separation from Antonina, so Anatol went down to Moscow and making what excuses he could, delivered Antonina into the arms of her mother and sent the two of them to Odessa. At the Conservatory Nicholas Rubinstein was sympathetic, and the lifted eyebrow was not in evidence. Definitely, though, Rubinstein made it clear that he hoped the recovery would be rapid and the Conservatory would soon see its best professor reinstated in the classroom. The two agreed concerning the desirability of spreading a proper story: Tchaikowsky was ill and going abroad; his wife would follow as soon as she could arrange it.

Lucky that the patient himself, in Petersburg, could not hear those last words! He got out of bed, and with unsteady hands tried to count his money. How many of those shiny things did it take to get a man onto a train and over the border? Perhaps Modia had some money, or Tolia. Tolia was gone though, they said. Down to Moscow. . . . Moscow! That Peter had learned to call home; with what terror the name of Moscow inspired him now. Round in his head whirled visions of Moscow, crazy, distorted visions. Streets were one long bridge over black bottomless waters; when he ran upon the wooden planks, pursued by nameless horror, his steps made no sound, and at its further end the bridge led off into nothingness. . . .

Peter screamed aloud. . . . Voices spoke his name, soothingly. On the crazy pain that was his head, something cool was laid. . . . "I remember very little of my stay in Petersburg," Peter Ilyich afterward told Kashkin. "I remember cruel nervous attacks. I remember Balinsky, my father, my brothers, and them only."

In eight days from the time of his arrival in Petersburg, Tchaikowsky was well enough to attempt a journey. His brothers got him up and onto the Berlin express; Anatol was to make the journey with him. Neither Peter nor Anatol knew their exact destination, nor how long they would stay; but one thing they both knew, and Modeste, waving good-bye from the station platform, knew it too: A vast relief to be increasing the distance between Peter Ilyich and the woman known as Antonina Ivanovna Miliukoff Tchaikowsky.

10

The Refugee

FROM Berlin, the brothers hurried to Switzerland. Clarens, on the shore of Lake Geneva, was a favorite resort for Russians. Not so much resort as retreat; many political prisoners found refuge there from the persecution that was becoming more acute with each year of Alexander II's reign. If, in his walks about Clarens, Tchaikowsky met Russian faces, heard Russian spoken, he did not welcome it. Intensely loyal to a Tsar who was his helpful patron and admirer, Tchaikowsky hated all revolutionaries. But not one of these compatriot refugees was fleeing a spectre so strange as that which had driven Peter Ilyich to these high chaste mountains. . . .

A few days after his arrival in Clarens, Tchaikowsky wrote a long letter to Nadejda von Meck. A month had passed since his last word to her, written the morning after that first night in the Moscow flat with Antonina. "Death," he had said, "is in truth man's greatest blessing, and with all my soul I pray for death." The very next line, however, had naively revealed that Tchaikowsky's prayer was not for death so much as for death's sister—escape. "My one desire is to find a chance to run away somehow, somewhere . . ."

The letter from Clarens is more consistent in tone than any Tchaikowsky has written since his bachelor days. It is not only more consistent, but it is honest—always, with Tchaikowsky, a symptom of mental health. He is still frightened, but he writes frankly and naturally, making no excuses:

Clarens, Oct. 23, 1877

"Nadejda Philaretovna, you will be surprised to get this letter from Switzerland. I don't know whether you have had the letter written soon after my arrival in Moscow and addressed to you at Naples. I have had no answer to it. This is what has happened since.

"I spent two weeks with my wife in Moscow. Those two weeks were a series of the most unbearable mental agonies. I saw right away that I could never love my wife, and that the *habit* on which I had counted would never come. I fell into despair and longed for death, which seemed the only way out. I had moments of madness in which my whole being was filled with such terrific distaste for my poor wife that I wanted to strangle her. I could not carry on my work either in the Conservatory or at home. My mind began to go. Yet I knew I alone was to blame. My wife, whatever she may be, is not responsible for my encouraging her and bringing us to the point of marriage. My lack of character, my weakness, blundering and childishness were responsible for everything. In the midst of it I had a telegram from my brother telling me to come to Petersburg for another production of *Vakoula*. Happy to escape even for a day from the whirlpool of lies, pretense and hypocrisy in which I was caught, I went to Petersburg. At sight of my brother, all I had hidden in my heart during those endless two weeks came out. Something terrible happened, what, I do not remember. When I began to recover I found that my brother had had time to go to Moscow, talk to my wife and Rubinstein, arrange matters so that he could take me abroad and send my wife to Odessa, of which last nobody will know. To avoid scandal and gossip, my brother agreed with Rubinstein to spread the rumor that I was ill, that I was going abroad, and that my wife was to follow.

"Now I find myself in the midst of beautiful country, but in a most dire mental state. What will happen next? I cannot return to Moscow. I cannot see anybody. I am afraid of everyone. Finally, I am idle, unfit for any occupation. There is no place in Russia where I can go. I am even afraid of Kamenka. Besides my sister's family—and she has a grown-up daughter—Kamenka houses Leo Davydoff's mother, his brothers, many people who are working in the plant, and others. How are they going to feel about me? How could I defend myself? I am not yet fit to talk to anybody about anything.

"I must stay here for a time, rest, and let the world forget me. I must arrange for my wife's comfort and think over my future relations with her.

"I need money again, and again I can ask no one but you. It is terrible, it is painful and lamentable, but I must do it, must again have recourse to your infinite kindness. To bring me here, my brothers procured a small sum by telegraph from my sister. They are far from rich; to ask them again is impossible. And money had to be left for my wife, various kinds of bills had to be met, the trip here paid for, and as if by design, our exchange is low. I had hoped Rubinstein would be able to forward a sum, but my hope was vain. In a word, I am spending the last of my small means and have only you in view.

"Is it not strange that Fate brought you into my life just at the moment when I, having made a long series of crazy mistakes, must ask for help three times? Oh, if you only knew how it torments me, how painful it is! If you knew how far removed I am from any desire to exploit your kindness. I am too wrought up and excited to write calmly. Everyone must despise me for cowardice, weakness, and stupidity. I am terribly afraid that something close to scorn may occur in you. That is the suspicion of a sick mind. Actually, I know you will intuitively understand that I am an unhappy man, but not a bad one.

"Oh, my good sweet friend, in the midst of my tortures in Moscow when I thought there was no way out but death, when I gave way to unlimited despair, there were times when I felt that you could save me. When my brother came abroad with me, I realized I could not exist without your help and that again you would come forward as my saviour. And now as I write this letter, tormented with shame before you, I still feel that you are my real friend, a friend that can read my very soul, in spite of the fact that we know each other only by letters. I should like to tell you a great deal, to describe my wife in detail, explain to you why a life together is impossible, why all this happened, and what brought me to the conviction that I could never adapt myself to a life with her. But it is impossible as yet for me to tell a calm story.

"Why have you not written to me from Naples? Were you ill? It troubles me very much.

"Good-bye, Nadejda Philaretovna. Forgive me. I am very, very unhappy.

"Your,
"P.T."

And while Peter Ilyich was writing this letter, Nadejda von Meck was leading her retinue—her four children, her servants and governesses and the faithful Julia—across the continent northward to Moscow, whither she arrived some days after Tchaikowsky's departure. Not having heard from him in nearly a month, Nadejda had no idea Peter Ilyich had left either Russia or Moscow; no doubt she looked forward eagerly to being in the same city with him now that winter and the Conservatory term had begun. She loved to be able to send and receive quick letters by messenger, and surely, thought she, the young wife would not prevent this, would not come between them now. On the contrary, Peter Ilyich seemed more than ever to need counsel and friendship.

It was truly a blow to find her friend vanished from Moscow and Russia—and no word to tell of his whereabouts. Surely, he might have left a message for her! Horrible rumors reached her. . . . His letter from Clarens did not arrive for several days and the widow, painfully anxious, had recourse to the nearest source of information. How cannily the interview with Rubinstein was conducted, will be seen from the widow's own account:

Nadejda to Peter Ilyich

Moscow, Oct. 29, 1877

"How glad I was to have your letter, my sweet, dear friend! When I came to Moscow, I was so frightened to find you gone that I truly did not know what to think, nor could I understand why I had not known about it before. Now I know everything that has happened, my poor friend. It makes my heart ache to think of your suffering and of how your life has been spoiled. Yet I am glad that you have taken a definite step—it was necessary, the only thing to do. I did not let myself tell you before what I truly thought, because it would have seemed like gratuitous advice, but now I believe I have the right, as a person so close to you in spirit, to give you my real opinion. And I repeat, I am glad that you escaped from the hypocrisy and lies—not for you, these things, and not worthy of you. You tried your best for another's sake, you fought to the end of your strength, certainly without profit to yourself; a man like you can perish in such circumstances, but he can never reconcile himself to them. Thanks be to God that your nice brother came in time to save you, and that he was so energetic.

"As to my feelings toward you, my God! Peter Ilyich, how can you think for a moment that I despise you when I not only understand all that has happened, but feel it as you feel it; I myself would have done the same, only I would surely have taken the step of separation earlier, because it isn't natural to me to make such a sacrifice as you have made. I live in your life and your sufferings; everything you feel and do is comprehensible and precious to me.

Dear Peter Ilyich, why do you vex and offend me by torturing your-self with the material side? Am I not close to you? You know how I love you, how I wish you well. I think that not blood and physical ties, but feeling and spiritual kinship give one the right to help, and you know what happy moments you grant me, how deeply grateful I am for them, how indispensable you are to me, and how I need you, exactly as you are; therefore it is not you I help, but myself. Agonizing over it, you spoil my joy in taking care of you, making me seem no more than a stranger. Why do you do it? It hurts me. If I needed something from you, you would give it . . . ? So then, we are quits, and please do not interfere with my taking care of your affairs, Peter Ilyich.

"Nicholas Gregorievitch" (Rubinstein) "has just been here to tell me he had a letter from you, and that you are in Clarens. He came because when I arrived in Moscow and was so shocked to find that you had gone abroad, and was told such horrors, I was desperate and wanted to know where you were. I asked my brother to inquire of Rubinstein. N.G. said, Geneve, Poste Restante, but the next day I had your letter, and the third day he came to say that the address is Clarens. I don't know how you feel, Peter Ilyich, but I prefer not to have anyone know of our friendship, so with N.G. I talked about you as of one about whom I was quite indifferent. As though I knew nothing and with ingenuous interest. I asked him for how long you had gone abroad and why. I had the impression that he wanted to awake warmer sympathy for you, but I kept within the cold limits of a simple admiration for your talent. He told me some of his plans for you which I imagine you must know, and also that your nerves are in bad shape. But you are better now, Peter Ilyich, are you not? With God's help you will soon recover, you will take up work on our symphony, music will again interest you and fill your life. Oh, how I desire all to be well with you! You are so dear to me. All will be well—you will rest, recover, and all the suffering you have lived through will seem a dream that can never repeat itself. But surely I have tired you—I cannot write briefly to you. Is it true that you have a sister in Switzerland? That would be nice for you just now.

"N. v. M."

"The cold limits of a simple admiration for your talent. . . ." There are times when social training and the privileged "distance" of aristocracy stand a lady in good stead. "Some" of Rubinstein's "plans" no doubt referred to the proposition that Tchaikowsky be appointed delegate to the Paris Exhibition in January, a scheme very dear to Rubinstein's heart because Tchaikowsky's name would advertise the Moscow Conservatory abroad. Also, the position would carry a substantial salary, and when Anatol had gone down to Moscow and asked for an advance of money to take Peter Ilyich abroad, Rubinstein had been forced to refuse. Rubinstein was genuinely fond of Tchaikowsky, but the Chief (as the members of the Conservatory called Rubinstein)—preferred to keep his friendships on the debit side; this attitude—and especially the Exhibition plan—was soon to cause a serious quarrel between himself and Tchaikowsky. Nadejda must have discerned something of the kind; anyway she was careful not to call Rubinstein's plans by name. Was it her love for Peter that made her so intuitive, and caused her again and again to sense, across half a continent, those things that lay nearest her friend's heart?

But before Tchaikowsky had Nadejda's letter, a note came from Rubinstein, a friendly missive. "Calm yourself," he wrote. "Take care of your health and don't fear anything or anybody. You are too highly estimated as a musician to be compromised by anything outside of music."

Tchaikowsky wrote back immediately, reporting that he was at work on his opera. "Friend Petia," Rubinstein replied. "I am very glad you are recovering and have begun to work a little. Soon I shall have to kill the fatted calf for the prodigal's return. I am extremely interested in what you say about *Eugene Onegin*. Please assign the parts. Even if we have to change the casting a bit, it is most important to know your preferences. Can I count on the symphony too? I saw Frau von Meck and we had much to say about you. She will probably send you another commission, or money direct."

She did. She sent him the letter of October 29th from Moscow describing Rubinstein's visit, and she enclosed what the Chief so aptly called money direct—in the shape, not of a casual gift, but the first installment of what was to be an annual allowance of 6000 roubles. But Peter did not receive it immediately; their letters crossed; he received, instead, Nadejda's letter from Venice written on October 8th, promising to forward a sum large enough to enable Peter to stay abroad for a few months and rest. What Peter wrote in reply is what he will write Nadejda many times in the future: an expression of gratitude and love, of shame, a reminiscence of terror as though by telling his nightmare, a man could disperse it. He speaks of freedom, and truly he was free for the moment, there on his mountain fastness—free from Antonina, from gossiping tongues, from all responsibility save that one burden he loved—the urgent duty of his talent. Lastly, his letter expresses that nervous restlessness which will cause him to wander from country to country, from scene to scene, in search of a peace no scenery can ever afford to one whose nature must forever deny peace, forever repudiate it even as the search seems ended. The letter of November 1st has a vagueness of tone that is somehow irritating to the reader; in this mood, Peter Ilyich is not at his best.

To Nadejda von Meck

Pension Richelieu, Clarens, S.
Nov. 1, 1877

"Today I received several letters from Moscow, forwarded after I left there. Among them was yours from Venice, dear Nadejda Philaretovna. How I have come to rely on your friendship, how I believe in you as an instrument of Providence sent to save me in this miserable period of my life! Your every letter shows an excess of generosity and kindness toward other people's mistakes. Have you ever reproached me for all my madness? You understand and forgive everything, Nadejda Philaretovna. You offer me means to rest. In my last letter, which you have by now, I anticipated your offer; I asked your help once more. How hard it is! The more generous and kind you are, the more shameful is a further appeal to you. Your letter today has relieved my mind. If you only knew how very, very much you do for me! I was standing on the brink of an abyss; the only reason I did not plunge into it was because I put my hope in you. I owe my salvation to your friendship. How shall I repay you? Oh, how I hope that sometime I may be of use to you! What would I not do to express my gratitude and love. I shall stay here until I receive from you the means to go to Italy, which attracts me strongly. It is very agreeable here, very quiet, but a little depressing. The first days I could not get my fill of gazing on the mountains. Now those same mountains begin to frighten and oppress me. I long for space. Some three days ago it started to rain, the sky is hopelessly grey, the sun hidden from morning to evening.

"You write that one cannot buy freedom at a price. In truth, entire freedom cannot be bought. Yet the limited freedom I have now is for me a supreme delight. At last I can work. Without work, life has no meaning for me. And to 'work with a person near me outwardly so close, inwardly so far removed, was impossible. I went through a terrible ordeal, and think it a miracle that I emerged with my spirit not destroyed, only deeply wounded.

"My sister, as clever as she is kind, writes that she went to Odessa, found my poor wife and took her to the country. My sister has promised to talk with my wife about our future relationship, and here my wife's wonderfully placid disposition will come in very handy. She who, by threats of suicide, forced me to come to her—endured my flight, our separation and the news of my illness with an indifference simply incomprehensible to me. Oh, how blind and mad I was!

> "My good, dear, best friend, thank you.
> "Your
> "P.T."

And now came Nadejda's letter written in Moscow after she had seen Rubinstein, and enclosing not merely a casual sum, but the promise of an annuity. To Peter Ilyich, 6000 roubles a year spelled more than riches; it spelled freedom, peace, easement from fear. It meant that he could choose his life, it removed the menace of home and Moscow. In a word, it released him from the intimacies of marriage. Antonina could never pursue him across a continent. If his daily bread was not dependent upon the Conservatory, he need never have less than five hundred miles between himself and that girl. She would forget him; one of her colonels would come along—surely some of them must be real? Yesterday, here in Clarens, Anatol had received a letter from Antonina in which she announced that on the train between Kursk and Kiev, a colonel had fallen in love with her. Tchaikowsky wrote a short note to Nadejda telling

her of this. Next day, after he had read her Moscow letter, Peter
sat down and wrote Nadejda again—words that must have made
the recipient very happy:

"I doubt if the opportunity will ever come," wrote Peter Ilyich,
"for me to prove my readiness to make any sacrifice for you—you
will never be able to ask of me a great enough service. And so I
have no recourse but to serve you with my music. Nadejda Philaretovna, from now on, every note that comes from my pen will be
dedicated to you. When desire for work renews itself with redoubled
strength, it will be owing to you, and when I am working, never,
never, for one second shall I forget that it was you who gave me
the chance to go on with my career. Much, much remains for me to
do. All false modesty aside, everything I have written up to now
seems weak, unfinished, in comparison with what I can and must
do. And I will do it."

Warm words, and heartfelt. And how quickly, how instantaneously warmth is gone—turned to ice with the first mention of
Antonina! Nadejda had asked for a word-portrait and Peter gave
it at some length, with an obvious effort at objectivity which broke
down at the end of every sentence, no matter how charitably begun.

Antonina was blonde, wrote Antonina's husband—without, however, once using Antonina's name. It is noticeable that Tchaikowsky
never wrote Antonina's name to Nadejda, referring to her at first
as "my wife," later in vaguely legal terms as "the known person," and
still later, to his brothers, in epithets more specific and less attractive.

Antonina was blonde then, she was of medium height, her eyes
were a pretty color, but expressionless. Her lips were thin, her
smile unpleasant, her complexion clear. . . . She was called pretty,
but her mannerisms, her many affectations of speech and gesture,
robbed her of all charm. . . .

"In her head and heart," went on Peter Ilyich, breaking down
completely, "is absolute emptiness. After having assured me that
she had been in love with me for four years and that she was a
good musician, can you believe that she knew not one note of any
of my compositions, and that on the day I left, she asked me what
piano pieces of mine could be had at Jurgenson's? It was this above

all else that made me feel our life had run into a blind alley and could progress no further. I was no less astonished to find that she never went to the concerts and quartet performances of the Musical Society, where she knew surely that the object of her four years' devotion could be met, and where she could so easily have come.

"You wonder, perhaps, how we passed the time when we were alone? She is very talkative, but everything she said led inevitably to: The numberless men who loved her (which she repeated continually), most of them generals, nephews of famous bankers, well-known actors, or members of the Imperial family. The vices, baseness and detestable behaviour of her relatives—with all of whom she is at swords' points—were described with the strangest fury, most of it being aimed especially at her mother."

Strange indeed, Peter Ilyich, and more than strange! Whether or not the nineteenth century had words for nymphomania and persecution complex Tchaikowsky, more shrewdly than he knew, had selected for characterization, traits that were more than merely irritating; they were dangerous. Antonina's friends, it seemed, rose and fell dizzily in her estimation; Antonina's husband found himself hurled against his will into quite furious quarrels. His mother-in-law wrote him complaining of her disrespectful daughter, whereas the last time he had seen them together they had been as doves. And when after those two horrible weeks he had fled to Petersburg, and when Anatol, leaving Peter under the doctor's care, went down to Moscow to tell Antonina of her husband's illness and flight, Antonina received the news with completest indifference, pouring into Anatol's astonished ears, stories of other men who were in love with her. . . .

"Nevertheless," continued Tchaikowsky to Nadejda, recapturing objectivity with an effort, only to lose it before the sentence came to a stop— "It is fair to add that she tried in every way to please me, sincerely desired my love, never opposed any of my plans or ideas and lavished her caresses on me to satiety.

"After this you must be amazed that I could have bound my life to such a strange companion. I myself cannot explain it. Some madness must have come over me. I imagined that I would surely be affected by her love for me, in which I then believed, and that on my side I could learn to love her. I know now that she never loved me

But one must be just—her wish to marry me, she mistook for love. And then, I repeat, she did everything she could to make me love her. Alas, the more she tried, the more she alienated me! I vainly fought this feeling; I knew she did not deserve it, but what could I do with my unruly emotions? Dislike grew not by the day, the hour, but by the minute—little by little becoming a huge, ferocious hate such as I never before felt and of which I did not think myself capable. At last I lost the ability to control myself. What happened next you already know. Just now my wife is with my sister, and soon she will choose a permanent place to live.

"Yesterday my brother had a letter from her in which she appears in an absolutely new light. From a gentle dove, suddenly she turns into a very ill-natured, demanding person, a liar. She levels many reproaches at me, the gist of which is that I have shamelessly duped her. I have written to her explaining that I do not wish to start any argument, because it will lead us nowhere, and taking all guilt on myself. I begged her to forgive me the wrong I had done her, and said that I yield beforehand to whatever decision she may make, but that live with her I never shall—this I said positively. Certainly it is understood I will see that she is not in need, and I asked her to accept means of support from me. I await an answer. I have sent money enough to take care of her for some time.

"This is all I have to tell you about my relations with my wife. Looking back on the short time we lived together, I have come to the conclusion that the 'beau role' is entirely hers, not mine. She acted honestly, sincerely and consistently. She deceived herself by her love, and not me. She was sure, I imagine, that she loved me. As for me, though I had carefully told her that I bore her no love, yet I had promised to do everything I could to love her, and as I arrived at a somewhat contrary result, I was guilty of deluding her. Anyhow she deserves pity. Judging from yesterday's letter, offended pride has awakened, and has decidedly begun to speak.

"Little by little I have started to work, and I can say definitely that our symphony will be finished not later than December, and then you shall hear it. Let this music, so closely connected with your image, tell you that I love you with all my soul, my best friend, my friend-above-all-friends.

"Good-bye. Thank you, thank you, dear Nadejda Philaretovna.

"Your

"P. Tchaikowsky

"P.S. I am very glad that you did not let Rubinstein feel that you know me well."

Peter Ilyich put down his pen and all that day rejoiced with his brother over his new good fortune. But by next morning he could contain himself no longer; he must share this wealth. Modeste, back in Russia, needed money; when did Modia not need money? And when, from now on, would Peter Ilyich ever refuse to supply it?

To Modeste Ilyich

Clarens, Nov. 6, 1877

"Just when you need money, Modia, I have suddenly become, if not rich, at least comfortably off for quite a long time. The person you know of has sent me three thousand francs, and will send me a thousand and a half every month. It is all arranged with such wonderful delicacy and kindness that I feel very little embarrassment. *Dieu!* how kind that woman is, how generous, how tactful. And at the same time, wonderfully clever, because while she does me great service, she does it in such a way that I cannot for a moment doubt that the service gives her pleasure."

Back in Moscow, the European post must have brought relief to more than Modeste Ilyich. Nadejda read the long, merciless description of this wife of Peter's and knew that not the wife but she herself had conquered. Peter had declared himself unequivocally; this was no lover's quarrel; this husband hated his wife, scorned her and would scorn her forever. His frankness gave Nadejda the right to declare herself in turn. Concerning Antonina, she need never again show the conventional, careful attitude of the outsider toward a marriage. She could say what she chose, and from now on, she said it. Not one sigh of pity did Antonina rouse in the widow's breast; on the contrary, to her the girl was a viper, an opportunist, a stupid scoundrel. And every intelligent person knows that a stupid scoundrel, by reason of that very insensibility, can be more dangerous than a clever one. A leech had fastened itself upon genius, and she, Nadejda Philaretovna, would reach out and tear the thing away—slowly, carefully, if need be, but with a never-faltering grip.

Nadejda to Peter Ilyich

Moscow, Nov. 12, 1877

"Thank you very much for writing me a portrait of your wife, Peter Ilyich. I found her just as I expected, and that is why I never wanted to send my daughters to any Institute. One very rarely remains oneself there—good natures are apt to become spoiled, bad ones to grow worse, and the lazy to become completely idle. I feel very badly, Peter Ilyich, that you blame and disturb yourself by pitying your wife. You are not guilty of wronging her in any way, and you may be sure she will not suffer at all from the separation. She is one of these fortunate ones, exaggerated by her education, who never suffer deeply or long because they cannot feel anything deeply. They live an objective, completely material life—which you have taken care of—the ideal life for such natures. To eat well, and even better, to sleep—this you have made possible for your wife and you deserve only gratitude from her. Such natures cannot be unhappy because they are satisfied with themselves, and so they always flourish in soul and body. Even if something irritates them, it is merely another sensation. They have no feelings; things slip over the surface without wounding. If someone should tell you that she weeps, don't be disturbed, Peter Ilyich; be sure it is only for show. Any woman who is married, especially if she loves the man—and who does not want to have a child, has no heart. I must confess that I myself am no dreamer and have no sympathy for dreamers—I am a realist; my nature needs the most fervent poetry, but it must be founded on reality. The joy of having a child is full of that real poetry, and I feel it passionately."

In justice to Peter Ilyich, let us picture him as blushing slightly when he read those last lines. He had told Nadejda that Antonina did not like children, but he had not meant to convey a scene where he as potential father, had urged the young wife on to duty . . . Nevertheless, it was as well the widow had put her own interpretation upon the thing and it was gratifying to have somebody thinking of him as a potential father. Certainly, Antonina did not! The deception had been unintentional; let it remain deception. In the eternal ledgers, what mattered one more falsehoood chalked against a soul that since manhood had been forced to live a perpetual lie? Also, letters from Antonina were beginning to come; a man must turn to any philosophy that would permit him to face this pursuit with a measure of confidence and self-respect. Religion? When, the fugitive asked himself, had he thought of God, that God he had accepted in childhood?

To Nadejda Philaretovna

Clarens, Nov. 11, 1877

"Thinking over all that has happened, more than once I have been convinced that Providence has watched over me. When death seemed the only solution, I did not die, and now things are well with me and a new dawn of happiness is rising. As to religion, I confess that my nature is divided and that to date I have found no way to reconcile this difference. On one side, my mind obstinately refuses to be convinced by dogma, either the Orthodox or any other Christian sect. For instance, I never could find any sense in the tenet of punishment and reward, according to whether a man is good or bad. How can one draw a line between the sheep and the goats? Rewards for what, and punishments for what? Also, belief in eternal life is difficult for me to grasp. The Pantheistic view of immortality attracts me strongly.

"On the other hand, my education and the ingrained habits of childhood, combined with the poetry contained in the story of Christ and his teaching—all persuade me, in spite of myself, to turn to Him with prayers when I am sad, with gratitude when I am happy. I should like to know you from that side, my dear friend. You surely have achieved harmony and found the Truth. Could you (if it is not impudent of me to ask) just briefly explain your ideas of religion? Good-bye, my dear and best friend. There are no words to tell you my love and gratitude.

"Your
"P. Tchaikowsky"

Truly, Tchaikowsky was more artist than philosopher. His response to God, his search for God, was intuitive rather than thoughtful. He did not dare repudiate God intellectually; vaguely he sensed that this would do violence to his essential nature. Therein he was to prove himself wiser than Nadejda. . . .

But before he had time to hear from Nadejda concerning her religious philosophy, or from his sister at Kamenka concerning her proposed reformation of Antonina, Peter Ilyich, overtaken by his old digestive complaint, made a hurried trip to Paris in search of medical help. Anatol persuaded him—Anatol was soon to return to Russia and did not like to leave his brother in bad physical condition.

Tchaikowsky's account of his visit to the doctor is ludicrous and he seemed to recognize it as such; possessing one of those delicately lined digestive tracts in which every tremor of "nerves" is reflected, it was only natural that prolonged emotional strain should break down this weakest part of his physique. Probably the cynical doctor recognized the type at a glance and needed no case history to know this was a man who must be his own physician.

Paris, Nov. 14, 1877

"Nadejda Philaretovna! It turns out that my doctor, Saligoux, does not practice in winter; his address is not to be found. Yet I need very much to see a good doctor, because all yesterday I felt rather badly. So I asked the owner of the hotel to recommend a good doctor. He gave me the address of a Dr. Archambault, who he says is very famous. Today I went there. The famous doctor did not impress me very favorably. I am suspicious of doctors. I like to deal only with those who regard their patients as suffering human beings— not as something that complains and must pay a certain fee. That is why I wanted to see Saligoux so much, for he treated me with affection and sympathy.

"M. d'Archambault made me wait a long time in a beautiful sitting-room, then, appearing from under a portière, invited me in. I had barely begun the history of my illness when he said coldly, with a sneer: *'Oui, je sais tout cela par coeur. Vous n'avez pas besoin de me le dire.'* Then, instead of questioning me, he himself named the different symptoms of my ailment. At last he sat down to write his 'prescription,' and then, standing up, he said: *'Monsieur, votre maladie est inguérissable, mais on peut vivre avec elle jusqu'a cent ans.'* Having listened to his 'prescription,' which consisted of: 1. Taking a particular chalk before lunch and dinner; 2. Drinking a glass of Hauterive water an hour before meals; 3. Taking *'des bains de Barèges';* 4. Avoiding a terrific number of different foods— I put the fee on the table and went away far from reassured, having no faith in the prescription, and feeling that I have been not to a real doctor but to some salesman of doctor's advice.

"So my trip to Paris was wasted. It is most, most unfortunate. I have made rather a large detour and got very little for it. To tell the truth, I could kick myself now for not going straight to Italy. It is hard to tell you just what it is that irritates and disturbs me. I feel somehow apologetic, Nadejda Philaretovna, as if I have done something wrong. Don't reply to this—I know beforehand that you forgive me! I tell you this awkward feeling because it is pleasant to tell you everything.

"The queerest thing of all is that Archambault did not even ask what my occupation was, or why I am so nervous. A doctor should know all that. He only asked my nationality, and when I said I was Russian, he remarked, 'Le climat y est bien rude.' Well, the Lord be with him.

"Good-bye, dear Nadejda Philaretovna. If I were not afraid of being tactless, I should ask whether I annoy you by writing too often. I think about you much these days. I love you dearly.

                                        "P. Tchaikowsky"

Nervous men are always thinking they can be cured by doctors, and always disappointed when the Archambaults appear from under their portières and shake their medical heads. More than disappointed, Peter Ilyich was thrown into a panic, perhaps not so much at the doctor's words as at finding himself once more adrift in the world. The brothers went down to Florence, and Peter wrote the widow in despair. Imagine, said he, he was going to Rome! Rome would be awful; why, the number of things a tourist must see in Rome was frightening—Peter used the German word, Sehenswürdigkeiten. Were all Russians like this, he wondered? If he went to Rome it would be to work, not to run about with a Baedeker in his hand. And yet he would never be able to work in Rome; he knew it! Why had he ever given Rome as a forwarding address to all his Russian correspondents? Now he would have to go there! Why did he leave peaceful Clarens? What will happen to him when Anatol goes home to Russia, as go he must very soon? "Why did I leave Switzerland?" cries Peter Ilyich. "Why did I go to Paris? Why am I here in Florence? Stupid, stupid, horribly stupid!"

So the sick man cries out his reproaches—who was it said remorse never visits the healthy? And in the midst of it, he received a note from Nadejda spurring him to hardness against Antonina, and suggesting it might be time for the homeward journey.

Peter Ilyich replied that she was quite right; he ought to come home. But where, in Russia, could he go? Not Petersburg, where his old father lived. . . .

"You know that one reason for my marriage was to fulfill an old and ardent wish of his. My flight from Moscow, my illness and departure for abroad all had to be concealed from him; even now he does not really know what happened. He was told only that my nerves were upset, that I had gone abroad with my brother because my wife could not go for business reasons of her own, and that she was to join me at the first opportunity. He did not like it and could be quieted with difficulty. I think he will probably never know the truth. It is hard for me to lie to him and I would eventually be forced to answer his questions about my wife and why I live without her (he liked her very much), and to tell him the truth would be dangerous. Heaven knows how it might effect him. Also, I hate Petersburg; the mere sight of it plunges me in gloom."

And Moscow? Moscow would be even worse. He loves Moscow, really loves it, but every corner houses a friend or relative, all of whom would expect him to carry on his daily work at the Conservatory. How could he, when even the most casual personal encounter fills him with dread and "excruciating agony?" To go to Moscow just now would be to condemn himself to madness. . . .

"I can't tell you, dear Nadejda Philaretovna, the terrible tortures I suffered there in September. I was within a hair's breadth of going under. The wound is still too fresh. I am not yet ready for my old Moscow life—I am still ill—I could not stand it.

"The only place I should really like to go is Kamenka, but even Kamenka is closed to me now and for some time to come. When my sister learned what had happened, she immediately went to my wife in Odessa. I see clearly now that she made a great mistake in inviting my wife to Kamenka instead of confining herself to a meeting. My sister is very kind and very clever, but this time she did the wrong thing. Knowing me and immediately perceiving what my wife was, she began with wonderful enthusiasm to re-educate her, trying to persuade me by letters of my wife's many good qualities, and how in time she would make a splendid life companion. More than once I wrote her that because all guilt is on my side, mine also is all responsibility and that I accept the future consequences of my thoughtless behaviour, but I begged her for God's sake not to mention the possibility of our ever living together again. I don't understand what got into my sister at the time. What she could not see was that my hatred for my wife, even though unwarranted, is an unhealthy state of mind, that I must be left in peace, and that not only should she not describe her, but not even mention this woman whose very name and everything that reminds me of her drives me mad. The result was those letters from my wife of which I have already told you, in which she appeared either servile and insincere, or humble and loving, or accused me of baseness and dishonesty, or out and out implored me to love her. It was terrible.

"My sister, who thought to influence my wife for good, has succeeded only in raising her spirits to such an extent that my wife wrote my brother here that she is very gay and that a colonel has fallen in love with her. It is all very awkward; the very woman who unwittingly has done me so much harm lives now at my sister's, the one place that is home to me, that has always been my refuge from worry and, for me, the warmest place on earth.

"Well, enough of this dismal subject,
"P. Tchaikowsky"

Back in Kamenka, the kind Alexandra Davydoff was in truth having far from an easy time. Kind sisters of erratic brothers seldom do have an easy time, and while Alexandra's was not a nature to look for ease, she certainly had not expected, when she went to Odessa and fetched the weeping Antonina home under her wing—to find herself sheltering an incubus. Alexandra did not realize, at first, what this girl was; as the happy mother of a household, Alexandra's sympathies were all with the abandoned wife. How the girl cried! Perhaps it would cheer her to be occupied; let her teach little Natasha Davydoff to read and write. God knows how long she would have to wait for brother Peter, and if he did turn up, it would only make things worse. The girl certainly did not look the twenty-eight Petia said she was—poor young wife who had promised to make no wifely demands, had sworn to be content with the status of sister! Who could blame the girl for breaking such a vow? Indeed, if Antonina had not tried to break it, Alexandra Davydoff would have thought her unworthy the name of wife.

So reasoned Peter's sister, and Peter knew it and was afraid to come home.

But not for long. Day by day Alexandra, generous though she was, lost patience with this wife of Petia's. What a woman! One thing to cry, another to cry all day, dropping great tears on little Natasha's spelling book, frightening the child and making no explanation. More than tears dropped on these pages and on the letters Antonina wrote. They were spotted with blood; Antonina was a nailbiter and it was not a pretty thing to see. The way she went at it as well as the condition of her fingers, proved it to be an old habit, long antedating Petia. Hardly the person to have in a household of children. What a misfortune that Petia, himself a bundle of tortured nerves, should have tied himself to a creature even more emotionally unstable than he.

Oh, but far more unstable! Petia, for instance, was often sick with nerves, but in all his relationships he was loyal, or had been, up to now. Of course, he was much too quick to take offense at personal criticisms of his music and cherished such offense for years, ridiculously. But his friends were lifelong friends, his devotion to his brothers and to all his family, unswerving. Whereas Antonina's life, by her own description, seemed submerged in excited quarrelling. Antonina could not keep to one plan or one occupation longer than an hour. . . . Now Petia, while flighty emotionally and liable to the wildest excitement over nothing, was a worker, regulating his days like a clock and hideously distressed when this routine was broken. Oh, an impossible combination, these two, and any comparison between them, mere folly . . . Quietly but with determination, Alexandra began to question her guest as to future plans. . . .

But Antonina, it seems, was not interested in plans. She desired to stay where she was, and said so with greatest cheerfulness. She seemed more than sure of her welcome at Kamenka and what was more embarrassing, she had nowhere else to go. With her own brothers and sisters and various friends she was not at present, she said, on good terms. . . . No, no, said Antonina. "I like it here, and here I shall stay."

From grandmother to child, the Davydoffs were kindly folk, accustomed to deal gently with their little world. Husband and wife held a conference, the result of which was a letter from Leo Davydoff to Anatol Tchaikowsky in Venice, bidding Anatol be sure to stop by at Kamenka on his way from abroad—and take this woman to her mother down in Moscow.

Leo was a mild letter-writer, but "for God's sake" echoed in every line.

11

Onegin and the Fourth Symphony

ALEXANDRA DAVYDOFF did not, however, write to her brother. She disliked Peter's wife—but this did not absolve Peter himself from guilt. Her position would need time to define itself. For another month, therefore, uncertainty was to be Peter's portion and his punishment. Afraid to come home and face the criticism, afraid to have Anatol leave him, he began, fortunately, to recover balance in spite of himself, and the measure of his recovery lay in the music written. His work was desultory. Nevertheless, what he did was good, and *Onegin* progressed slowly to the point where the first act would be ready for Anatol to carry back to Russia.

And in Moscow, two persons awaited the Italian post with eagerness; Modeste, to whom his brother's welfare meant as much as anything his life held, and that other person on the Boulevard Rojdestvensky, busy with her children and her affairs, supervising as usual the condition of the fifty begilded, beplushed rooms—but living, now, for news of Peter Ilyich. As her anxiety concerning him decreased, the tone of her letters became lighter; she wrote advice, and she wrote the talk of the town:

"Please, Peter Ilyich, if you must drink that bad Italian water, mix it with wine, and always drink a little wine at lunch and dinner. Don't eat grapes without washing them. . . . Like you, I have a feeling against doctors and hardly ever call them for myself, but I have a big family and for that reason have had to deal with doctors all through Europe. Take care of your health, dear Peter Ilyich. Your life gives so much happiness to others."

(Could any remark have been more tactful to a man who knew he had just ruined a girl's life?)

"Yesterday," Nadejda continued, "I went to the Symphony Society. The best number was Beethoven's Seventh; Grijmaly played Vieuxtemps' First Concerto. Do you know that Hubert married Miss

Batalin last Wednesday? She certainly married him *'par dépit
amoureux,'* because I hear she was in love with you. When I was in
Petersburg lately, I heard your opera *Vakoula.* What a delight!
How lovely the tenor part, and how beautiful the dances! The theatre was full. You cannot know with what impatience I await your
new compositions!"

Not once, during these dangerous times of Tchaikowsky's unbal-
ance, did the widow cease urging him to write music. She never told
him to forget his music for a while if it would not come, and to rest,
be gay and talk to people. No—she said a righter thing. "Take care of
your health, Peter Ilyich. I await your new music impatiently." She
had no one now, to give her news of Tchaikowsky; Modeste was in
Moscow but she did not know him, and Nicholas Rubinstein was energetically touring Russia for the Red Cross—Russia still being in a
state of armament;—the latest Turkish War was progressing painfully toward its painful climax, the Congress of Berlin. As soon as the
widow received Tchaikowsky's letter asking about her religion, she
sat down to answer at enormous length; her letter is so vague as to be
almost incomprehensible. She declares herself a "realist," an "idealistic materialist," a believer in man and man's nobility. "My heaven
and hell exists on earth only, and I do not regret the joy of heaven because whenever on earth I find the kind, the true, and the good, I enjoy such happiness as I doubt if heaven can give." Even music she
looks upon as a physical, earthly thing. "I love music passionately; I
don't deny myself this pleasure, but I never dream meaning into it. I
feel a purely physical pleasure that is so delicious I regret its passing."

No wonder she loved the music of Peter Ilyich, devoid as it was of
mysticism or indeed of spiritual exaltation, and filled with an emotion which needs no intermediary between itself and the heart. Nevertheless Tchaikowsky, in his answer to the widow's long letter, quarrelled only with this one point—her definition of music as purely
physical. Throughout his life he mistook his own emotionalism for
something rarer. Let it be remembered that his musical god was
Mozart, the purest classicist of them all, the one composer of history
who might be chosen as the very antithesis of Tchaikovskianism.

ᐧeter took Nadejda's letter with him from Florence to Vienna and read it on the train. It inspired him, he said, with a great desire to answer at length, but he would not have time until he completed the first act of *Onegin*. The voices and bar-signs must be written in so Anatol could take it home. Peter Ilyich has said little about work since his departure from Russia, but the completed sketch for *Onegin* had been in his pocket when he left home, even the orchestration was definitely planned. What he had done in Switzerland was mostly routine and the composer never said much about his compositions when they reached this final stage. The rest of his letter would seem to show that Tchaikowsky understood the widow's so-called "realism" more clearly than she did herself. Or perhaps his mind, better educated than hers, was more agile at definition. Because Nadejda's days were businesslike, it does not follow that her mind was as neat; so-called "practical women," whose education has been consummated politely in the home circle, are seldom capable of logical discussion; particularly impossible for them is the definition of any abstraction such as philosophy.

Tchaikowsky's letter is straightforward and clear and by that same token, remarkably devoid of the *clichés* and catch-words of the time. Realism, it will be remembered, was the *ism* of the day. Zola was already internationally articulate; Tolstoi, Dostoyevsky and the great romantic "realists" were about to burst upon a world prepared for them by such as the widow von Meck. Peter Ilyich writes from Vienna:

Vienna, Dec. 3, 1877

"First I must ask how you can imagine that your *'profession de foi'* could change my feeling toward you or diminish my fervent love and devotion to your candid, intelligent, infinitely kind self? Is it possible that a little discord in views and opinions can change our feeling for one another? Just as I, who have not changed one jot in my unending devotion to you after reading your confession, so you, I hope, won't cease feeling friendly toward me if I allow myself to object to some points in your letter.

"One thing is clear to me—theoretically, you have broken with the church and dogmatism. I see that after many years of thought you have created for yourself an independent system of religious philosophy. But I think you are mistaken in declaring the building you have erected in place of the ruins of your former blind faith, to be sound, strong, and fully able to replace religion for you. The tragedy of the man inclined to skepticism is that, searching for something to replace the traditional faith he has discarded, he vainly flings himself from one philosophical theory to another, hoping in each to find that strength with which the believer is armed against the struggle of life. Don't say a word! To believe—not because of the usual lack of mentality—but to believe with a vision that can reconcile every misconception, every contradiction suggested by the critical mind—this is a great joy.

"The intelligent man who sincerely believes in God (and there are many such), has a shield against which the blows of fate are absolutely vain. You say that you have discarded established religion, that you have found a substitute. But religion implies reconciliation with life. Have you that? I answer 'no,' because if you had, you could not have written me as you did from Como. Do you remember? That sadness, that dissatisfaction, that undefined aspiration toward an undefined ideal, that alienation from people, that capacity for finding only in music (the most idealistic of arts) the answer to vital problems—all was proof that your own religion does not bring you real spiritual peace. Do you see what I mean? I think you are in accord with my music because I too am filled with yearning for the ideal. Our conflicts are the same. Your doubts are as strong as mine; we swim on the shoreless sea of skepticism, looking for a harbor we never find. Isn't it because of this that my music means so much to you and is so near your heart?

"I think also that you are mistaken in calling yourself a realist. If by realist one means a person who hates all pretense and every insincerity in life and art, then surely you are a realist. But, keeping in mind that the true realist will never look to music for consolation and peace, as you look—I should prefer to call you an idealist. You are a realist only in the sense of not being sentimental, not liking to waste your time on the fruitless and commonplace dreams that are natural to many women. You dislike empty phrases, insincere words, idle sentimentality, but that does not mean you are a realist. And you cannot be one. Realism implies a certain narrowness of mind, an ability to satisfy very easily and cheaply the desire, the quest for truth. Deprived of that thirst for knowledge, for an answer to the riddle of life, the realist denies even the necessity to search for truth, and is skeptical toward those who look for peace in religion, philosophy or art. The realist is not interested in art—music especially—because it serves as answer to a question that in his restricted being, simply does not exist. This is why I think you are mistaken in trying to enlist under the banner of realism. You say that music gives you an agreeable physical sensation, and nothing further. Permit me to protest! You deceive yourself. Is it true that you like music as I like 'Yquem' and salted cucumbers? No, you love music as music should be loved, which means that you give yourself to it with your whole soul, submitting yourself without reserve to its magic influence.

"Perhaps it is odd that I allow myself to question your own self-portrait, but my opinion is: first, that you are a very good person, and have been so from birth. You love truth because you have a deep natural affinity for it, and as deep a hatred of falsehood and evil. You are clever, and so you are a skeptic. A clever person cannot help being a skeptic—at least his life must contain a period of cruel skepticism. When natural skepticism inevitably brought you to the point of denying dogma and tradition, you began to look for a way out of the labyrinth of doubt into which you had fallen. You found some help in your pantheistic ideas of the world and in music, but full peace you did not find. Hating evil and falsehood, you walled yourself within the narrow circle of your family as a defense from the spectacle of human degradation. You do a great deal of good, your passionate love of art and nature makes doing good a necessity for a noble spirit such as yours. You help your neighbor, not as a bribe for future happiness in a heaven which you do not credit—yet do not quite deny—but simply because you are so created that you cannot resist doing good.

"But I see that if I go on and attempt to finish all I have to say, this letter will take me all day. I have already been working; I am tired and to write more is an effort.

"Sweet, dear Nadejda Philaretovna, if it is stupid and naive of me to try to prove that you don't know yourself as well as I do, if my assumption that I can explain your nature is ridiculous and impertinent, forgive me. I can tell you that your letter brought you somehow much closer, made you even dearer to me. Oh, how I love you, and how very, very eager I am for you to know it. Alas! words are never adequate.

"Tomorrow I shall write again and try to tell you my own religious ideas. And I will explain why I can't return to Russia just now.

"Good-bye, dear friend."
"Your
"P. Tchaikowsky"

This is flowery language, but to the point nevertheless. Not only had Nadejda's skepticism never brought peace, but it would some day bring her the very negation of peace. "Hating evil," wrote Peter Ilyich, "you wall yourself within the narrow circle of your family as a defense against the sight of human degradation." Now Tchaikowsky, for all his refusal to assume the ordinary responsibilities of life, for all his fleeing from the consequences of his own acts, had never denied life and the world, and shut himself from it. He loved the world and was by nature extremely friendly, so much so that Moscow in late years had become a very difficult place in which to work. Friends were to Peter a temptation and because they took time and strength from his work —a dissipation. Nadejda's withholding of herself, on the other hand, was done without purpose and for its own sake; it followed rather than denied her inclination; its source lay in fear and therefore it was dangerous.

It is more than possible that Tchaikowsky sensed this, and in his letter to Nadejda, gropingly tried to express it without offense. Could he have foreseen the extremes to which the widow's isolation would lead her, could he have dreamed that this very trait, unwholesomely fostered, would turn inward until his friend was ready to deny not only the world but her heart and the person nearest her heart, his warning would have been even more insistent. His next letter, written a day or two after the first one, is directed rather toward himself than his friend; very evidently he had been seeking, in the midst of his trouble, to recapture the fresh unquestioning faith of his childhood— and was finding, instead, his real religion: music.

Peter Ilyich to Nadejda Philaretovna

Vienna, Dec. 5, 1877

"To continue my answer to your letter:

"I feel quite differently from you about the church. For me it has kept much of its poetic appeal. I go to Mass quite often—the liturgy of John of Chrysostom is, I think, one of the greatest of artistic creations. If one follows our Orthodox service attentively, with full understanding of every rite and symbol, one cannot remain spiritually untouched. I love the evening service too. To go on Saturday to some small ancient church, to stand in that half darkness all filled with the smoke of incense, to meditate, searching an answer to the eternal questions—Why, When, Where, and To What End: to be wakened from contemplation by the choir's—'From my youth many passions fight within me,' and to abandon oneself to the magic poetry of that psalm, to feel oneself overflowing with quiet ecstasy when the King's doors open and 'Glorify the Lord from Heaven!' resounds—I love it all and it is one of my greatest joys.

"So, a part of me is bound with strong ties to the church, and part has, like you, long ago relinquished all belief in dogma . . . Eternal life—how can one imagine it as endless delight? The charm of life lies in its rapid alternation between joy and grief, light and shade, in its conflicts between good and evil . . . But opinion is one thing, instinct another. In spite of strongest conviction against personal immortality, I can never reconcile myself to the idea that my mother, whom I loved greatly, and who was such a saint, has disappeared forever and that I shall never have the chance to tell her that after twenty-three years of separation, I love her as much as ever.

"You see, my dear friend, that I am made up of contradictions, and though I have lived to a very mature age, have not settled my mind nor appeased my restless spirit either with religion or philosophy. Truly, there would be reason to go mad were it not for *music!* Music is heaven's greatest gift to man—poor wanderer in the dark. Only music can interpret, pacify, and quiet. Music is no straw to be grasped as a last resort, but a faithful friend, patroness, and comforter. For her sake only can one live on earth. In heaven perhaps there will be no music. Let us then live fully on this earth.

"Your

"P. Tchaikowsky"

Nadejda's reply is spirited; this time she defines her position more coherently. Writing again from Moscow she declares herself pleased that Peter Ilyich did not treat her long letter lightly, but tried rather to comfort her by evoking some remnant of the old childhood beliefs. This, she says, is impossible; many people have tried to convert her but not only can she not agree with them, she cannot even sustain the pretense of agreement which is necessary to maintain social relationships.

"My alienation from people is a result of this difference between my ideas and the world's. . . . Yet I believe so strongly in the existence of right, of goodness and of truth (my own conception of truth) that if, like Galileo, I were tortured for it, I should say as he said when he left the torture chamber 'and yet it turns.' . . . You think, Peter Ilyich, that the rich are never really put to the test; let me remind you that the rich care even more what the public and their friends say about them than the poor do. You must remember that I have not always been wealthy; sometimes I am frightened; but my creed holds me up and I do not bow my head before injustice or even ridicule—which people fear especially."

Thus far Peter Ilyich must have read with mounting admiration— he who so bitterly feared ridicule, and was so conscious of his fear. Nadejda went on then; to describe another tenet of her creed: namely, her hatred of convention, of what she called "externals." Her revolt against this extends, she confesses, to a denial even of personal beauty in mankind; to admire a pretty face as though it were carven of marble and needed no inquiry into the soul behind it is, she thinks, the mark of vulgarity, the very denial of nobility! "Perhaps, Peter Ilyich, you will put this down to the fact that I am an old woman, but I reply that I was not always old, and these opinions have been fixed for a long time. If perhaps, you should also lay my denial of dreaming daydreams and reveries to old age, I can tell you that I ceased to be a dreamer when I was seventeen—upon the day of my marriage."

An old woman, Nadejda von Meck, at forty-five; to be handsome and wealthy did not subtract a year from woman's age in 1877. Had not Peter Ilyich just spoken of his own thirty-seven years as a "very mature age?" More than her times conspired to call Nadejda old at forty-five; Russia is very close to the East; what a little span—as history counts time—had passed since the ladies of Moscow went walled in palanquins through the streets! And to the Orient, a lady is indeed old at forty-five. When the widow talks like this it is amusing and a little pathetic that Peter Ilyich, in his return letters, never denies her statement. But then, no coy interchange ever takes place between the two; once in a while—a very great while—Nadejda forgets herself and sends out instinctive feminine feelers; giving voice to a cry for help, for masculine gallantry, she receives in response the most serious, passionate assurances of gratitude and friendship—and nothing more.

One statement, however, Tchaikowsky will refute, and vehemently: the widow's repetition of her belief that musical sensation is purely physical. "I ask you, Peter Ilyich, is it a moral effect that a bottle of sherry has on a person? It is even considered immoral by some, with which I absolutely disagree. Music effects me as does a glass of sherry, and I find the effect most wonderful! That longing for something mysterious, inexplicable and at the same time marvelous, intoxicating —one would like to die experiencing it. A short time ago I played your *Andante* to the First String Quartet (I accompanied the violin); this music always leads me into the mood I described and at the end sends a shiver through me from head to foot. No one can understand the despairing agony that it expresses; it takes my breath away."

But with all her expression of shivers and agonies, the widow brought reasonable testimony to her case. She enclosed in her letter a newspaper clipping describing the soldiers' love of music down in the Crimea: surely, she urged, no conscious moral agent was at work here? Again, was Peter Ilyich ready to argue that music ennobled the characters of professional musicians? On the contrary—

"You, Peter Ilyich, were not born to that *milieu* and will never belong to it. You are a musician by vocation and inspiration. You were born to something different than those gentlemen, you were educated to other traditions and have worked out your opinions under different influences than they. Among them are a few honest people; but it is curious that the more generations which devote themselves to the musical profession, the worse its descendants prove."

Her letter affected Peter Ilyich profoundly. In the first place, the very sight of the envelope was reassuring; it was registered, which meant money enclosed—and Peter was down to his last cent. Five days before, Anatol had left him in Vienna and gone home to Moscow with the first act of *Eugene Onegin* in his pocket—and undoubtedly a railroad ticket bought with what remained of Nadejda's last check. Peter had travelled alone to Venice, sunk in gloom and terrified of solitude. At his hotel was waiting a telegram from Nadejda; he tore it open, expecting an order for money, but all he found was a cheerful message concerning the capture of Plevna from the Turks! Peter sent the widow a gloomy letter of thanks for her thoughtfulness in wiring him the good news—and on the same day wrote Anatol that he was reduced to his last ten *lire* and had received from Russia "nothing as yet save news of Plevna." Day after day passed, another Russian mail came without the *lettre chargée*. Kashkin wrote that all their friends had met in Rubinstein's rooms to hear the score of *Onegin,* which Taneyeff * had played on the piano. The music was marvelous, said Kashkin; it had left the hearers breathless. Even Rubinstein was enthusiastic; more than that, he was much relieved. From Clarens not a month ago, Peter had written that he was *homme fini.* . . . "Something is broken in me," he had said; "my wings are clipped and I shall never fly very high again. Now I am working hard at *Eugene Onegin* and my symphony, but I work at the instrumentation of them as though they had been conceived by someone else. . . ."

Certainly, thought Rubinstein and the friends assembled, this music of *Onegin* was not the creation of a broken man! They rushed out and telegraphed Peter Ilyich—but nothing they said could raise him from gloom. He was alone and penniless in a far country. Exactly three *lire,* he wrote Anatol, remained now in his pocket. So he wrote Nadejda and told her how lonely he was—with never a mention of money. He was ashamed to be forever complaining; he simply could not, he declared, keep anything from her. Why, he asked (carefully keeping the only important point from her) was a man of his age so weak and silly as to sit all day in magic Venice weeping and lamenting, instead of going about enjoying himself?

"Meanwhile," the letter went on, "I have put in a second day of steady work on the symphony. Work, I hope, will little by little crowd from my heart this longing for my dear brother. How everything here reminds me of him! How painful it is to look and walk in a town where so recently we wandered side by side. He telegraphed from Kamenka to say that my wife is leaving my poor sister at last. The latter made me very happy yesterday with a long letter in which she admits that at first she could not forgive me

* Taneyeff, Tchaikowsky's most talented pupil, was a strict classicist, an indefatigable counterpoint scholar whose works are only now beginning to be known. Sabaneyev calls him the "Russian Brahms."

because in process of crippling my own life, I hurt an innocent and loving woman. Now she understands there was no love, only a desire to marry. My brother-in-law writes me the same.

"I have also had the very good news that the first act of *Onegin* delighted my *confrères,* beginning with Rubinstein. I was quite fearful of their verdict, and what they say is therefore very, very pleasant. And yet I am sad, terribly sad because my brother is not with me.

"Good-bye, dear Nadejda Philaretovna,

"Your

"P. Tchaikowsky   .

"I have not yet received your letter."

The postscript was delicate, but unavoidable. Nadejda could have no doubt as to what it referred. Nevertheless it was unnecessary; on the day he mailed it, salvation arrived. Peter Ilyich instantly wrote the good news to Anatol: "My God, what would I do without Mme Meck! Have received a letter from her with an order; she sent me enough for two months in one—an eight-page letter, again on philosophy, but much clearer and better written than the first one. May she be a thousand times blessed!"

Nadejda's long confession affected Peter Ilyich profoundly, and in more ways than the financial. He was genuinely moved by her frank and spirited avowal of religious skepticism—a skepticism which seemed only to strengthen her deep faith in mankind. Immediately he read it, Peter regretted the letter he had sent from Vienna, rebuking his friend for her personal philosophy.

"It was very naive and clumsy of me to write as I did," he apologized under date of December 17. "People are only too disposed to judge their neighbors by themselves. Because I have not the strength to evolve a sound solution of my own, because I vacillate like a weather-cock between traditional religion and the critique of reason, I simply wanted you to swim in that ocean of doubt with me. I forget there are people like Spinoza, Goethe, Kant, who can manage without religion. (Have you read the book by Louis on Goethe? If not, read it. What a great figure!) And I have forgotten to mention those giants—of whom there are plenty—who know how to create for themselves a harmony of thought that can replace the old religion. I can only envy those people. It seems that I am destined all my life to doubt.

"Compared with you, how weak I am, how powerless to fight! I don't say that as a pose, but as frank confession of my spiritual weakness. I am sure that from my confession you must have come to somewhat the same conclusion, and I am ashamed. With you I feel the way a small person feels in talking to a very tall one. I mean it. Since reading your letter my respect and love for you has become if possible, stronger.

"Much of what you write appeals to me. I like your proud attitude toward public opinion. When I was my normal self, before my present breakdown, I assure you that my disdain for the 'qu'en dira-t-on' was every bit as strong as yours. Now, I must confess, I have come down to average in this. Well, I am ill, which means my spirit is ill too. I too have always disliked publicity, have always been uncomfortable when too much notice was taken of me. The story of my marriage, flight, and illness must have sharpened tongues, and the thought irritates me. Unfortunately, my work as an artist necessitates publicity, and the part of an outsider, a disinterested spectator, is impossible for me."

Here Peter Ilyich, who deserves the title of perfect letter-writer by virtue of invariably answering every question put him—tackles Nadejda's statements concerning the vulgarity of external beauty. He flounders a bit; obviously, he *likes* pretty people—"Yes, the beauty of a person certainly influences me." He then argues briefly and far from convincingly that beauty must come from inside, and hurries onto surer ground:

"In your letter there is only one thing with which I will never agree—your opinion of music. I dislike especially your comparing music with intoxication. I do not think such comparison possible. A person takes wine to fool himself, to give himself an illusion of satisfaction and happiness. And he gets that illusion in an expensive way. The reaction is terrible. Wine, it is true, gives momentary forgetfulness—but momentary only. Is it so with music? Music is not illusion, but revelation. And she is victorious because she reveals to us elements of beauty, otherwise inaccessible, to experience which is no transitory thing but means permanent reconciliation with life. Music is a lucid and happy thing. It is very difficult to analyze the experience of musical delight, but it has nothing in common with intoxication. It is not a physical thing. Certainly the nerves, and consequently the physical organs, take part in the reception of musical impressions, and in that sense, music pleases the body. But a definite line between the material and spiritual side of man is, as we all know, very difficult to draw. Thought is a physical process because it is one of the functions of the brain. After all, this is only a quarrel of terminology. No matter how differently you and I define musical experience, one thing is clear: we both love music with equal depth; in both our lives it plays an equal part. For my part it is enough to have you love so warmly, and call divine, the art to which I have devoted my life.

"Last night I was reading the third volume of Thackeray's beautiful novel *Pendennis*. One of the characters, Major Pendennis, often reminds me of Kondratieff. I came across one incident that was especially characteristic of my friend. I jumped out of bed and filled with the most unnecessary fury, wrote him a letter in which I attacked him banteringly but with a resentment plain enough to see. After reading your letter, I was ashamed. I immediately wrote Kondratieff again, begging him to forgive me for such inordinate and unbecoming anger. So you see what a good influence you have on me, my best of friends, my providence and my comforter."

The end of the letter is very characteristic. Peter Ilyich was not an intellectual man; he was an artist. What he thought, what he felt, his nature compelled him to translate into music or action of some sort— and translate immediately. What a relief, to jump out of bed at a bound and at a bound, forgive Kondratieff!

Peter's spirits went rapidly up. Not only were his pockets filled with money and his heart with assurances of Nadejda's love, but other good fortune was on the way: Modeste and his deaf-and-dumb pupil were coming over from Russia to join him, perhaps spend the winter in Italy. Peter himself had engineered it a week ago, before leaving Vienna. The minute Anatol left him, he had sat down and written Conradi, the father of Modeste's pupil, and with the eloquence born of desperation had urged the benefits of Italian sunshine for young boys. The result, a telegram from Modi received in Venice: "You have conquered Conradi; we are coming soon."

Telling Nadejda the good news, Peter expressed himself as "unbelievably happy." And all through this man's life, happiness brought the same result; a great outpouring of music. A few moments peace, a little respite from worry with something pleasant to look forward to, and Peter Ilyich was charged with music, trembling with it, almost suffocated with the desire to get it out of himself and onto paper. Artists differ strikingly in the mood that makes for creation. In the midst of misery and spiritual desperation one man will write a song brimming with childlike gayety, while another, for money and nothing but money, will produce a symphony that echoes rather the rustle of angelic wings than the clink of gold coins. With Tchaikowsky the condition for musical creation—no matter what misery had preceded—was always and invariably the same: a sense of well-being, of security and peace. Nadejda von Meck knew this; from the very first she recognized it, and posterity blesses her name accordingly. She needed Tchaikowsky's music herself and she desired the world to share it with her, but she laid upon the man no test, no trial of strength, no fabricated spur of uncertainty or fear. "I am your friend," said she, again and again. "I will give you money. You can count on me. Be at peace, Peter Ilyich; it is my privilege to befriend a great man."

Two days after Tchaikowsky had her long, kind letter with the remittance, and also the news from Modeste, he wrote Nadejda of his happiness—adding: "I am working enthusiastically on the symphony" (Tchaikowsky referred to the Fourth, the one he called "our symphony"). "The first movement is nearly ready. I can confidently declare it the best thing I ever wrote."

And the next day:

Venice, Dec. 21, 1877

"I have not only worked steadily at the orchestration of our symphony, but I am engulfed by it. Never before has any orchestral composition cost me such labor, but never before have I loved any work so much. At first I wrote simply for the sake of finishing the symphony, plowing through all difficulties—but little by little I was agreeably surprised to feel enthusiasm take possession of me, and now it is hard to stop working. Dear, sweet, Nadejda Philaretovna, perhaps I am mistaken, but I think this symphony is something out of the ordinary, the best thing I have done up to now. I am very happy that it is yours, and that hearing it, you will know how at every measure I thought of you. If it were not for you, would it ever have been finished? In Moscow, when I thought all was ended for me, I wrote on the first draft the following, which I had forgotten and only found here when I started work: "In case of my death, I desire this paper to be given to N. Philaretovna von Meck." I wanted you to have the manuscript of my last work. Now, thanks to you, I am not only alive and safe, but can give myself fully to work, conscious that from my pen comes something that, I think, is destined for remembrance. Yet perhaps I am wholly wrong—enthusiasm for one's latest work is natural to all artists.

"Anyway, at the moment I am in high spirits with such interesting and fascinating work to do. I put up quite calmly with various small unpleasantnesses from my landlord. Dear friend, don't be vexed if I write you briefly and rather seldom until the work is done. It tires me so that by evening I find even reading difficult, and my eyes ache. The weather is beautiful but very cold. Yesterday little clouds appeared, but today is fair again. Good-bye.

"Lovingly and devotedly,
"P. Tchaikowsky"

To crown all this beatitude (no one can say that Peter Ilyich was not easily pleased) came further good news from home:

"Yesterday I had a most reassuring letter from Anatol. I am loved in Kamenka as before, so my mind can be quite at rest on that subject. I kept thinking they all pitied me, and it was a very bitter thought. The last letters I had were very comforting; yet what my brother has lately written gives me definite assurance that all the inhabitants of Kamenka who are so very dear to me, have forgiven and understand everything—that I acted blindly, with no malice of forethought. My wife is still there. She told my brother she wants to become a nurse and he says he will arrange it. I shan't go into detail, but everything I hear about her is balm to my conscience.

"Today I began the last half of the second movement of the symphony. The work becomes easier by the hour. In spite of interruption, I hope to finish everything for our New Year.

"Good-bye, dear Nadejda Philaretovna.
"Your
"P. Tchaikowsky"

Meanwhile Nadejda von Meck, in Moscow, was having her own troubles. The December weather had been too much for her, she wrote; she was down with a cold, and coughed all through the con certs of the Symphony Society. Letters from Italy were slow in coming; they had to go north to Vienna then eastward to Russia. While Tchaikowsky was writing in high spirits from Venice, his Vienna letters, therefore, were only just being delivered to Nadejda in her huge bedroom on the Boulevard Rojdestvensky. After the philosophic letters, others came from Vienna, entirely concerned with music and musical criticism. Tchaikowsky was never at his best as critic; moreover, from the vantage point of posterity, out-dated musical criticism is apt to make amazing reading. How, we ask ourselves, can these great men have failed so lamentably to recognize one another? A Tchaikowsky listening to a beautifully produced *Valkyrie*, or sitting down at the piano with a friend to go over the score of a brand new Brahms symphony—how and why was he so blind and so complacent? Beyond all men, the creative artist seems to suffer from lack of detachment, objectivity; perhaps, in an extreme individualist like Tchaikowsky, this is merely the defect of his quality. Of Tchaikowsky's contemporaneous composers, the only ones who could write both good music and good criticism were Schumann, Berlioz and that same giant whom Peter attacked so perversely—but with no heat of envy:

"What a Don Quixote Wagner is!"—wrote Tchaikowsky to the woman who would understand. "Why does he strain himself in pursuing the impossible when in his hands is a great gift from which, if he would only submit to its natural direction, he could extract a whole ocean of musical beauty? In my opinion, Wagner is a symphonist by nature. The man has a glorious talent, but affectation ruins him, his inspiration is always paralyzed by some new theory that he desires to put in practice and for which he would sacrifice anything. Pursuing realism, truth and rationalism in opera he has quite lost music, which in his last four operas is most conspicuous by its absence. Such kaleidoscopic, unrelated little musical pieces, following each other breathlessly, never pausing by some simple musical device to give the listener any slightest rest, I cannot call by the name of music. Not one broad, finished melody, not once is the singer given leeway. He must run after the orchestra the whole time, concentrating on not losing his one little note, which has no more importance in the whole than some little note for the fourth

Waldhorn. But that he is a wonderful symphonist is beyond all question.

"Let me prove by example how the symphonist in Wagner dominates the vocal and often the operatic composer. You must have heard his famous *Walkurhrenritt.* What an heroic, beautiful picture one has of those wild giants, flying with thunder and clamor on their celestial horses! In the concert hall it is invariably more effective. In a theatre, with board rocks before you, clouds made of rags, soldiers leaping awkwardly across the background, and finally a tiny theatrical sky to give us the infinite space beyond the clouds, this music loses all its imagery. The theatre, instead of making the picture more vivid, acts as a cold douche.

"Finally, I don't understand and never could, why the *Niebeiugen* is considered a masterpiece of literature. As a folk poem, perhaps— but as a libretto, no. All those Wotans, Brunnehildes, Frickas, and so on, are so impossible, so unnatural that it is hard to take a real interest in them. And how little action! Wotan scolds Brunnehilde for her disobedience for a whole three quarters of an hour. How tiresome! And yet what a wealth of strong, beautiful passages of purely symphonic character!"

But there was one musical characteristic which, whenever encountered, drove Tchaikowsky into a fury of irritation—what he called this new tendency, especially noticeable in Brahms, to chop off a melody at the moment it attained full swing. Melody being Tchaikowsky's greatest talent, he naturally believed in it with all his heart; when a melody came to him he enjoyed it and saw to it that the hearer would enjoy it—climbed right up on melody's back as it were, and let it ride blissfully off with him. What then were these Germans doing, eternally forcing song into technical development, sacrificing beauty for the sake of mass and thickness? Pure showoff!

"Yesterday Kotek and Modeste and I studied the new symphony of Brahms—a composer who is praised to heaven in Germany. I don't understand his attraction. In my opinion he is dark, cold and full of pretense, of obscurity without true depth. I think Germany is on the decline musically, and that the French are now due on the scene. They have many new men of great talent. I have just heard some new music, beautiful in its way, Delibes' ballet *Sylvia.* I knew it before from the piano arrangement, but in the wonderful performance of the Vienna orchestra it completely charmed me, especially the first part. My own *Lake of Swans* is simply trash in comparison with *Sylvia*. In short, I have known nothing in the last few years that has charmed me so much except *Carmen*. Perhaps Russia and the rest of Europe will soon have a new word to say. But in Germany music is positively on the decline, and Wagner is a great representative of the decadence."

All this was balm to Nadejda von Meck. She would say so, very shortly—but not until she had read the second half of the letter, written a day later. In Vienna there had been a big symphony concert, but Tchaikowsky had stayed at home, although he thereby missed the Third Symphony of Schumann that he loved so much. . . .

"I was afraid," read the widow in the ivory tower that was her chamber, "that I should meet some musicians of my acquaintance. If I meet only one of them, I shall have to wait on at least ten of the 'big guns' tomorrow, thank them for their kindness (last year they placed my overture to *Romeo and Juliet* on their program without being asked—which was unanimously hissed anyway). If I should call on the aforesaid big guns and pay them compliments, it would be a great help to the promotion of my compositions abroad. But my God, how I hate that kind of thing! If you only knew how offensively they try to patronize the Russian composers! One can read in their eyes, 'Though you are a Russian, I am kind and indulgent enough to honor you with my attention.' God be with them. Last year, against my will I had to pay Liszt a visit. He was polite to the point of nausea, but the smile on his lips said the above words plainly enough. At the moment I am certainly less than ever disposed to pay my respects to those gentlemen."

Nadejda was entranced with every word of this. She replied instantly. She would never have believed that persons not united by ties of blood and education could have such similar tastes, feelings and sympathies.

"Dear friend of mine, our patriotism is not only alike in character and intensity, but shows itself in the same way. Our feeling for music instinctively, deep within ourselves, is absolutely the same, only our name for that feeling differs." (Just yesterday, she had been telling Julia how she felt about Brahms.) "I was saying that what I desire in music is life, emotion, vitality, imagery, and that I hate dry theories, philosophic preaching and those exhibitions of knowledge that become so technical one gets dizzy listening. I do not like Brahms, hate Wagner, and believe that at the moment, Russian music is in the lead. I should not, like you, put French music foremost; the French cling so obstinately to the old classicism that they prevent their own advance.

"How the art has progressed lately in Russia. . . . !" And Nadejda goes on to ask Tchaikowsky's opinion of the Russian composers, all so busy turning out music at the moment—Borodin, Rimsky-Korsakov and the rest. She gives them short shrift, ending up (to everyone's satisfaction no doubt) "but *you* I adore, my friend . . . You write that they are pleased with your opera *Onegin*. How could they be anything but pleased? They are not barbarians in music (although they are on every other count)!

"This is the sum total of my feeling toward our composers. Correct me if I am wrong, Peter Ilyich—but not concerning the last named composer! *That* love is already in my veins, it has become part of my flesh and blood, part of my being. It is a necessity of my nature; to lose it now would plunge me in a spiritual, fatal illness; I should, though still living, lose my life.

"With what delight I read of your distaste for meeting the 'bigwigs,' and seeking their good graces! *Mon dieu,* we feel the same about everything! We even make the same mistakes."

Waiting for this letter, which was slow in coming, waiting also for Modeste's arrival, Peter Ilyich lost heart once more, once more was plunged into black remorse, into that pit so vividly portrayed by a contemporary pessimist of another nation. For the attainment of greatness, said Nietzsche, a man must first become acquainted with "profound self-contempt, with the martyrdom of self-distrust, with the misery of the defeated."

The martyrdom of self-distrust. Even in the midst of good fortune, this was a chasm which, for Tchaikowsky, yawned ever at hand; and now, at the lowest ebb of his career, defeated by his own crazy act of marriage and his graceless flight from home—any slightest hint of criticism from the world or any imagined neglect from friends, sufficed to hurl the victim downward. Nadejda's letter then, came as a hand from the bright fields above. How he had longed for it! Peter confessed to Anatol:

"Mme Meck had not written me for a long time, and with my usual misgivings I imagined she had ceased to love me, that she had found out about *The*, and wanted to break off all connection. Up to this morning even, I was sure of it, but I just had a letter from her, so sweet, so kind, with such sincere expressions of love! A saintly person is that Philaretovna!"

To Nadejda, the composer replied warmly: "I can't tell you what a comfort your letter was. I need expressions of affection and friendship so much just now, and your dear letter was lavish with them." As to Nadejda's questions concerning the Petersburg composers, he would answer them one by one, said Tchaikowsky. But first he might as well say that they were all dilettantes—Balakirev, Borodin, Rimsky-Korsakov, Moussorgsky and Cui. Posterity bears him out—the Five were indeed dilettantes, in the sense of anti-professionalism in art. They were amateurs, as Glinka had been before them. But what amateurs! Talent and more than talent was there abundantly. Their parade of anti-scholasticism was to Tchaikowsky, of course, the crassest folly; they were like children, convinced that play far out-valued lessons. He was well aware of their feeling toward him and the Rubinsteins, knew the Five cried fie upon them all three and upon every theory held by the Conservatory.

"Borodin?" Tchaikowsky began. "Greatly talented, but he is already fifty, and blind fate brought him a Chair of Chemistry in the Academy of Medicine rather than an active musical career. He cannot write a line without somebody's help." Cui? His music is "elegant, coquettish and meticulous, but what can one expect of a Professor of Fortification, busy lecturing in all the military schools of Petersburg?" Moussorgsky is the exact opposite; he revels in crudeness for its own sake, flaunts his musical ignorance and boasts that his genius is the richer because he has refused training. "Yet he has flashes of real talent, not without originality."

Tchaikowsky's severity regarding the Five was in no way derived from personal pique; his relations with them were, as we have said before, friendly. But between his almost femininely sensitive nature —intense though it was—and the virile, furious genius of a Moussorgsky, there lay an impassable gulf. In his life of Moussorgsky, Oscar Riesemann gives an amusing letter written by Moussorgsky to Stassov the Petersburg critic, describing a musical evening at a friend's house. The nickname given Tchaikowsky, "Sadyk-Pasha," was borrowed from a notorious bandit chief of the day and the *Oprichnik* was of course, Tchaikowsky's opera.

"My dear Generalissimo,

"For some days I have been in the company of the worshipper of *absolute beauty* in music." (To the Five, Art was for Russia's sake —not for art's sake.) "Our conversation left me with a strange sense of internal void! The *Oprichniky* was not performed on Sunday because the composer had not brought the score with him. In its place we did several things, in the following order:

"*Thisbe*—a fiasco!

"*Mlada* was a success, with the exception of *Morena,* which fell flat.

"*The Nursery* made no impression as a work of art; they all declared that the composer's rendering of it made one forget the deficiencies of the composition—otherwise there was nothing in it.

"*The Tramps*—a fiasco!

"The parrot story—a furore!

"Sadyk-Pasha seemed to be half asleep and half-awake—probably he was dreaming of sherbet; perhaps too, of Moscow kvass—at any rate, he looked quite as sour while the extracts from *Boris* were being played. I was watching my audience—always an instructive pastime! —and saw Sadyk-Pasha grow sourer and sourer, till I quite expected him to begin to ferment! This actually happened after the parrot scene—he began really to boil, and the bubbles he threw up burst with a dull, hollow sound that was very unpleasant. All I could gather from these sounds (they were not many) was the following: 'He has power' (you can guess whom he meant), 'but his powers are wrongfully employed—it would be useful—to work at a symphony' (in strict form, of course). The powerful one thanked the Pasha profusely and the incident closed. Next day I met the Pasha at Bessel's; 'twas the same old story: 'Our aim in music must be beauty —nothing else but beauty'!"

Posterity knows the truth—that both men were seekers after beauty, and both found it. These musical wars—what a waste of energy!—we exclaim. And yet—perhaps not entirely waste. A nature like Moussorgsky's needs a war, needs, as whetstone to creation, a visible enemy. Whereas Tchaikowsky—but we know what Tchaikowsky needed. He would have written his own music in any age; in the midst of whatever artistic war his individualism, his artistic eclecticism, would have ridden stubbornly neutral, stubbornly triumphant. On the very field of battle he longed not for weapons but for peace, and fled ruth lessly and shamelessly to where peace was to be found. It was a long letter he wrote Nadejda about the Five. After disposing of Moussorg- sky, he went on to Balakirev, leader and, according to Peter, "the greatest personality of the Circle. Unfortunately, he stopped before accomplishing much. He has great talent which has been lost because some fatal event made a little saint of him, after he had for so long prided himself on his atheism. Now he scarcely steps out of church, fasts, says his prayers, bows to the relics, and has time for nothing else. In spite of his great gifts he has done much harm. He ruined Rimsky- Korsakov by assuring him that study was harmful. . . ."

"They are all infected to their very marrow with the most terrific conceit and with the dilettante's confidence in his superiority over the rest of the musical world."

Rimsky-Korsakov, Tchaikowsky admits, is an exception. Already at thirty, a composer of repute, Rimsky-Korsakov had realized he could go no further without a deeper knowledge of musical theory, har- mony and counterpoint, and four years ago had appealed to Tchai- kowsky himself for guidance. . . . Peter tells Nadejda the story, well known now to musical history, of Rimsky-Korsakov's brave plunge into the severest and most elementary musical studies. In one summer the young man wrote sixty-four fugues—perfect in their way, says Tchaikowsky, but the reaction was too sudden. "Soon after, his sym- phony and quartet appeared. Both compositions are full of tricks and as you have quite justly observed, marked by a dry pedanticism. He is passing through a crisis, and how that crisis will end it is hard to say. Either a great master will emerge or he will sink definitely into contrapuntalism."

A great master did emerge; it is most interesting that Rimsky- Korsakov, in his memoirs, confirms his teacher's—and Nadejda's—

comments on his quartet. In the quartet, says Rimsky-Korsakov, he fell between two stones; he tried contrapuntal tricks, but while they succeeded as musical juggling, they were not music. "The technique," he wrote, "had not yet entered my flesh and blood."

These long letters concerning music and philosophy and the good life were salutary for Peter Ilyich; perhaps the widow knew it and asked her questions with a purpose—that in replying, her correspondent might take momentary leave of his personal troubles. After Vienna, Tchaikowsky did not permit himself to be alone again but sent to Russia for his servant, Alexis Safronov, and to everyone's surprise, that stolid and highly unimaginative person found his way from Moscow without mishap. But two weeks in Venice was more than enough for Peter Ilyich, even with Alexis for companion—the two went everywhere together. "Those Venetian ruins!" cried the composer to Nadejda, from Milan, whither he had fled. And the empty hotel with nobody in it but himself and Alexis! His only consolation during the Venetian two weeks had been his good health, due in no small part to his symphony. "Working on it cheered me greatly. When I knew Modeste was coming from Russia and when I plunged into work, I was suddenly at peace. Three movements are now ready. I don't know how long this enthusiasm for my latest work will last, but just now I look upon these three movements as the crown of all my musical efforts. Can you read between the lines to whom thanks are due that I could begin it? Must I tell you that those thanks are endlessly, deeply sincere? Better to say nothing when a thing is so obvious."

In Milan, Tchaikowsky heard Marchetti's opera, *Ruis Blas*. The music was agreeable, but the fat, ungraceful performers made him fear for his own newly completed opera, *Eugene Onegin*.

"Where shall I find Tatiana, as Pushkin imagined her and as I tried to portray her in music? Where is the artist that can even approach the ideal Onegin, that cold dandy, socially correct to the marrow of his bones? Where can we find Lensky, an eighteen-year-old youth with thick curls, with the impulsive and original manners

of a young poet like Schiller? How Pushkin's charming picture
will be vulgarized when transformed to the stage with its routine,
its stupid traditions, with veteran players taking the part of sixteen-
year-old girls and beardless youths. The moral is: Writing instrumental music is far more satisfactory, has fewer disappointments.
How I agonized over the production of my operas, especially *Vakoula!*"

From Milan, Tchaikowsky wandered down to San Remo to await
the coming of Modeste and his boy pupil. He had the usual hideous
time trying to settle down; finding himself at first in a big, fashionable
hotel, he sent Nadejda a shocking list of prices for room and board.
Furthermore, on going down to dinner late, what was Peter's horror
to run into at least a hundred elaborately dressed guests coming out
of the dining-room. They all seemed to know one another and they
looked him over from head to foot with a superciliousness indubi-
tably British. The fact that they were British was enough to repel any
self-respecting Russian. At this very moment, was not an Englishman
—the wicked, wily Disraeli, trampling mercilessly upon Russia in
the Congress of Berlin?

Peter fled the British and ran about San Remo looking for rooms;
Alexis was less than useless in these crises. A Frenchmen urged the
two to come—at huge expense—to his house; as inducement he said
he was a political refugee, "like Rochefort, condemned to death." All
this threw the composer—himself a refugee—into frantic gloom and
homesickness.

"Why is it," cried he to Nadejda: "that the simple Russian landscape, a walk in summer through Russian fields and forest or on
the steppes at evening, can effect me so that I have lain on the ground
numb, overcome by a wave of love for nature, by the indescribably
sweet and intoxicating atmosphere that drifted over me from the
forest, the steppe, the little river, the faraway village, the modest little
church—in short, all that makes the poor Russian natal landscape.
Why . . . ?"

Yet home, Peter said, was closed to him. And when at last he found
a place to live in San Remo, he laughed at his own misery: "I am like
the old woman in Pushkin's story--the more reasons I have to be

happy, the more miserable I become! But now that you are my friend, dear Nadejda Philaretovna, may I not tell you all, all that takes place in my poor sick soul?"

There is but one answer to that question, and Peter Ilyich knows it. Never, never can he confess to Nadejda the deep, basic sickness that underlies all his misery. Among confessions, that is the one confession that cannot be made to womankind. Alexandra knows, but Alexandra is a sister, with a sister's forgiveness. One other woman knows— would God, breathes Peter Ilyich, that she did not! By her knowledge of *The*, Antonina can ruin him, tear his good name to tatters. Oh, pray heaven the news will never reach across Moscow to that other lady who loves him with such blind, mistaken confidence!

12

A battle with the Chief. Onegin completed.
Nadejda inquires about love

So from city to city, day by day, Peter fled his phantom, and from Moscow to Switzerland, from Switzerland to Vienna, from Vienna to Paris, to Venice—Milan—San Remo—forever the phantom pursued him. But all the time, he was working at *Onegin* and the Fourth Symphony, and during those times when he felt incapable of sustained effort, at songs and short pianoforte pieces. And then, with the arrival of a new year—1878—something tangible appeared for the composer to worry about, something in no way concerned with Antonina or with womankind.

Peter had been away from home for three months now, and his world had let him blissfully alone, the more surprising because in his world Tchaikowsky was a not inconsiderable figure. The Moscow Conservatory and indeed all of musical Russia had come to depend upon him; if they permitted him this holiday it was because Nicholas Rubinstein so directed it, Rubinstein being one of the very few who knew the facts.

For Tchaikowsky, Rubinstein represented not the inner check but the outer; Rubinstein was public opinion, he was the world, responsibility, a job. He was what a man must face if he is to call himself a man, and the fact that the Chief was a despot and Peter Ilyich was temperamentally unequal to any out-and-out personal fight, gave the advantage wholly to Rubinstein. When he commanded, there was no choice but to obey; during eleven years therefore, Tchaikowsky had taught musical theory for twenty-six hours a week at the Conservatory. Under such a régime, no man who was not a very packhorse for work could have composed four symphonies and three operas, not to speak of dozens of songs and short pieces and published a *Manual of Harmony* that had proved of much value to the

Conservatory. Rubinstein knew all this and knew also who held the whip hand—until Nadejda von Meck appeared on the scene.

But now, with so powerful and sympathetic a friend behind him, the hardworking subordinate could afford to lean back and take a slightly longer view of the Chief. From San Remo, Tchaikowsky, at Nadejda's request, sat down and wrote her his candid opinion:

"Nicholas Rubinstein is not as much of a hero as he is often made out to be. He is a wonderfully gifted man, intelligent, though poorly educated, energetic and clever. He is not small by nature, but has become so because of the silly, servile admiration that surrounds him. All these defects come from his mad love of power and unpardonable despotism. But N. Ph., what services he has rendered to music! Because of it, we can forgive everything. Whatever his Conservatory—artificially planted in the Moscow earth—may be, it is the source of sane musical ideas and tastes. Twenty years ago Moscow was a wilderness as far as music was concerned. I am often angry with Rubinstein, but when I remember his tireless work, I am disarmed. Even granted that he did most of it for the sake of ambition, still the ambition is praiseworthy. And one must not forget that he is an excellent pianist (in my opinion, the first in Europe) and a very good conductor.

"My relations with him are very strange. When he has drunk a little wine, he begins to be as sweet to me as possible, and accuses me of lack of feeling, lack of love for him. But normally he is very cold to me. He loves to make me feel that I am under obligation to him for everything. The truth is, he is a little afraid that I despise him. As I am not expansive, he sometimes imagines that I try secretly to get the position of director from him. He has tried several times to get a confession from me about this, and when I frankly tell him I would rather be a beggar than a director because nothing can be more unsuited to my nature than such an occupation, he calms down, but not for long. In short, though remarkably clever by nature, he becomes blind, stupid, naive, when the idea occurs that anyone wants to usurp his position as the first musician of Moscow."

Barely had Tchaikowsky mailed this when Alexis, informing his master beamingly that the Russian post was in, handed him a large official envelope bearing the stamp of the Imperial Government.

Peter Ilyich, his heart sinking, opened it—and knew instantly whose scheming lay behind its contents.

Shortly before he left Russia in the autumn, Tchaikowsky had been appointed musical delegate to represent his country at the Paris Exposition which was to begin on January 1st, 1878. Well aware that he was nervously and temperamentally unequal to such a position, Peter had put off the onus of a definite refusal by saying he could not afford to go. And now, in San Remo, four months later, he received notice that the Minister of Finance had appointed him delegate at a salary of a thousand francs a month, that his country was proud to afford him the honor of such an appointment, and that he was to proceed to Paris immediately and stay there eight months!

Had he been ordered hung at sunrise, Peter Ilyich could not have been more dismayed. Babylon, it would be—he cried to Nadejda, and he would be a madman in Babylon. "The very thought of appearing before the Chief, of meeting all the musicians, dragging myself to dinners and musical soirées, having no time to write (my only weapon against my malady) makes me ill; it is beyond my strength." A huge questionnaire accompanied the official letter from the Russian Government; how many concerts would Tchaikowsky arrange? What quartet societies, what choral societies would appear?

Questionnaire? How could he fill out five sheets of paper marked A, B and C.? Was he not already plunged in work—his own work? Was *Onegin* to be laid aside for eight months, and the Fourth Symphony? To put them by for eight months, now at the height of creation, would be to kill them forever. What could Rubinstein be thinking of, to urge such a plan—for it must be Rubinstein, pertinent and definite as always, who had suggested the very pertinent and definite thousand francs a month.

As well to have offered him the post of Minister of Finance! Now, if they had asked for music, if they had said, "Peter Ilyich, write us a piece for the Exposition and put in plenty of noise and trumpets," he could have complied, no matter how great his personal distaste. He was always able to fulfill a musical commission. But all this organizing! Nor was it a help to realize that Russia's political position in Europe was extremely unfavorable. Victimized by England in the person of Disraeli, by Germany in the person of Bismarck, Russia had not yet begun to make friends with France. In Paris they would hiss the Russian bear as they had hissed it before. For this very reason, Peter knew it to be his patriotic duty to advertise Russian music abroad; up to now, only the brothers Rubinstein had advertised it. But he could never do it. He knew he could never do it. He was no salesman, and the showmanship that was the very essence of Rubinstein had in him no part. He paced his room in San Remo, crying aloud with the eternal, anguished cry of the creative artist: *Leave me alone! Let me prove my patriotism as I prove my soul—by the music I write.*

The artist has always been an apolitical individual, sentimentally patriotic, but oblivious of the machinery of government until it hinders him in his creative output. Tchaikowsky could write Nadejda how he had lain face down upon Russian soil, numb with the ecstasy of love for country, but when through Rubinstein his government invited him to do it a public favor entailing loss of time and strength that might be applied to creative work, Peter Ilyich fell into a passion of hate for the government and Rubinstein too. All his life, Tchaikowsky's only enemy was that person who interfered temporarily with his creative artistic flow, whether this enemy were the Russian government, an utter stranger encountered during a composing walk, a colleague, or a wife.

For three days therefore, Peter roamed the bright San Remo streets in a torment of indecision. The fact that he recognized his indecision as part of his nature, did not decrease his discomfort—a discomfort that can be understood only by persons who, like Peter Ilyich, go through life saying yes to every invitation, and then spend hours of precious time and energy trying to squirm out of the noose. It was difficult for the world to guess—even difficult for Rubinstein who knew him so well—that this man, so charming at a dinner party, endured tortures of fatigue and self-reproach after every social gathering. To Anatol he wrote now:

"Tolia, I have hidden something from you. Since the day you left me in Vienna, every evening before bed I drink several glasses of brandy, and during the day I drink a lot too. I can't live without it. I am calm only when a bit tipsy. I have come to depend upon this secret drinking, so that the mere sight of the little brandy bottle I keep always by me gives me pleasure. I write my letters better when I have had a drink. It is a proof I am not yet well. In Paris, to keep going I should have to be drinking from morning till night. My hope lies in Modeste. A quiet life with someone I love and work to do is what I need. In brief, for God's sake forgive me, but I cannot go to Paris. I should be worthless there, both to myself and others."

On the same day—but omitting all mention of the bottle, Peter wrote Nadejda:

"Whether I am being cowardly or wise, I see clearly that I cannot go to Paris. If you or my brother had seen my condition today, you would have said, 'Stay where you are.' Today I shall answer officially, saying I am ill and asking them to name another delegate. Now, until I have your approval and my brothers' and sister's, I shall be in torment. Another thing . . . if I had accepted the position I could have lived entirely or at least partly without your help. And however kind you are, however rich you may be, the sum you send is too large at the present rate of exchange (which will now go lower due to England's mean tricks). It will torment me that I am taking too much from you . . . Everything does; I have become sickly suspicious. Perhaps I shouldn't say that; please forgive it. I swear it has never for a moment occurred to me that you could regret the money. No, absolutely no! Yet I must do all I can to protect such a kind and generous friend from expense. . . ."

Rubinstein himself was touring Russia for the Red Cross and knew nothing of this insubordination; never dreaming of a re- fusal, he had not even written Peter Ilyich. But as soon as the Mos- cow Conservatory group had the news they began telegraphing San Remo in remonstrance. Karl Albrecht intimated that the Chief would be furious. So Peter sat down and wrote Rubinstein a friendly enough letter, reminding him that a man who even in health was incurably shy and no organizer, could hardly be a credit to his

country in the guise of musical ambassador. Then he wrote Albrecht.
Let me alone, all of you!—he cried.

"I shall do nothing whatever to advertise my wares. If they wish
to play and sing my music, let them; if they don't, very well. I spit,
spit, spit upon it all!!! Must I tell you again that if I were rich I
would live in a desert, rarely visiting even Moscow, which I love
deeply? In August I shall take up my professorship again (which
I might say I loathe with all my heart). I shall live out my life in the
White City" (Moscow) "in quiet and seclusion, with a few intimate
friends—you among them. And until my last breath I shall spit
upon the world, its opinion, its fame and its honors.

"One thing I know from bitter experience: no man can force his
life into a mold contrary to his real nature. And all my nature, each
fibre, each cell, protests against the post of delegate.

"Karlushka, let me recommend my newest child," (the Fourth
Symphony) "which I hope has already arrived in Moscow. For God's
sake love it, for I shall have no peace if you don't. Perhaps you don't
know how very greatly I value your opinion. Thank you and Kashkin
for your warm words about *Onegin;* they are a million times dearer
to me than the condescension of some —— Frenchman. I embrace
you both, and Rubinstein too. As to fame, I spit, spit, spit upon it."

And now the Chief returned to Moscow from his Red Cross tour,
and now the thunder began to roll in earnest. He wasted no time in
writing Peter Ilyich, nor did he spare anyone's feelings. Blaming
Tchaikowsky bitterly for his refusal to go to Paris, Rubinstein accused him of cowardice, laziness and a willingness to sit in the sun
with the widow's bankroll in his pocket.

It can be imagined with what feelings Peter Ilyich read these
words. In the first place, the Chief's accusations were far from just;
since his departure from Russia, Tchaikowsky had not only worked
hard but had accomplished much. The first act of *Onegin* finished,
the Fourth Symphony completed and both works delivered to Moscow. And the worst of it was that the Chief was evidently trying to
do a little spade work over on the Boulevard Rojdestvensky. Peter,
with Rubinstein's letter in one hand, sat down and wrote Anatol
with the other:

January 20, 1878, San Remo

"Last evening I had a disturbing letter from Mme Meck, filled more than ever with expressions of affection but complaining of something unpleasant that has happened. Without actually saying who is responsible for her feeling so badly, she writes in a bantering sort of way, bedecking Rubinstein with sarcastic phrases that, combined with other hints, lead me to conclude it was surely Rubinstein who offended her. From what she says I even understand that R. went to see her and talked about me. Comparing what she says with his letter, my guess is that R. tried to persuade her to stop sending me money, telling her I am growing lazy, etc. A nice gentleman! Fooh, what a bounder!"

The Chief was clever, the Chief knew Tchaikowsky's nature—and Tchaikowsky was aware that he knew it. To have a professor from his own school at the Paris Exposition would be a bright feather in the Rubinstein cap, and now here was Peter Ilyich actually daring to refuse! Such a refusal might go further than the Exposition, it might mean eventual desertion of the Conservatory itself. Nicholas Grigorievitch had not lived six years in the house with Peter Ilyich for nothing. Peter said he was shy; the Chief did not believe it—but what he did believe was that, given a loophole, Peter was always inclined, for some crazy neurotic reason of his own, to flee the world, even when the world offered success and praise and money. Up till now, there had been no loophole. And here was the widow von Meck offering, apparently, to keep the man in idleness for the remainder of his days. . . . The only thing to do was to stop this loophole which the Chief by his introduction had all unwittingly carven out.

This train of reasoning, Tchaikowsky told himself, undoubtedly lay back of Rubinstein's visit to Nadejda von Meck. Raging up and down his room in San Remo, fortifying himself with wine, Peter Ilyich got ready to tell the Chief what he thought of him.

To Nicholas Rubinstein

January 26, 1878

". . . As to Mme Meck, you are cruelly mistaken concerning her character and her relations with me. Secondly, your reproach for my accepting her help, even supposing it was the result of any action of yours—I should find unfitting. It would be useless to tell you the long history of my connection with Mme Meck. I ask only one thing—that no one but you and Karlusha (Albrecht) shall suspect anything. It would be extremely disagreeable to have it come back to her that through me, someone knows of our relationship.

"I must add that your *insinuations* about her, regardless of your friendly intentions, for which I am very grateful, can only harm my relations with her and disturb her very much, as from remarks of yours she has concluded you know of my past association with her, which she wanted to keep the greatest secret. . . . In regard to that lady, I must tell you that never has kindness, delicacy, generosity, and infinite tolerance been united so fully in anyone. I owe her not only life but the ability to continue work, which for me is more precious than life. I am indignant that you understand her as little as you do. Certainly she is not erratic. To me she is simply the eternally kind hand of Providence. One must know her as I know her now, to believe there are people so unbelievably kind and trusting. My role in regard to her is not to be envied. I simply exploit her kindness—an agonizing realization, were it not that she knows how to pacify and stop the pricks of my conscience."

After heaving these letters into the Russian mail system, Peter Ilyich felt better, and said so to his friends. He felt even more cheerful next day when Nadejda's letter came—during all this time he had not heard from her concerning the Exposition.

"My dear, sweet friend," she wrote; "please don't let the fury of the Thunder-hurler distress you. Think only of your health and peace, take care of yourself, because that is your duty to society as a composer and a man who gives delight to others—and to your country as our best representative of ability and talent. It was not worth your while to waste yourself on such a thing as the Exposition; you cannot stand the work of a hunting-dog; you would have excited yourself God knows how much, and that you have no right to do. Thank God you refused. Nor is it worthwhile to quarrel with Rubinstein. How can he understand you? If he becomes unbearable, it is always easy to say farewell to him. He and the poor Conservatory will be the losers; not you, certainly. You will be welcomed anywhere, *à bras ouverts.*"

The widow went on to joke a little about Rubinstein. Here he was, back in Moscow after a tremendously successful tour for the Red Cross which everybody had ascribed to patriotism, and now she found that patriotism had been a mere side issue. "What do you suppose he was after, Peter Ilyich? A title of nobility! 'Nicholas de Rubinstein!' *Dieu*, how absurd it sounds! It would be interesting to know what brand of title he will receive: of Jerusalem, or simply of the Universe? I have an idea it irritates him greatly that the proceeds from these concerts 'wet his moustachios but do not enter his mouth.' All he gets is a dinner at the English Club, given him by the members."

Ridicule of one's enemy reads sweetly from the pen of a friend, but no amount of ridicule on the part of Nadejda could persuade Peter Ilyich to look lightly upon the Chief's anger. He waited anxiously for Rubinstein's reply to his own furious letter—and was surprised to have his antagonist turn the other cheek. Rubinstein answered with words of peace, even of apology. Said this shrewd scion of a shrewd family, "The trouble is, Peter Ilyich, I haven't the knack of expressing myself properly in writing."

Tchaikowsky replied in kind, and all was seemingly forgiven. But no amount of mutual apology nor effusion of friendliness could hide the fact that the relationship of these two men was altered, now and forever. The Chief had commanded, the subordinate had disobeyed—and well the Chief knew why. Peter Ilyich, sick and penniless, would never have composed the high-handed letter written by Peter Ilyich, sick indeed but with the greatest of curative agents behind him—*money* behind him, real money, wealth inexhaustible.

How had Peter done it, the Chief wondered. This woman was around Peter's finger; very possibly she had pensioned him for life —and the two had never even met! The notorious Tchaikowsky charm must be powerful enough then, to work its magic even upon letter paper. Well, give the boy credit, thought Nicholas, maybe it was music paper, not letter paper; certainly the widow seemed utterly fascinated by Peter's music. But Peter had been a white-livered fool to turn down the Exposition, with all the glory it entailed

Knighthood lay behind such services as that. So-ho, if Peter wouldn't go to Paris, Nicholas knew who would, and put on a real show, worthy of the Conservatory and of Russia.

Perhaps, thought Nicholas (de Rubinstein) this affair (confound Peter's talented, lunatic hide!) would turn out for the best after all. . . . But what next? If the widow Meck continued to support Peter Ilyich, the Conservatory would lose its best professor. No doubt of it, Peter hated teaching; perhaps he (Rubinstein) had laid it on a little too heavy these ten years. With what snare could Peter be lured back upon the debit side, money being out of it forever? Peter always paid his debts. He must win the man's gratitude then, anew; Peter was a very fool for gratitude. Rare trait among mankind! Throw Peter a bone and he would do more than wag his tail, he would bring back two bones to his master. . . .

Rubinstein smiles; one eyebrow moves ever so little. He has a plan, and characteristically, the plan is much kinder than the reasoning that has inspired it. What the plan is, Peter Ilyich will find out next autumn when the Chief comes home, crowned with laurels, from the Exposition. . . .

And while Rubinstein in Moscow is plotting to turn defeat into victory, while Nadejda in the same cold white city is coughing her way through luxurious rooms, overheated in this January weather —Peter Ilyich in Italy is hurrying northward from San Remo to meet Modeste and his young pupil, due in Milan on the evening train from Russia. "To see my brother and his sweet boy was light and warmth to my soul," he wrote Nadejda. All night the two sat up, talking as only Russians can talk, inexhaustibly, until the pale early sun filtered through the shutters.

Next day they planned festivities in the city, but at three in the afternoon Milan heard the news of Victor Emanuel's death, and the theatres were closed.

"I was very sorry to hear of the King's death," Tchaikowsky's letter continued, "but thanks to that sad event, I was able to finish what was yet undone in the symphony,* which I had brought with

* The Fourth, which the composer was now orchestrating.

me especially to get a metronome in Milan and mark the exact tempi. After working all evening and part of the night I was able next morning to wrap up a completed symphony and send it to Moscow. So our symphony is now flying at full steam to Rubinstein. With the title I put the dedication, 'To my best friend.' What will the story of that symphony be? Will it live long after the author has disappeared from the earth, or will it fall quickly into the abyss of forgotten things? I don't know, but I know that at the moment, with a blindness perhaps natural to parents, I am not capable of seeing the defects of my youngest child. Also I am sure that in structure and form it marks a step in my development, which goes very slowly. In spite of my mature age" (Peter was thirty-eight) "I am far from reaching the limit of my capacity. Perhaps that is why I value life so highly."

Now that he had Modeste, everything pleased Peter Ilyich; even Rubinstein and Moscow lost their terrors. The little party went to Genoa and looked at pictures; there was no use, Peter wrote, in his trying to like pictures. But Modia liked them and Modia, said Peter proudly, *knew* about them, too! For the moment, Peter Ilyich is proud of Modia, of Modia's pupil, of himself. "My sweet and dear friend," he writes Nadejda, "I owe you all my happy moments. . . ."

Peter and Modia and little Kolia and Alexis their Russian servant walked about Genoa looking conscientiously at pictures—but had they an idea, one wonders, what a strange picture they themselves presented? Perhaps Alexis did not go to galleries, he had been quite ill in San Remo and had caused his master dreadful anxiety by coming out all over in spots. Peter Ilyich had spent a lot of money on doctors, but Alexis said the spots came from not having enough to do; there was no wood to chop in San Remo! But now he was better and walked out often—the only average, day-to-day person in the group. Peter and Modeste were fine-looking men, especially Peter, but they were excitable and talkative and their Russian speech no doubt attracted attention from the passersby. If it did not, their gestures must have, for young Kolia was stone-deaf, and sign-language had to be employed. Also he was dumb except for the halting speech so painstakingly taught him by Modeste; when tir or out-of-sorts he could barely be understood. There is somethi touching in Modeste and Peter's love for the delicate, unfortunate boy and their complete obliviousness to the unattractiveness of his disability. Peter became so fond of him that ten years later upon Kolia's coming-of-age, he proposed him as a husband for Nathalia, the youngest Davydoff niece—much to that young lady's horror!

As to Alexis, he was stolid and good-natured and extremely devoted to his master. He it was who would some day inherit the furnishings of Tchaikowsky's house at Klin, would with his own funds buy the house and help establish it as a museum. Tchaikowsky supported not only Alexis, but eventually, Alexis' wife and family. What were the qualities that made his master so dependent upon him it is difficult to trace. But we know of one great asset possessed by this incomparable servant; namely, a complete unmusicality. Where music was concerned, Alexis might have been deaf as Kolia; and this was fortunate because Tchaikowsky was extremely shy about composing and while at work would permit no one in the room. No one, that is, but Alexis, who could dust and set things in order while his master played or wrote. Only once, Alexis broke through; Tchaikowsky was playing the *Chorus of Maidens* from the third scene of *Onegin* when Alexis suddenly burst into applause. Peter Ilyich was appalled: did this mean an end to musical privacy? Was criticism henceforth to lurk perpetually in corners with a duster? Fortunately, records Modeste, this was the first and only enlightenment that ever struck into the musical darkness of Alexis Safronov.

Behold them then all four, the blue-eyed Tchaikowsky brothers with their servant Alexis and the tall, fair, deaf boy, paddling happily about Genoa in the mild January weather, returning to their hotel for supper, putting the boy to bed and then sitting down to write their letters home. And behold in Moscow the widow von Meck receiving happy letters and herself replying happily in spite, she says, of a terrible headache that has tortured her for two days. She is delighted, that "our symphony" is finished, and she hastens to send a money order for the printing. Would Peter Ilyich care to publish the symphony abroad as well as in Russia? "Do as you think

best," she finishes. "I should like to promote your works abroad;
I should like to show the world what good things we have in
Russia."

Fifteen hundred francs fell out of the envelope and the brothers
Tchaikowsky sighed with relief. Last quarter's allowance, it seems,
had long since disappeared—had "dissipated itself," is the way Peter
expressed it in writing. In fact, the four of them were living on what
remained of Modeste's monthly salary from Kolia's father. Perhaps
Nadejda Philaretovna intended this money solely for the printing
of the symphony? But that would be unnecessary. Jurgenson would
print it without charge, and to have Klindworth make a four-hand
piano arrangement would cost only five hundred francs. "I myself
am not clever at such arrangements. After completing the hard and
complicated work of the score itself, to begin again writing the
music in another form is difficult. It makes me impatient and hasty,
hence the clumsiness and awkwardness of execution that character-
ize my own arrangements of my scores."

The conditions under which a man recovers and maintains health
are as authentic an indication of his essential character as can be
found: for Peter Ilyich, these conditions were quiet days devoted
to creative work, as now; and with nature accessible and a brother
at hand, this was a life as nearly ideal as the man would ever know.
The little party of four returned from Genoa to San Remo and
settled down, the time passing so quietly, wrote Peter, that it was
hard to tell one day from another. At eight in the morning they
rose, had coffee and a little walk, then separated for their daily tasks,
which for himself meant orchestrating the last act of *Onegin*—Anatol had taken only the first act to Russia. Modeste tutored Kolia,
Alexis had found wood to saw. Lunch at noon, a walk until perhaps three-thirty, then work again until early dinner. After dinner,
reading, letter-writing and another short walk after which Kolia was
put to bed, and at eleven, the brothers bade each other good-night.

Sometimes Peter took his afternoon walk alone, climbing the hills
behind San Remo in search of that perfect solitude to be found only,
he wrote Nadejda, in communion with nature. It was a pleasure to

be had so easily in Russia, but he had despaired of it here in San Remo where all the world promenaded the sea wall in the hard bright sun, chattering and laughing—and called it taking a walk. But up in the hills behind San Remo was the little town of Cola, nearly two hours walk, and Peter Ilyich one afternoon followed the Cola path, meeting not so much as a peasant gathering olives. He went briskly and when he was tired, rested under a tree, gazing down through silvery olives to a glimpse of incredibly blue sea. . . . "It was a magnificent quiet," he wrote; he had felt a sudden up-rush of happiness, an ecstasy and a gratitude which immediately craved to communicate itself to Nadejda. So Peter got up and started home to write his friend, and what did he come upon but a whole glade of violets! He was so pleased, he said. He had been buying them on the streets for some time but had not been able to find one growing; he had picked as many as he could carry. . . .

Back on the Boulevard Rojdestvensky, in her boudoir over the city street where sleighs slid silently by on the hard-packed snow, Nadejda von Meck opened a crinkly envelope and six bits of fragrance fell into her lap. "They will remind you," she read in the beloved handwriting—those precise, thin strokes, delicate as the stems in her hand—"of the South, the sun, sea, warmth. . . . There in the woods I was completely happy, and immediately it was very necessary to tell you about it."

Nadejda read the words and reread them; there was more about flowers, quite a discussion as to the relative merits of violet and lily-of-the-valley; to Peter the lily was queen of flowers, but Modeste preferred violets, and the brothers often disputed the subject. Nadejda shook her head; not upon such subjects had the men of her acquaintance been wont to dispute. Karl George's discussions had centered upon bridges and struts and the relative merits of cantalever over suspension; even when she herself had joined in, it had been to suggest that they were underestimating the cost. . . .

The widow von Meck put the dry sweet petals in her handkerchief and went to her desk. She adored flowers, she wrote Peter in reply. Particularly those with perfume, and in her choice of words was revealed the deep but always self-denied sensuousness of her nature: "Flowers intoxicate me; I breathe their aroma with a kind of fierce joy." Nevertheless she preferred trees to flowers; there was more power in trees, she said. More strength. . . .

Nadejda was a despot. Like all despots she worshipped strength, power—and like all despots, surrounded herself with persons weaker than herself, whom she could rule. Any deviation from this, any crossing of her will by another will as strong, only drove her into greater seclusion and illness. She admired the oak, symbol of strength, and said so, yet it was not to strength that her love went out; Peter Ilyich had her heart, and the small gentle Volichka would soon have it—these were no oaks! Nadejda had formed an idea of herself, had built up a *persona:* she saw herself as an atheist needing no God, a woman alone, needing no mate. In short, she saw herself in a role, and for anyone—for woman especially, this is a reckless business, a trafficking with the devil. Tchaikowsky was her relief, her safety valve; to him alone she confessed occasional weakness, occasional defeat of the spirit. She often asked his advice concerning her young sons. At this particular time she was worried because the boys, although naturally bright, had been doing badly in their studies. She knew of Tchaikowsky's great love and understanding for children.

Tchaikowsky replied in the tranquil, domestic mood of Uncle Petia:

"Perverse though it sounds, for myself I don't want your Kolia and Sasha to be first in their class. The usual type of first pupil does not attract me. Most of them are the kind of boy that is known as obedient and clever, lack of personality and cowardice being mistaken for obedience, and the ability to learn by rote being mistaken for cleverness. After graduation, first pupils usually disappear in the crowd of the mediocre and ungifted; on the other hand, the clever ones are often the last in their class. Certainly one cannot tell this to the boys, but one must not say too much about being upset and disappointed, providing their first failure was not due to lack of conscience or laziness. . . .

"My symphony, sent from Milan to Moscow on the 10th of Janu-

ary, has not arrived. I tremble . . . Albrecht writes that it is to be
played at the concert on the 22nd of February. God grant that you
will be quite well on that day and able to go. To have it performed
without you would be a great grief to me. . . .

"I feel very well, never healthier, and my spirit is alert and strong.
Looking upon myself, listening inwardly to myself, I feel quite sure
that my recovery is complete. But, my friend, the rumor of my madness was not quite unfounded. Remembering all I did, all my crazy
actions, I cannot escape the conclusion that temporary madness,
from which I am only just emerging, overtook me. Many things of
the near past seem to me a dream, terrible and wild like a nightmare
in which a man wearing my name, appearance and character behaved just as one behaves in a dream, senselessly and wildly, without
reason. This was not I, with a consciousness of my identity, with a
healthy will, guided by reason and logic. All I did then was marked
by that pathological disconnection between reason and will which
spells madness. During that strange and terrible time, during the
nightmare that blinded my reason, to save myself I reached for the
hands of some who are dear to me, who came forward to rescue me
from the abyss. To you and my two sweet brothers I owe the fact that
I am not only alive, but healthy, physically and mentally.

"If my love and gratitude to you ever finds opportunity to show
itself, know that there is no sacrifice I would not make for you,
N. Ph.—"

He closes, as so often, with a kiss for Nadejda's little daughter,
Milochka, "if she permits." He too, has a child to care for now and
it makes him happy, he says. "How nice our Kolia is! On the whole,
all children are nice."

But if all children were nice, all adults were not. Tchaikowsky
had been abroad four months now, and the news of his hiding place
had leaked out. Musicians knocked at his door, Italians and Russians, and neither Modeste nor Alexis seemed able to turn them
away. A former Director of the Petersburg Conservatory, living in
Nice, sent an emissary to find out (Peter said his mission could be
read in his eye) whether Tchaikowsky were really as mad as the
newspapers had said. The Director himself would follow in a day
or so, and then more of the curious, "who love," wrote Peter
miserably, "to look upon a madman."

The Director came—and found his madman fled. The party of four, after solemn conference, had escaped to Monaco. The Director sat down and waited. He was waiting when they returned, the hotel concierge told them. They tiptoed past the desk, up the carpeted stairs and reaching their rooms safely, dared not emerge until noon of next day when the visitor was gone. . . .

Nadejda read this story and saw nothing funny in it.

"How well I understand it all!" she wrote. "How many flights and lies did I not tell until at last I accustomed people to doing without me! From now on this danger will threaten you rather more, because as spring approaches, there will be more tourists. Don't let them bother you; run away! You will derive no benefit from living with people, so better be rid of them. Then at least you can say, 'God be with them, I am not to blame for their misfortunes.' I was never in Monaco, but there is a great attraction for me there—roulette. I like all games of chance, and I have studied roulette so that I know how to win without fail. Abroad I played in Hamburg and in Switzerland, and at Fontarelli in Spain. Before I learned, however, I lost, but won it back again."

"To win without fail." How the widow loved to tempt providence with these flauntings of infallibility, and how disastrous her spurious optimism was later to prove! Not so with Peter Ilyich, confirmed pessimist and admirer of Schopenhauer. Forever expecting the worst, the composer was naively astonished, doubly pleased, when success descended upon him. Like a child, he seemed to possess no sense of retrospect; today's disaster, today's honor was never connected, for him, with yesterday's impulse or yesterday's action.

But those who flee the world seek ever a haven; far more than do the easily gregarious, these shy ones desire the all-protecting bosom of love. For Tchaikowsky, a maternal bosom was the desideratum. For Nadejda von Meck, something more was necessary—the sublimation of a natural passion that her forty-seven years and the bearing of twelve children had not been able to dilute. She was still subject to sudden storms of passion; even now in the dead of Moscow winter, ill, coughing, wrapped against the cold draughts of her huge house, with spring far off—the mere mention of Tchaikowsky's music carried her onto dangerous ground. What if, next week, she were too ill to attend the first performance of the Fourth Symphony? "Our symphony," what emotion the words evoked! The widow's pen, replying, lingered on the word Poetry, forming capital letters, on the words Love and the Meaning of Love: "Dear heaven," she proceeded, sensing a faint flutter of alarm, "why did I begin talking of music and poetry? My head and heart are wrought to such a state that I cannot continue my letter today. Peter Ilyich, have you ever loved? I think not. You love music too much to love a woman. I know of one love in your life, but I think such love platonic (although truly, Plato never loved so!). A half-love, a love of the imagination rather than the heart, not the feeling that is part of flesh and blood, without which a man cannot live."

If this was dangerous ground for the widow, it was even more dangerous for Peter Ilyich. Nadejda's mention of a past love must have referred to the singer, Artôt. All Moscow knew of that affair, dead ten years ago, and even at its height, not very serious. Concerning Nadejda's questions—had Peter known physical love—plainly, the widow knew nothing about *The*. Even in face of the gossip that had raged around Moscow since his marriage and flight, Nadejda apparently had remained ignorant. Nobody, in short, had dared whisper it to her.

And this was not at all unnatural. The widow von Meck, in spite of her protestations of atheism and expressed hatred of convention, had a moral bias that was purely Victorian. She was, in fact, a Victorian lady and in those days a lady, however emancipated, was not on familiar terms with the words that describe sexual perversion. Court circles in Imperial Russia accepted homosexuality with the same shrug of the shoulders with which a small, highly sophisticated society has accepted it everywhere in all ages of history. But Nadejda did not belong to Court circles nor would she have cared to belong to them. As a von Meck, her position was that of *haute bourgeoisie* rather than aristocracy, and nothing is more conservative morally than your small nobility, however wealthy. There had been a time when the von Mecks were aristocracy, but poverty had forced Karl

George to work, and in an Imperial society, work for pay was utterly incompatible with real aristocratic position. Nadejda loathed "society" and the fashionable world; often in her letters to Tchaikowsky, she deplored its loose morality.

No wonder, then, that Peter was terrified for fear Nadejda learn about *The*. While her wealth and ingrained autocracy gave her the bearing of a woman of the world, Tchaikowsky, graduate of the snobbish and morally corrupt School of Laws, was far ahead of the widow in worldly sophistication, and knew it. Who indeed, would have dared hint scandal to this lady? Certainly not Kotek nor any of the other young musicians from the Conservatory whom she employed to teach her children and play duets with her. It would have meant the instantaneous and ignominious loss of a job. Outside of her own family then, only one person was in a position to dare such intimacy and take the chance of mortally offending the widow. For this one person, the risk would have served no purpose, and when had Nicholas Rubinstein ever acted without purpose?

No doubt some of this reasoning filtered through Tchaikowsky's mind when he sat down, that February evening in San Remo, to answer the widow's dangerous questioning. One thing was certain: in Nadejda's nature was no room for insinuation or hint; if she questioned him about love she could have done so only in good faith.

"You ask," he wrote, "if I have known non-platonic love. Yes and no. If the question were put a little differently: have I felt the happiness of fulfilled love, the answer would be no, no, no!!! I think the answer to your question lies in my music. Ask whether I understand the power, the immense strength of that feeling and I can answer yes, yes, yes, reiterating that I have tried my best more than once to express in music the torment and delight of love. Have I succeeded? I do not know, or better, I leave it to others to judge. I disagree with you absolutely that music cannot fully express the feelings of love. On the contrary—only music can do so. You say that words are needed. No, words alone are not enough, and where they are powerless, comes full-armed a more eloquent language—music. That form of expressing love to which the poets have recourse, is a usurpation of a function belonging wholly to music. Words in the form of poetry cease to be simply words: they become music. The best proof that the poetry which tries to express love is more music than words (as, for instance, Fet, whom I like very much), is that when such poetry is read attentively as words and not as music, the words have almost no meaning. Yet in reality they possess not only meaning but deep thought—not literary but purely musical. I am glad that you put instrumental music so high. What you say about words harming music, often dragging it down from unscalable heights, is absolutely true and I have always felt it deeply—perhaps that is why I have succeeded better with instrumental compositions than with vocal.

"Until the next letter, my dear friend. Very, very often, without exaggeration, every minute—I think of you, and with all the power of an ardently loving heart, I call all kinds of blessings upon you. May you be very happy.

"Loving you devotedly,
"P. Tch."

Deftly enough, Peter had turned the subject from love to music— but this was not wholly hypocritical. To his very marrow, this man was aware of a fact that he had himself expressed more than once: his music alone redeemed him for manhood. Also, it is the way of musicians to refer every subject back to music; perhaps more than any other artist, the musician is guilty of this intense preoccupation with his art.

Nadejda read his letter and was satisfied. She never reopened the question.

As to Peter Ilyich, writing under a Riviera moon, he was getting well, and to be healthy in exile is to be restless. On the 13th of February, 1878, he mailed a completed opera to Moscow: *Eugene One-gin* was finished. On the same day he wrote Nadejda; ought he to go home now and take up his duties at the Conservatory? Was it possible that Rubinstein had been right in accusing him of laziness? Was he wrong to use Nadejda Philaretovna's money to remain abroad and rest? Would it be better for his pupils for him to stay away until he felt ready to give them something more than the thinly healed nerves he had now to offer? Surely, if his classes had done without him all winter, they could do without him until autumn. . . .

"In short, I believe I could again take up my old occupations, but it would be very hard. I want very, very, very much to have more rest and to return in September completely refreshed, having forgotten—as far as one could forget—the unhappy event that darkened my life half a year ago. Truly there is a queer contradiction in my appealing to you thus for advice. I ask you for the truth, begging you not to let other considerations confuse your judgment as to what is my duty—and in the same breath you can feel me saying, 'For God's sake, don't demand my return to Moscow because I should be very unhappy.'

"Yes, I want you, dear friend to tell me once more that there is nothing harmful in my rest, in my 'idleness,' and that I am not wrong in using your money to live here. Only now do I quite appreciate the tremendous benefit of these four months' isolation—the sojourn in a foreign land, which in the beginning was sometimes hard, making even Rome seem unbearably irksome, but which now quite satisfies my unconquerable desire to live away from everyday contact with people, Anyway, I shall not permit myself to give in to my *far niente* for too long. Believe me, I have an instinctive distaste for idleness in the real sense, and if one can call the way I now live idle (because I work for myself and not for others, to satisfy my own desire to write) it will not last long.

"I shall not hide from you, precious friend, that I feel a great joy today in the knowledge that I have finished two big compositions in which I think I have gone ahead, and very much ahead. The rehearsals of the symphony will start soon after you receive this letter. N. Ph., if you are quite well then, won't you find time to go to one of the rehearsals? When you have heard a big new composition twice, you will understand it better and more intimately. You cannot get a clear idea from hearing it once; hearing it twice everything becomes clear, and many things that slipped by the first time, catch your attention the second. Details stand out, important ideas take on their true meaning in relation to secondary ones. It would be splendid if you could find an opportunity to do this.

"As to the opera" (*Onegin*), "I am actually glad the Conservatory has postponed its performance. Next year they can give it in full, and in the meantime they can learn it.

"I am in a most rosy mood, happy to have finished the opera, happy that spring is coming, happy to be well, free and safe from people and social life, and most of all, happy that I have such strong supports in life as your friendship, my brothers' love, and the knowledge that I have the chance to perfect myself in my career. If conditions are favorable—and today I want to believe they will be—I can leave a sound memory behind me. I hope this is not an illusion, but an honest estimate of my powers.

"Give Milochka a tender kiss on the forehead, my friend. Thank you for everything, everything.

"Your
"P. Tch."

Whether or no this is the letter of a healthy man, certainly it is the letter of a happy one. Heaven reserves for some men a rare talent for hope; a steel-fibred capacity for rebirth after disaster. One senses in the words of Peter Ilyich more than health—as though his pen were borne along by that extra life, that upsurge of unreasonable joy which is the privilege and the birthright of genius.

Zest, said a philosopher, is the last gift of the immortals to man.

13

The Fourth Symphony is performed. Peter gives it a program

A<small>LEXIS</small> chopped his wood in the hard San Remo sunlight, his ears assailed by the slight sound of the Mediterranean sucking against a pebbled beach. His masters walked and rewalked every promenade; fleeing at times to the olive orchards behind the town in search of Russian forest shade and Russian country stillness. Reading in the guidebook that full-blooded, excitable people should not live in a place where the colors were bright and the air stimulating, the Tchaikowsky brothers looked at each other, nodded simultaneously and ordered Alexis to pack their bags. Florence, no doubt, would have a more tranquil shadiness. . . .

Behold them then, all four, settled comfortably enough in their Florentine apartment and enjoying eagerly every sight and sound of the coming Italian spring. Already on the streets the girls were selling Peter's favorite flower, the lily-of-the-valley. The very sight of those shy blossoms on his table was enough, Peter wrote Nadejda, to give a man love of life. He was resting now, for a week or two. *Onegin* and the Fourth Symphony were gone from under his hand and he was not ready for another big work. On the 22nd of February, he went alone to his room, and sitting down, watch in hand, awaited the moment when, hundreds of miles away, the trumpet notes of his symphony would sound the motif that the composer himself had characterized as the relentless voice of fate:

On that day, under Nicholas Rubinstein's baton, the orchestra of the Moscow Conservatory gave the symphony its first performance, and on that day Nadejda braved snow and ice and cold and illness to make her way alone to the balcony of the concert hall, where sne might sit unseen and unmolested by friends. *To my best friend* was written on the symphony, but only one person in the audience knew who the best friend was—although that suave gentleman with the baton could have ventured a guess.

It was two days before the composer received any slightest news of the reception accorded his favorite child:

To Nadejda Philaretovna

Florence, Feb. 24, 1878

"I received your telegram yesterday morning, my dear friend, and it gave me unspeakable pleasure. I was uneasy, first, that your health might interfere with your being at the concert, second, that you might not like the symphony. Even if you had not liked it much, it was very possible you would have sent me congratulations just out of kindness, but from the tone and wording of the telegram, I see clearly that you are satisfied with what was written for you. In my deepest heart I am convinced it is the best thing I have written. It seems a little queer to me that I have not had any word of the symphony from my Moscow friends. The score was sent more than a month and a half ago. With your telegram I had another, signed by Rubinstein and all the rest, and saying that the symphony was perfectly performed—not a word as to its quality. Perhaps that is to be understood. Thank you for the news of my beloved child's success, and for the cordial words of the telegram. In imagination I was present at the concert. I calculated the exact minute when the introductory phrase would resound, and all the details followed as I tried to imagine what impression the music would make. The first part (the most complicated and the best) probably seemed long to many, and not quite easy to understand the first time."

Tchaikowsky waited a week, two weeks, and still no word—after the telegram—from his Moscow friends. He walked the streets of Florence, alone or with Modeste, trying to conceal his chagrin from his brother and from himself. Out from a hundred towers, bells flung their voices on the wind, calling the hours. The bells at home

had deeper, slower voices. . . . But in Moscow there would be no
flower girls with fragrant February violets to sell, no sudden heat of
sun striking a man's bare hand with summer strength. Peter turns
to his brother. "Modia," he asks with anxious voice, "are you sure
the first movement of my symphony is not too long?"

Over and over in the composer's head the trumpets blare that fate-
full call, mingling with the bells of Florence, drowning the bells.
The man who has made this music knows that it is good. But will
the world know it? Walking the streets with his quick, nervous
step, how can Peter Ilyich know that this motif, these trumpet voices
that follow him, will haunt as inexorably the memory of every man
who hears them even once?

At last came a letter from Nadejda, a huge, fat roll of paper that
answered eagerly all the questions Peter Ilyich, writing a month ago
from San Remo, had asked concerning his future. Page after page,
assuring him of her undying friendship, begging him not even to
think of returning to the Conservatory for a long, long time, beseeching him to accept from her the money to live.

"In my long life I have come to the conclusion that if a genius is
to develop and gain inspiration, he must have security from material
want. Without it he will deteriorate, stagnate, grow weak, whining,
helpless. And you know, my wonderful friend, how precious your
talent is to me, how I long to take care of it. In your music I hear
myself, my moods, the echo of my feelings, my thoughts, my grief.
So how could I *not* take care of you? We are far apart only in distance; but for that we should be nearly one person; we feel the same
about everything, usually even at the same time."

Friendly words, and reassuring—but was Nadejda not going to
so much as mention the symphony? Surely she had heard the performance; why then did not her letter begin with news of it? Why
was not her first word concerned with this thing that meant more

to Peter than life itself? Page after page before the word *symphony* fell upon Tchaikowsky's eye—and only those who have submitted a self-created symphony or book or picture to a friend, can realize how eagerly and how desperately Peter searched for this word.

"The public received your symphony very well," he read at last, "especially the *Scherzo*." (This was the *pizzicato* movement for which the composer had said he had great hopes.) "Applause was great and at the end they called for you. It must have been Rubinstein who came out; I didn't see because I had started to go out. But I believe the composition was somewhat marred by a poor perform-ance; the orchestra was worse than I ever heard it. Usually they give a good performance, but this time surely they did not rehearse enough."

Faint praise this, from a lady whose natural style was furiously extravagant. Nevertheless Peter Ilyich was grateful; perhaps he sensed that Nadejda was not experienced enough for immediate comprehension of this music—although he could not know that in a few months, when she had the piano arrangement under her fingers, she would go nearly mad with joy over this symphony. But if Tchaikowsky was disappointed over her first response he did not show it, but replied eagerly. With Nadejda's help he could, he wrote, return to the Conservatory next autumn and to his teaching—not as a hateful chain to drag but as something he had himself chosen.

"Once and forever, N. Ph., I tell you that I will accept from you without false shame anything you want to offer me. I know that you are wealthy, but wealth is relative. A large ship needs large waters. You have great means, but because of that, great regular expenses.

"Your letter today gave me such joy, my priceless Nadejda Philaretovna! How immeasurably happy I am that the symphony pleased you, that my music entered your heart and you experienced the feelings that filled me in writing it!

"You ask if the symphony has a definite program. Ordinarily, when asked that question concerning a symphonic work, I answer, 'No, none whatever.' And in truth it is not an easy question. How can one express those vague feelings which pass through one during the writing of an instrumental work which in itself has no definite subject? It is a purely lyrical process, a musical confession of the soul that, filled with the experiences of a life-time, pours itself out through sound, just as the lyric poet pours himself out in verse. The difference is that music is an incomparably more delicate and powerful language in which to express the thousand vari-colored moments of the spiritual life. Usually the seed of a future musical creation germinates instantaneously and most unexpectedly. If the soil is eager, if there is a disposition to work, that seed takes root with amazing power and speed, appears above ground as a little stalk which puts forth leaves and branches and finally, flowers. This simile is as near as I can come to a description of the creative process. If the seed appears at a favorable moment, the main difficulty is past. The rest grows of itself.

"Words are vain to tell you the boundless joy that comes over me when a new idea is conceived and begins to take definite shape. One forgets everything; one is a madman, trembling and quivering in every organ, with scarcely time to outline the sketches, so rapidly does one idea pursue another. Sometimes in the midst of this magic process an outside shock wakes one from this state of somnambulism. The bell rings, the servant enters, the clock strikes, reminding one that the business of the day must be attended to. These interruptions are inexpressibly trying. Sometimes, inspiration takes flight, one has to seek it again—often in vain. Frequently one must rely here upon a quite cold, deliberate technical process of work. Perhaps such moments are responsible, in the works of the Great Masters, for those places where the organic coherence fails and where one can trace artificial coherence, seams and patches. But this is unavoidable. If that spiritual condition of the artist called inspiration, which I have tried to describe, should continue uninterrupted, the artist could not survive a single day. The strings would snap and the instrument fly to pieces. One thing however is indispensable: the main idea of the piece, together with a general outline of the separate parts, must not be found through searching but must simply appear—a result of that supernatural, incomprehensible and never-analysed power called inspiration.

"But I digress from your question. Our symphony has a program definite enough to be expressed in words; to you alone I want to tell—and can tell—the meaning of the work as a whole and in part. You will understand I attempt to do so only along general lines. The Introduction is the germ of the entire symphony, the idea upon which all else depends:

"This is 'Fatum,' the inexorable force that prevents our hopes of happiness from being realized, that watches jealously lest our felicity should become full and unclouded—it is Damocles' sword, hanging over the head in constant, unremitting spiritual torment. It is unconquerable, inescapable. Nothing remains but to submit to what seems useless unhappiness:

"Despair and discontent grow stronger, sharper. Would it not be wiser to turn from reality and sink into dreams?

"Oh, joy, at last the sweet and tender dream appears! Some bright clear human image passes, beckoning me on:

"How delicious and how remote, now, the distressing first theme of the Allegro. Little by little, dream possesses the soul. Forgotten is sadness and despair. Happiness is here! But no, this was only a dream, and 'Fatum' awakes us:

"So life itself is a persistent alternation of hard reality with eva-
nescent dreams and clutchings at happiness. There is no haven. Sail
on that sea until it encompass you and drown you in its depths. This,
approximately, is the program of the First Movement.

"The Second Movement expresses another phase of suffering. It
is the melancholy that comes in the evening when we sit alone, and
weary of work, we try to read, but the book falls from our hand.
Memories crowd upon us. How sweet these recollections of youth, yet
how sad to realize they are gone forever. One regrets the past, yet
one would not begin life anew, one is too weary. It is easier to be
passive and to look back. One remembers many things—happy moments when the young blood ran hot and life fulfilled all our desire.
There were hard times too, irreparable losses, but they are very far
away. It is sad and somehow sweet to sink thus into the past.

"The Third Movement expresses no definite feelings, rather it is
a succession of capricious arabesques, those intangible images that
pass through the mind when one has drunk wine and feels the first
touch of intoxication. The soul is neither gay nor sad. The mind
is empty, the imagination has free rein and has begun, one knows
not why, to draw strange designs. Suddenly comes to mind the
picture of a drunken peasant, a brief street song is heard. Far off,
a military procession passes. The pictures are disconnected, like those
which float through the mind when one is falling asleep. They are
out of touch with reality; they are wild and strange.

"The Fourth Movement: If you truly find no joy within yourself,
look for it in others. Go to the people. See—they know how to make
the best of their time, how to give themselves up to pleasure! A
peasant festival is depicted. No sooner do you forget yourself in this
spectacle of others' joy, than the merciless Fatum reappears to remind you of yourself. But the others are indifferent to you; they do
not so much as turn their heads toward your loneliness and sadness.
Oh, how gay they are! And how fortunate to be ruled by such simple,
immediate feelings! Here one sees the existence of simple, deep joys;
enter into them and life will be bearable.

"This, dear friend, is all I can tell you about the symphony. Of
course what I have said is neither clear nor complete. This follows
from the very nature of instrumental music, which does not submit
to detailed analysis. 'Where words cease, there music begins,' as
Heine said.

"It is late. I shall not stop to write about Florence except to say
that I shall keep the most agreeable memories. At the end of next

week I think of going to Switzerland to stay quietly through March and work upon a number of short pieces.

"P.S. Just now, putting my letter into the envelope, I reread it and was horrified at the muddy and slipshod program I am sending you. This is the first time in my life I have tried to transpose musical ideas and images into words, and I have certainly not been successful. All last winter while writing the symphony, I was suffering from terrible hypochondria; it is a true echo of the way I felt. But it is no more than an echo. How then can I translate it into clear and definite words?

"Already I have forgotten many things about that time, I have only a general recollection of the horror and intensity of what I felt. It will be very, very interesting to know what my Moscow friends think of my work."

A day or two later Tchaikowsky sent Nadejda another letter from Florence, writing at night, with only a bare postscriptum mention of the symphony—a sad little letter, breathing homesickness and nostalgia.

"I have worked until I am tired, and now I come home to talk with you, my peerless and my dear friend. The window is open; how delightful to breathe the coolness of the night after a hot spring day! How odd, how strange but at the same time how sweet to think of my far-away, inexpressibly beloved home! There it is winter. You are sitting in your study, perhaps at an open fire. Muscovites, men and women, walk by your house wrapped in furs, the quiet is not disturbed even by the noise of carriages, the sleighs slide silently by.

"How terribly far we are from each other! You in winter, I in a country where the trees are already green and where I can write this letter at an open window at eleven in the evening. And yet I think of that winter not with aversion but with delight. I love our winter, long and steady. One waits and waits for Lent to come, and with it the first signs of spring. What a miracle is our spring, with its suddenness, its rich power! I love it when the streets run torrents of melted snow and the air is vital and vigorous. With what affection one greets the first green grass! How one rejoices at the coming of the rook, and after, the larks and the others, foreign summer visitors! Here the spring comes on slow feet, little by little—one cannot say exactly when she has arrived. And I cannot be moved by the sight of green grass when I have had it before my eyes in December and January.

"Do you remember I wrote you from Florence about the boy I heard one evening on the street, whose beautiful voice so affected me? Three days ago, to my great joy I found the boy again, he sang for me again *Perchè tradir mi, perchè lasciar mi,* and I was in ecstasy. I don't remember when a simple popular song has had such effect on me. This time he introduced me to a new Florentine song, so charming that I want to find him again and make him sing it several times, so that I can write down the words and music. It runs approximately, so: (It is about one Pimpinella; what does it mean? I don't know, but will surely find out.)

"How I pity the child! He is much exploited by his father, uncle and other relatives. Because it is Carnival time he sings from morning till evening, and will sing until his voice is ruined forever. Even now the voice is a little cracked, compared with the first time I heard him. It adds a new charm to its wonderfully sympathetic quality, but it will not be for long. If he had been born into a rich family, he would perhaps become a famous singer. One must visit Italy to see its absolute pre-eminence in the vocal art. At every step one hears beautiful voices in the streets—this very minute a very pretty voice in the distance is singing, with open throat, a song in a high chest tenor Even if the voice is not lovely, every Italian is a naturally good singer They have the right *émission de voix* and the art of singing from the chest, not through the throat and nose, as with us.

"Imagine, I haven't had one word from my Moscow friends about my symphony! It is very strange.

"Good-bye, my dear.
"P. Tch."

Pimpinella is still sung; its melody transports one not only to the streets of Italy but to another time, an age of innocence more remote than the intervening years would warrant. There is about Tchaikowsky's arrangement of the song an ornament and a melancholy wholly Victorian. This is evident in many of his lesser songs, and is even more pronounced in his piano pieces. The latter have not a trace of the composer's fury and abandon—and not a trace of his power. He wrote a great number of them, and one and all sound as though designed for ladies to play on *salon* pianos at evening parties Who that was born before the turn of the century but recognizes these nostalgic strains—hears the troika bells, the horses galloping romantically over the snow:

In Florence, that year of 1878, after shipping the Fourth Symphony and *Onegin* to Moscow, Tchaikowsky wrote many of these short piano pieces, dedicating them to Modeste, his companion at the time. One of them, Number 12, was a Venetian melody that had been sung under his window during that lonely week in Venice just after Anatol had left him to return to Russia. To Anatol he dedicated five songs published with *Pimpinella,* among them the still popular *Don Juan's Serenade.*

Florence in March was beautiful and brilliant, but it was no place, Peter wrote Nadejda, for a composer who wanted to work. The street songs were lovely and so were the bells, but other sounds were not. He had tried to write systematically, working on short pianoforte pieces, but English ladies in the hotel "played eternally on the piano, across the streets someone boomed exercises on the trombone and in the streets they screamed as well as sang." Restful in a musician's memory loomed the high still mountains of Switzerland; would not little Kolia also—Peter asked his brother—profit by a change to Clarens?

Modeste was never difficult to persuade; a day or so later—March 7th—the four of them took the night train for Geneva and after an anxious trip with a tired small boy, arrived at Clarens, Tchaikowsky's old retreat. Here they found winter; snow was underfoot and in the air, but from the moment they stepped from the train, the stillness delighted Peter Ilyich. At the hotel, mail was waiting from Russia; Peter glanced eagerly through it for the handwriting of his

Moscow musical colleagues—and did not find it. He waited a few days longer and then wrote Nadejda:

To Nadejda Philaretovna

Mar. 12th, 1878

"This is going to be a confession. I am deeply chagrined, offended, and amazed by the incomprehensible silence of all my friends concerning the symphony. I have had no news except from you, and indirectly, through Kotek, who told me that his friend Porubinofsky, a pupil of the Conservatory, was very much pleased with it. I expected this symphony would at least interest my musical friends, even if it did not stir and move them. I expected them to understand how impatiently and greedily I awaited sympathetic criticism, and that each would describe in detail his impressions, as you have, my dear friend. I needed it very much. And, imagine, not one word except a telegram to say the symphony was performed perfectly—an assurance, as I see from your last letter, that was not true!

"And yet how can one help being offended? Let us suppose that I am quite satisfied with your enthusiastic report and that I can live without their encomiums—it is not flattery I need, but friendly attention. If it were not for your letters I should have been quite ignorant of anything about the symphony. And is it not strange that of all the Conservatory only the voice of a bassoonist pupil, Porubinofsky, should reach me, and that indirectly? It is hard to describe how happy even that made me; at least one person from the institution of which I have been a part for twelve years responded, and very warmly. It gives me something to think of.

"Again you appear as my consoler. If it were not for your friendship, which repays me a hundred times for the neglect of my colleagues, I should be disappointed beyond words—desperate. You understand me, dearly loved friend. You understand that, having written a big composition into which I put my whole soul, I knew that of the crowd which heard the composition there would be only a few who would be able to appreciate it even in part. One consoles oneself with the thought that friends will understand, cheer one, appreciate. And then, not a word, not one word of congratulation from them. It is painful and very mortifying.

"I wrote you about the boy singer whose wonderful voice in Florence touched me so. I heard him once more on the eve of my departure and wrote down the words and music of a little song, which I send you, with my accompaniment. Is it not a sweet little song? And what queer words!"

> "Good-bye, my dear.
> "Your faithful friend,
> "P. Tch."

Nadejda's reply makes one glad that Peter Ilyich had such a friend, and glad also that he had confided in her. At last she seemed to understand his real grief at Moscow's silence concerning the symphony.

Nadejda to Peter Ilyich

Moscow, March 18, 1878

"I had just sat down to write you, my sweet, beloved friend, when your letter came enclosing the song, *Pimpinella*. Thank you, my dear, for that lovely thing. . . . I quite sympathize with your distress at the neglect of your friends, my sweet, my dear, because I know that the greatest sorrow can come not from enemies, but from those we count as friends. I understand how painful it is, but to tell the truth I did not expect anything better from any of them, and if what the lower hierarchy thinks can give you pleasure, I can tell you the opinion of one of the cleverest, most mature and ardent lovers of music, your pupil Pahulsky" (The same Pahulsky who afterward married Nadejda's daughter, Julia.), "whom I see very often and of whose sincerity and depth of feeling I can judge absolutely. He is mad about your symphony. For several days he could speak of nothing else, think of nothing else, every five minutes he would sit at the piano and play it. He has a very good musical memory, and I owe to him my close acquaintance with our symphony because he plays it constantly to me now. He has a real passion for music and was an admirer of Wagner before hearing your symphony, but after the first rehearsal he came to me in such a state of excitement that I thought something had happened to him. 'That is music!' he said, 'What is Wagner now, and why do *we* all exist on earth?'

"From what he says I see that you are mistaken, dear friend, in thinking that you have not known how to inspire your pupils with love for their work, because I see with what respect and gratitude Pahulsky remembers your course. He says that a word of yours even in rebuke, meant ten times more than the orations he hears now. With what enthusiasm he tells how you would come into the class and before starting, sit down at the piano and strike several chords. 'But, my God, what chords they were!' he says. And I hear from him that the greater number of pupils miss you very much. You see, my dear, those that envy you are the only ones that do not love you; so be indifferent to the neglect of the Moscow friends. They are friends as far as their natures permit them—one cannot expect more. Your symphony certainly pleased them, it could not be otherwise, but envy prevents their expressing it.

"As to the public, certainly it is hard for it to understand such a composition immediately. Pahulsky tells me that in the intermission, before the symphony was played, a gentleman, unknown to him, not of the Conservatory, explained to a gathering around him that it was doubtful if the public would like this composition because they could not understand it. If it was clear to me on hearing it the first time, it is because I know by heart the character of your creations. I am not disturbed or confused by the suspensions and tied notes, and organ points because I have grown accustomed to them, and the daring sequences, the wonderful harmonies, thrill me before others have got accustomed to these new sounds. Yet they too, will someday appreciate it."

No sooner had she mailed this than Nadejda received Tchaikowsky's letter from Florence, explaining the emotional program of the Fourth Symphony. She was delighted. What Peter said was proof that in writing this music he had been moved by true inward inspiration, the quality for which above all other qualities she revered him as a composer. Only the other day, some musicians had tried to convince her there was no connection between the notes of a symphony and the inner feelings of the man who wrote it. The whole thing, said they, was a matter of mechanics, of technique. Writing again to Peter Ilyich, Nadejda quotes her own shocked reply to these false prophets:

"'Is it possible,' I asked, 'that *Tchaikowsky* composes in that way?' They said, 'surely.' I suffered for the sake of my dear art, and yet held to my opinion that the inner bond between composer and composition must exist, and you, my dear sweet soul, confirm my opinion. You personify my image of a composer by inspiration from within. I am happy that I can say '*E pur si muove.*' . . .

"Your symphony made just such an impression on me. The first

part affected the heart, deeply, sadly, tragically—what a theme! What
an audacious sequence of chords! It is like an electric shock. What a
conclusion! One could go mad, it is so beautiful. The second movement"—and Nadejda goes off into a panegyric undoubtedly genuine,
even though one regrets that she did not give way to it the day she
heard the symphony performed, rather than now, nearly three weeks
later. She is especially entranced by the Russian quality of the symphony and asks the composer whether this effect is instinctive, or
placed there by design? Because Tchaikowsky does not roar his
Russian-ness to the skies by way of newspaper columns, she often
hears criticism of him as being anti-patriotic, a man without musical
roots. Now Wagner, for instance—"shouts to all Europe how he has
created German music, and they believe him and give him honor,
while they doubt you who remain silent. Well, God be with them in
their naïveté. I am convinced that Glinka is the creator of Russian
music, you its greatest builder."

And as far as sheer Russian-ness is concerned, posterity confirms
the widow's belief. For all their championship of nationalism, for
all their loud repudiation of western music and conscious insistence
upon Russian folksong as a basis for every phrase they wrote, not
one of the Petersburg Five, the nationalists, composed music more
deeply Slavic than Tchaikowsky's. Stravinsky himself has vouched
for this. "Tchaikowsky was the most Russian of us all," he said.

Tchaikowsky's answer to Nadejda is in his best vein. How well
he himself knew that he was at his best only when his "specialty,"
as he called it, was concerned.

To Nadejda Philaretovna

Clarens, Mar. 17, 1878
"I have your letter, my beloved friend, and read it with the greatest
pleasure. Let me answer your questions in order. It is very pleasant
to talk with you about my method of creation. I have never before
revealed these mysterious manifestations of the spirit—partly because
not many have requested it, partly because those that asked did not
inspire me with the desire to answer. But it is very good to describe
the process of composition to you because you are unusually sensitive
to my music. Never has anyone, except perhaps my brothers, made
me as happy as you with your sympathy. If you only knew how

precious that sympathy is to me, and how little I am spoiled by it!

"Do not believe those who tried to persuade you that musical creation is a cold, purely mental exercise. Only the music that pours from the depths of an artistic soul, moved by inspiration, can touch and take possession of the hearer. There is no doubt that even the greatest musical genius has sometimes worked unwarmed by inspiration. It is a guest that does not come on first invitation. In the meantime one must work, and an honest artist cannot sit with his hands crossed because he is not inclined to compose. If one waits for inclination instead of advancing to meet it, one easily drifts into laziness and apathy. One must hold fast and have faith, and inspiration will come.

"This happened to me only today. I wrote you that I had been working regularly, but without enthusiasm. If I had given way to a lack of inclination, I would surely not have accomplished anything for a long time. But faith and patience never desert me, and today, ever since morning I have been possessed by the inexplicable, mysterious fire of inspiration of which I told you, thanks to which I know that all that I wrote today will enter and affect people's hearts.

"I don't think you will accuse me of self-praise when I tell you that the apathy of which I spoke comes very rarely. I believe this is because I have patience and have trained myself not to surrender to inertia. I know how to conquer myself. I am glad I have not gone the way of my Russian brothers,* who, suffering from lack of self-confidence and self-control, lay their work aside at the smallest difficulty. That is why, in spite of great talent, they write so little and with so amateurish a result.

"You ask how I work in regard to orchestration. I never compose in the abstract—never does the musical idea come to me except with suitable exterior form. So I find the musical thought simultaneously with the orchestration. When I wrote the *Scherzo* of our symphony, I imagined it just as you heard it. It is impossible if not performed *pizzicato*. If played with the bow it would lose everything. It would be a soul without a body and all its charm would disappear.

"As to the Russian element in my compositions, it is true that I often begin to write with the intention of using one or another popular song. Sometimes (as in the *Finale* of our symphony) this happens of itself, quite unexpectedly. As to the Russian element in general in my music—the relation to the popular songs in melody

* The Five in Petersburg—Borodin, Moussorgsky, etc.

and harmony—I grew up in a peaceful spot, saturated from earliest childhood with the miraculous beauty of Russian popular song, so that I love to the point of passion every expression of the Russian spirit. In short, I am a Russian through and through.

"I must thank you for your new care of me. With impatience I await the books and hope they will come tomorrow. A thousand thanks, my dear. I feel perfectly well today and very happy; my work was very satisfactory. Beside the small pieces I am writing a sonata for the piano and a violin concerto, and hope to go home well-provided with sketches. Be assured that I shall be very careful in my choice of words for the Romances," (songs) "and I hope you will be pleased.

> "I love you without end,
> "Your
> "P. Tch.

"Please give my kiss to Milochka. Thank her for the candy."

14

The Violin Concerto. Peter defends his Symphony

A<small>ND</small> now a Russian visitor arrived in Clarens—a welcome one this time. Kotek, the young violinist who had once been go-between for Nadejda and Peter Ilyich, and who had lost his position in Nadejda's household by gossiping about the messages entrusted to him. Peter had pled his cause with the widow in vain; now the brothers welcomed the young man joyfully, and the mountain-top resounded to much sonata-playing—nor is it unlikely that Kotek's violin was help and inspiration in the first sketching of the Violin Concerto. Any fiddle player who has lived under a composer's roof knows how often he is called upon to try out a passage. "Is it violinistic?" asks Peter of his guest. "Go get your instrument. . . . There—does that passage lie well for the hand?"

"Thanks to my work and the agreeable company," Peter wrote Nadejda, "I don't know where the time goes, or whether it is winter and snowing outside. The sonata and concerto interest me immensely. It is the first time in my life that I have begun anything without finishing what preceded it. I have always kept firmly to this rule. But I could not control the desire to write sketches for a concerto, and then I became so interested I put the sonata aside, but from time to time I still return to it.

"I have no news of the symphony from Moscow. Not one word of sympathy or a compliment. Jurgenson writes that Rubinstein will play my concerto." (The B Flat Minor Concerto Rubinstein had criticized so severely in 1874.) "Do you know the concerto? If not, I should very, very much like you to hear it. It is one of my favorite children. Why does Rubinstein consent to play a concerto he thought so impractical before? Anyway I am grateful. He will certainly play it perfectly. . . .

"Being a little superstitious and remembering that not very long ago, good fortune seemed a quite impossible occurrence, I am frightened sometimes and the consciousness that luck is fickle darts through my head quickly, like lightning. But then I remember you, and joy and peace return. The first movement of the Violin Concerto is ready; tomorrow I begin the second. From the day I began to write it, this favorable mood has not left me. In such a spiritual state, composition loses all aspect of work—it is a continuous delight. One does not notice the passing of time, and if nobody came along one would sit writing the whole day. But I do not renounce my settled routine, and the last two days, thanks to the beautiful weather, our after-dinner walks have been very long and delightful."

The sonata Tchaikowsky mentions at the beginning of this letter was the G major Piano Sonata. It was not important and, like the rest of his solo piano compositions, is seldom heard today. But the Violin Concerto was another matter and proved more than worthy of Tchaikowsky's optimism concerning it. A reliable "hit" on every virtuoso violinist's repertoire today, it is a thorn in the side of those intellectuals who shudder at the rich deep yellow of Tchaikowsky's most Slavic self. It is undeniably effective, eminently violinistic, gorgeously rhythmic and colorful. Young Kotek must have been a good fiddle player to compass this difficult concert music; one envies him his position of passage-prover. How strange those wild Russian strains, those long overwhelming melodies floating thus, new-born, from the window of a Swiss chalet. . . .

To Nadejda

Clarens, March 22, 1878

". . . As I write, Rubinstein is giving his concert in Moscow. Were you there? I imagined you sitting in a corner of the balcony. It would be very good to know that you were there and heard my concerto! And isn't it better to hear music from the balcony than in the orchestra with all the elegant people who are less interested in music?"

Nadejda had indeed been at the concert. "What a joy your concerto is," she wrote, "and how that man Rubinstein can play! Superhumanly! So well that one forgets not only the world, but the player's defects. He rises to godhead, and one ceases to judge him. True, this charm disappears the moment the ear ceases to influence the heart; one can adore him for two hours only. But your concerto! One cannot forget that as long as the heart beats! It is hard to say what is best in it." (Here Nadejda says at some length what is best in it). . . . "I need not add that the hall was full of people and the applause more than necessary. Two crowns of laurel were presented with other more substantial gifts, but I don't know the sum.

"Rubinstein will play your concerto again in Petersburg for the benefit of the Red Cross. I am very glad; I should like so much to have your compositions promoted more abroad—here my Russian pride speaks. It is maddening that they know (Anton) Rubinstein well, that cosmopolitan composer, and have no opportunity to know our Russian '*pur sang*,' national composer, our pride—you, my sweet friend! And Rubinstein has now had his *Maccabees* performed in Vienna, causing a furore. He gives two concerts there too. I should like to promote Russian music that has two such pearls as Glinka and Tchaikowsky, and now one cannot even buy your compositions abroad. Tell Jurgenson, my dear, that he should sell more to the foreign market. I am so glad that they will play your *Snow Maiden* again at the last concert. You ask, my dear, whether I know your concerto —how could I not know it? I often play the last movement myself. I have all your compositions.

"Yours with all my heart,
"N. v. M."

Tchaikowsky replied that his friend need not disturb herself about his fame abroad. It would come of its own accord, or not at all. Rather than curry favor with the great European conductors, he would remain forever in obscurity. . . .

"Only you and my brothers really understand me. My Moscow friends cannot reconcile themselves because I refused to be a delegate at Paris. I feared just those blows to my pride that I should inevitably have suffered there every moment. They cannot understand that such names as Liszt, who will be the musical delegate from Hungary, Verdi, etc., would crush me by the greatness of their reputation. Any one of the foreign musicians that come to Paris would ignore me in the presence of those celebrities, among whom I should have to crawl. My friend, I have a reputation for modesty, but I must confess that my modesty is nothing less than a hidden but very, very great pride. Among all living musicians there is not one to whom I freely bend the head. But nature, in putting so much pride into my soul, did not give me the skill and talent to sell my goods well. *Je ne sais pas me faire valoir.* I am abnormally timid, perhaps from too much pride.

Not knowing how to advance my fame and achieve it through my own initiative, I prefer to wait until it comes of itself. . . . For long I have reconciled myself to the thought that I shall not live to see universal recognition of my talents.

"You speak of (Anton) Rubinstein. Can I compare myself to him? He is the first pianist of our time. In R. great virtuosity is united with great talent for composition, and the first carries the second. I shall never in my life achieve a tenth of what Rubinstein has achieved, because he begins by being the greatest virtuoso of our time. I can say this of Anton Rubinstein—as my teacher (I studied composition and orchestration under him) nobody knows better my musical nature and nobody could help more in promoting my fame in western Europe. Unfortunately, that especial 'bigwig' has always treated me with unapproachable hauteur, bordering on scorn, and nobody has known how to inflict deeper wounds to my pride. His manner to me is unfailingly amiable and pleasant, but through that amiability and pleasantness he has always managed to convey that he does not think me worth a cent. The only bigwig that wishes me well is Bülow. Unfortunately, because of his illness he has practically left the artistic world and cannot do much. Thanks to him, though, I am better known in America and England than anywhere. I have a whole file of articles about myself that he sent me, written in the two countries which he has recently visited.

"Good-bye, dear, sweet, peerless friend.

"Your
"P. Tch."

And now approached the Ides of March—dangerous time for a full-blooded lady like Nadejda von Meck! Official spring was still far ahead of Moscow's calendar; snow would lie in the streets and along the corners of northern walls until April. But there was a charm that could carry spring to the widow's heart at any hour, in any clime—the music of Peter Ilyich. And the more torrid his music, the more Tchaikovskian—the higher the widow was transported. One night while the composer was still in Switzerland, Nadejda fared forth to a concert and spent a delirious hour; coming home late, she committed the reckless extravagance, the usually-to-be-regretted-indiscretion, of writing at two in the morning to the man she adored:

Nadejda to Peter Ilyich

Moscow, March 14, 1878
2 o'clock A. M.

". . . I have been to the concert, where I heard your *Marche Slav*" (composed the previous year). "I cannot express my feelings as I listened; sheer delight brought tears to my eyes. I was unspeakably happy at the thought that its author is in a certain sense mine, that he belongs to me—that no one can take him from me. For the first time since I have known you, I heard a composition of yours in unusual surroundings. In the Hall of the Nobility I somehow sense many rivals, sense that you prefer many friends to me. But here, in a new setting, surrounded by strangers, I felt that you could not belong to anyone as fully as to me, and that no one could rival me. 'Here I possess and love.'

"Forgive this delirium—do not fear my jealousy; it binds you to nothing—it is my own, and ends with me. From you I need nothing more than I receive now except perhaps a little change of formality. I should like to have you treat me as one ordinarily treats friends—use 'thou.' In a correspondence it should not be difficult, but if you find it awkward, I shall let it pass because I am happy just as we are; may you be blessed for that happiness. A moment ago I wanted to say that I embrace you with all my heart, but perhaps you would find it strange; so I will say as usual—good-bye, my sweet friend.

"Yours with all my heart,
"N.v.M.

"If this seems improper, take it as the delirium of an abnormal imagination, excited by music. Never be astonished at such paroxysms in me—truly my mind is unwell."

And in truth the *Marche Slav* was bad medicine for a lady emotionally constituted as was Nadejda von Meck. It is a heavy purple moment, as the many who have heard it will testify—and Nadejda was susceptible to purple. But Tchaikowsky's treatment of her outburst was both honest and kind. For the Anglo-Saxon reader not born to the tender usage of the second-person singular, Tchaikowsky's reply defines in a peculiar way his relations with Nadejda. He could write, "Loving you greatly," and sign his name underneath; he could declare he adored Nadejda "with all the strength of his

soul"—but at the sound of that small intimate syllable *thou,* he re-
treated.

Peter Ilyich to Nadejda

Clarens, March 24, 1878

"I had mailed you a letter, dear friend, just before receiving yours,
which touched me deeply. The happiest moments of my life come
when I see that my music enters deeply into the hearts of those I love,
and whose sympathy is dearer to me than fame. Is it necessary to tell
you that I love you with all my heart? Never before have I met a soul
so closely related to mine or one that so sensitively responded to my
every thought, every heart beat. Your friendship has become as necessary as air. Whatever my thought, it always includes the image of my
far-away friend, whose love and sympathy has become the corner-
stone of my existence. When I compose, one idea is ever in mind—
you will hear and feel what I am writing, and this compensates in advance for all the misunderstanding, all the unjust and sometimes hostile opinions that I am fated to hear from the crowd—not only from
the crowd but from my so-called friends. In vain do you imagine I
can possibly find anything strange in the endearments you express in
your letter. In accepting them from you I have only one fear—that I
am not worthy of them. I say this, not as empty words or because of
modesty, but simply because at such moments all my imperfections,
all my weaknesses, appear in higher relief.

"As for the change to 'thou,' I simply have not the courage for it. I
could not bear any falsity or pretense in my relationship with you, and
feel it would be awkward to address you with the familiar pronoun.
We imbibe conventions with our mother's milk, and however we
should like to rise above them, the smallest infraction produces uneasiness and the uneasiness, falsity. I want to be myself with you always, above all else I prize absolute frankness. So, my friend, I leave
it to you to decide. The uneasiness of which I speak will certainly pass
as I become used to the change, but I think I should tell you that in
the beginning I should have to force myself. Whether I use you or
thou, the substance of my deep love and affection will never change.
It is hard not to fulfill immediately your smallest wish, yet on the
other hand, I cannot use a new form without your taking the initiative. Tell me what to do. Until you answer, I write you as before.

"Loving you greatly,
"P. Tch."

One feels in this letter no constriction of falsity; it flows easily and directly, the way words should flow between intimate friends. And how well Peter understood the widow, with her ecstasies and her black glooms and her two-in-the-morning deliriums. Next day she would regret her indiscretion—who should know this better than he?

Nadejda did regret it; on the last day of March she wrote again:

To Peter Ilyich

Moscow, March 31, 1878

"I have just had your letter, and thank you with all my heart, my dear, incomparable friend, for your sincerity and frankness. Those very qualities are what I love so much in you. I prize them highly, they inspire me with infinite confidence in you, and the most precious thing in our relationship is that I believe in them. And you understand that I, less than anyone, am spoiled by sincerity.

"Now let me explain why I desired the change in form. While writing, I was in such an abnormal, exalted state that I had even forgotten what planet I was on—I was aware only of your music and its creator! In that state, it was distasteful to use 'you,' the refined creation of decorum and convention, which often covers hatred and hypocrisy. At that moment, I hated saying 'you'—but the next day, when I returned to normal, I regretted what I had written because I realized it put you in an awkward position, and I feared greatly that you might consent against your will for the sake of indulging me. I thank you the more, my precious friend, that you freed me from the guilty knowledge that I had abused another's kindness, and I thank you too for thinking so well of me and expressing it so frankly. And so, let the matter be buried in fact and in memory.

"After this, I shall answer your letters in order. One cannot but be astonished at the identity of our ideas and thoughts. Lately I have been thinking how splendid it would be if you would write a violin concerto—when suddenly comes a letter saying it is already under way. And how quickly you work, my dear friend—the first movement completed already!

"Milochka is playing round me with two air balloons, and says in French, 'One has burst and still the other flies. . . .'

"Good-bye, my dear, peerless friend.

"Loving you deeply,
"N.v.M."

And now at last, onto Peter's Swiss mountain-top came news of the symphony. Taneyeff wrote it, Taneyeff the faithful, the conscientious. Once a pupil of Tchaikowsky's, now a teacher and composer in his own right, Taneyeff's musical scholarship commanded Tchaikowsky's respect fully as much as did the Rubinsteins' pianistic virtuosity. And Taneyeff deserved respect. Amid the notoriously convivial, easy life of Moscow artistic circles, Taneyeff, in his house on the outskirts of Moscow with his old nurse, lived like a monk, like a saint, devoted to music as to a religion. Sabanayev in his *Modern Russian Composers* says Taneyeff was a great teacher and a great force, believing in a rationally constructed musical beauty—a perfectionist. Best of all Russian music he loved Glinka and Tchaikowsky, but of Scriabin, Ravel, Debussy, Strauss, he would say bitterly, "Murky waves are running in music." After Taneyeff's death, stacks of manuscript were found in his house, things that had not satisfied him—no less than three completed symphonies, six quartets and a mass of minor compositions. Those who know his music say that it is excellent, those of us who have never heard it look forward eagerly to the time when, like all good music, it will come into its own.

Here is what Taneyeff found to say about Tchaikowsky's "favorite child," his Fourth Symphony:

From S. I. Taneyeff to Tchaikowsky

March 31, 1878

"The first movement is too long in proportion to the others; it gives the effect of a symphonic poem to which the composer has slapped on three more movements and called it a symphony. The trumpet fanfares that make up the Introduction, and that afterward appear from time to time, the changes of tempo in the secondary theme—all give an effect of program music. Anyway, I don't much like the first movement. The rhythm ♩♩.♩ is repeated too often and becomes tedious.

"The *Andante* is lovely although I don't care much for the middle part. The *Scherzo* is wonderfully, absolutely successful. But the *Trio* sounds like a ballet dance and I don't like it at all.

"N.G." (Rubinstein) "prefers the *Finale,* with which I disagree. Knowing what you can do with a folktune when you want to, the

variations here on *In the field there stood a birch tree*, don't strike me
as important or interesting.

"There is one defect in this symphony to which I shall never become
reconciled: every movement contains places that remind one of ballet
music—the middle section of the *Andante*, the *Trio* in the *Scherzo*,
and the suggestion of a march in the *Finale*. Listening, involuntarily
I see Mme Sobeshansky pirouetting, or Hillert II, and this annoys me
so I cannot appreciate the true beauty of the music.

"This is my honest opinion. Perhaps I have expressed it too frankly,
please don't be angry with me. It's not surprising that the symphony
does not wholly please me. If you had not sent *Onegin* at the same
time, I should probably have been entranced with the symphony. It is
your own fault! You composed an opera that puts even quite meritorious music in the shade. *Onegin* gave me so much pleasure, I spent
such delicious moments with the score that I cannot find one thing
wrong in the whole of it. A wonderful opera. And yet you announce
that it's time for you to stop writing music! You never wrote so well.
You have achieved perfection; profit by it and take heart."

Reading this, any lover of the Fourth Symphony is indignant.
For the despised First Movement, one is pleased to record that the
world now regards it as the finest of four very fine movements; as
for the "tedious" rhythm ♪♪.♪, it is so dramatically successful in
its presentation of the menacing, inexorable call of fate, that one's
blood curdles at the sound, and the hackles rise. . . . The lovely
woodland melody:

Taneyeff chose to ignore entirely, although the *pizzicato Scherzo*
apparently reached his consciousness as did the gentle melancholy
of the *Andante*. Above his faint praise, one senses the professor's
frown. As to Nicholas Rubinstein's preference for the very orchestral, brilliant *Finale,* it was natural; Rubinstein loved anything
showy.

Taneyeff admired *Onegin,* and truly, the years have proved that
the opera fulfilled its aim. Tchaikowsky did not call it an opera, he

called it "Lyrical Scenes" from Pushkin's poem, and as such it is
completely and quite magically charming. Lenski's aria to his own
dead youth, the duet of maidens in the first act, the famous waltzes,
are nothing short of delicious. But to put it above the Fourth Symphony, and so unconditionally above it, was a strange mistake for
a musician like Taneyeff to make.

Tchaikowsky wrote back immediately, and with a touching humility. Nevertheless he defended the "ballet music" charge with
spirit. In truth, this tendency to burst suddenly into waltzes is very
typical; Tchaikowsky does it in nearly every big composition, sometimes in highly inappropriate places, as in the elegiac piano trio
written some years later in memory of Rubinstein, and in his opera
Pique Dame, just when the story is blackest. But the waltzes are so
rhythmic, so melodious—in fact, so irresistible—that one welcomes
them, appropriate or not, with a smile of pleasure.

Tchaikowsky to Taneyeff

Clarens, April 8, 1878

"Dear Serge,

"I read your letter with the greatest pleasure and interest. As answer
I ought to send you a detailed criticism of your own score, but this I
shall have to postpone. . . . Don't be afraid you were too severe in
your criticism of my Fourth Symphony. It was your honest opinion
and I am grateful for it. What I need is criticism, not dithyramb. Yet
much that you said surprised me. I don't in the least understand about
the 'ballet music,' nor why you don't like it. Is ballet music, to you,
any gay melody in dance rhythm? If so, you must have little sympathy with most of Beethoven's symphonies, in which one finds such
melodies at every step. Are you trying to say that my *Trio* is written
after the style of Gerbes and Pugni? I don't think it deserves that!

"Speaking generally, I can't read anything censorious into the expression 'ballet music.' Ballet music is not always bad, it can be good,
as in Delibes' *Sylvia.* And when good, isn't it good whether Sobeshansky dances it or no? I can only conclude that you dislike my ballet
places because they are ballet, not because they are bad. Perhaps you
are right, yet I can't see why a symphony should not contain occasional dance tunes, even with an intentional whiff of the street—*rude
comiseni.* Beethoven used this effect more than once. Again, I rack

my brains to find any ballet music in the *Allegro*. It is a complete puzzle to me.

"As to your remark about my symphony being programmatic, I quite agree but don't see why you consider this a defect. To the contrary, I should be sorry if symphonies that mean nothing should flow from my pen, consisting solely of a progression of harmonies, rhythms and modulations. Most assuredly my symphony has a program, but a program that cannot be expressed in words; the very attempt would be ludicrous. But is this not proper to a symphony, that most purely lyrical of musical forms? Should not a symphony reveal those wordless urges that hide in the heart, asking earnestly for expression? Furthermore, I must make a confession: in my naïveté I imagined that the idea behind my symphony was obvious, that everyone would comprehend without any definite program. Please don't think I am trying to parade myself as a person with deep feelings too great for utterance. I did not try to express any new idea; as a matter of fact the work is patterned after Beethoven's Fifth Symphony—not as to musical content but as to the basic idea. Don't you see a program in the Fifth? Not only does such a program exist but there is no question as to what it means. My symphony has much the same basic idea, and if it does not appear clearly, it only means that I am not a Beethoven—which is no news to me.

"Let me add that there is not a line of my symphony that was not deeply felt, an echo of the sincerest part of my nature. Perhaps this does not apply to the middle of the first movement. Here, seams can be discerned, gluings and forced passages that have a labored artificiality. I know you will laugh when you read this, skeptic and mocker that you are! In spite of your love for music, you never seem to believe that a man can compose solely from inner compulsion. But just wait —your time will come! And when it does you will begin to write, not because others claim it from you but because you yourself feel the need to write. Then and only then onto the fertile field of your talent (if I sound florid I am only saying what I feel) will fall the seed of glorious fruit. Meanwhile your field awaits the sower. I will write more about this another day; your score has some beautiful details. . . .

"My next letter will be about you and not me. . . . I was much interested in Cui's criticism of my *Francesca*. What he said about the first part resembling a Russian folk-song did not originate with him— I told him that myself, last year. If I hadn't, he would never have noticed it. His remark that I wrote it under the influence of the *Nibelungen* is very true; I recognized this myself when I was writing. If I'm not mistaken, this influence is seen especially in the Introduction.

Isn't it strange that I let an artistic work that I really don't care for, influence me?

"Since I wrote you I had given up hope of composing, many things have changed in my life. The devil of authorship suddenly and quite unexpectedly returned to take possession of me. Please, Serge, don't read any sign of annoyance in my defense of my symphony; naturally, I should like to please you with everything I write, but I am quite satisfied with your unfailing interest. You can't believe how happy I am that *Onegin* pleases you. I value your opinion greatly, and the franker you are, the more it really means. So, thanks from my heart, and don't ever fear to see me wince; from you I need just that edged knife—the truth—whether favorable or no."

Tchaikowsky said nothing to Nadejda about this correspondence concerning the symphony. It was nearing time for him to return home, and he had more personal subjects to discuss with his "best friend." Antonina, for instance. All this time in Clarens he had mentioned Antonina but rarely—when he did, although only a line, it was a line of fury.

"Of my own free will," he wrote now, "in a fit of madness afterward incomprehensible to me, I inoculated myself with an insufferable plague, and I cannot rid myself of it! I have learned how a man, not wicked by nature, can become a criminal. I have learned how one human being can long passionately, madly, for the death of another. It is wholly bad and wholly stupid, nevertheless in this thing, reason abandons me. At the bare thought of the terrible phantom that will persecute me always, always—until I am in my grave—I fall into inarticulate hatred and fury. Then the days go by; little by little I forget, gain control—until some new blow shatters everything."

And it was not only Antonina that Peter Ilyich dreaded to find awaiting him in Moscow next month—Rubinstein would be there, and classroom after classroom of pupils. Peter would ask the Chief to reduce his hours of teaching. Rubinstein had, went on Peter, "a kind of passion for unnecessarily dividing the pupils into extra classes, as much as to say, 'You who are paid to teach, go on and teach as long as possible, whether it is necessary or not.' If only they could find a substitute teacher of harmony! Someone who could take these raw youths of fifteen and explain to them, day after day, that a triad consists of a third and a fifth. The boys are bearable because, stupid or no, they expect some day to make music their profession, but the girls!—O Lord!" Out of sixty or seventy in Peter's classes, perhaps five were musicians, the rest were as stupid as they were industrious. They learned the rules, and then when something came up that required initiative, they were utterly at sea. "I lose my head," wrote Tchaikowsky, "and burst right out in fury. A more patient teacher would be so much better for the Conservatory! Nevertheless I am needed there, and I shall go back."

All this pleased the widow extremely. "Your decision to continue your work at the Conservatory," she wrote, "makes me very happy, my dear friend. You do a great work there, and absolutely no one can replace you. God grant that your health and strength will permit you to carry out your decision. I have heard before of your antipathy for teaching young girls and I quite sympathize and like you exceedingly for it, because it proves that in art nothing can corrupt you, not even young girls. One hears that some of the professors are attentive to them. How disgusting! On the whole, the morals of the Conservatory are such that not only would I not send a daughter there, but I would not send my son. . . ."

And while the widow penned this reassuring but perhaps slightly inaccurate portrait of Peter's morals, Peter himself was enjoying himself hugely on his mountain-top. He and Modeste and Kotek had been playing over *Onegin,* the whole of it, and to the composer's delight, both men were much impressed. As for the performance by the Conservatory next autumn, he did not fear it, wrote Tchaikowsky. But in the state theatres, which operated on the prima donna system—featuring one soprano and letting the other parts fall—the ensemble would be terrible. Now, if Anatol's flame, Mlle Panayeff, could have the part of Tatiana, the opera would be—according to Anatol—a roaring success. But Panayeff's parents refused to permit her to go on the stage as a professional artist, and not another Tatiana existed in the whole of Russia.

Nadejda wrote gloomily from Moscow; she was ill again, and complained of "heart cramps," which Peter assured her were due to nervous tension; he himself often suffered from them. Don't he down, he advised Nadejda. Walk about your room with the windows open; even a cold in the head is a thousand times preferable to one such cramp. Secondly, put compresses of cold faucet water on the heart, and thirdly (Peter liked to classify both advice and confession with these hortatorial firstlies, secondlies and thirdlies), thirdly, drink a large glass of *good* wine—Sherry, Madeira, Malaga or even Port. This, of course, not as cure but as palliation: "Even the strictest hygiene," concluded Peter Ilyich from the depth of hard experience, "is helpless against nerves, because no health measure can defend us from the anxieties which Fate devises and springs upon us suddenly."

This was written from Clarens on April 11th, and this morning, said Peter, he had finished the Violin Concerto entirely, orchestration, corrections and everything. Only a few days remained before they would start home; Kotek was already gone. He would use the few intervening days to rest, not beginning any new music. . . .

During these rest periods from composition, Tchaikowsky, if he had a piano available, spent much time reading music, old and new, and always, in the evening, wrote Nadejda about it. Now, on his mountain-top, he played Chopin—how the Petersburg Nationalists scorned the Chopin in Tchaikowsky! And now he went back to his adored one, his god, Mozart. "This sunny genius, whose music even in remembrance moves me to tears." Only a week ago he had written those words to Nadejda, and she had replied indignantly, as she always did to eulogies of Mozart:

"I am astounded, Peter Ilyich, that the man who wrote such an amazingly beautiful thing as the first movement of the Fourth Symphony, could admire that epicurean, Mozart. Tell me, would the soul of a criminal shudder in listening to Mozart's music? Not a bit; on the contrary, in it he would find himself justified. But hearing yours, he would break down. Do you realize what that means? My God, it is not something to be explained in words. Indeed, how can one compare you with Mozart? I must stop or I shall talk on for three days."

Nadejda was not bored by Mozart's music, she was shocked by it, and this was a natural reaction for a romanticist—especially a Vic-

torian romanticist like Nadejda, to whom art, if it was to justify itself, must be the vehicle either of emotion or morality. Mozart's
pure classicism, the sheer abstraction of it, the lucid perfection of
its form was to her a dangerous sophistication and she bridled
against it, perceiving here a whisk of the devil's tail. Her own emotions had never received the balance of a serious scholastic education as had Tchaikowsky's; emotionalism in art was to her a principle, a test of its creator's sincerity. . . .

Tchaikowsky replied that hereafter he would refrain from trying
to convert his friend to Mozart, yet such a silence would be very
difficult! Here was a composer who possessed all the qualities he
himself lacked. Well Tchaikowsky knew that his great talent for
melody and orchestration did not extend to musical form, and more
than once he had acknowledged that his best works were marred
by sudden descents to chaos and helpless confusion. To him, Mozart's classic clarity conveyed the very opposite of what it conveyed to
Nadejda von Meck:

"You say," he wrote, "that my worship for Mozart is quite contrary
to my musical nature. But perhaps it is just because—being a child of
my day—I feel broken and spiritually out of joint, that I find consolation and rest in Mozart's music, wherein he gives expression to that
joy of life which was part of his sane and wholesome temperament,
not yet undermined by reflection. It seems to me that an artist's creative power is something quite apart from his sympathy with this or
that great master. For instance, a man may admire Beethoven, and
yet by temperament be more akin to Mendelssohn. Could there be a
more glaring instance of inconsistency, for instance, than Berlioz the
composer and champion of ultra-romanticism in music, and Berlioz
the critic and adorer of Gluck? Perhaps this is just an example of the
attraction which makes extremes meet, and causes a big strong man
to fall in love with a tiny delicate woman, and vice versa. Do you
know that Chopin did not care for Beethoven, and could hardly bear
some of his works? I was told this by a man who knew him personally. At any rate, dissimilarity of temperament between two artists is
no hindrance to their mutual sympathy."

Now, on the eve of departure for Moscow and all the emotional
turmoil that Moscow would contain, Peter seemed more than ever

to need the deep, healthy simplicity of classicism. He sealed his letter, convinced that he really would stop bothering Nadejda Philaretovna about Mozart (in a month he was at it again) and wrote a note to his publisher, Jurgenson. Whenever Tchaikowsky had been long away from home, he sat down and wrote someone a meticulous report of his musical accomplishment during the vacation. This time he had been away six months and had completed two big works, he told Jurgenson, and a violin concerto. "In fact you will have to face quite a few new compositions of mine. Seven short pieces are ready, two songs and a pianoforte sonata" (G major) "on which I have begun work. By the end of summer I shall have to engage a whole railway truck to send it to you. I can hear you tell me, with your usual energy, to go to the devil."

Tchaikowsky had a strong consciousness of the value of time; to him, time that did not produce music was time wasted. In this one matter his conscience was merciless; neither illness, "nerves," nor tragedy justified more than a few days away from the writing table. And now that he was well and knew himself well, any interruption was maddening. The day before they were to start home via Lausanne and Vienna, the door of Tchaikowsky's room at Clarens burst open and a loud voice asked in Russian for Peter Ilyich. It was a general from Moscow, searching, Peter wrote Nadejda, for the mad musician described by the home newspapers. The general seemed definitely disappointed to find everybody entirely sane, and not even a bit "touched." Hours passed before the man took his leave, and all during these hours Peter Ilyich swore to himself that when he got home he would be so rude, so blatantly disagreeable that no casual visitor would seek him out twice.

Hopeless vow! Had he possessed the kind of nature that could hold to such a resolution, Peter Ilyich would never have committed the foolish act of compliance that had driven him from Moscow in the first place. Nor would he, left alone for one day in Clarens before joining Modeste in Lausanne—Modeste had gone ahead with his pupil—have been so afraid of solitude that he dared not enter the rooms his brother had just vacated.

Mid-April was here and it was time to go: escape had been sweet, but escape is always temporary. Peter looked out on the high white mountains of his retreat, and sighed. How inexorable the fates that force us thus to face our destiny, that return us always to the consequence of our acts! If the gods would permit a man to expiate his sins in music—ah, thought Peter Ilyich, what a symphony could he not write!

15

Home again. Tchaikowsky tells his methods of composition

PETER ILYICH came down alone from his mountains and, meeting Modeste with his pupil at Lausanne, crossed the neutral borders of Switzerland. No matter what personal trials faced him, it would be good to be home again, to hear Russian spoken and to be able to speak it without frowns from the passersby. During that spring of 1878, not one European hand was stretched in friendship toward Russia. England, gathering her spiked skirts in maternal protection over that sweet chick of European contention, the Dardenelles, had outmanoeuvred the Northern bear, not in battle but in the resultant "peace." Under the sharp diplomatic heels of Disraeli and his sovereign mistress, Russia was ground down, completely humiliated.

No amount of friendly family feeling between the reigning sovereigns could mend the breach dug so skillfully by Bismarck and Disraeli. In their letters, Tchaikowsky and Nadejda raged helplessly against Europe in general, but especially against England, that "shameless nation that has passed the limits of decency." "How I hate that awful race!" cried Tchaikowsky. "And I!" replied Nadejda, "and with it, Austria and Roumania."

And as though this international humiliation were not enough, Russia was in bad case also from within. Alexander II, tightening daily on the conservative checkrein, was unwittingly causing the beast to rear higher. Princes of anarchy, wearing their shirts bloused outside their trousers, endeavored thus thinly disguised, to return to the soil and induce a bewildered peasantry to rise against the government. From below, terrorism, arson and bombs—from above, the over-severe punishments characteristic of a frightened and tottering monarchy.

Tchaikowsky and Nadejda were loyal monarchists, nevertheless they were not blind to the state of affairs.

"How Russia would revive," wrote Tchaikowsky, "if the Emperor would finish his wonderful reign by giving us political rights! It is wrong for them to say we are not ready for constitutional reforms. They used to say we were not ripe for the new courts of justice and when the courts were being established, how often we heard regrets that we had no attorneys or lawyers. Yet both were found. Deputies and electors also will be found."

And again: "Anatol assures me from Petersburg that the student riots and our internal conditions in general are very serious, and that we can expect new outbreaks any day from the unrest of the young intellectuals. How sorry one feels for our poor good Emperor, so sincerely concerned for the country's welfare, yet meeting such mortal disappointments and anxieties!"

Indeed, it was not a pretty time for a Russian to be going home. Disease was rife; typhus, that scourge of spring, raged in Petersburg; the schools were closed. In Moscow, diphtheria and small-pox were terribly prevalent; Nadejda wrote that her house reeked of carbolic and liquid germ killer. The only disease that spared them was cholera, which was waiting for autumn and the swampy mists that would lie over Petersburg. The twentieth century Western world, accustomed to see its schools closed for measles or chicken-pox, would do well to remember what a little time ago it was that death walked hand in hand with a child through the city streets. Not chicken-pox but typhus, cholera—black-hooded phantoms of a terrible death. Nineteenth century Russian memoirs are shocking in their casual frequent mention of this grim menace. Tchaikowsky's mother had died of cholera; his father caught it from her and nearly died. Tchaikowsky was fourteen at the time, and he had adored his mother with a desperately dependent love. As a still younger boy he had barely entered school in Petersburg when scarlet fever broke out; some cousins took him into their home—and in his hand the small Peter carried death. He himself did not fall ill but the eldest son of the house, pride of his parents, caught scarlet fever and died. Because of it, terror and a sick conscience for long pursued Peter Ilyich.

And did Tchaikowsky, on his long journey from Switzerland on

that April day of 1878, think on these things? At home, Modeste
reminded him, the rivers would be flooding; thaw and mud—ferocious mud that hardened at night into hub-high ruts—would make
the outskirts of Moscow impassable except on foot. Nadejda von
Meck had written that she could not leave town because of it, and
had added indignantly that if Moscow landlords who were so
meticulous about carbolic indoors, would refrain from flinging their
garbage onto the streets, the plague might go away more quickly!
The only pleasant public news she had to tell was the incident of
fashionable Petersburg refusing in a body to call on the British ambassador during the holidays. The first honest gesture, Nadejda intimated, that society ladies had ever been known to make.

Well, home would be home anyway, mud and typhus notwithstanding. And the nearer the three travellers came to the Russian
border, the more relieved was Tchaikowsky that he was going
straight to Kamenka rather than to Moscow, where Antonina and
Rubinstein would have confronted him. Surely, his sister had forgiven him; Anatol said she had! The first sight of her face would
tell him; she was a Tchaikowsky and could not hide her heart.
Modeste was like that, and as to Tolia, what his face did not reveal,
his tongue did. If Alexandra was still a little distant, well, maybe his
injury would melt her. Peter Ilyich, who never accomplished a
journey without accident, had in Vienna rolled bodily down a steep
flight of steps and hurt his right hand; it was bandaged impressively.
To Nadejda he had made light of it; in proportion to his fear of
emotional and nervous discomfort, Peter always made light of definite
physical pain. It would be fun to give the family their presents; as
usual, he had brought home a whole trunkful of delightful surprises. At the Russian border a tipsy policeman and three cold-
hearted customs officials tried to part him from some of them but
Uncle Petia, with Modeste to support him, held surprisingly firm.
. . . Merely because a man lets himself be pilfered for seven months
by Italian hotel porters and Parisian medicos, does not mean he
cannot defend himself in his own country.

Peter Ilyich to Nadejda Philaretovna

Kamenka, Wednesday,
April 24, 1878

"We arrived at last, yesterday evening. All day I had been very nervous, wondering how I would be received at Kamenka. My sister, Anatol and the rest of the family met us. They all expressed so much love and sympathy that I calmed down very quickly and began to feel I was in a cordial and friendly atmosphere. As my sister's house is crowded, she has prepared a quite separate house for me—very pleasant. It is a clean, cozy little cabin, rather far from the settlement and the Jews, with a view of the village and the winding river in the distance. The garden is full of sweet peas and reseda which will bloom in two months and spread its wonderful aroma. . . . My cabin is arranged very conveniently and comfortably. Even a piano has been procured and put in the small room next to the bedroom. Work will be a pleasure."

Though Peter vowed he was so calm, Anatol dared not stay more than a day or two in Kamenka before hurrying up to town to put the divorce wheels in motion. And now began weeks of struggle: attacks, counter attacks and all the bitter recrimination of a divorce suit. The difficulty was to persuade Antonina to file suit; briefly but passionately, Nadejda had written Tchaikowsky to pay the woman off, and to be quick about it. Antonina was told that Leo Davydoff, Tchaikowsky's brother-in-law, was shouldering the bill; Leo Davydoff believed it was the Moscow Musical Society.

At best, divorce is not a pretty proceeding, and this time it was far from pretty. Peter's position was not a dignified one. The mail waxed heavy with letters about "the matter," as they called the divorce, and "the known person" as they called Antonina. As for Antonina, she lost her head completely, writing to each member of the Tchaikowsky and Davydoff families alternate letters of appeal and abuse, always insisting that a great many men were in love with her, and conspicuous among them, Peter Ilyich.

Nadejda urged Peter to ask Rubinstein's help. Why not write frankly, asking Rubinstein to use his persuasion with the girl, and at the same time, telling him why a life with Antonina was impossible—that the two were utterly unsuited. "I don't like," said Nadejda, "the way people are talking; why should the girl acquire this undeserved aura of martyrdom? If any one is a martyr, Peter Ilyich, it is you."

Nadejda's letters were a wonderful comfort to Peter just now. In his little cabin below the big house at Kamenka, he tried to work on the G major Piano Sonata he had begun in Clarens, but he was too anxious and nervous for any real accomplishment. Fever and nightmares pursued him. "Come away from there, my beloved friend!" cried Nadejda, from Moscow. "They tell me you are growing thin, and that you have done no work. My estate at Brailov is empty; will you not be my guest there, quite alone, until it is time for me to go south? Now that the weather is warm one longs to go far away, back to nature, to the forest and the nightingales over the river. Only music can surpass nature. . . . I press your hand. Do not forget her who loves you with all her heart . . ."

Tchaikowsky asked his sister what to do, and Alexandra said they would miss him dreadfully, but of course to go down to Brailov. It was the middle of May when Peter made the journey—and the instant he attained the country, care fell from him. What a miracle these emerald fields, after the snows of Switzerland, the pale olive trees of Italy, and the ploughed acres of Kamenka farm! Brailov was a gorgeous estate of twelve thousand acres, situated in the Ukraine among the foothills of the Carpathians. On it were farms and forests and beet-sugar factories and much coming and going of superintendents. There were huge, beautiful gardens and a river for boating. Horses to ride and drive; in short, all the extravagant fairyland of an old-fashioned Russian estate. Even without wealth, the Ukraine in May was paradise; lilacs bloomed, nightingales sang in the wood, shepherds played their pipes, leading their flocks over fields all pink with clover.

Tchaikowsky stayed two blissful weeks, writing daily to his hostess in Moscow; it is to be doubted which of them enjoyed his visit the more. His life fell into a delightful routine of garden walks, forest walks, tea by the river, coffee on the terrace, long evenings alone in the moonlight. At mealtime in the huge dining-room he was a bit timid, he confessed to Nadejda, feasting before so many servants, but he could feel their good will and knew they were trying to make him comfortable. He liked to play Nadejda's harmonium, especially he enjoyed experimenting with the overtones. He had amused himself composing some short pieces, romances and violin pieces; would his hostess permit him to leave them here as a small testimony of his love for Brailov and Brailov's hostess?

Of these three pieces, one was the original *Andante* of the Violin Concerto. Together the three make a melodious but unimportant package; musically they correspond to those books placed in the guest-room by the bed-lamp. Tchaikowsky called them *Souvenir d'un lien cher*. Separately they are, *Mélodie, Méditation,* and *Scherzo.*

Rubinstein had been right; Peter Ilyich always paid his debts. Soon, very soon now, he would have to face the Chief and those hungry rows of students waiting to devour his strength. But here, for the moment, was heaven, solitude; Peter feared but one thing and that was the mail. And even that, when it came, proved favorable: Antonina wrote that she would divorce him! Peter was beside himself with joy; he ran round the garden for an hour and a half, he told Nadejda, capering, leaping, singing—anything to "stifle by sheer physical weariness the pain of my happy excitement."

"Thank God!" wrote his hostess immediately, from Moscow. "Hurry, Peter Ilyich, hurry! Shape the iron while it is hot; the person may change her mind! Telegraph me what money you will need for this so I can send it without delay. I shall be very happy when you are free. God grant it may be soon."

Peter prepared to leave, but first he went to Mass at the nearby Monastery and forgot everything in his intense interest in the nuns' choir. The old lady that led them had such a wonderful face, wrote Peter, and she sang with notes, showing she must be educated musically. Peter Ilyich, standing alone in the dim church, built a whole romance around her, then he ran to the house and told Alexis to pack their bags for Moscow. In the usual state of pre-journey fluster he sent off several telegrams wrongly addressed, finally blundering onto the train in a condition of complete gloom, which by no means diminished with the northward mileage.   •

Moscow was awful. By some especially designed malignancy of fate, the Chief had a birthday that week, and Tchaikowsky could not avoid going to the party. Everybody was there. *Everybody*— Tchaikowsky's letter fairly groans. They shouted, they drank healths, they exclaimed over Peter Ilyich, resurrected after eight months; they embraced him—and they asked questions.

As to the Chief: "I read in his eyes that he has little sympathy with me, and that only expediency makes him bear the sign of friendship. He cannot forgive me for refusing to be a delegate to Paris, which from his point of view, I ought to have accepted as a great kindness. He does not like people who do not consider themselves under obligation to him; he would prefer everyone around to call themselves his creations. In short, I am not *persona grata* to him, and he could not hide it."

And immediately Peter Ilyich made his escape from the birthday party, he fell into a hotter fire. At five o'clock the Clerk of the Consistory was waiting to tell him what a man must do to get a divorce. Anatol had arranged this meeting the day before, and all during Rubinstein's party it had been hanging over Peter's head. Anatol went along; like a prisoner led to execution Peter walked to the appointed spot. It was terrible, he wrote Nadejda. This clerk was a horrible man, cynical and sordid, who recited the instructions with a face either leering or indifferent. Lies would have to be told, false witnesses procured to enact a scene the details of which he simply could not—Peter wrote—repeat to Nadejda.

"The consistory is a living survival of the old Court. All is done by bribery, and in that little world the tradition of bribery is still so real that nobody shows the slightest shame at naming the necessary sums. Each step in the case has its tax, and each bribe is divided immediately between clerks, scribes and the priests who admonish the couple to lead a better life!"

Nadejda must, one feels, have read this description with mingled pity and amusement. What a child Peter Ilyich was, so surprised and shocked at the world's wickedness! For herself, if she had wanted so deplorable a thing as a divorce she would have gone ahead and got it, handing out bribes as cold-bloodedly as the clerks received them. Nadejda was a Victorian lady, but like many of her sisters, she believed the end justified the means. . . .

As to the Certain Person herself, she was nowhere to be found —something between a blessing and a curse. It would have been horrible to see her, but on the other hand, a man cannot divorce a ghost. She was undoubtedly hiding—to what purpose only heaven knew—and Jurgenson had undertaken to find her and with Anatol, manage everything. Tchaikowsky waited and fumed and despaired, and when nothing happened and Antonina did not appear, he fled. Let the case rest until autumn—he cried, and went down to Leo Davydoff's private estate at Verbovka, just south of Kamenka.

Jurgenson found the Certain Person and concentrated all his tact, all his business ability and experience to persuade her to the divorce she had at first agreed to and then repudiated. He failed in some bewilderment; the conversation turned, he wrote Peter, like a squirrel in a cage. In all his life he had never met a more ignorant and difficult person. She insisted that Jurgenson was one of the divorce lawyers and said she would talk with no one but her husband. All the Tchaikowskys and all the Davydoffs—including Peter's sister Alexandra—were villains who had schemed against Antonina since the beginning. Indeed, she was convinced the whole divorce had been planned before the marriage ever took place. "Plotted," said Antonina, "by Anatol Ilyich, Rubinstein and Alexandra Davydoff." If these wicked people would remove themselves, Peter Ilyich would fall at her feet. . . .

All this Jurgenson reported to Tchaikowsky and Tchaikowsky reported to Nadejda von Meck who had by now gone down to Brailov for the summer. Here she found the violin pieces, *Souvenir d'un lieu cher,* and professed herself charmed with them—although one senses a reservation of her usual unconditional praise. She wrote that she knew she would like them better when she could hear them played on the violin; Pahulsky was with her, but he was so near-sighted he could not read over her shoulder on the piano rack and had not yet made his own copy of the violin part.

Peter wrote from Verbovka that he would not need the ten thou-sand roubles Nadejda had offered, because in the end the Certain Person had refused Jurgenson the divorce, declaring that if wit-nesses came forward to swear to her husband's infidelity, she would shout his innocence to the court. This was dangerous ground for Peter Ilyich, although he did not say so to Nadejda. If Antonina began explaining to the court about her husband's innocence of adultery, to what lengths might she not elaborate his inabilities! A third of the original sum—say three thousand roubles—would be enough, Peter told Nadejda, to persuade Antonina to leave Moscow forever. At least, so Antonina herself said, and the matter of a regular annuity could be arranged later.

Nadejda replied sympathetically as always. But for the present she saw there was no more to be done. It was becoming plain that Peter Ilyich simply was not of a calibre to deal with this creature. The burden of the widow's advice was always, treat the woman more harshly! And in all her advice gleamed the hard imperious-ness of conscious wealth. This was a shield unknown to Peter Ilyich; to cast off responsibility without incurring public disgrace, requires not little bits of money but enormous, inexhaustible wealth.

His very hatred was a handicap. "I cannot see her," he wrote Nad-ejda now from Verbovka. *"C'est plus fort que moi.* At thought of her I fall into such fury, such disgust, such desire to do her violence, that I am afraid of myself. It is a disease for which there is but one remedy: not to see her, not to meet her, and to avoid as much as possible any connection with her. Even as I write these lines, involuntarily the hated sight rises before my eyes and I become excited and suffer—I am angry and hate her—and hate myself not less than her. Last year, there was an evening in September when I was very near—Oh, within a step of that blind, mad, sick hatred which can lead to crime. I assure you that only some miracle saved me, and now at thought of her the same feeling begins to boil in me and makes me fear myself."

For the moment, Antonina had won, and everybody knew it. Even Nadejda dared not press the matter further. Naturally, all this told upon Tchaikowsky's health, and tedious though health symptoms may be in the telling, they are inescapably significant in the analysis of a personality like Tchaikowsky's, where every occurrence of daily life registered physical reaction. Was he victorious—then the man did not know the word fatigue; he could write music for twenty hours at a stretch. Did he suffer defeat—symptoms appeared —and always the symptoms were symbolic of desire to escape.

Peter Ilyich to Nadejda Philaretovna

Verbovka, July 16, 1878

"I quite enjoy all the health one can wish, except for a new and very strange thing that occurs every evening. At nine o'clock, unbearable sleepiness with complete loss of strength comes over me, so that I can neither talk nor listen. I want to run and hide myself—to disappear, cease to exist. Yet I know from experience that I must fight this sleepiness if I don't want to have heart cramps all night, with nightmares and painful dreams. The struggle continues all evening. Of course, it is only a question of nerves to which one must pay no attention. Strength of will and a glass of wine save me from it.

"The work progresses rather slowly, and not as successfully as I could wish. The sonata has been ready now for a long time and today I began to copy several romances, some of which were written partly abroad, partly at Kamenka in April. One of the romances I copied today is composed to Lermontoff's 'The love of the dead man.' I wrote it because in one of your letters you used that poem as proof of your contention that poetry and music are related."

But defeat at the hands of Antonina had its compensation. At least, Tchaikowsky did not have to sit all summer in the heat and dust of Moscow, waiting upon the pleasure of the Consistory. Verbovka was pleasant, prettier in its surroundings than Kamenka. Uncle Petia plunged into family activities. A play was in preparation in honor of Anatol who was visiting them and everyone was to take part—all the nephews and nieces and cousins. The peasantry was to be invited as public. Uncle Petia was musician and prompter.

"In the meanwhile," he wrote Nadejda, "the rather tedious work of copying my music progresses slowly. Four things are ready, including Brailov's violin piece. Now to begin the series of children's pieces, then copy the Mass, and after that I shall take your advice, and rest. Then I shall be thinking of something new and big to write. I don't know why, but I have grown cold to 'Undine.' I want to find an operatic subject that will be deeper and more exciting. What would you say to Shakespeare's *Romeo and Juliet?* True, it has been used many times both as operatic and symphonic canvas, but the richness of that tragedy is fathomless. Rereading it, I became enthusiastic about the idea of an opera in which I would preserve Shakespeare's plot and action throughout with no changes or additions, as in Berlioz' *Juno.*

"My health is perfect. I don't know when I have felt so well. But at moments I am gripped by my old longing to be far from everyone and everything. I think of Moscow with foreboding, fear and constriction of the heart."

Nadejda herself was not sorry to forget Antonina for a while, and return to a correspondence about music. She always wrote cheerfully from Brailov; the country was a happy place, with one's children running in and out. She wrote inquiring as to Tchaikowsky's methods of composition; did the melody come first to him, or the harmony? Did the proper orchestration occur with the musical idea or afterward? And in opera, which was primary inspiration, the literary subject or the musical theme?

Tchaikowsky loved these questions and answered not with one letter, but three:

To Nadejda Philaretovna

Kamenka, July 6, 1878

"I have your letter, dear N. Ph., and hasten to answer. You want to know my methods of composing? My friend, that is a rather difficult question, because the circumstances under which new compositions are born vary extremely. Yet I shall try to tell you in a general way how I work, and in order to explain the process of composition, I must first divide my compositions into two categories:

(1) The ones I write on my own initiative because of sudden inclination and urgent inner need.

(2) Compositions inspired from outside, such as the request of a friend or publisher, or commissions, like my *Cantata* written for the

Polytechnic Exhibition or the *Marche Slav,* written for the Red Cross concert.

"I hasten to explain here that experience proves the value of a work does not depend upon which of these categories it belongs to. Very often a piece that was artificially engendered turns out quite successfully, while pieces invented wholly on my own inspiration are sometimes less successful for various incidental reasons. The circumstances surrounding the composer at the time of writing, upon which his state of mind depends, are very important. When he is creating, the artist must have calm. In this sense, creative activity is always objective, even musical creation, and those are mistaken who believe the artist can use his talent to relieve himself of specific feelings of the moment. The sad or happy emotions which he expresses are always and invariably retrospective. With no especial reason for rejoicing, I can experience a happy creative mood, and conversely among the happiest surroundings I may write music suffused with darkness and despair. In brief, the artist lives a double life, an everyday human one and an artistic one, and these two lives do not always coincide. Anyway I repeat that for composition, the important thing is to rid oneself temporarily of the troubles of everyday existence, and give oneself unconditionally to the artistic life.

"For compositions belonging to the first, or inspired-from-within category, not even the least effort of will is necessary. It is enough to submit to one's inner voice, and if the everyday life does not rise up to crush the artistic life, then work proceeds with the strangest ease. One forgets everything, the spirit quivers with sweet excitement, and before one has time to follow the swift flight to its end, time has gone by unperceived. In this state is something somnambulistic, *'on ne s'entend pas vivre.'* It is impossible to explain these moments. Whatever emerges from the pen at such times, or simply remains in the head, is always of value, and if not interrupted from outside, will be the artist's best work.

"For commissioned work one must sometimes create one's own inspiration. Very often one must first conquer laziness and lack of inclination. Then different impediments arise. Sometimes victory comes easily, sometimes inspiration evades entirely. But I believe it the duty of an artist never to submit, because laziness is a strong human trait, and nothing is more harmful to an artist than to let laziness get the better of him. One cannot afford to sit waiting for inspiration; she is a guest that does not visit the lazy, but comes to those who call her. Perhaps there is a foundation to the charge that the Russian nation lacks creative activity, that the Russian is terribly lazy. He loves to postpone things, he has natural talent but has also a natural lack of self-discipline. One must acquire this, one must conquer oneself and not fall into dilettantism, from which even so colossal a talent as Glinka's suffered. That man, dowered with great original power of creation, lived to a mature age, yet wrote amazingly little. Read his memoirs and you will see that he worked only as a dilettante, at leisure, when the mood came. We are proud of Glinka, yet we must admit that he did not fulfill the task his genius put upon him.

"Both his operas, in spite of marvelous and quite original beauty, suffer from striking inequality of style. Pure and gracious beauty is followed by childish naïveté and insipidity. What would have happened had Glinka been born to another stratum of society, and had lived under different conditions, if he had worked as an artist who, recognizing his power, feels it a duty to perfect his talent to its very limit, rather than composing music as a dilettante, simply because he had nothing else to do?

"I hope, my friend, you will not suspect me of self-praise when I tell you that my appeal to inspiration is never vain. I can only say that this power, which I have called a capricious guest, has long ago become so accustomed to me that we live inseparable, and she leaves me only when she feels herself superfluous because my everyday human life has temporarily intruded.

"But always the cloud dissolves and she reappears. So I may say that in my normal state of mind I compose music always, anywhere, at every moment of the day. Sometimes I watch with curiosity this busy flow of creation which, quite by itself, apart from any converse I may be having at the moment, apart from the people I am with at the time, goes on in that section of my brain that is given over to music. Sometimes it is the elaboration, the melodious detail of some little work planned beforehand, another time a quite fresh, original musical idea appears and I try to retain it in my memory. From whence it comes is a mystery.

"Now I will sketch for you the actual process of composition—but let me postpone it till after dinner. *Au revoir*. If you only knew how difficult it is to write you thus, yet how agreeable!

Two o'clock

"I write my sketches on the first piece of paper that comes to hand, sometimes a scrap of notepaper, and I write in very abbreviated form. The melody never appears in my head without its attendant harmony. In general, these two musical elements, together with the rhythm, cannot be conceived separately; every melodic idea carries its own inevitable harmony and rhythm. If the harmonies are very complicated,

one must indicate the voice parts in the sketch. If the harmony is very
simple, I often jot down the bass, or write out a figured bass; at other
times I don't need even that. It stays in my mind. Concerning instrumentation, if one is composing for orchestra, the musical idea carries
with it the proper instrument for its expression. Yet one often changes
the instrumentation later. Words must never be written after the
music, because it is the text that calls out the suitable musical expression. One can of course adapt the words to a little melody, but for
a serious composition such a procedure is impossible. So what you
tell me about the *Life for the Tsar* cannot be true. Nor can one write
a symphony and then find a program for it, because here again, each
episode of a chosen program evokes its own musical illustration. The
preliminary sketch of a work is extremely agreeable to do; sometimes
it affords a quite inexpressible delight, but it also means anxiety and
nervous excitement. One sleeps badly and often quite forgets to eat.
But the actual execution of the project is done very calmly and quietly.
To instrument a composition that is already ripe, having been worked
out in one's head to the last detail, is a very jolly business. One cannot
however, say as much for the composition of piano pieces or songs
or little pieces in general. These are annoying to work on; just now I
am busy with such work.

"You ask if I stick to established forms. Yes and no. In certain
compositions, such as a symphony, the form is taken for granted and
I keep to it—but only as to the large outline and proper sequence
of movements. The details can be manipulated as freely as one
chooses, according to the natural development of the musical idea.
For instance, the first movement of our symphony is handled very
freely. The second theme, which tradition places in a related major
key, is here minor and unrelated. In the recapitulation (same movement) the second theme appears only in part, etc. The *Finale* also
deviates from conventional form. In vocal music, where everything
depends upon the text, and in fantasias (like *The Tempest* and
Francesca), one can create one's own form. You ask about melodies
built upon the common chord. I can prove to you absolutely, and can
give you examples to show how by means of rhythm and the shift-
ing of notes, one can build a whole million of new and pleasing
combinations. This concerns of course, only homophonic music, in
polyphonic music such a melodic structure would destroy the independence of voice parts.

"The melodies of Beethoven, Weber, Mendelssohn, Schumann and
especially Wagner, are frequently built on the notes of the triad, and
any talented musician can always thus invent a new and pretty far

fare melody. Do you recall how pleasing the Sword motif is in the *Nibelungen?*

"I am also very fond of a melody of Verdi's (a very gifted man) from his opera *Bal-Masque:*

"And how charming and fresh is the principal theme of the first movement of Rubinstein's *Ocean Symphony:*

"If I searched my brain, I could give you a mountain of examples to prove my point. Talent is what really does it; and talent knows no limitations but can create pleasing music out of nothing. What could be more vulgar than the following melodies? Beethoven's Seventh Symphony:

Glinka's *Jota Aragonese:*

"Yet what a wonderful musical structure Beethoven and Glinka built upon these melodies!"

To Nadejda

Kamenka, July 7, 1878

"This is a continuation of yesterday's letter. You say you are afraid you don't use the correct technical expressions when you write to me about music. With my hand on my heart, I swear that even if, perhaps, you have happened to use some musical term not quite correctly, you were so little off the track that I never noticed it, it has never distracted me from what you wanted to say. Even when you do express yourself inaccurately, I always understand what you are trying to tell me. At any rate I never once smiled at your musical opinions; on the contrary you display a technical knowledge rarely found even among the most educated amateurs. Please, dear friend, never be troubled when you write me about music. In case a musical term is used incorrectly, I promise to mention it and point it out.

"Talking with you yesterday about the process of composing, I did not express myself clearly concerning the work that follows the first sketch. This phase is especially important: what has been written with passion must now be looked upon critically, corrected, extended, and most important of all, condensed to fit the requirements of the form. One must sometimes go against the grain in this, be merciless, and destroy things that were written with love and inspiration. Although I cannot complain of poor inventive powers or imagination, I have always suffered from lack of skill in the management of form. Only persistent labor has at last permitted me to achieve a form that in some degree corresponds to the content. In the past I was careless, I did not realize the extreme importance of this critical examination of the preliminary sketch. For this reason, the succeeding episodes were loosely held together and seams were always visible. That was a serious defect, and it was years before I began to correct it, yet my compositions will never be good examples of form because I can only *correct* what is wrong with my musical nature—I cannot change it intrinsically. I know also that I am very far from achieving the full maturity of my talent. But I see with joy that I am progressing slowly, and I ardently desire to take myself as far along this road to perfection as I can go. Therefore, I was inaccurate yesterday when I said I wrote out my compositions unhesitatingly from the first sketches. It is more than a copy, it is a detailed, critical examination of the first plan, corrected, rarely added to, and very often cut.

"I have something to propose. You say you would like to see my sketches. Will you accept from me the manuscripts of *Eugene Onegin*? In the autumn the pianoforte arrangement will be published, and perhaps you would be interested to compare my sketches with the published work. If so, I shall send you the manuscripts on your return to Moscow. I suggest *Onegin* merely because I never wrote anything else so easily; the manuscript has so few corrections that it is not hard to read."

To the suggestion at the end, that Nadejda accept the manuscript of *Onegin,* the widow made her own terms: "My dear, wonderful one," she began, with a barrage of her marvelous and wholly naïve Russian superlatives, "if you consent to let me have the manuscript for five hundred roubles, I shall be most happy to take it, but I beg you to tell me without reservation whether that sum is equal to its worth."

"The manuscript has no price!" vowed the composer in return. And anyway, was he not a hundred times in Nadejda's debt? "For the first time in my life, I find a person who is interested in my unfinished work. And I am far from being so famous that my handwriting has a price."

Nadejda accepted the manuscript—but her conscience, she said, would always reproach her. Tchaikowsky, however, knew well enough when money was due him; a few days later he sent Jurgenson a businesslike bill:

To P. I. Jurgenson

Verbovka, Aug. 10, 1878

"Dear Friend,

"By now you have my manuscripts—not a little material for your engravers. I sent you five pieces, besides which I shall soon send you three pieces for the violin that have been requested here by an amateur." (*Souvenir d'un lieu cher*, the pieces written at Brailov for Nadejda.)

"I should like to receive the following fees:

1. The sonata	50	roubles	($ 25.00)
2. 12 pieces @ 25 roubles	300	"	(150.00)
3. The Children's Album	240	"	(120.00)
4. Six songs @ 25 roubles	150	"	(75.00)
5. Violin pieces @ 25 roubles	75	"	(37.50)
6 The Liturgy	100	"	(50.00)
	915		457.50

"Or in a round sum, 900 roubles, but seeing that I submit so much at one time, I will take 800. Please, my dear, find out and let me know the state of our mutual debt, including what you have payed out to Antonina Ivanovna for me. If you owe me very much, you need not pay me all at once, just little by little."

Nadejda was somewhat alarmed by Tchaikowsky's account of how he composed; was not all this frightfully fatiguing? Should he not rest more? "Reserve your powers, Peter Ilyich; give yourself a chance to reach the apex of your talent and to remain there as long as possible for the glory of your art and the joy of mankind. If my anxiety has any effect on you, and if you will restrain yourself even a little for me, I shall be very happy."

"My dear," replied the composer, "nothing could be more reasonable than your advice as to resting more and using one's inventive powers less. But how can I? Once the sketch is outlined, I cannot rest until I finish it, and then the moment the composition is done, I feel an irresistible desire to begin a new one. For me, work (*that* work) is as necessary as air. I have only to give myself up to idleness to be possessed by unhappiness, doubt that life will give me the chance to bring my talents to whatever perfection they are capable of reaching, dissatisfaction with myself, even self-hatred. The thought that I am good-for-nothing, that only my musical work redeems my defects and raises me to manhood in its truest sense, begins to overwhelm and torture me. The only means of escaping these tormenting doubts and self-flagellations is to start a new task. So I turn like a squirrel in a wheel. Sometimes a quite unconquerable laziness comes over me, apathy, disappointment in myself—it is a very deplorable condition, and I fight it as hard as I can. I am much inclined to hypochondria, and know that I must control my inclination toward idleness. Only work saves me. And I work. Still, thank you for your friendly advice. I shall try to follow it as far as possible."

Peter Ilyich was becoming daily more dependent upon Nadejda. Let her neglect him for a week, and he fell into panic. It happened now; he waited for a letter as long as he could, and then wrote suggesting they mail their letters on stated days, every so often. Nadejda was pleased, but she said her headaches might cause her to fail him; every month she had one—a ferocious, blinding pain that lasted three days. Today she had only just recovered in time for great festivities at Brailov. They were celebrating, as they did every summer, the combined name-days of Nadejda's brother, her eldest son Vladimir and his small new son,* Volichka, "a charming little creature. The garden has been illuminated, fireworks and Bengal fires have been prepared. It is effective—the pavilion on the pond is all lighted, the pond itself is bordered with lights, and a little boat in the middle is hung with colored lanterns. We always open the gardens to the public and people swarm in. . . . Keep well, and don't forget her who loves you with all her heart.

                                          "N.v.M."

"P.S. I think *Romeo and Juliet* much better as an operatic subject than *Undine.*"

Tchaikowsky replied in much embarrassment; how could he have been so naive as to ask a busy woman of affairs to have a writing pact with him! She had urged him again to Brailov; she herself was going abroad and the entire estate would be vacant; he accepted with pleasure. But before he left Verbovka he wished to report on the work he had done:

To Nadejda Philaretovna
                                    Aug. 5, 1878

"I write you, my dear sweet friend, with a light heart, happy in the knowledge of work more or less successfully accomplished. Today I wrote the last page of the *Liturgy,* and so all the lengthy and annoying work of copying is done. Now I shall rest and recover new strength. Do you know what I think? People who work feverishly and hurriedly are really the laziest people in the world. They hurry to gain the right to be idle. Now my secret weakness for doing nothing at all will have full freedom. It is more than time, because I broke down a week and a half ago and have not yet returned to normal. I feel myself quite well only to feel ill again immediately after."

Kamenka in late August was flat and hot and dusty. In Leo Davydoff's fields, smoke rose menacingly from the stacks of burning beetles. Peter Ilyich was glad to give Alexis the order to pack

* Vladimir II, afterward husband of Barbara von Meck.

the boxes for Brailov. And if Brailov had been enchanting in spring when last they saw it, how gorgeous it was now in the full panoply of summer! To sit on the terrace above the garden was to be drunk with color—dahlias, chrysanthemum and the flaming "fire-bush." "I am intoxicated with beauty!" cried Peter Ilyich. And what fun to have all these books at hand in Nadejda's library; next to the books, he enjoyed the dogs. Nine of them took a walk with him yesterday, he wrote, and if he had not feared for the furniture he would have had all nine in his living quarters for company!

Peter stayed about ten days at Brailov and returned to Verbovka, in his pocket the sketch for five movements of a brand new orchestral suite. This was to be the first of three suites for full orchestra. At his brother-in-law's Tchaikowsky worked on this music with furious delight; only a few days remained before he must return to Moscow; the Conservatory would soon open for the autumn term.

"I cannot tear myself from work," he wrote Nadejda. "Yes, beloved, best of friends, who advised and prescribed rest for me, I have broken my promise to devote some time to rest. I am not at all tired, which is always true when I have worked with no pressure other than the heart's urge. I think I have no right to fight my nature when it lights with inspiration, and so I beg you not to be cross because I did not keep my promise. As I worked, my thoughts were always with you; again and again I asked myself if these passages would please you, or these melodies move you. So it can be dedicated to no one but you. *To my best friend;* either I shall put it in the heading, as with the symphony, or if you prefer, put nothing on it at all, that the dedication may be known to none but ourselves.

"From now on, my friend, address me in Moscow. At least I shall return there a normal and quite healthy man, which I owe to you, and never for a second shall I forget it.

"Good-bye, my dear and sweet N. Ph.,

"Your
"P. Tch."

"Address me in Moscow." No light words these, from the pen of a Peter Ilyich. First, he must go north to Petersburg to see his father and have a talk with Anatol, then south again to Moscow. But no matter what is ahead of him this winter, if only he can write music,

Peter knows he can live. "For God's sake go on with your novel!" he writes Modeste, following any man's habit of prescribing his own best remedy to another, and recalling the pleasant days at Clarens when work had made all four of them happy.

"For God's sake go on with your novel. Work alone can distract one from the '*misères de la vie humaine*.' Besides, by it you will win independence. I can hear you reply that you have no time for writing because you are busy all day with Kolia. Yet I say, write, write, write! I could point to myself as example. I used to have about six hours a day of killing grind at the Conservatory, besides living with Rubinstein near the Conservatory; not only was Rubinstein's way of living a hindrance to me but I had to compose amid the constant disturbance of scales and exercises. In spite of it all, I wrote. It is true that your lessons with Kolia are more demanding than my theory classes, yet I say—write! Meanwhile I embrace you, my dear Modia. Nothing matters when people love each other as you and I do (forgive my self-assurance)."

16

Autumnal Petersburg

In September, 1878, Tchaikowsky, Nadejda von Meck and Rubin-stein were geographically far apart. Nadejda was in Switzerland, at Interlaken, driving out twice a day to look at the view. Russians whose lives are spent on the wide northern plains seem to have a craving for mountains; those who can afford it go to Switzerland periodically, as one would take a cure. And they are as exhilarated by the eventual descent as by the first sensation of altitude—not surprising, considering the amazing Russian response to stimuli of all kinds. Conversation, vodka, music, scenery—when these things seize upon him, your Russian is himself a whole charge of Cossacks; a hundred devils of vitality inhabit him and he can talk or walk or drink or sing any Anglo-Saxon to shame. In her younger days, Nadejda herself must have possessed this quality of inexhaustible vitality; illness had undermined it and she tired like ordinary mortals. As to Nicholas Rubinstein, with a spring in his spine worthy of ten Cossacks—he was in Paris, waving his country's flag at the Exhibition; whether or no he was to draw shouts from a hostile populace, Nadejda herself would soon bear witness.

And Peter Ilyich, with a cold in his head, was on the train from Verbovka to Kiev, the first lap of a northward journey—and he was miserable. At a way station he picked up a newspaper, and turning to the music page, read the most horrible attack upon the Moscow Conservatory. Not upon its music but upon its morals and professional intrigues. In fascinated horror he read and reread, searching breathlessly for his own name. M. Tchaikowsky, said the paper, was too busy with his music to take part in intrigue. . . . Heaven and a kind reporter had been with Peter this time, but in truth any attack on the Conservatory was an attack on himself; he was too much part of the institution to escape. Nicholas Rubinstein was torn

to pieces; the entire Conservatory, it seems, was no more than a sink-
hole to be fumigated.

"It was like a blow on the head!" Tchaikowsky wrote Nadejda.
At Kiev he changed trains. Settling down in a compartment occupied by three strangers, he threw away the newspaper and told himself he was a fool to be so sensitive. In the old days he had been able
to pass over such scurrilous attacks as if they were nothing; vacation,
he told himself, must have softened his hide. Most certainly he would
have to harden himself, and rapidly, if he were to live in Moscow. . . .

Peter shook his head, and decided to relax. He gazed out the carriage window at the familiar landscape flying by. The fields that
in Brailov had been green with summer were browner here, autumnal as they sped northward. A light rain fell—Petersburg would
be foggy and grey and horrible. . . .

In the compartment Tchaikowsky's fellow travellers were talking; their voices droned on. . . . What were they saying, what were
those names they repeated? Napravnik, Davidov. . . . These were
Petersburg names, Petersburg musical names. Davidov, (no relation
to Tchaikowsky's aristocratic brother-in-law) was Director of the
Conservatory there. Obviously, the travellers were Petersburgers. . . .
And concerning the musical world they were all too well informed.
Their voices rose, they laughed, they were having a good time
and Peter Ilyich, every nerve taut, listened for his name. It came.

Followed a nightmare. . . . The gentlemen did not leave a stone
unturned; the only thing about Tchaikowsky they did not see fit to
mention was his music. All about his marriage, all about his madness, just what kind of madness, how it came on and why. . . . It
wasn't actual insanity that had seized Tchaikowsky, said one of the
gentlemen, eagerly. . . . The composer was still entirely capable for
daily life and for music. There was no violence about what ailed
him, but on the other hand, it was incurable. . . .

The train stopped at a station. Peter got out quickly and moved
his things to another compartment—but no sooner had the train
started than the people in the seat opposite recognized him and

although he had never laid eyes on them before, began to question him intimately.

"I was seized with an indescribable, unconquerable desire to run away and hide, to leave it all." (How Nadejda, reading this, must have trembled in sympathy for this hunted creature whom she loved!) "There came over me an inexpressible fear and horror of my future life in Moscow. Naturally, I began immediately to plan for a definite break with society. At moments I was seized with a longing and thirst for absolute rest—death. Then it passed and there reappeared the old desire to live, to do my work and to say to the end all I have not yet said. But how to reconcile one with the other—how to save myself from contact with people, live apart from people and yet to work, forge ahead—?"

Outside the train windows it was dark—nearly nine in the evening now, and they would soon be in Petersburg. Tchaikowsky felt better, the people had stopped talking, and after all, they had seemed very glad to greet him and to know he was come home. In the darkness, lights flashed by; there was a roar; pungent cindery smoke filled the compartment as the train slowed down to enter the Warsaw Station. Peter Ilyich picked up his bag and walked out and down the train steps. . . . Just a year ago, Anatol had met him at another Petersburg station, had dragged from the platform a babbling, weeping stranger they said was his brother. . . .

And now, a year later, down the platform a man came running—"Tolia!"—"Petia." "Oh, my dear brother . . ."

This time it was Anatol who broke down. Peter put his arm about the younger man's shoulder and spoke quietly. "Don't cry, Tolia. Don't feel so. I am home again, and I am well. . . ."

Peter was touched by his brother's emotion, but he was also a bit alarmed, he told Nadejda. Tolia had cried with such audible sobs! "His nature is like my own," wrote Peter Ilyich. "Healthy, but quivering with nerves. I am convinced a man can conquer this kind of nervous sensibility. Tolia is ten years younger than I, and it should be easier for him to make the fight."

Brave words, induced by a reserve of health and the sight of someone temporarily weaker than himself! Peter Ilyich would indeed never go to pieces as he had upon that dreadful night a year ago; but in spite of health, in spite of nerves braced for shock, the city terrified him; no man recovers wholly from a breakdown such as Tchaikowsky had experienced. He and Anatol installed themselves in their eldest brother Nicholas' apartment. Nicholas was in the country. After four days Peter wrote Nadejda a letter so long that it must have consumed all night in the writing. In part he said:

"My dear, do you know what I fear? I fear that the Moscow life, the feeling I tasted on the train to Petersburg, the Conservatory with its uncongenial surroundings and the deadly, irritating class work, will unavoidably bring on an attack of misanthropy as soon as I take up my contracted profession and outside relations with people —that it all will possess me so completely I shall be helpless to fight it. It cannot yet harm my health—that is still strong enough to withstand much. What I fear is apathy, disgust for work, and if that should happen I would be no more than a worthless melancholic. I give you my word not to let myself go. I shall fight. But you can do me a great service by your advice and guidance. When I plan my life, I continually revert to the thought of you! What will N. Ph. say, what would she advise?

"Answer one question, my dear friend! What would you say if after a short time, I should quietly leave the Conservatory forever? What if, in a year, two years, I should make my home far away from the former scene of my active life? Up to now I have always considered it somehow my duty to remain at the Conservatory because of the dearth of people qualified to teach my specialty; that, however uncongenial the work, I ought to sacrifice myself. Lately, I have had my doubts about this. First, I was and always shall be a bad teacher because in every pupil, man or woman, I see a sworn enemy, created to torment me.

"Secondly, is it not my duty to give all my time and strength to the work I love, which for me embraces all the meaning and significance of life? You will ask perhaps, where and how I should settle down if I decided to leave my teaching. At present, while my ties to those about me are unsettled, I cannot answer this question definitely. Nothing would induce me to live in Petersburg or Moscow. I could never endure Petersburg; Moscow I love, but with some pain and bitterness. I like it as a place, as a city—even its climate—but you know why Moscow, more than any other place, is difficult for me. I should like to live the greater part of the year in the country, at my sister's and at

Brailov, if you would allow me to come there in spring and autumn. It would be pleasant also to spend some time in Clarens or Florence. In short, I should like the same nomad life I have lived for the last year. My God, what freedom to work, how happy I should be; how much and how well I would write, what a calm spirit I could have, far from the sordid gossip of my former life!

"A final reason—only in the country, only abroad and when free to change residence at will, am I protected from meeting the person whose nearness will always disturb and burden me tragically. I am speaking of the person you know of, the living monument of my madness, whose aim is to poison every minute of my life if I do not go far away. So my friend, what would you say if I left the Conservatory? I have by no means decided. I shall go to Moscow and try to become used to it. But I must know how you feel about it all. Not for anything in the world would I do anything contrary to your advice and opinion. Please answer my question."

And while Peter Ilyich sat imploring his friend through the black Petersburg night, Nadejda, in Paris, was writing to him. She had gone there for the Exposition which was still in full swing. She wanted to tell Peter Ilyich all about it and about Rubinstein's part in it. But Peter would wait a long time for a reply to his letter, and during those three weeks of waiting he would again and again beseech his friend's advice; until he knew whether Nadejda approved his decision to resign at the Conservatory, Peter could not leave for Moscow and Kamenka. He was obviously wholehearted in his effort to obtain Nadejda's real opinion and not merely her pity or sympathy; no one, he repeated, was so well-equipped as she to understand his horror at personal contacts, his incapacity to deal objectively with the world.

And the more helplessly Peter wrote about how he could not get on with people, the more enthusiastically people decided they could not get on without him. The world knocked at his door, yet he seemed incapable of believing that the world came in good faith and not in derision. At the moment he was not, of course, in a normal position socially—with an abandoned wife somewhere, nobody knew where or why. But while Tchaikowsky in no way exaggerated the amount of gossip that was raging round his name, he greatly exaggerated the malignancy of it. He had enemies of course; what famous man has not, while jealousy walks the earth? But he was too essentially unworldly to absorb the fact that nobody cared in the least what happened to Antonina Miliukoff, or who had wronged her, if anybody, and why. Whereas all Russia was glad to welcome home a great musician. Scandal or no scandal, Tchaikowsky was one of his country's biggest assets. His country knew that Rubinstein, in Paris, was playing Tchaikowsky's music to the world, but unfortunately Petersburg had not yet had the true facts about these concerts as no personal mail had yet come through, only newspaper gossip.

If he could bury his head in music, wrote Peter to Nadejda, he might forget his troubles, but unfortunately, Petersburg afforded no hiding place.

"Because of the Russian concerts in Paris just now, the newspapers are full of my name and the more publicity pursues me, the more I dread it. I cannot meet even strangers without real distress, and as my acquaintance in Petersburg is wide, I have to hide all day to avoid chance meetings. In the evening I dare not go to public places. My life is like that of a fugitive from the law! I have become quite a misanthrope, my friend, and seem to have lost the ability to live with other people. Ah, well, you understand this better than anyone."

Moreover it was September, and the dark days were approaching. All through the winter, lamps would flare except for a brief sun at noon.

"Petersburg," wrote Tchaikowsky, "has the most mournful, oppressive effect on the spirit just now. The weather is terrible—foggy, endless rain, dampness. One meets Cossack patrols at every step, as though we were in a state of siege. And the return of our army" (from Turkey) "after paying a shameful price—all of this is depressing. These are terrible times, fearful times. On the one hand an absolutely terrified government, so abandoned to fear that Aksakoff is exiled for a brave, truthful word. On the other hand, unhappy, mad youth, exiled in thousands without a trial—exiled where even the crow brings no bones. And between these two extremes, a public indifferent to everything, sunk in egotism, looking on without protest."

No doubt that Nadejda would agree with all this. "Petersburg!" she once had written him. "That foreign city—how I hate it!" And had she not lately deplored the stupidity of a society that would not lift a finger to help its government, and that sat supinely by "until thunder crashed, and then made the sign of the cross."

Ordinarily, September and early October—the so-called "golden autumn" is a pleasant time in Petersburg. On the North shore of Russia, set in a swamp, the city is reclaimed land, created artificially as a "modern" capital by Peter the Great. By mid-October the mists begin to rise from the lowlands; on this particular autumn the wet weather came early. To a nature like Tchaikowsky's, Petersburg would eventually have proved uncongenial no matter what the climate; it was as unlike Moscow as Chicago is unlike Charleston and the old South. Upon Moscow, built on seven hills, clung the slow colorful dust of centuries; Petersburg is flat, traced with canals; its palaces of bureaucracy line the river's edge.

And Petersburg was a bureaucracy. There lived the Tsar and his court; there was housed the machinery of government with its thousands of clerks and sub-clerks. On the twentieth of the month everyone, high and low, was paid; Petersburg, it was said, lived according to the "psychology of the twentieth." Ambition was furious, merciless—and ambition strode the streets in uniform. Everyone had a uniform; not only the tall and gorgeous officers of the Tsar's Guard, but all the pupils of the privileged schools: the Alexander Lyceum, the School of Pages, the Naval School. As a member of the School of Laws, Peter Ilyich himself had once worn a stiff braided serge collar. Even the Academy of Art, the University, the theatre, were submerged by uniforms. To Petersburg the Tsar was sun—art as well as science lived in his warmth. Had His Majesty not patronized art, there would have been no art; it did not spring spontaneously from the people, as in Moscow.

No wonder Peter Ilyich was lost in this life, and no wonder he implored Nadejda von Meck's support in his decision to leave it—and Moscow—for freedom and work. He was not even sure of Nadejda's whereabouts; he knew she had intended to go to Paris, but he had not heard if she had really arrived. Meanwhile the newspapers continued to report the Exposition, each according to its particular reportorial bias, and Tchaikowsky, aware that Rubinstein as delegate could make or unmake his reputation in Europe, was naturally anxious as to which way the Chief might jump.

"I cannot get at the truth," he wrote Nadejda. "Some newspapers say my compositions had great success in Paris. Others say they failed. From all that appears here in the papers about these concerts, I see without astonishment—but not without bitterness—how many enemies I have. I have never been interested in intrigue and always tried to keep out of it. I can truly say I have never intentionally harmed anyone in my life; yet I have enemies who rejoice at my failures and who minimize and poison every success. There are moments when I not only wish to live far away, off the beaten track, but when I want to stop writing even—to cease having any part in the social scheme. Of course, this feeling is temporary. If I can only get into surroundings that protect me from contact with strangers, I can work.

"But here I am, talking about myself again. It depresses me to hear nothing from you. I myself am to blame; I should have arranged to have all letters that were sent to Moscow, forwarded here. Now it is too late. Day after tomorrow I go to Moscow, and no doubt I shall find a letter or telegram from you."

And the very day before Peter Ilyich thus voiced his misgivings as to the Russian concerts at the Exposition, Nadejda had been to one of them. Rubinstein was having a spectacular success in Paris. Europe may have despised Russia, but Europe "yielded submissive," as one newspaper phrased it, "to the compelling power of a Rubinstein." The Chief, wily old fox who knew what he wanted and why, had played Tchaikowsky's B Flat Minor Piano Concerto, the very piece he had once condemned so flatly as unplayable. Wildest enthusiasm had greeted it. Nadejda missed that concert, but she did not miss the next. This is what happened to her:

"When we entered the hall," she wrote, "I was in a state of great nervous excitement and agitation. I wanted so much to have our Russian music, particularly your music, known and appreciated in Europe! I feared the opinion of Paris. First came Rubinstein's overture to *Ivan the Terrible*. The orchestra and the volume of sound drove me to despair, and with horror I thought of what they would do to your *Tempest,* that *Tempest* that made such an impression on me first, which charmed me so, and which is so dear to me in every way. But when the opening notes sounded, I forgot everybody and everything. Dead quiet reigned in the hall, no one breathed. When the chord with the suspension sounded, I trembled through all my nerves, and Paris, the stupid public, patriotic pride—the whole world—faded further and further away—only *The Tempest* existed, love, and its invisible author, pouring forth great, luxurious sound, capable of filling the world, giving happiness, blessing and delight. O, my God! I can never tell you what I feel when I listen to your music! I am ready to surrender my soul, you become a god: everything from the depths of my spirit, responds. What I love especially are the times when you speak from your heart, so eloquently, so charmingly, that one could listen forever. There is such a place in *The Tempest*—according to the program, in *Ile Enchantée.* It is the part in which you have all the violins go full blast—what richness, what delight, and how hard to have it end! When *The Tempest* ceased, I had left my body . . . I wanted them to play the Fourth Symphony, I wanted the *Marche Slav,* I wanted your compositions only. The audience was satisfied.

"The third concert will be on Saturday, and I shall probably go again. I had hoped they would play our Symphony, but they say no, Bartsevitch will play only your *Waltz* and *Serenade.* Beloved friend, I have not yet heard that *Waltz.*"

She broke off to thank Peter Ilyich for dedicating his latest orchestral suite to her; would he please print the dedication right out on the page, as he had on the symphony, so that she might have the pleasure of seeing the sweet words, and realizing they were for her? And again about the concert, a scandal had occurred! The trumpeter had tuned his instrument a tone and a half too low, or so she had been told. "Whether it was true or not," she added, "the chord delighted me."

What, after all, was a mere tone and a half to the widow von Meck? Always his chords would delight her; she pressed both his hands, she said. With all her heart she was his. . . .

Unfortunately, this letter was three weeks finding its way home. A pity Peter Ilyich could not have received it sooner, he was in deep need of just such fervent, uncritical devotion. In Petersburg he called on Davidov, Director of the Conservatory founded by Anton Rubinstein. During the evening, gossip raged concerning Nicholas Rubinstein, and Tchaikowsky was glad to get away. He might criticize the Chief privately, but in his heart he still felt grave discomfort at such public disparagement.

Peter Ilyich took the train for Moscow, and the bad taste of last evening's talk remained with him. Anatol saw him off at the station and behaved well; the boy was evidently in better control of himself than a fortnight ago. "Take care of yourself," the brothers told each other simultaneously at the train-steps. "Be calm, be always calm"— and laughed at the coincidence of their warning. Settling himself alone in the compartment, Peter smiled again; what a relief to be leaving Petersburg and the fog and the Cossacks and the interminable Tchaikowsky cousins!

Rolled in his rug on the carriage seat, Peter slept fitfully. Early next morning, descending at Klin Station with the other travellers for a hurried glass of tea, he felt tired but strangely content. In the train once more, he watched eagerly for the Moscow hills to rise, listened eagerly, descending at the Nicholas Station, for the clash of bells from a myriad golden towers.

17

Moscow once more. The Chief prepares a surprise party

THE Moscow bells rang, the Moscow dogs barked, every street corner called a welcome. Tchaikowsky's hotel was near the Conservatory and all his old friends came to see him, tramping up the broad stairs and down the carpeted corridor to his door. Peter tried to make them welcome. But his smile was strained, his fingers uneasy in the palm of a friend; the visitors sensed it and took offense. This meagre smile, this sudden darkening of the blue eyes that in the old days had been so gay, so candid—how could anyone know that not ingratitude cast this shadow, but fear?

Moscow!—that had been home and that was home no longer. The bells he had once loved—each stroke, each deep tolling reminded him now of things a man must forget if he was to keep his reason. Only a year ago those bells had tolled outside the windows of the stifling room where he sat a prisoner with one whose name he could no longer pronounce, so terrible was the sound of it in his ears. Only a year ago . . . And where was she now, this woman? Here in Moscow? Those footsteps in the corridor approaching his door. . . . That knock—how could he tell whose face would greet him if he answered that knock, if he dared open the door of his chamber?

Peter Ilyich to Nadejda

Moscow, Sept. 24, 1878
2 A. M.

"I cannot sleep, and so talk to you, precious, beloved friend. People have just left me (Laroche and Kashkin) whose society was once pleasant to me. Why was I so annoyed with them that I couldn't hide it, and both remarked on it several times? Why do the three days spent here seem three endless years? My whole spirit is centered now on one idea, one aim—to leave here somehow; a gulf has opened between my past and future, and I must cross it or fall into depths of misery, anger, and disgust for life.

"I wanted to tell you about my conversation with Davidov" (Director of the Petersburg Conservatory). "The situation is this: Here in Moscow I have to work not less than twenty-six hours a week; it has never occurred to the head of our Conservatory to consider my work as a composer, to save me from exhaustion and give me a chance to devote more time to the beloved work. He has never made any distinction between me and the crowd of other teachers. Davidov, with tears in his eyes, told me that if I would change to Petersburg I should have only four hours to work, and would receive twice as much pay. He would arrange a class in advanced theory—free composition—and would not insist that those four hours be given within the walls of the Conservatory. He could not believe that for twelve years I have been teaching harmony and have been obliged to give the Conservatory twenty-six to twenty-seven hours. Several times previously, indirect propositions to leave Moscow for Petersburg have been made to me, but this is the first direct offer.

"The conversation made a great impression on me, although the change of service attracts me very little. However advantageous Davidov's offer may be in comparison, it would still not give me freedom. Not for anything would I let myself be tempted by bigger pay for less work, hurt Rubinstein's feelings and make him an enemy for life. On the other hand, the conversation with Davidov opened my eyes to many things and helped fortify my resolve to drop this work that I find so uncongenial, in a city where life has become unbearable. You can imagine how agreeable it is to teach for four consecutive hours (as I did today) the laws of the triad to forty girls who don't understand anything and don't want to understand anything, when I know that in another conservatory, I would have only two or three talented pupils from the advanced class. And only four hours a week of it!

"I could tell you much about all this, but it would only take time and irritate me. Let me say one thing: even if in my secret heart I have always suffered because the Moscow directors refused to single me out from the general run of teachers, only now do I understand how little they cared to encourage my composing. I shall not say a word of this to Rubinstein. First, it would only bring about a misunderstanding between him and Davidov. Second, it would spoil his picture of himself as everyone's benefactor. Third, already having decided to leave here, it would be foolish to inject more poison into our already poisoned relationship. Fourth, poor Rubinstein has been so venomously and incomprehensibly set upon by the newspapers that I feel sorry for him (he is very sensitive to newspaper criticism). Fifth, I owe him much as an energetic exponent of my work, and should like to part with him as friends.

"In short, it is equally impossible for me to stay here or go to Petersburg. One thing remains—to resign the position of professor without publicity or fuss and become free as a bird, if not forever, then for two or three years at least. My God! Is such happiness possible? I shall await your opinion with great impatience and a trembling heart. I should like so much to convince you concerning my decision to leave Moscow—I am so afraid you will not approve; still, I feel that persuasion and fear are unnecessary. You can read my heart from half a word, from a hint. I think you will approve.

"*Mon Dieu,* how awkwardly and stupidly I write today! My nerves are strained to a high pitch. I want to say so much, but words are lacking. Ah, my friend, my dear sweet one, I want to go somewhere far away—I cannot think of work now. Until I come to some definite decision, until I am able to decide the time of my departure and can count the days and hours until that happy moment, I shall have no relief."

Poor Peter Ilyich, for whom a decision was always as painful as though the operation were done with knives upon his own flesh! At last he received Nadejda's letter about the Paris concert and *The Tempest.*

"You cannot imagine," he replied, "what an effect your praise has upon me; if you only knew how rarely I hear praise! I am so happy that my music moves and touches you. No one has ever said what you often say of my music. Always, now, when I write anything I have you in mind, wondering what will stir you, what will leave you untouched. A famous actor said that he always selected one sympathetic person from the audience and played for him. I write music for you.

"I have just had to spend three hours with Fitzhagen, a kind and affectionate, but dull and petty German. Every day I force myself to talk with and even visit people who are either dull or uncongenial. What can one do when living with wolves—one must howl as a wolf! But how much it all costs me!

"Good-bye,
"Your P. Tch."

Peter, unfortunately, was no wolf; his howls were invariably mistaken for overtures of friendship. Other musicians, notably Taneyeff, his monastic and scholarly pupil, could live in Moscow unmolested, but not Tchaikowsky. He tried to escape into apathy; he had "ceased boiling and raging," he told Nadejda in the next letter, and had become "bluntly indifferent." This is about as easy to believe as though Peter Ilyich had declared six-point antlers suddenly bristling from his shoulders.

To Nadejda Philaretovna

Moscow, Oct. 2, 1878

"Beloved friend!

"A week has passed since I came here, and it seems an eternity. My way of living is absolutely a nightmare. At the designated hour I appear at the Conservatory, go straight to the class-room, sit through my time, and then like an arrow hurl myself into a cab and go somewhere out of town: either to the Neskuchny Garden, or to Kunzevo, or Sokolniki. Only there do I find peace. I am very grateful to the Muscovites for not caring for nature. I found complete solitude in all those places, especially in Kunzevo, where I once stayed from ten in the morning until six in the evening without meeting one living soul in the beautiful alleys of the park. In the evenings I lock myself at home or wander in a far corner of the Zamoskorechie and give myself up to the saddest thoughts. The worst of it is that I cannot work at all, and must therefore kill time. And how to kill it! It is awful to see the hours pass one after the other without accomplishment, without significance.

"I want to tell you all the tragi-comic episodes of my flight from the world. For instance, for three days, sitting in my bedroom, I heard the singer Korsoff, a man I can't abide, scolding my Alexey and me because in answer to his question 'Is Peter Ilyich at home?' he was told, 'Not at home.' At last we met. It so happens that he needs me to write a song to put in his part. I said I had no time, was not in the mood and could not write anything good. 'Well,' says he, 'if you can't write anything good, I will make you do it over until it *is* good.' Were it not for the laws about crime, I think I would have hired some *bravo* to kill that impudent man.

"I feel myself a guest at the Conservatory—everything there is strange to me. I have ceased boiling and raging, and look with blunt indifference upon everything that once irritated me so painfully. I feel things cannot go on this way, cannot last, and that I shall leave

Moscow. I tell you frankly that if it were not for that thought, for the assurance that somehow I shall soon be free, only one thing would be left—to take strong drink often and without restraint.

"Ah, my friend, if you knew how hard it is for me and how ashamed I am to distress you by my complaints and my dissatisfaction with life! You do so much for my happiness and yet I always complain, I never find lasting happiness or tranquillity so that I can work steadily. And why did I have to return? Why did I have to arrange everything here without being sure in advance that I would be able to breathe the atmosphere of Moscow? Alas! it seems I cannot.

"I have been wanting to go to your home on the Rojdestvensky Boulevard, but, believe it or not, I have not had the energy. I fear you will not believe it when I tell you that I haven't once been in that part of the city, beyond the Conservatory. I have limited myself to my own street and the Zamorskorechie. Fear of meeting someone has become a mania. And truly, I am a maniac."

In the midst of Peter's distress came a telegram from Nadejda in Paris, saying she was writing, and he would soon have a letter. Immediately his tone changed: "A great light shines in my soul," he said. "Every word from you gives me energy, strength and hope . . . Rubinstein will be here in a few days, and as soon as I have your letter I shall form some plan of action and begin to carry it through."

But before Nadejda's letter was received, Nicholas Rubinstein returned from the Paris Exposition—a conquering hero. Moscow loved nothing better than to welcome home such a one and to crown him with bay. A great dinner was given in his honor at The Hermitage; toasts were drunk, everybody embraced everybody. Rubinstein himself was in fine fettle—and he knew exactly what he was doing. The banquet was long, the food abundant and extravagant. As the first toast was proposed—"To Nicholas Grigorievitch, who has done our country a great patriotic service, etc. etc.,"—Rubinstein got to his feet and instead of bowing his thanks, turned directly to Tchaikowsky, waved a hand, and smiled. . . .

Peter Ilyich, his empty glass in his fingers, knew every eye in the room suddenly upon him; his smile froze on his face. He heard the Chief's voice, silky, insinuating; "*there* is the man to whom your praise is owing. Not to me . . ." Not Rubinstein's playing but Tchaikowsky's music had captured Paris; the Piano Concerto, *The Tempest*, the *Serenade* and *Valse*, the *Chanson sans Paroles*— Ah, but the Conservatory had reason to be proud of its son, its premier professor, its pre-eminent artist whose compositions had carried the name of Moscow thus to Europe! Where would Russian music be without Peter Ilyich Tchaikowsky? *Where would the Moscow Conservatory be?* Was not Tchaikowsky's the name that made the world aware of our Conservatory, and would it not be so for years to come?

For years to come—so this was it. This was the Chief's scheme; every word was a stone in Peter's prison wall. After weeks of struggle he had made up his mind to resign forever from the Conservatory and had only awaited the Chief's return so to inform him. Their last meeting had been far from cordial; Tchaikowsky had persuaded himself that Rubinstein would not care much whether he left the Conservatory or no. . . . And now here was the Chief on his feet, purring praises. . . .

Rubinstein sat down; The Hermitage roared applause and called for Peter Ilyich. . . . Peter got to his feet, looked once at Rubinstein and began to speak his thanks . . . "I came home absolutely desperate," he wrote Nadejda. "After the services Rubinstein had rendered me in Paris, after this ovation arranged by him at the dinner, it would be blatant ingratitude on my part to cause any difficulty for him by leaving the Conservatory."

Not only was Tchaikowsky's carefully nursed indignation against the Chief completely undermined by this stratagem, but he carried now a genuine burden of gratitude; there was no doubt that Rubinstein had played his concerto magnificently in Paris—and if Tchaikowsky remained in his service, it would be played again as gloriously.

Peter spent a bad night—what there remained of night. Next afternoon he went to see Rubinstein, and the Chief's first question disarmed him further. "What is the matter, Peter Ilyich? You seem gloomy. Are you ill? Karlusha (Albrecht) says no one ever sees you. Why do you hide yourself? Will you not talk frankly with me?"

"I could not lie to him," Tchaikowsky wrote Nadejda. "I told him nearly everything. I became terribly excited, confessed that my life here was unbearable, that a mania of misanthropy had seized me and I could never conquer it. I said right out that I could not stay here long."

Rubinstein's reply was surprising in the extreme. Tchaikowsky expected expostulation, persuasion, expected to be told it was all imaginary, this misanthropy, and with courage it would disappear. Nothing of the kind took place, Rubinstein laughed, shrugged his shoulders, remarked that the withdrawal of the Tchaikowsky name would mean a loss of prestige for the Conservatory—and was silent.

Peter left the house chagrined but relieved. Evidently he was not valued at all as a teacher, only as a composer. Well, he would be a composer, and nothing else. Nevertheless in his heart, Tchaikowsky knew he was a good teacher. What then, was in Rubinstein's mind, what game was he playing? Next day Peter wrote Nadejda:

"I saw Rubinstein again today; he was friendly and seems as gay and serene as on the day of his arrival. Last year he said I was mad, and that the madness would pass. Does he still think it will pass? Alas, he is badly mistaken! Every hour, every minute I am convinced this madness will never leave me. The worst is that I cannot work here, and without work, life loses all meaning for me.

"The person you know of has not appeared, I don't even know where she is. But her mother bombards me with letters, consisting of expressions of tenderest love! She wants me to come and visit her—she even wants me to be nuptial godfather at her daughter's wedding; she says my blessing will bring luck! ! ! Oh, God, to be away from all this! If only your letter would come! I can do nothing until I know what you think."

At last Nadejda's letter came; she had taken her household down from Paris to San Remo; there she found Tchaikowsky's frantic letters forwarded from Paris. Instantly she replied—and without equivocation:

"Of course, Peter Ilyich, leave the Conservatory! For a long time I have thought it absurd that a person of your brains, training, education and talent should be at the mercy of a man inferior to you in every way" (Rubinstein). "A man despotic and unscrupulous. I purposely gave you no advice before, but all the time I sincerely hoped you would yourself decide to drop a position that involved continual submission to our mutual friend.

"As to the usefulness of your teaching to future generations, I believe you will give them much more by your compositions than by combining fifths and octaves in the class-room. Many exist who can do nothing but that—whereas you can leave monuments in art that will be the best guide and example for studious youth. In a word, to abandon a position that is not in keeping with a man's dignity or talent, seems to me quite right and accords with all my principles."

Nadejda must have written this with a fiercer joy than carries on paper. Had she not, many years ago, used all her force to persuade her young husband, Karl George, to abandon a stupid government position and follow his natural talents for engineering? And that had been a more desperate gamble than this of Tchaikowsky's. Peter Ilyich had no twelve children to feed. . . .

"What you have done has my blessing, dear friend," wrote Nadejda. "As to your plans for spending half your time in Russia, half abroad, it is what I have desired for you. I too shall spend the winter abroad. If you could come somewhere near me, beloved friend, how happy it would make me! Why could we not both settle in Como and live on the shore of the Lake, a mile or two apart? How good it would be!"

Was ever relationship stranger than this? Many a man and woman have fallen in love by correspondence, but none before or since have arranged a *ménage à deux* at a distance of two miles. Nadejda regretted that Peter Ilyich had not accepted her invitation to live in her Moscow home while he was in the city. She had even ordered a small apartment prepared for him. Surely he could have forestalled gossip by telling Rubinstein that Mme Meck's brother had tendered the invitation? (Here the widow's desires for once over-ruled her worldly judgment, or had distance caused her to forget the sardonic Rubinstein smile?) But if Peter Ilyich would not live in her vacant house, would he do her the favor of stopping in for a few moments some afternoon? No one would see or speak to him: the order had been given. If he would just go in, play her pianos, smoke, look at the pictures, it would please her greatly. Again she reassures him about his plans for leaving the Conservatory:

To Peter Ilyich
San Remo, Sept. 20, 1878

"I had only just finished my letter to you when yours of September 12th was brought to me. Davidov's offer" (of a position in the Petersburg Conservatory) "delights me beyond words, my dear Peter Ilyich, because it proves there are people who appreciate you. But I agree that you must not accept, especially as there is no risk of forfeiting such favorable terms. I am quite sure you will always be able to get them all over Europe, but full freedom and plenty of time for rest are necessary to you as a composer with such rich imagination. You say quite rightly, beloved friend, that I can understand what you feel from half a word. More than that—I understood your present state and the necessity for a change before you yourself felt it. For a long time I have wanted you to be *quite free*."

How gay, how relieved was Peter Ilyich when he read these words!

"Your letter has come at last, my best, my ever kind, beloved friend," he wrote. "This is just a line to thank you for giving me, as my good genius, the chance to free myself from hateful slavery. How I shall work, how I shall try to prove to myself that I am really worthy of all you do for me! Very, very often, I am troubled because you give me too much happiness. Then if I don't write, don't work, I begin to despise myself and fall into great despair because of my nothingness and unworthiness, and because of the discrepancy between your idea of me and the real 'I.' When I work, when what I do has satisfied me, then the abyss fills and I reach the measure of all the kindness and affection you have given me. And I shall work! My God, what happiness, freedom! I will go to your house today. Good-bye, my beloved friend.

"Your
"P. Tch."

What then, could he do for Nadejda Philaretovna, besides words upon paper? Peter Ilyich put down his pen. She had saved him from madness a year ago, and now the madness threatened once more, and once more she came forward. . . . Oh, thrice blessed the name of this woman, protectress who stood between him and a terrible, teeming world! He would write music and more music, the best that was in him—that was what Nadejda Philaretovna wanted. But he could not begin now, this minute. He must see Rubinstein again. . . . Oh, a thousand things remained to do before his shackles would fall! But he must show his gratitude now, instantly; he would burst if he could not do something. . . .

Peter Ilyich puts on his black felt hat and his grey overcoat and swings over to the Rojdestvensky Boulevard. If Nadejda Philaretovna wants him to visit her house, by God he will visit it. What if he does meet everyone he knows on the way? Now he has nothing to fear. He is free. *Free!* Why, even if he meets Antonina—Peter's hands are rigid inside his gloves—even if he meets Antonina, he can just tell her he is going abroad, indefinitely. *Indefinitely!*

To Nadejda Philaretovna

Moscow, Oct. 12, 1878

"Yesterday—at last—I was in your wonderful house, my dear. Ivan Vasilievitch" (Nadejda's steward) "met me with great cordiality and let me wander freely through the rooms. I stayed two hours and looked over everything very carefully. Needless to say I am absolutely delighted with the beautiful hall and other formal rooms, but your private apartments pleased my heart most—also the rooms in which you suggested that I live. I found them quite ready to receive a guest. What a wonderful little place! With what pleasure I could live in those rooms, as cozy as they are luxurious. Unfortunately, it is impossible. Being a professor at the Conservatory, under obligation to others, I cannot hide myself in your sweet little retreat. My address must be known, and what would they say if I began living at your house! And yet I can't imagine anything more convenient than that little corner in your home, inaccessible to everyone.

"In spite of the prospect of near freedom, in spite of the foretaste of happiness that your letter gave me, I have been ceaselessly pursued by a strange, painful, acute, and maddeningly vague fear and terror. It forces me to avoid human society, persecutes me even at home, everywhere and all the time. At your house—and there only—I spent two hours quite free from it—I can also relax out of town. I liked your pictures exceedingly. Of them all I preferred *Ingano e Amore,* for its design and color rather than for its rather melodramatic subject. But the ones in your bedroom and the room next to it are charming. I couldn't get a good view of one picture that interested me because of the way it was hung. Yet it caught my attention because it is really an illustration of the first movement of my first symphony." (*Winter Day Dreams*.) "It portrays a broad road in winter. It is lovely. The head of the old man over the door is a joy.

"I played on your instruments: the Bechstein and Steinway are beautiful. The Deben organ is very good both as an instrument and a piece of furniture. I ended my first visit to your house by asking Ivan Vasilievitch to show me everything down to the smallest detail. I went in every room, even your beautiful bathroom. An upholsterer is working in the house just now. Iv. Vas. begged me to come again when everything is in shape. Of course I shall; it was all so pleasant and inviting! Why is it being put into complete order when you are spending the winter in Italy?"

The reason it was being put in order was because Nadejda liked to feel—wherever she was—that if she became too ill or too homesick she could fly instantly to Moscow. And flight, for the widow von Meck, was seldom undertaken without every comfort waiting at the other end. The maintenance of two or three houses, always staffed and in readiness, went by some other name than extravagance with Nadejda.

But Tchaikowsky knew none of this reasoning. At the moment he knew only that he had enjoyed Nadejda's house, nor had he any more consciousness than she of the queerness of his lonely visit, of the strange picture of a man—moreover a distinguished man—sitting happily smoking his cigarette in a big house empty of a hostess who would herself never receive him. He went home to his hotel and enjoyed the visit again in his letter to Nadejda, going on to tell his plans about leaving the Conservatory. To avoid publicity, he and Rubinstein had hatched an elaborate plan. (This time, the Chief knew he was really beaten. Having plotted to keep Peter Ilyich in the Conservatory he now turned and plotted quite as energetically to get him out with the least possible disturbance.)

The plan was for Tchaikowsky to disappear quietly to Petersburg. From there in due time he would write the Chief saying that ill-health prevented his return. In the meantime Rubinstein could himself take over some of the harmony classes, and Taneyeff could take the rest. Only a month of prison, then, remained, yet what an eternity a month would seem! "Good-bye, my friend," Peter's letter ended. "Thank you a thousand times for words that brought me back to life. What is my friend Milochka doing? Give her a kiss for me.

"Your

"P. Tch."

Nadejda replied enthusiastically; she was happy that Peter Ilyich had freed himself from the yoke of the Tartar, "in the shape of our respectable and undoubtedly meritorious friend, from whom it is always better to be separated." She was glad Rubinstein did not stage a scene—"peace, cheaply won, is preferable to a good quarrel." Thank God her friend had escaped! She regretted only that he must now endure the official farewells, the "dinners, speeches, tears."

Tchaikowsky regretted it also; in fact, he decided he simply could not endure it. Once launched, Tchaikowsky's flights were always rapid.

To Nadejda

Moscow, October 14, 1878

"My dear!

"Here is what occurred to me last night. Why should I remain here a whole month for no good reason? My life now is so senseless that even a month of it is hard to bear. I wanted to stay for two reasons: first, to give Taneyeff time to prepare himself to take my place; second, the first concert of the Russian Musical Society is scheduled for the third of November, and Rubinstein is going to play my piano concerto. As to the first, it so happens that the advanced classes in harmony will be taken not by Taneyeff but by Hubert, who needs no preparation. Taneyeff is quite prepared for the first course in harmony. As to the concert, I would not go to it for anything in the world, so shall not hear Rubinstein play anyway.

"Other reasons kept me here, mostly a feeling of embarrassment toward the Conservatory. I didn't want a hurried departure to advertise how little I care for my *soi disant* friends here. After all, I have reasons for disregarding questions of delicacy, and secondly, all argument falls before the fact that my life is now so blatantly nonsensical, so unbearable, so stupid that I cannot stand even a month of it. I shan't conceal the fact that I have had to fortify myself with wine. Well, in a word, *j'ai precipité les evènements*. Today I told Rubinstein that I would leave at the end of the week.

"So my friend, in less than a week I shall be *free!* My plan is to stay in Petersburg during October and go abroad to Clarens in the beginning of November.

"I shall arrange my departure quietly, without farewells and celebrations. My address will be: Petersburg, New Street, corner of Nevsky Prospect, No. 78, Apt. 30, care of Anatoly Ilyich Tchaikowsky. I shall surely receive the *lettre chargée* today or tomorrow. Thank you, my friend.

"Your
"P. Tch."

The week passed; time moves apparently, even when wine fails to rally the heart.

"I held my last class yesterday," wrote Peter on October 19th "I go to Petersburg today, a free man! The sensation of freedom is indescribably joyful. And it is good that no disagreeable feeling is mixed with it. My conscience is quite clear; I go with full assurance that the Conservatory will not suffer from my absence. The thought that I am not being ungrateful makes me happy, though I don't doubt there are some who accuse me of ingratitude. Thinking over all my years of work in the Conservatory. I cannot but realize that nothing was ever done to relieve me or encourage the only part of my work that gives point or value to my life. On the other hand, I go at peace with Moscow. I shall remember with gratitude that here my artistic strength developed, here fate ordained that I should meet the person who was destined to become my good angel."

That same afternoon, Tchaikowsky made his farewells; not the least of them was a last visit to Nadejda's house. Ivan, the steward, received him like an old friend and let him wander at will through the big silent rooms, but Ivan could not know that this smiling, friendly gentleman was here to pay his respects, and take quaint *congé* of Ivan's absent mistress.

That same evening Peter dined with his old friends: Rubinstein—whom he now could afford to call friend—Albrecht, Jurgenson his publisher, Kashkin and Taneyeff. Their genuine regret at the parting touched him, he wrote Nadejda, and he himself felt sad at the breaking of ties which had endured twelve years.

At midnight, Tchaikowsky took train for Petersburg, a free man. Free, that is, from the Conservatory and the teaching he had found so irksome. There remained but one central duty: to write good music, and that was a responsibility imposed not from without but from within. Around this responsibility Tchaikowsky's days and nights would henceforth circle, toward it his every energy would henceforth be strained—and with what plenitude of joy, what never-failing gratitude toward the woman who had made this duty possible.

Nadejda was in Florence when she received Peter's Moscow letters. Only one thing worried her—what he had said about "fortifying himself with wine." She replied seriously and with directness. She well understood, said she, the state of nerves in which wine becomes a necessity, but she knew also the frightful and irreparable harm that wine can do. "My dear, my kind one," pleaded the widow, "if you really want to do something for me, don't use that dangerous remedy. Control yourself, have a care for your talent—if not for your own sake, for the sake of others. Your destiny is high, and worthy the sacrifice of a moment's relief from depression and un-happiness—especially as the best treatment for that unhappiness lies in the very occupation with which you will attain your destiny! Believe what I say, my priceless one."

Tchaikowsky did believe what she said, and knew also that there was real foundation for her fears. All his life, Peter drank quite heavily. It was difficult not to when his friends, especially his Moscow friends, spent half their time over wine. It was part of the régime; long nights around the café table, discussing art, life, love—and how much higher and further a man can soar, fortified by wine! To "trans-cognac oneself," the composer Moussorgsky used to call it—poor Moussorgsky, who trans-cognacked himself finally into the grave. Rimsky-Korsakov's memoirs bear witness to Tchaikowsky's virtuosity in this respect: "He could drink a great deal of wine and yet keep his full powers, both physical and mental. Few of us could keep up with him in this respect."

Tchaikowsky may have kept his full powers while in company, but this kind of indulgence always told on his health both as to nerves and digestion. He was always making resolutions not to drink; his diary records many such. . . . "From now on," he replied to Nadejda's admonitions, "I give you my absolute promise to think of you when I am tempted, and in your friendship I shall find strength to hold out. But now that I have attained freedom—that greatest blessing—I do not believe I shall ever again reach the point where I have to look to wine for oblivion."

Tchaikowsky wrote this letter from Petersburg. His old opera, *Vakoula,* was to be produced at the Imperial Theatre and rehearsals were in progress—much impeded by a temperamental tenor who refused to sing. Peter found comfort in seeing his father once more, who was "wonderful in his angelic kindness. The dear old man sobs with joy each time I appear. His health is good; yesterday he went to the theatre and it did not tire him at all."

As for writing music, he was getting nothing done at all, complained Tchaikowsky, and he would not stay in Petersburg another minute, *Vakoula* or no *Vakoula,* were it not that Anatol was so nervous and queer he was afraid to leave him. Petersburg was filled with cousins; one ran into them at every step. "They talk about music!" moaned the composer. "They try to find out when I shall be promoted to the position of Director of the" (Petersburg) "Conservatory! They ask me to play for them! They are all State clerks and look upon me as a musical clerk, professing themselves astonished at the injustice of the powers in not making me a director."

And now once more the kind sister Alexandra Davydoff came to the rescue with a warm invitation to Kamenka. She offered her brother a brand new cottage, sunny and quiet. Peter replied that he would come right away, and he came. How quiet the autumnal countryside, the thin snow lying white against his cabin door in the early morning, the farm-hands singing on their way to the barn.

After the long, arid period of Petersburg and Moscow, inspiration returned, and Tchaikowsky found himself working again on the orchestral suite (Suite Number One) that he had sketched upon his last visit to Brailov. He liked the suite, he said. "Our symphony is being printed," he reported to Nadejda, who was now in Florence. "Taneyeff spent a long time on the piano arrangement. The Sonata" (G major Piano Sonata) "is also being printed, and the *Liturgy* and children's pieces" (twenty-four easy pieces for piano). "Also twelve other things (these were also piano pieces) and the Romances" (six songs dedicated to Anatol). "All will be ready shortly."

This list, with the important exception of *Onegin* and the Violin Concerto, nearly comprised the sum of Tchaikowsky's work since he had begun to know Nadejda von Meck, eleven months before. He did not mention here the three violin pieces composed at Brailov and dedicated as *Souvenir d'un lieu cher,* nor the *Skobeliev March,* composed at Kamenka on commission for Jurgenson and signed—because Tchaikowsky considered it worthless—by a pen name.

Here arises an inevitable question: Has there been any noticeable change in the quality of Tchaikowsky's work since he has known Nadejda von Meck? *Onegin,* the Fourth Symphony, the Violin Concerto—are they better or worse than his preceding compositions? Are they different in emotional quality from what he used to write—brighter, sadder, richer? And if so, was the change due to Nadejda?

When a composer comes under the influence of a woman, this question is always asked. But it is impossible to answer; even a composer himself cannot trace his love-life in his work. Music is too abstract an art to be underwritten by the name of woman—either woman in general or a specified Helen. Of Tchaikowsky's three famous symphonies (Fourth, Fifth and Sixth) the Fourth, while gloomily Tchaikovskian in the first movement, has about it a happy, pastoral quality the other symphonies do not possess. To many it is the most appealing of the three. Yet Tchaikowsky wrote it just before and after his marriage, completing it during the most harried months of his life. *Onegin* was written at about the same time, and *Onegin,* although supposedly a tragedy, is in effect a charming series of lyrical outbursts, combining gayety and melancholy as naturally as the nightingale combines them. If ever Tchaikowsky was under Nadejda's influence, it was while he was composing *Onegin* and the Fourth Symphony.

The greatest composers have borne witness that music—even program music—does not develop from concrete thought or from concrete experience. Tchaikowsky himself testified in a letter to Nadejda, concerning objectivity at the moment of creation. A phrase is born, the phrase begets a second phrase, and so on to the development of a symphony. Did not Brahms confess that his best ideas came to him while brushing his shoes in the morning? To hint that a B minor Mass is a thing of mechanics or physics is not to deny the thing called inspiration, nor to belie the spirituality of a Johann Sebastian. . . . Bach was a deeply religious man, and his music is deeply, gloriously religious. Tchaikowsky was an emotionalist, a nineteenth-century romanticist, and it shows in every line he wrote. A great man's music is like his destiny—heaven and hell come not fortuitously, from without, but are defined by himself, his character and his physical being. Therefore it is fruitless to ask whether Nadejda von Meck influenced Tchaikowsky's music. Without Nadejda. Tchaikowsky would have written nothing at all that dreadful year. He would have gone mad, he would have killed himself—and likely enough, would have killed Antonina too. Nadejda saved him. Her money gave him freedom from Antonina and from fear. It gave him back his full strength that heretofore had been sapped by the gruelling routine of teaching. Nadejda herself did not aspire to wield a personal influence over Tchaikowsky. That she saved him rather by her money than, say, her personal magnetism, she knew well.

For her—and for us—it is enough that she saved him.

18

Florentine Idyll

A<small>ND</small> while Tchaikowsky sat in Kamenka enumerating his year's work, Nadejda von Meck in far-away Florence was hatching a daring plan. Here she was, queen of the Villa Oppenheim out on the magnificent Viale dei Colli—among the hills, looked after by Ivan, her Moscow steward, who had come out to her, the faithful maid Lucretia to comb her long hair, three other Russian maids, three Italian servants (and slippery rascals they were, too). For the children, a German governess who, fortunately, could play the piano, not to mention butler's helpers, "cooks, extra cooks, two lackeys and two coachmen." Writing to Tchaikowsky, she mentioned them all. Gardens and terraces, she went on to say, surrounded the villa, and the gardens were peopled by ancient, weather-beaten statues. The Archangel Michael himself stood guard over her silent fountain! Beyond and below Michael, below the silvery olives and the groves still flaunting their November scarlet—lay Florence, and on beyond Florence rose the dark Apennine Hills. Here at dusk—the magic, clear blue dusk of autumnal Florence—if one sat quite still one could hear faintly the river Arno, moving cityward to be received by the glory of its ancient bridges. Even on wet days it was all so lovely. At the garden's edge, poplars rose golden through the fog, and at night the city lights gleamed soft and far away. . . .

It brought tears to the eyes, said Nadejda! It was heaven, but for one great omission, that want of one incomparable friend. Peter Ilyich could repair that omission—nobody else. Why, therefore, should he not come to Florence now, right away? She would prepare an apartment for him, either in town or somewhere out here among the hills. He would have no care in the world but one—the only real care either of them had anyway—his music! "Come, my dear!" said Nadejda.

Tchaikowsky read these words in Kamenka not long after he had posted a letter to Florence asking Nadejda not to send a *lettre chargée* this month because living cost him nothing at his sister's. When he had read the invitation, he did not hesitate a second. He telegraphed a joyful acceptance, and then he sat down and wrote what came close to being a love letter. "What greater delight than to think of living where you can be with me?" (Well Tchaikowsky knew she would not be "with" him!) "To make you happy, to be of service to you, I would come not only to Florence, but to the most distant ends of the earth."

Nadejda read this, and her heart beat high. Her long self-restraint, was about to bear golden fruit. Peter trusted her enough to come to her city, live in the apartment she would prepare, upon the money she was to supply: he knew she would not overstep her boundaries, would never by hint or outright plea, force the relationship further and demand to see him. . . .

She set about Florence instantly with her lackeys on the box, threading her clattering way through narrow, twisting streets to hunt a home for her incomparable one. She found two apartments, one in town and one out in the hills, about a quarter-mile from her own villa: she sent Peter Ilyich the plans of both. Would he please decide, and let her know?

Tchaikowsky replied that he would much rather be out of town, but would it be possible for Nadejda's agent to make sure there would be no musical neighbors? Any other kind of noise is bearable, but he cannot write his own music while other people are playing theirs. And would it be too much to ask that the piano be ready on his arrival, so that he can start work immediately? He can of course compose without a piano, but it is very agreeable to have one to amuse himself with.

Peter Ilyich made his travelling arrangements and then retired as always before a journey—for a day's nervous dysentery. (This rather violent and frequent disorder played too large a part in Tchaikowsky's life—and death—to be left politely un-mentioned.) He was to leave Kamenka on Tuesday, November 26th. All day

Friday and Saturday he wandered about his rooms, hoping the "symptoms" would disappear before train-time. On Saturday night he was feeling a bit less pallid when Leo Davydoff, vigorous, handsome and hearty, came in. Peter, it seemed, was to have a treat tomorrow. A big hunt had been arranged; everything was ready—keepers, dogs, beaters. . . . It was going to be wonderful! said Leo in his big voice. Yes, he *did* remember what had happened to Petia on that last shoot when he got so sick and had to be helped home, but lord, man!—that had been four years ago. A mere accident. *This* was to be a real send-off, a good healthy Russian memory for Peter to take to those effete Italians. An all-day hunt, beginning at sunrise. Alexis must be sure to get his master up at five o'clock. "Isn't that right, Alexy—you coming too?" roars Leo, and Alexis grins assent.

"Splendid!" says Peter weakly, who can not endure the sight of blood or suffering. "And what are we hunting, Leo?"

"Wolf!" says Leo with beaming eye. "Wolf and fox and wild goat. Of course we may not have much luck with the goat; they're getting very scarce and shy these days, you know."

Breathing a silent prayer that the wolves may be even scarcer and shyer, Peter Ilyich spends a sleepless night and is up and dressed—after the nature of nervous persons—long before anybody else. In the cold dawn everyone pounds him on the back, congratulates him, and all morning he stumbles blindly through the woods, gun on shoulder. Snow is falling. So much the better for hunting!—cries Leo. By noon Peter Ilyich would give all his money and all his friends and all his talent for a warm bed and a hot brick at his feet. Not an inch of him that does not ache, and his eyeballs flame so he can hardly see. Impossible to ask any of these men to abandon their sport and see him home. Why did he come? Why is he out here staggering round with this infernal gun when by a mere word to Leo last night, he could be in a warm room now, and working? Work! Will he ever, ever, *ever* be where people cannot ask him on wolf hunts or on anything else?

"I remained with the hunt," he wrote Nadeida next day, "until

five in the afternoon, in spite of increasing pain and weakness.
Finally I got home, with a pain in my head so awful I can't describe
it, and nausea and weakness. I threw myself on the bed and there
came on the most dreadful nervous attack I have ever experienced.
I thought I was dying. I can't remember how or when I finally got
to sleep. Today my body hurts all over. I know it was nothing but
migraine, but it was bad all the same!"

Peter cancelled his plans for leaving Tuesday, but sick or well, he
was determined to be gone by Wednesday. In another minute it
would be Sunday, and who knows but Leo might stage another
wolf hunt? So on Wednesday Uncle Petia was put on the train, and
with a sigh of relief said good-bye to the snow and the cold and the
kind relatives who planned treats and wolfish send-offs. Alexis,
grinning, carried his master's luggage up the train-steps to the compartment. One place was the same as another to Alexis, provided
there was plenty to eat and another servant to gossip with in Russian. And there would be; Ivan Vasilievitch, Mme Meck's steward,
was in Florence with his mistress, and Ivan was a good fellow. . . .
From Kiev to Vienna across the Carpathians, then a day and night
in Vienna, a telegram dispatched to Nadejda Philaretovna to say Peter
would not stay in Venice but would come straight through. And
then the train again and the long journey down through Austria
and across the hills into Venice.

And as he sped southward, a faint uneasiness troubled Peter
Ilyich; deepening as he drew ever nearer to Florence. Who would
meet him and Alexis at the station tonight? Ivan Vasilievitch with
Nadejda's horses and the Russian lackeys on the box? Or Pahulsky,
the Polish violinist, once his own pupil, who had taken Kotek's
place in the von Meck household since Kotek's loose tongue cost him
his job? Whoever met him, would they take him straight to his own
apartment at the Villa Bonciani, or would he—uneasy thought—
be required to stop off to pay his respects at the Villa Oppenheim
on the way?

He had been more than a little reckless, thought Peter, engaging
to spend three weeks not half a mile from Nadejda Philaretovna,

and on the self-same boulevard. If she invited him to call, he would simply have to comply, and even if she did not require an actual visit, it would be more than likely they would meet accidentally, out walking. And then an end to this safe and comforting relationship, an end to all his security. What a fool he had been to come here and jeopardize everything! He might have known that no woman on earth, not even a saint like Nadejda Philaretovna, would be able to keep her distance forever. These misgivings he voiced afterward in a letter to Modeste.

When the train at last drew into Florence, Pahulsky was waiting eagerly on the platform. They drove straight to Tchaikowsky's apartment and Pahulsky left him there. Peter Ilyich flung off his coat and explored his new home. It was almost magnificent. A dining-room, two bedrooms and a dressing-room furnished for his comfort to the minutest detail—and a drawing-room with a splendid grand piano. Flowers were everywhere to greet him; there was a big table where he could write music, with every kind of stationery, pencils and pens, and propped against the inkstand, a note from his hostess. Peter Ilyich tore it open: "Welcome, my dear, beloved, wonderful friend!" he read.

"How glad I am, *mon Dieu*, how glad that you are here! To feel your presence near me, to know the room you are in, to admire the same scenery, to feel the same temperature as you, is a joy that cannot be expressed! I hope you will like the place I selected—*soyez-y le bienvenu, mon délicieux ami.* You are now my guest, beloved and dear to my heart. But if anything should be in the least inconvenient for you, please let me know immediately. I am not bound by any lease and you could move at any moment.

"What a coincidence—you came on the same train as my daughter Lydia! We have been looking for them for some time. This is why I sent Pahulsky to meet you, because Ivan Vasilievitch, who knows your apartment, had to wait and have tea ready for Lydia when she came from the station, and my other man, a Frenchman, had to meet them at the station to get their luggage. I hope my sending Pahulsky did not disturb you. If you need anything, my dear, good friend—a carriage, books, no matter what—please come directly to Villa Oppenheim as you would to your own home, and be assured that I shall be pleased and delighted. Julia remembered that the tea was very bad here, so we always have a supply of Moscow tea—we do not drink foreign tea anywhere, therefore we shall prepare Moscow tea for you too; let Alexis take care of it. He is probably *fort dans le ménage*.

"In regard to walks, let me recommend, as nearest you and most charming, the walk to the monastery of Campo Santo and the Piazza San Miniato. This is a delightful place. You go there by way of our Viale. We walk every day, no matter what the weather; we always go out at eleven and walk a little beyond Bonciani, where you live, my dear friend. There we return the same way exactly, at noon, for luncheon.

"I have put newspapers and periodicals in your apartment. In two of them you will find accounts of yourself. Besides these, all our newspapers and periodicals are at your service.

"*Au revoir,* my dear friend beyond compare! Peter Ilyich, take a good rest. It worries me the way you are so often a little ill. Heaven grant that your sojourn here will benefit your health.

"Devotedly,
"N. v. M."

Now what a woman!—thought Peter Ilyich; was ever man so blessed as he? She had thought of everything; that bit of information about the walks, giving the exact time and place where she was to be found every morning, was the very height of consideration; she had given it so he would not be afraid to go out. Peter was tempted to sit down and write her that very minute, but it seemed foolish when Alexis could pop over with a note early in the morning. . . .

Peter Ilyich to Nadejda Philaretovna

Florence, Dec. 3, 1878
"Truly, dear friend, I cannot find words for my complete delight in everything that surrounds me here. I could not imagine more ideal conditions of living. Last night I was a long time getting to sleep, and roamed through my charming apartment enjoying the wonderful stillness, aware that below my feet was the lovely town of Florence, and that at last I was near you. When I opened the shutters this morning, the charm grew. The quaintness of the outskirts of Florence attracts me greatly. As to the apartment, its only fault is that it is too comfortable and spacious! I am afraid of growing spoiled. One invaluable asset of the apartment is that I have a large verandah where

I can walk and enjoy the fresh air. This means a lot to such an ardent lover of fresh air as I. Yesterday I enjoyed this for a long time, and I can't describe my delight at the complete stillness of the evening, in which one hears only the roaring of the waters of the Arno, falling and tumbling somewhere in the distance. The weather was beautiful, but today to my regret, it is rainy; I have brought you bad weather.

"Thank you, my ever kind friend, for the joy you are giving me. I shall not avail myself of your offer to betake myself to the Villa Oppenheim with a request for horses and carriage. I am a great lover of walking and I am glad one has to walk to reach town. If I should feel tired I can always hire a cab in the town to take me home. I need nothing beyond what is already furnished in my apartment. My trip from Vienna to Florence was as agreeable as my trip from Kamenka to Vienna was unpleasant and tiresome. I suffered from toothache all the way to Vienna, and felt generally sick. In Vienna I had a rest, and changed my mind about going to Venice. This time Italy welcomed me. The weather was quite summery, the sun shed its rays brightly on the countryside, the air was transparently clean and soft.

"I intend to have a good rest from the journey today, and to look round and arrange a scheme of life. I shall begin work tomorrow. Pahulsky can come at two o'clock for a lesson. While you are here I want to acquaint you, at least partly, with my new suite, or better, *ours* (like the symphony). To this end I am arranging some of it for four hands—I shall show Pahulsky the tempo and will send it to you. But first the manuscript must reach me from Petersburg.

"How strange that I rode on the train with Lydia Karlovna and did not recognize her! I noticed only a Russian nurse with a child, and a Russian gentleman, but I did not see your daughter—I would have recognized her from her picture.

"I shall be very much obliged, dear friend, if you will send me the Russian newspapers from time to time. Take care of yourself. A thousand thanks.

"Yours,
"P. Tch."

Alexis took the letter down to the Villa Oppenheim next morning—and thus was inaugurated one of the strangest fortnights ever spent by intimates. That afternoon, Peter Ilyich and Alexis decided to walk to town for the mail, fog or no fog. They passed Nadejda's villa, where from the garden they heard children's voices. The Russian mail was in that day; quite a lot of letters, among them one from Anatol that Peter read on the way home. Tolia had been to a party in Petersburg and had seen his old flame, the too-rich and too-beautiful Panayeff, and was infatuated anew. It troubled the elder brother, this wild tendency of Tolia's to fall madly in love every two weeks; he decided to write Nadejda about it and ask her advice.

At home a note was waiting from the Villa Oppenheim:

"I cannot express, my dearest Peter Ilyich, how happy I am that you like the apartment and that we are so near each other. Since last night my rooms appear even pleasanter and my walk more agreeable. Today I passed your house, looked at all the windows and wondered what you were doing. I am awfully sorry the weather is so bad, but you did not bring it, my dear, it is so nearly all the time. Tomorrow or the day after, the sun should certainly appear.

"I don't know how to thank you for the pleasure you offer me with *our* suite. How much charm the word 'our' contains. *Mon Dieu,* what happiness, to have something in common with you—and at present we have much in common— How good it is! When you are out walking, beloved friend, go by our villa sometime and see where I live. At present my house is full of people. Lydia has two children—there is no Russian nurse, but there are three Germans, including a Czech wet-nurse. Write me, my dear friend, your daily schedule. Just now I played the *Canzonet* of your Violin Concerto, and was delighted beyond description. Today I received the printed piano arrangements of *Onegin* and *Vakoula.*

"Is your apartment warm, my beloved friend? What temperature do you like? I was afraid it would be cold and ordered a fire in the fireplace. I am exceedingly grateful to you, my dear Peter Ilyich, for your willingness to help my protégé Pahulsky; I see in it a proof of your friendship that is beyond price. *Au revoir,* dear neighbor. Now I shall often write you short letters. I will send the newspapers tomorrow, they did not come today.

                          "Loving you with all my soul,
                                    "N. v. M."

Dinner at the pension was excellent that evening, only Peter Ilyich had forgotten to buy cigarettes in town, and the rest of his evening would be ruined. . . . When lo!—like grace from on high appeared Ivan Vasilievitch, in search of a good Russian heart-to-heart talk

with Alexis—a whole package of marvelous cigarettes from Nadejda
under his arm.

Priceless woman! Peter Ilyich sat down and told her so, on paper
she had provided. Told her also about Tolia's amours, and then gave
her the quiet schedule of his day, which he declared had already inspired him to write music. He wanted to finish orchestrating the
suite as quickly as possible. An idea had come to him for a new
opera. "Namely," he wrote, "the *Maid of Orleans,* by Schiller. It
contains wonderful themes for music, and the subject is not yet
worn threadbare. I have thought of it before, and during my last
stay in Petersburg dreamed of it again, but now it begins to attract
me seriously."

Nadejda was of course pleased about the new opera, but her next
letter was mostly concerned with Anatol Ilyich. She did not deplore
his amatory tendencies at all.

"Thank God that he is gay," she wrote. "Let him flutter from flower
to flower; a man like that must not be permitted to be bored, and
above all, must never marry, because then he will let go and be helplessly unhappy. I know more than one such man, prone to melancholy
over nothing; marriage is always fatal because then he has nothing
to look forward to, no more fun! And for the wife it is terrible, having a gloomy, discontented man around all the time. Nothing can
help such a man. As long as he is unmarried, a vague romantic future
sustains and amuses him; a young lover like Anatol dreams of marriage twelve times a year and never has the blues except when he is
temporarily out of love! Don't worry over him, dear friend, and don't
show him too much sympathy; it will be dangerous! The more one
humors a man like that, the more he will let himself go; you should
tell him to pull himself out of his depression, because nobody else can
do it for him."

Daily, now, the two grew into closer intimacy, and ever nearer to
the danger line of meeting. The surroundings alone were enough to
soften anybody's heart. To walk among these hills with their glorious
towers and lichened, sprawling walls, to enter Florence and hear
the noises of the street echoed so strangely at every turn—the horses'
hooves, the cries of street venders. To see flowers everywhere, hung

even upon the walls for sale, and then to walk again into the hills at dusk, watching those three great stars—what were their names?— come softly into view over the cypresses. . . .

"There is a wonderful stillness here," Tchaikowsky wrote his publisher, Jurgenson. "Especially I love the evenings, when I linger on my verandah and revel in the complete absence of all sound. That is strange, you will say; how can one enjoy sound that is absent, or indeed anything that does not exist! But if you were a musician perhaps you too would be permitted to hear, in the night stillness a sound, as though the earth in its flight through space intoned a deep bass note. But this is nonsense. . . ."

Frequently, Nadejda von Meck drove by Tchaikowsky's house. She loved to pass at night, when the light in his windows told her exactly where her friend was, whether he had finished his dinner and gone back to the study, or if he was out somewhere. (The *pension* sent Tchaikowsky's meals upstairs to his apartment.) Peter thrived under this constant care. Has he fruit at dinner? the widow inquires. Will he promise to let her keep him supplied with cigarettes? He must smoke none but the best Turkish tobacco because that is good for the nerves. She will let Ivan bring him three kinds so he can choose. She is so pleased that he saw her villa; will he not come over sometime when she is out, and let Pahulsky show him around?

Tchaikowsky replied at midnight. He could not thank her enough, he said, for her invitation to the villa.

"But forgive me, queer fellow that I am, if I do not avail myself of it until you are gone from Florence. I know that if you tell me I shall meet no one, it will be as you say. But it would all embarrass me terribly—the knowledge that everyone was hiding from me! Please let me come the instant you are gone, and do not be angry. In your house at Moscow, and in Brailov too, I had such a happy feeling of communion with you, all undisturbed by anxiety, and I should like to repeat the experience here."

Nadejda was equal to this refusal as she had been to other rebuffs—because, gently though he always phrased it, Tchaikowsky had refused her more than one. She was quick, this time, to assure

him that she had regretted her invitation even before she had had
his reply. She knew she had promised an impossibility, because the
house was full of children and no one could contract to keep children
invisible. She would be so glad to have him come after they had all
left Florence. . . .

Peter Ilyich, it will be remembered, loved all the world of make-
believe. Indeed, a man who could write the *Nutcracker Suite* and
the waterfall music in *Manfred* must have been more at home in
cloudland than in the marketplace. And so it proved now. The boulevard that ran by his house and Nadejda's was new and wide, paved
on both sides for pedestrians. One afternoon when Peter Ilyich was
out walking, swinging along with his quick, easy stride, an open
victoria approached, drawn by two spanking roans. A lackey sat
beside the driver on the box, and in the back sat two ladies, one in
white with a flash of color, the other all in black.

Tchaikowsky's heart beat high; he tried to look southward over
the roofs of Florence to the far Tuscan hills—but his eye was drawn
irresistibly to the approaching carriage; he fumbled in his waist-
coat for his pince-nez on their black ribbon. . . .

Sure enough, it is Nadejda Philaretovna! And the lady with her
must be her married daughter, Lydia Karlovna. Peter Ilyich bows;
for one instant his heart ceases to beat. Will they stop? The ladies
bow vaguely in return, the driver and lackey touch their hats and the
carriage is gone, rolling down to Florence.

Nadejda, apparently, had not recognized him; she was near-
sighted. Peter went home and wrote her, and his words are the words
of a child that has just seen an angel. To have this spirit, whom until
now he has seen only—and how often!—with his inner eye, appear
thus for an instant and then in an instant be gone from sight—how
strange and how exciting! "Like some enchantment," wrote Peter
Ilyich.

A few nights later he saw Nadejda again, at the opera, and this time
they both enjoyed it. "Hopeless for me to try and say how happy this
made me," wrote Peter, "especially as I knew you had been sick the
day before and this meant you were recovered. I sat just where you

thought you saw me" (Nadejda had not been sure it was he) "right near the trumpets and trombones which are always so extremely active in an opera! Like you, I left after the second act."

As for Nadejda—"How I love you!" she wrote, "and how happy I am to have seen you at the opera! Rising in the morning, my first thought is of you, and all day I am conscious that you are near; your presence seems to inhabit all the air about me! No matter how cold it is, this is where I want to be; your nearness is a never-ending delight. Dear one, you won't leave Florence before I do?"

Happiness has no story, and these two were, for this brief fortnight, happy. Again and again they saw each other at the theatre; sometimes Nadejda took her little daughter Milochka, and Peter Ilyich would put up his opera glasses and watch the two converse. "What can the small one have been telling you?" he asked Nadejda after one of these evenings. "She never stopped talking for a second, and with such animation! Is there anything more captivating than the face of a charming child? Tell Milochka, my friend, that she has a fervent admirer!"

The two became quite used to seeing each other, as time went on. Peter Ilyich, perfectly secure, certain now that Nadejda would never force a meeting, used to watch for her to pass his window. Every morning at twelve o'clock the little procession went by, while upstairs Peter stood behind his shutters. First came Milochka's black poodle, frisking gayly along the pavement, nose to every crack. Then Milochka herself, with her older sister Sonia and the two small cousins, then sometimes, the German governess whom Nadejda found so congenial because she could play piano duets, and lastly, Nadejda herself, tall and distinguished in rich black silk, fashioned as always a little behind the mode.

And as they walk by, does Nadejda look up, does she make a sign to her beloved friend? It is unlikely; Peter's letters never mention a greeting. Perhaps she looks up once very quickly, and then away, her heart beating wildly, and perhaps the small Milochka gazes upward, turning her head backward as they pass, her hand pulled by Fraulein . . . From first to last, Milochka is filled with curiosity concerning this mysterious Peter Ilyich, and so is Sonia, pretty blonde coquette that she is. The time is not far off when Milochka will scheme a daring plot concerning her mother and Peter Ilyich, and will carry it through. . . .

December came and with it a cold, continuous rain, but nobody's spirits seemed affected. Good news arrived from home, too. In Petersburg the Fourth Symphony had been performed with brilliant success. Tchaikowsky sent Modeste's telegram immediately over to the Villa Oppenheim, and with it a letter. "All day," he wrote, "I have been possessed by our symphony, humming it, remembering where and under what circumstances this or that was written. It carries me back two years—how glad I am that now is now! How much has happened since I wrote this symphony; when I began it, I knew you but slightly, but I remember well that every note was written for you. By some intuition I knew that no one would respond to my music so warmly as you, that our souls were kindred, and that many things expressed in this symphony are more comprehensible to you than to anyone in the world. This symphony is my child and I love it greatly, nor am I afraid of its ever disappointing me."

One day, Nadejda sent Lalo's violin concerto around for Peter Ilyich to look through. He wrote her a long letter, criticizing the concerto severely and comparing it unfavorably with Moussorgsky. The widow sent back a quite furious reply; how could Peter compare anyone with Moussorgsky, that barbarian, that musical charlatan? Tchaikowsky replied that he was sorry he had been so intense, but he still insisted that no Frenchman had it in him to "reach those pillars of Hercules which are accessible to the wide and turbulent Russian nature."

Peter's meaning was clear: Moussorgsky might be undisciplined, but he was strong. "Between your opinions and mine," he explained to Nadejda, "a middle path must be chosen. In me there still sits stubbornly the professor of harmony, who daily for twelve years corrected mistakes; hence my extreme sensitiveness to those mistakes.

But never again shall I compare Lalo to Moussorgsky—except to say that in a few details Lalo almost reaches Moussorgsky!"

In other words, the professor of harmony did not retreat one inch from his position.

Every few days, Pahulsky came round from the Villa Oppenheim for a harmony lesson. This was Tchaikowsky's way of repaying the widow for her entertainment here in Florence. It touched her deeply and she was profuse in her thanks. (Pahulsky afterward married Nadejda's favorite daughter, Julia.) The composer's day-to-day criticisms of Pahulsky's musical progress give the lie to Tchaikowsky's own repeated assertions of his inadequacy as a teacher. Very likely the inadequacy extended only to uninteresting pupils.

To Nadejda Philaretovna

Villa Bonciani
Thursday evening Dec. 12, 1878

"I have already written you about Pahulsky, but let me say further that his success in the difficult tasks I set him testifies to a fine instinctive understanding of musical form. Young men who have spent two and three years in harmonic and contrapuntal exercises often flounder hopelessly when they are first required to handle not only the perpendicular harmonic relationships, but the relationship of theme to theme and the symmetrical distribution of these in the whole. Here is where industrious but ungifted pupils are blocked, because brains and industry are not enough; musical sensitiveness is required. And he who lacks it will go no further than aimless, fruitless filling of a vacuum with harmonic and contrapuntal exercises. I am certain now, that Pahulsky can *write music.* Whether he will ever do something really original, time alone will show.

"At the risk of being accused of stubbornness, I return to Lalo. Again I refute what you say about that place we discussed: if the concerto had been written for piano accompaniment, you would be partially right. In comparison with orchestral *timbre,* the note of a piano is, one might say, still-born—a whole note—four beats, cannot be sustained on the piano. Not so in the orchestra. While Sarasate plays his trill on *la,* therefore, the orchestra holds its whole note, *sol,* and at the end, this *sol* will be as vivid as at the beginning—contrary to a pianistic effect. However, my quarrel is not with the actual combination of these two sounds—*la* and *sol*—but I maintain the dissonance has no right to be there, no part in the scheme. Dissonance in itself is the greatest power of music; without it music would be eternal bliss— lost to us would be the privilege of telling in music all our passion and our pain. Consonance is powerless to move and stir us, therefore the tremendous significance of dissonance—but it must be used knowingly, artfully, and with taste.

"When we discuss music, for God's sake, dear friend, don't think I set myself upon the artist's pedestal and enjoy only my own opinions! Of course, it is distasteful to listen to the impertinent chatter of ignorant people who in their blindness deny all that is beyond their comprehension—those who have decided that everything which is not Offenbach is not music but science, the result of mathematical calculation! But to discuss music with you, who are not only dear to me personally, but who possess so much sympathy with my musical ideas—is highly agreeable. Besides, I don't really believe at all in the infallibility of musical specialists. They are too often one-sided; their knowledge paralyzes their senses and while tracing the technique of a piece, they neglect the very essence of music. Whereas an amateur like yourself, a veritable lover of music, gifted with unusual sensitiveness and understanding, is a companion worthy of the most distinguished and learned musician.

"Therefore, my dear, don't hold back your musical opinions. You could never offend my professorial dignity! Many of your musical judgments are original and interesting. For instance, what you said about Anton Rubinstein." ("His music," Nadejda had written, "possesses not one jot of originality, yet it appeals because of its actual physiological agitation, a passionate nervosity that is expressive of the man himself.") . . . "No one" (went on Tchaikowsky) "has defined Anton Rubinstein so precisely before. Professional critics, like Laroche, chant an eternal hymn before the man, never pausing to denote his real place in the world of musical composition.

"Often, you and I do not agree, for example, about Mozart. But what does it matter? Many authoritative musicians share your opinion there."

Only a week remained, now, of this strange intimacy that was so careful to keep without the bounds of reality. As though in fear of parting, the two redoubled their protestations: "I love you with all my heart," wrote Tchaikowsky, throwing caution to the winds; "with

all my soul and with all my strength." Again and again he speaks
of his dependence upon her: "During the last ten years, it seems to
me that I have not made much progress. I don't say this to tempt you
to encourage me; what I mean is that I am no more satisfied with
myself now than I was a decade ago. I have not written one thing, no
matter how short, of which I may say, 'This is perfect.' Not one
measures up to what I *could* do. Perhaps this is salutary, a stimulus to
work; if I were pleased with myself, maybe I should never work
again! Please make no reply to all this; I know well that I shall never
lose your support in what I do. And the knowledge of your sympathy
has become a habit with me, so that while I write, you are always in
my mind. When I write well, it is pleasant to think you will like and
respond to what I have written. In short, I do not believe I could ever
write another line of music, if I did not know that no matter what the
world thinks, my friend will hear and understand."

Nadejda sent books and newspapers and magazines, and Peter
returned them so quickly that Nadejda commented on it. It was true,
Tchaikowsky replied, that he read very quickly, and his friend would
have to set it down as merely one more manifestation of nervousness. "I do everything with feverish haste, as if I feared the book I am
so much interested in would be torn from my hands, or the paper on
which I write my score. This hurry shows itself afterward both in
reading and composing. I forget what I have read so soon that I might
as well never have read it!" .

On December 17th, at half-past four in the afternoon, Tchaikowsky
wrote: "I have spent every moment today until this one, at a new composition. With fear and trembling I have begun, beloved friend, the
opera" (*Jeanne d'Arc*).

And once begun, Tchaikowsky was obsessed with this work. As
usual, he had hideous trouble with the libretto. He would have to go
to Paris, he said, and see the libretto of *Jeanne d'Arc* as it was performed five years ago in Paris; here he had only Joukovsky's translation of Schiller's play and kept running against passages he felt sure
were more dramatic in the original. He is drowned in this libretto,
he says; he cannot find his way in or out.

To Nadejda Philaretovna

Villa Bonciani, Florence
Sunday morning, Dec. 22, 1878

"Let me tell you, beloved friend, that yesterday my heroine, Jeanne d'Arc, managed to get me into a painful state of excitement, and I had a bad night. First of all, I was depressed before the immensity of the task I had set myself. Secondly, although I was satisfied with the scene I had just finished, I by no means felt at peace. This always happens when I have a big and fascinating work ahead. It is not at all easy to explain this condition: I want to write quickly, quickly. Ideas come so fast my head cannot hold them. One grows desperate, at such a time, in realization of human weakness. Before me I see with anguish long days, weeks, months before the thing will be done, before I can even have it on paper to go over and rewrite. I should like to finish it now, this minute, at one stroke of the pen!

"And then in the evening, excited as I was, I picked up the book you had sent, and when I came to the last days of Jeanne d'Arc, to her torture and execution and that first trial when she lost strength and confessed to witchcraft, I was completely crushed. For me her sorrow was suddenly the sorrow and the pity of all mankind. Utterly useless to think of sleep. Early in the morning I took a glass of wine and that helped; I fell asleep.

"Forgive this detailed recital; somehow I feel impelled to make it. Not for nothing do artists call their work their children. Giving birth to them, one experiences the pain and delight of real travail, and at the same time one joyfully anticipates birth."

The book Tchaikowsky spoke of was a luxuriously illustrated volume about Jeanne d'Arc. Nadejda begged him to accept it as a present, but Peter Ilyich sent it back by Ivan. What would a wanderer, a homeless gypsy like himself do with such handsome possessions?

And now Christmas draws near, and Nadejda must go up to Vienna to meet her boys. Her brother Alexander is bringing them over from Russia for the holidays. From now on it will always be the widow who makes the first move. Tchaikowsky has no responsibilities and must fit his plans to hers. Let no reader, therefore, think of Nadejda as a lonely lady following a man about Europe; on the contrary her hours "with" Peter Ilyich are snatched, a result of much plotting, from the manifold duties of her daily life.

Having lived lavishly at the Villa Oppenheim, the widow has trouble parting from her landlord. Tchaikowsky is furious over this. "The rascal!" cries Peter Ilyich. "Can we not wring his neck?" Failing that, let "N. Ph." carry out the man's unjust demands to the letter and then leave him high and dry, minus the generous tip she had planned to bestow. And now that she is really leaving, says Peter, he wants to leave himself; he will stay on just one day to see the Villa Oppenheim, and then Florence will have nothing further to attract him.

"Good-bye, my beloved, incomparable friend!" writes Nadejda. "I write you for the last time from Villa Oppenheim and from your dear neighborhood. I should be very happy if I could think that sometime, somewhere, this happiness might be repeated. My dear, thank you for everything, for all your goodness and kindness to me here. All my life I shall remember with delight this time spent so near you, in constant communion with you."

Two hundred lire were enclosed in the letter, to settle Tchaikowsky's expenses at the Villa Bonciani, and two thousand French francs to have in readiness should he care to publish the new orchestral suite in Paris. Tchaikowsky accepted the Italian money and paid his bill, but the two thousand francs he returned to Nadejda with the fervent plea that she be not angry with him for so doing. Jurgenson would print the suite without cost; moreover, he has money now, 2700 francs in gold, enough to live in wildest luxury until January when Nadejda's quarterly allowance falls due. "I give you my word of honor," finishes Peter Ilyich earnestly, "that I have nothing to spend all this money on, and if need arises I will turn to you without hesitation."

He goes on to thank his friend for the wonderful days here in Florence. She is the source of all the good in his life, and how can he make her realize it? "I was happy here, and at peace; it was light and bright in my soul, and the nearness of my best friend gave a special charm to all my surroundings. Although, due to the manuscript of my suite arriving so late from Petersburg, I did not accomplish my ambition of leaving Florence with a completely finished suite, nevertheless I began an opera and wrote one of the principal scenes. There fore I did not spend my whole time in idleness and can take away with me, not only wonderful memories, but a quiet conscience."

Thus they parted, Nadejda for Vienna, where no less than a crowd of Petersburg friends and relatives awaited her. Peter Ilyich stayed on in Florence. And it is to be doubted which of the two bore the parting harder; time was when Nadejda had been the aggressor in all matters of affection, but that time was definitely past. The widow gathered up her children and her servants and Pahulsky and her thirty boxes—and her daughter Julia—and departed. Peter Ilyich, alone in the Villa Bonciani with the stolid Alexis, gazed upon the empty hills and mourned, half in nostalgia for happier days, half in panic because his best friend was gone.

19

Colonne plays The Tempest. First Orchestral Suite. Antonina again

It was a few days before Christmas when Nadejda herded her retinue onto the Vienna train, carefully distributed in compartments according to sex; she and her three daughters and two Russian maids in one, Pahulsky and the men servants next door. And then the kind of thing began to happen that one had to expect on railroad journeys in 1878. As they went northward it grew colder and colder—blizzards, zero temperature. Nadejda, who loathed the cold, cried out that they might as well be in Moscow, and bade her maid light the stove. First they were suffocated with smoke, and then as Lucretia poked it, flames burst from the iron door. Nadejda leaned out the window and beat with her umbrella on Pahulsky's window, but the train was so noisy she could not be heard. Finally a frantic bang roused Pahulsky; he fetched the conductor and brakeman and after much shouting and furious action the fire was put out.

During the rest of the journey they all froze, and Nadejda arrived in Vienna with a severe cold, fever and headache. Twenty rooms had been reserved for her at the Hotel Metropole, and the hotel director was at the station; he and she being old friends. It was a joke in the family that this man always addressed Nadejda as Excellency, so when Milochka saw the portly form on the platform, she shouted, "Mama, here is your Excellency!" and everyone was much embarrassed.

They trundled in cabs to the Metropole, and soon the boys came shouting in from the Petersburg train with Uncle Alexander, and everybody became noisily busy over the Christmas tree.

Meanwhile Peter Ilyich languished in Florence, too gloomy to so much as walk by the Villa Oppenheim, let alone think of going through it. Weeks ago, he had told Anatol to mail the first three acts of his orchestral suite from Petersburg. He dared not leave Florence until the manuscript arrived, and he could not work further on *Jeanne d'Arc* without seeing the French libretto. It rained and rained, and Peter Ilyich, for want of occupation, wrote a poem! A wild business, he told Nadejda, for him to be writing poetry; it came very hard but he would finish and send it to her. Finally, even the poem ceased to console him and Peter fled northward to Paris, sure that the suite was lost. He would of course rewrite the suite, he said, but not until the new opera was finished. The owner of the Villa Bonciani and all its servants bade him the most cordial farewells, beseeching him to return; his usual "railroad fever," as he called it, was mitigated by the fact that he and Alexis had a compartment to themselves. Nobody asked him a question and nobody stared or whispered that here was a crazy man.

In Paris, Tchaikowsky did the necessary research for *Jeanne d'Arc* convincing himself that Schiller's tragedy, while not historically accurate, was in point of psychologic truth far superior to all other accounts of Jeanne. Early in January, with Schiller's book in his pocket, the composer left Paris for his old retreat, Clarens, in Switzerland. Here, fortunately, the manuscript of his suite arrived from Petersburg after long delay, but Tchaikowsky was too absorbed in the opera to work on anything else.

To Jurgenson

Clarens, January 26, 1878

"Something very interesting has just happened. There exist three remarkable personages, well known to you. The rather bad poet M.N.V.* who wrote some verses for your editions of Russian songs. (2) B.L.† former musical critic for the Russian news. (3) The composer and ex-professor, M. Tchaikowsky.

"About an hour ago, M. Tchaikowsky invited these two gentlemen, who live with him, to the piano and played for them the second act of his opera, *The Maid of Orleans*, on which he is now working. M. Tchaikowsky, who is on the most intimate terms with N.V. and

---

* These were the initials under which Tchaikowsky translated Rubinstein's German songs.

† Tchaikowsky's signature to his newspaper articles.

B.L., conquered his natural timidity and played his new work with great enthusiasm, inspiration and artistic effect. Anyone seeing the delight of these two gentlemen would have thought they had composed the opera themselves! They strutted proudly round the room, openly admiring the music. It ended by the composer, who up to now had successfully simulated modesty, being suddenly overtaken by a spasm of joy, and all three rushed like madmen onto the balcony to cool their disordered nerves in the fresh air and to forget their impatience to hear the other acts—as yet not completed. In vain N.V. and B.L. reminded Tchaikowsky that operas cannot be tossed off like pancakes; he continued in despair over the weakness of human nature and over the impossibility of getting onto paper in one night all the music that had accumulated in his head. At last these kind souls calmed the mad composer and he sat down to write a letter to a certain Moscow publisher. . . ."

But while he professed himself much pleased with the musical half of the opera, Tchaikowsky was impatient with the work of arranging Schiller's play into a libretto. "This literary endeavor will certainly shorten my life by several days," he wrote Nadejda. "I cannot tell you how it exhausts me, nor how many pens I have chewed before I could wring one or two lines from myself! Time and again I left my writing table in despair of finding the proper rhyme or meter, or because I simply could not make the people say the right thing at the right time. As for rhymes, it would be a charity for someone to publish a rhyming dictionary; I believe one exists in German. If there is a Russian one, I have never seen it.

"About the poem I wrote in Florence—my author's heart is filled with pride. Modeste and the others say they like it. May my libretto be as successful!"

But it was not successful. Tchaikowsky wrote, in all, eight operas, and of these only two are known today: *Onegin* and *Pique Dame*. Himself the most subjective of composers, totally incapable of identifying himself with characters unlike himself, Tchaikowsky had a fatal propensity for plunging into operatic subjects that were quite foreign to his natural talent. He seemed to think that he, or a paid librettist, could by sheer force of will and of work, manipulate the stories from large to small, or from black to white. In this he was like

Rameau, who used to boast that he could put the *Gazette de Hollande* to music—and then try it, and fail.

From Vienna, Nadejda wrote a little cautiously about the verses, but she threw caution to the winds in describing Brahms' new violin concerto, which she had just heard Joachim play for the Vienna Musical Society. It was awful!—said she. Even Joachim's marvelous playing could not redeem it; why, it was not a violin piece at all, it was a symphony, with the first themes warring and entangled, then a *cadenza,* then a long, dreamy theme, *pianissimo,* during which everybody went to sleep, including the orchestra. The last movement—well, it was a bit livelier, suggestive of gypsy music, but it was never permitted to move and flow. It was watered wine—said Nadejda, with two exclamation marks. And to think that all those people applauded until their gloves must have cracked, calling for Brahms and shouting bravos, and then calling for Joachim!

No doubt Tchaikowsky, had he been at the concert, would have agreed with Nadejda. As for the kid gloves, both the widow and Peter Ilyich, used to the informality of concerts at home, were impatient with the European custom of dressing for opera and theatre. What, Peter wrote, had the hearing of music to do with white ties and ball gowns? As for the widow's scorn of Brahms' music, let us of a later century remember that Brahms' violin concerto is not easy to comprehend even on second hearing. To the ear of 1879 it must have been doubly difficult.

And the more Nadejda disliked German compositions, the more anxious she was to have Europe become acquainted with Tchaikowsky. Why does he not advertise himself a little, she asks?

Tchaikowsky to Nadejda Philaretovna

Clarens, Feb. 7, 1878

"I will follow your advice and send Bülow" (the famous German orchestral conductor) "a copy of *Onegin.* Usually I hate to push myself with musical celebrities, but Bülow is different because he is really interested in Russian music and in me. Indeed, he is almost the only German musician who admits any musical competition from Russia. You remember what happened to my *Francesca Overture* in

Berlin last winter. Bilze played it twice, really an act of civic courage, seeing the unfortunate fantasia had been severely criticized by all the newspapers after its first performance. The audience did not hiss, they just sat in silent hostility; all modesty aside, I know this was merely prejudice. It is admittedly improper for a Russian name to adorn a German musical program. However, this does not disconcert me; I believe that my time will come, although perhaps long after I am dead."

And now Tchaikowsky, having made sure that Nadejda was going to Paris, told her from Clarens that he had only been waiting to know her plans before making his own. He would come to Paris too, and finish the opera there, where he could be near her.

What a victory for the widow! To know that of his own accord Peter Ilyich was seeking her out, to prepare as in Florence, an apartment for him, to direct the landlord as to his comfort and finally, to send Pahulsky to the station to meet Peter's train! No longer need she fear that she could not make him happy; the Florentine adventure was proved, now: Peter Ilyich was hers forever.

As to Peter himself, he said a dramatic farewell to Clarens. The landlady wept, the landlord embraced him, the chamber-maid wept (so Peter wrote Jurgenson) and finally Peter broke down and wept with them. In Paris he was quite stunned with the magnificent apartment Nadejda had chosen, but learning the rent, he soon fled horrified to more modest quarters, assuring Nadejda by letter that he did not require the surroundings of a prince. And anyway, princes' parlors face the street, and although that means sun and air, it means also the noise of carriages passing, and a man cannot write music against such a symphony.

"I have worked amazingly today," he wrote Nadejda after two weeks on his back street. "I did more than I usually can do in three days. If nothing uncalled-for happens, the opera should be entirely finished in another week. I have written it very quickly indeed; the secret being that I have worked every day with absolute regularity. This is one department of life where my will is iron; when I don't feel like working I can always conquer my disinclination, and persisting, I am soon carried away . . ."

Nadejda watched over him like an alert invisible hen. Are his rooms warm enough?—she asks. Why does he lacerate his nerves by reading such books as *The Brothers Karamazov.* Dickens' *Little Dorrit,* that Peter mentioned, is suitable enough, but Dostoyevsky is not for people like herself and Peter Ilyich. . . . Why doesn't he divert himself with pleasanter things? Has he been to call on Turgeniev, here in Paris?

Tchaikowsky's answer is one of the sincerest things he ever wrote:

To Nadejda Philaretovna

Paris, March 3, 1879
Monday

"My friend, you ask why I don't visit Turgeniev; it is a question that calls for a careful and detailed reply. But because you know me so well and because you will understand, I shall answer in a few words.

"All my life I have suffered from social contacts. Perhaps this suffering is due to a shyness severe enough to be called mania, perhaps I do not need social intercourse, perhaps I lack facility in the minor falsehoods necessary to conversing with a new acquaintance. In short, I cannot define what it is that causes me such pain, but I do know that for years I went about in society and pretended to like it, thereby tormenting myself incredibly. It was not all tragedy; I could tell you many funny things that happened. But God alone knows how I suffered, and if at present I am so happy and feel so much at peace, it is solely because I can live, whether here or in the country, alone, and need see only those persons before whom I can be myself. Never in my life have I gone one step to meet an 'interesting' person, and whenever by chance it has occurred, I have met only with disappointment, sadness and fatigue. Two years ago, Count L. N. Tolstoi, the writer, expressed a desire to make my acquaintance, as he was much interested in music. I made a feeble attempt to hide, but he went to the Conservatory and told Rubinstein he would not leave Moscow until I came down to meet him.

"Now, Tolstoi is a highly talented man, and what he has written is congenial to me; there was no way to avoid a meeting that the world in general would term both flattering and agreeable for me. We met, and I certainly played my part: i. e.: I told him how flattered, pleased and thankful I was to know him—oh, a whole series of the usual inevitable falsehoods. 'I want to know you better,' he said. 'I want to talk to you about music.' And he had barely shaken hands before he stated his own musical views. Beethoven was bereft of talent—this was the start. A great writer, a divinely-gifted searcher of hearts, began by giving utterance, in a tone filled with confidence, to nonsense that would have insulted any musician.

"What could I do? Argue back? Well, I did. I started a dispute. To tell the truth, he deserved a lecture, but how could I stand up and give him one, then and there? Maybe another man would have, but I only played my part, pretending to be serious and amiable. Later he called on me several times, and though I am convinced that Tolstoi is a sincere character, kindly and even to a certain extent sensitive to music (I saw him sob outright when I played at his request the *Andante* from my first quartet), still his acquaintance afforded me nothing but pain and trouble, exactly as any other acquaintance would have done. In sum, one can enjoy a man's company only when, due to years of acquaintance and to mutual interests (especially family interest) one may remain oneself. Otherwise, any company is a burden, insufferable to a nature like mine.

"This, my dear friend, is why I don't call upon Turgeniev or anyone else. There are a number of people here that I could visit; when Saint-Saëns, for instance, was in Moscow he made me promise I would look him up here. Anyone else in my place would already have made the acquaintance of the local musicians. It is a pity I can't do it; I realize how much I miss because of this lack of social ability. You cannot imagine how I have tried to fight this defect, and how I have suffered in the battle. I worked so hard at my own reformation!—and then I decided it was all hopeless. I was too old to change. Only then did I find peace. Three years ago, if I had spent some time in Paris, as now, probably I would even then have kept to myself, but it would have bothered me, and I should have felt remorse. Several times, Turgeniev has expressed sympathy for my music. Viardo has sung my romances. Common sense decrees that I should call on them; to do so would be to my interest. But I have become reconciled to the fact that my shyness has paralyzed my success in the world, and I simply do not care.

"On the other hand, dear friend, when I tell you I am happier now than I have ever been, the words come from my very heart. Yes, now that I may hide in my hole and always be myself, since books and musical notation have become my only society, I am very happy. And as for meeting famous people, let me add that experience has taught me that their books and their music are invariably more interesting than they themselves. But how foolish to write you all this, who know it without my telling!

"I beg, however, to correct one mistake which you share with many. Turgeniev is not married to Viardo, nor has he ever been married to her. She is married to Louis Viardo, and he is still living. Viardo is a very well-known writer, and moreover, the translator of Pushkin. Turgeniev and Viardo are united by bonds of very touching and absolutely pure friendship, which long ago became such a habit that they cannot live apart. This is absolutely true."

This story was obviously a very comforting analogy for Nadejda and Peter Ilyich. The whole letter appealed to Nadejda, and she sympathized with every word. A day or two later, Tchaikowsky wrote Modeste that, "quite unexpectedly," he had finished the opera.

"When you write the last word of your novel you will appreciate the profound joy of feeling that burden slip from one's shoulders. For ten weeks to sit down every day at fixed hours and squeeze music out of one's brain—sometimes with ease, sometimes with difficulty—is no simple matter. But how I shall luxuriate in my earned rest!"

Tchaikowsky wrote Nadejda that he would rest for a day or two, and then return to Russia. He did not want to go, but he must. So for a few days he strutted idly about Paris.

"Like a cock," he wrote his brothers, "You would laugh to see me walking the streets in a new coat (*demi-saison*) and most elegant hat. On my neck I flaunt a silk *plastron* with a coral pin, lilac gloves on my hands. As I pass the glasses on the walls of the Rue de la Paix or the Boulevards, I have to stop and admire myself. I see the reflection of my elegant person also in the windows. A mania for coquetry has seized me (as has happened before). I toy with the lovely thought of buying myself a gold chain and pin. I have ordered a new suit of clothes and a dozen shirts. The money is flying and soon I shall not have a franc in my pocket. But that signifies little as a gift from N. Ph. is due to arrive."

In the evening Peter went out again, feeling distinctly satisfied with himself. How bright and charming these streets, and how he loved this city! Especially fascinating was this new electric illumination installed since his last visit to Paris; he must write Nadejda Philaretovna about it and see if she liked it as well as he. Sauntering along the Rue de Rivoli, past the boulevards, the composer saw his name blazoned

on the billboards; Colonne was to conduct a full orchestral performance of his *Tempest Overture* next Sunday at the Chatelet. Although
Tchaikowsky had been notified of the performance, a warm glow
stole over him; why, these billboards were like home! But the concert
itself would not be like home; Moscow roared applause whether or
no his music pleased, simply out of kindness for himself. But Paris
would offer no wreaths and curtain calls; the music would be badly
played and would be hissed as all his compositions had been hissed
abroad.

Well, thought Peter, he would go to the concert anyway, incognito,
not letting even Colonne know he was there. If the performance was
a failure he could leave town; that was one comfort. To a bird of
passage, what matters his reputation in the most recently forsaken
nest?

As to Nadejda, she was much excited over the approaching concert,
even though Peter Ilyich informed her that the Parisian public would
show scant support to a "barbarian Muscovite." But on Sunday she
was ill and could not go. Peter sat alone in the hall as he had planned,
telling himself before the music began, that he really did not care
what happened. Let them love his music or hate it, they could not
stop him from writing more.

But the composer was due for a surprise, and not a pleasurable one.
In Peter's self-criticism and in the spirit with which he faced disappointment there is something touching; one discerns an artistic courage that does not belong to little men:

To Nadejda Philaretovna

Paris, March 8, 1879

"I cannot resist writing you my impressions about *The Tempest*.
The performance itself was neither very good nor very bad. My music
was greeted with meagre applause and a few hisses, none of which
surprised me because I had expected it. The thing that did surprise
me though, was my own reaction; I was hurt. I had thought myself
capable of more courage, namely, of complete indifference to public
failure. I was terribly excited—a thing I had not anticipated at all!

'But do you know, dear friend, I don't blame the Parisian public

for this. I did not like *The Tempest* myself, today. It is too long, its
form is episodic and unbalanced, the episodes themselves are ruined
because of lack of continuity. This is why I felt badly. I cannot attribute the failure to bad performance or to lack of understanding on
the part of the audience. It would seem that *The Tempest* was a poor
way of introducing myself to Paris. I cannot complain of Colonne's
part in the performance; he must have worked hard and enthusiastically, but it was obvious that the players themselves lacked confidence in my music. They seemed to know beforehand how the audi
ence would react; a few of them smiled and threw knowing glances
at the public, as much as to say, 'Excuse us for serving you so strange
a dish. It isn't our fault.'

"Immediately after *The Tempest* I left the hall and had to take a
long walk before I could compose myself. Now I feel a little sad, but
know that by tomorrow my grief will have passed.

"Anyway I feel very grateful to Colonne and shall write to him immediately. I shall have to trump up a reason for not thanking him in
person. I can tell him I am only passing through Paris and that I am
not feeling well."

Tchaikowsky did write Colonne in much the same words he had
used to Nadejda, and the letter was published in the *Gazette Musicale,*
with editorial comment concerning the "noble and sincere modesty
of this composer."

"As to the feeble applause and somewhat energetic hisses with
which the public greeted my unlucky *Tempest*"—said Tchaikowsky's
letter to Colonne—"they affected me deeply, but did not surprise me.
If a certain degree of prejudice against our Muscovite barbarity had
something to do with this, intrinsic defects of the work itself are also
to blame. The form is diffuse and lacking in proportion. In any case
the performance was excellent, and had nothing to do with the failure
of the work."

The contrast between these two letters and Tchaikowsky's next,
written from Berlin, is a perfect illustration of that moral childishness
and artistic maturity that was Peter Ilyich. After the usual farewells,
the composer had begun the long homeward trek to Russia. Nadejda
remained in Paris. He reached Berlin in brisk style with none of the
accidents that usually beset him en route—no falling downstairs, no

nervous seizures occasioned by farewell wolf hunts. But in Berlin he halted; he had to halt.

To Nadejda Philaretovna

March 16, 1879

"You will be surprised, dear friend, to learn that I am still in Berlin. Something has happened to place me in a very ludicrous light. Nevertheless I shall tell you, because I always tell you everything. In Paris I managed my funds so cleverly that after paying the hotel bill I had not quite enough left to take me to Petersburg, and when I got to Berlin I could not go any further! So I wired Jurgenson to telegraph some money he owes me. I can't imagine why he hasn't answered; I just wired him again. No doubt I shall have the money tonight or tomorrow morning.

"The whole trouble is that during my last days in Paris I was beset by a mania for elegance such as never before visited me, and I foolishly bought all kinds of clothes and linen. The fact that you know very well what a lot of money I had, makes me the more ashamed to confess this childish extravagance.

"But in spite of this incident I must tell you that my finances are in the most brilliant condition; Jurgenson owes me quite a large sum from the sale of my works."

Brilliant though his finances may have appeared, Peter could not leave his Berlin hotel without paying the bill; he waited two days. Nothing from Jurgenson, not a kopek, not a word; nothing from Nadejda. Berlin was a dreadful city!—he wrote. The most depressing and tedious place he had ever visited. Horrible music, performed in horrible beer halls! In one of these beer palaces he had heard his own *Andante* played, from the string quartet—played well, he had to admit, but why must these Germans inhale their music through tobacco smoke and the breath of boiled cabbage?

Finally he wired Nadejda in Paris. Instant relief! Back came her answering telegram, and following it like magic, a man from the banking house of Mendelssohn, calling upon the composer personally. In a frenzy of haste to be out of this hateful city—what city is not hateful to a man with empty pockets?—Tchaikowsky hurried to the bank. Where his friend the Mendelssohn banker disappeared to is unknown, but anyway Peter Ilyich could not get his money be-

cause he forgot his passport, his visiting card and all means of identi-
fication. He had to stay over another day.

So he wandered to the aquarium and watched them feed the croco-
diles. He loved it, he said; it was the nicest thing that had happened
to him in Berlin. Tomorrow before train-time they would feed the
boa constrictors; would he dare to go?—he asked Nadejda. Live rabbits, they gave them! He had seen it once, somewhere else, and it had
quite flattened him out. But if Nadejda should come to Berlin, she
must surely see the aquarium. . . .

With all accounts reckoned, Peter Ilyich abandoned Berlin and the
rabbits and hurried home to Petersburg. But the consciousness of his
shortcomings continued to trouble him. "Whenever I am in need
of money," he confessed to Nadejda, "it means that I am spending
lavishly and without sense. The funds you give me are *enormous;* I
never before dreamed of such richness, and the fact that I, at my age,
cannot keep within my budget speaks badly for me. I hope it will
never happen again. Thank you, thank you and thank you, my dear,
gracious, kind benefactor."

In the middle of March (1879) Tchaikowsky and his brothers went
down to Moscow to hear the Conservatory students give a first performance of *Eugene Onegin.* From a darkened theatre the composer
watched the dress rehearsal; between acts, his former colleagues
rushed to congratulate him. Even Nicholas Rubinstein, usually so
sparing of praise, admitted he had fallen in love with the music. As
to Taneyeff, Tchaikowsky's faithful admirer and severest critic, who
had taken over Tchaikowsky's counterpoint classes at the Conservatory, he could not speak his praise but burst into most unscholarly sobs
which touched Peter Ilyich to the heart. Anton Rubinstein and other
Petersburg people came down to Moscow for the performance—after
all, a Tchaikowsky first night was an event.

Before the curtain went up, Nicholas Rubinstein asked Peter to
come round behind the scenes, and there, to Peter's horror, stood the
whole Conservatory, pupils and teachers. Rubinstein produced a large
wreath of flowers, and coming forward, formally presented it, amid
shouts and calls for "Speech." . . . "God knows," Tchaikowsky told

Nadejda, "how hard this was for me." Between the acts he was called again and again before the curtain, but he knew it was himself they were applauding and not the music. Modeste attributed this coldness on the part of the public to an inadequate, semi-amateur performance, and musical history bears him out: *Onegin* is a favorite opera the world over; its touching lyricism, its waltzes, the gay simplicity of its sentimentality, have a peculiarly intimate appeal.

After the performance there was, of course, a supper for the composer at the Hermitage. Anton Rubinstein came along with his brother, but never a word would he vouchsafe as to whether or no he had liked the opera. Speeches and toasts and more speeches, until, Peter records, "everyone grew merry and I went home at four o'clock with a splitting headache."

He took his headache back to Petersburg, where he was living with Anatol—and a day or two later something happened to give him worse than a headache. While Tchaikowsky was out, the porter had received calls from a lady who would not give her name; also, he told Peter, he had seen a woman waiting near the house. Therefore when Peter, that afternoon, came in from a walk and went to his brother's study, he was more chagrined than surprised to find Antonina. She rushed at him, flung her arms around him, and for two hours told him not only how much she loved him, but how much he loved her. All the time, Anatol in the next room had an ear to the keyhole. Anatol, it will be remembered, had been through the School of Laws and knew the value of a reliable witness. At last Tchaikowsky, in despair of ending the scene, handed the girl a hundred roubles, "for a trip to Moscow." Instantly all her tears were dried and she became very sprightly, reciting stories of men who had loved her since last she had seen Tchaikowsky. Modeste and Anatol came in, she greeted them affectionately, whom half an hour earlier she had called her worst enemies.

"Nothing in the world," Peter wrote Nadejda, "can banish her delusion that I am in love with her and that sooner or later we shall be reconciled. She will not even hear the word divorce, and the man whom last year she commissioned to offer me—through my brother—

a divorce, she now calls a mean schemer who did it because he was in love with her.

"Modeste says she is not a human being, but belongs to a peculiar species which begins and ends with herself."

And now this girl, who from the calm distances of Switzerland and Italy had faded to a merely disagreeable shadow, began once more to assume immediate and terrifying proportions. Tchaikowsky told himself he no longer feared her: "She can bother me now only when she is actually within a few paces of me," he wrote Nadejda. Also, Anatol was ever at his side. But the trouble with Anatol was, he was not firm enough; Anatol was too much like his brother Peter, he would run rather than step on a fly. Anatol was too apt to assume the character of distressed witness rather than protector. Furthermore, Antonina apparently had no intention of remaining even a few paces distant. She had promised to go immediately to Moscow on the money Peter had given her at the last interview and Peter, guileless soul, thought that she had gone and breathed freely.

Anatol's little apartment was on the first floor. A week after he had given Antonina the money, Peter was at home one morning, trying to work; he had taken the manuscript of the orchestral suite— (Number One, in six movements)—out of his trunk and really felt now that he might be able to do something further with it. He played over a few bars, but the house seemed noisy; there was a bumping on the stairs as though boxes were being carried up; somebody new must be moving into the apartment above. . . . Peter put away his work and went out for a walk; he was somehow uneasy. . . .

He had reason to be uneasy. Those boxes were Antonina's; there was a note under his door when he came in, to tell him so. "In imagination I kiss you innumerable times," read Peter, his face stiff with horror. "I know you don't like it very well when done in fact. It was an accident, my moving into your house. Don't be afraid that I am running after you."

An accident! Either this girl was crazy, or she was a cruelly implacable woman. Peter sat down, the letter in his hand, and waited for Anatol. Light steps sounded overhead; Peter got up and crossing the room swiftly, made sure the hall door was fastened. A few more "accidents" of this kind, and he would be reduced to the old slavery of terror. Petersburg had become impossible; hurriedly he wrote Modeste in Moscow arranging that they meet there and go to Kamenka for a visit, taking the deaf and dumb boy with them.

Down went Peter to Moscow—and down went Antonina a day or so later. The night before he left Moscow for Kamenka, she "broke in" upon him—as he phrased it in a letter, and stayed an hour. In the end Peter promised her more money and she went away. Peter went out to dinner with a friend; on his return he found a note from Antonina asking for immediate funds. . . .

Writing an account of this to Anatol from Kamenka a few days later, Tchaikowsky's pen abandoned all dignity and let fly. He referred to Antonina neither by name, nor as "my wife" nor as the "certain person." What he called her—not once but twice, and in capital letters was: The Reptile.

This was written on the 21st of April. April in Kamenka was by no means spring; it was cold and rainy, but it was a place of comparative safety; Antonina could follow him there only by letter. Tchaikowsky worked hard at the orchestral suite, that same suite which had followed him around Italy by mail until it found him in Clarens, and which he planned to dedicate to Nadejda von Meck. Technically, he was satisfied with this, his first orchestral suite, as it progressed. (He was to write five suites in all, including the *Nutcracker*.) It was a free medium for virtuosity in orchestration, and Tchaikowsky knew how to use an orchestra. The work was in D major, a key the composer seemed to favor; he called it a bold, bright key, and he succeeded sometimes in doing very dark and sentimental things with it. But the First Suite, while it satisfied him technically, did not possess, somehow, that other quality Peter so frankly ascribed to his best compositions; it did not come "from the heart."

Meanwhile, letters from Antonina kept pouring in. . . . "Last night," Tchaikowsky wrote Nadejda, "I could not sleep, and today I am a raging fire—all because I saw that person's handwriting. I am ashamed of my weakness in all this."

"Does the Person *never* leave you in peace?" cried Nadejda in return. "Peter Ilyich, I will gladly send you ten or fifteen thousand roubles, if only it will buy you peace. . . . Energy, utmost energy, should be employed in the prosecution of this matter . . ."

But that particular kind of energy was a quality Tchaikowsky never possessed. When he was in a hole he sat there, shivering, until someone pulled him out. Not a pretty picture—until we remember that even when shivering, Peter's fingers could make musical notation. He had indeed, but one energy: artistic energy—and it was never-failing. Here in Kamenka he turned furiously to music, covering sheet after sheet with his delicate, precise penstrokes, as though by sheer force of musical creation he could exorcise the demon of this particular pit. He was wildly anxious to finish the suite so he could begin orchestrating *Jeanne d'Arc,* and he did finish it, and mailed it to Moscow. Finally, at Nadejda's insistence, he went down to Brailov for a brief visit; it was May now and the widow had returned from Paris to Moscow to settle her affairs before moving her family to Brailov for the summer. Peter had no thought of waiting for her there, the Davydoffs needed him at Kamenka; there was no doubt he was both a help and pleasure to all of them. To Anatol he wrote that even Brailov was ruined this time by thoughts of the Reptile. "Don't ever tell her lawyer about Mme Meck," he warned Tolia. "Laugh, and say that because Mme Meck has at times paid me well for musical commissions, it does not follow she can lend me thousands. Tell him the money comes from Leo Vas" (Davydoff, Tchaikowsky's brother-in-law).

But to the widow he wrote happy letters, enclosing lilies-of-the-valley picked on his rambles. He wrote, he told her, with the very pen she had provided for him in Florence at Bonciani. All the little objects Nadejda had put on the Bonciani desk for his convenience, he had brought home to Russia: penknife, eraser, inkstand and the little bell. He expressed himself as very pleased to find Brailov unaltered; except for a big new portrait of Nadejda in the entrance hall, nothing was changed. "This," he wrote, "has great charm for me. Returning to a place where one has been happy, one wishes everything as it was before, and the slightest displacement of objects is a grief. I liked so much being met by the same Marcel, driven by the same Ethim and if I am not mistaken, by the same horses, and to see the familiar face of the watchman. Entering the house I saw the same furniture and flowers, even smelled the same smells, characteristic of each mouse!"

This fear of change was a very noticeable trait in Tchaikowsky; when he moved from one apartment to another, or even from one hotel to another, Alexis was required to set up certain pictures and small objects in exactly the position they had occupied previously. Peter Ilyich seemed to derive therefrom a sense of security—that illusion of permanence without which no man can endure the humiliation of his own mortality. Tchaikowsky longed for roots, yet his nature forever repudiated those responsibilities which are the price of permanent relationships; to achieve roots, a man must sacrifice wings. For this great human privilege of being rooted, for the deep and healthy consciousness of being part of the continuity of life, linked to past and to future, fortune demands a price—and the man who dodges the price is forever a man outside of life. Refusing Nadejda's repeated proffers of gifts—handsome books, pianos, organs—Peter explained that he was a nomad, a gypsy, and what right has a gypsy to possessions?

In truth Peter Ilyich was less than a gypsy; he was a ghost, a phantom. And he walked the earth, he called man Brother, by one right only—by virtue of the great gift of music he had for mankind.

At Brailov, Tchaikowsky had planned to rest and had not brought the new opera with him, thinking he would do a better job on the big task of orchestration if he waited until he was back in Kamenka. So he walked and picnicked and talked to the peasants and villagers —but always, whether at church or in the forest or day-dreaming pleasantly on the river bank, music was in his mind.

Tchaikowsky to Nadejda

Brailov
May 17, 1879

"Yesterday, after writing you and brother Anatoly, I began to read the score of *Lohengrin,* which I had brought with me. I know you are not an admirer of Wagner, nor am I. Wagnerism as a principle can never have my support and Wagner as a personality provokes my distaste. But I must give due homage to his tremendous musical gift, which in my opinion shines at its brightest in *Lohengrin.* This opera is the crown of his creative stature; after it his talent began to crumble, disintegrated by his own satanic arrogance. He so lost his sense of proportion that everything he wrote after *Lohengrin* is impossible to comprehend, and will therefore, perish.

"But I am especially interested in *Lohengrin* just now from the standpoint of orchestration. Before beginning my own work I wanted to study the score of *Lohengrin* very carefully to see if I could use some of Wagner's orchestral methods. His mastership is amazing, but for reasons that would involve too much technical explanation, I shall not borrow anything from him. For vocal purposes, Wagner's orchestration is over-symphonic, over-rich and ponderous. The older I grow, the more convinced I am that these two branches of music, symphony and opera, are complete opposites. Therefore the study of *Lohengrin* will never cause me to change my manner, but for this very reason it has been of value as a study."

Within walking distance of the big house at Brailov was the Monastery where Tchaikowsky loved to attend Mass. He became much interested in the rebuilding of a Roman Catholic chapel on the estate, which had been interrupted long ago by a government that supported, of course, the Greek Orthodox Church. Tchaikowsky wrote Nadejda about this, pleading for her support; whatever her own beliefs she should, he insisted, encourage freedom of religion. Brailov should make no distinctions between ritualistic forms. . . . "I have just come from Mass at the Monastery," he wrote on May 21st. "The church and courtyard were crowded with people, and I heard the blind 'lyre singer.' The man accompanies himself on an instrument he calls a lyre, but which really has no relation to the antique instrument of that name. In the Ukraine, the blind have a refrain which they sing over

and over, always to the same accompaniment; I used this tune as a
theme in the first movement of my piano concerto" (the B Flat Minor
Concerto that Rubinstein had repudiated and then played with so
much success in Paris)—

Tchaikowsky stayed at Brailov for three weeks; this time he had
written no music to leave as a gesture of thanks to his hostess. So he
wrote a diary every day, and left that. Just before he started for Kamenka, something happened to please him. June was nearly here,
yet Peter had been able to find no lilies-of-the-valley, although he had
searched Brailov from end to end. And on this last morning came a
knock at the door, and there was Marcel, the estate superintendent,
smiling, his arms filled with crisp green and white fragrance. Peter
shouted aloud, from surprise and pleasure. "Where did you ever find
them?" he asked at once, and Marcel answered, "Two miles from
here, in the garden of the abandoned farm-house we call Simaki."

He had thought Brailov the summit of earthly happiness, wrote
Peter Ilyich to his hostess. What then was Simaki, but heaven?

He did not know that this particular heaven was for him but two
months distant.

20

Brailov à deux. The Maid completed, also the First Suite

It was nearly June; Brailov was ready to bloom with brighter flowers than the shy white bells Tchaikowsky loved. All the riot of a Ukrainian summer quivered beneath the wild bright green of the wheat—high time for Nadejda to bring her family south from Moscow. And if Peter had been so happy there in the manor, how much happier he would be at Simaki by the river, alone in his own little house! Heaven then, would be open to them both. . . . Nadejda wrote him so, begging him to occupy Simaki for the summer. "Nightingales will sing in your garden," said she. "You will have six rooms at your disposal, low-ceilinged, shaded by huge old trees. No one lives within sight, and although I shall not be able to walk near your apartment every day, as I did in Florence, still I can feel that you are near, and then I shall be gay and calm and fearless! Peter Ilyich, come, and I promise that you will never be disturbed; I will send you a light, pretty boat and your Alexis can take you rowing! Ten paces from your house the forest begins, and by moon light you can walk between the forest and the river. . . . Oh, my dear, kind friend, if you would consent to spend the summer there, just two miles from me?"

Nadejda sent this letter, and then set forth for Kiev at the same moment Peter Ilyich was boarding the train from Brailov to Kamenka. In the night, at Kazatino, their trains crossed, and for twenty minutes stood side by side at the station. Tchaikowsky was out roaming around the platform in the rain; he instantly recognized Nadejda's palatial private car. It was enormous, nearly twice as long as the ordinary car, and it was marked with the name of her own Kazan Railroad. All the curtains were drawn and Nadejda was sleeping; Peter waited to see if Pahulsky would perhaps come out and he could ask after Nadejda's health, but there was no sign, and soon the two were hurrying from each other through the night.

Nadejda replied to this news with a gay impudence unusual to her.
Had she but known how near he was, said she, she would at least have
peeked at him through a hole in the curtain. . . . But oh, what happiness to be in Brailov just after Peter Ilyich! It is next best to having
him as guest. Everywhere she feels his presence; in the forest, on the
cliff. The rooms he occupied have lost their anonymity; forever now
they will bear a title: *"Bedroom of Peter Ilyich. Parlor of Peter Ilyich"*;
the same nightingale has sung for them both, and she thanks God that
such happiness is hers.

And when in a few days Tchaikowsky replied that he would love
nothing better than to come to Simaki, Nadejda was willing to wait
another month until he could leave his family at Kamenka. She
agreed that he ought not to disappoint his sister and all the young
Davydoffs by cutting short his visit.

As to Peter himself, he had swung bodily into that state of half-
ecstasy, half-frenzy, which was his when working.

To Nadejda Philaretovna
Kamenka, June 4,
Ten P. M.

"I have begun working very hard. The orchestration of an opera is
pleasant and should not call for much strain. It is the kind of work
that would give me much pleasure if my nature did not require me
forever to hurry, forever to feel a despairing consciousness of the lack
of time and my own inadequacy. I want to be done all in a moment,
whereas to write a big orchestral score like *The Maid of Orleans* requires months of tenacious work. But in about ten days the first act
will be ready.

"P. Tchaikowsky

"With your permission, I shall write you only once a week for a while.
Until the opera is finished, I must plan all my days and my cor-
respondence with the strictest regularity. I shall write you every
Wednesday."

This sense of hurry was not, with Tchaikowsky, merely a nervous
restlessness. It lay far deeper; it was a consciousness of the value of
time, a deep conviction which was near to divination—that every
moment is God-given, more precious than any single gift man has
from heaven. It is a quality not found in little men, and Peter had it

at its most intense—a double awareness of the glory of life and the imminence of death. *Death looks over man's shoulder and says, Live! I am coming.* . . .

Three days earlier than his prophecy, on June 10th, 1879, Tchaikowsky finished the first act of the *Maid of Orleans.*

"It is a bulky score," he wrote Nadejda. "And what a pleasure to see it completed! For a musician, an orchestral score is more than a collection of notes and rests; it is a whole picture, in which the main figure and the secondary ones and then the foundation—the scene itself, is realized. Any orchestral score is for me not only prophetic of future pleasure to the ear, but direct and instant delight to the eye. I therefore observe meticulous neatness in my scores and suffer no erasure, corrections or inkstains. Some day I want to display my musical penmanship to you; very soon I hope to show you one of my scores. If, as I hope, I come to Brailov while you are there, I shall send the opera score to you at the big house."

Tchaikowsky had reason to be proud of his orchestral scores, and not merely on behalf of penmanship. He had a real mastery of instrumentation; even today, composers study his scores as he himself studied Wagner's, to see if perchance they may profit by his methods.

Two weeks later, on June 12th, Tchaikowsky reported further advance. He could not sleep, he said, but it was only his accustomed summer wakefulness, which did not interfere with the quality of his work.

"My work advances fairly rapidly. It tires me a bit, especially at this time of year because of the heat and the annoyance of flies. On the other hand, it gives me great pleasure. It is hard to express the delight I feel when an abstract musical thought assumes real form, transmitted to an instrument or group of instruments. This is perhaps the happiest moment in the process of creation. And when I can realize as now, that the music I am instrumenting is my own, there is a double pleasure. Besides, *Jeanne d'Arc* has another charm for me—every note reminds me of that last journey abroad which was so very pleasant. In about two days, I shall be transported thus to Florence and the Villa Bonciani, because I shall then set to work on the scene from which I began the opera in Florence."

Next day, Wednesday, 6 A. M.

"Twenty years ago today my mother died. This was the first real grief I suffered. Her death had tremendous influence upon the course of my life, and that of my family. In the full bloom of maturity, she died quite suddenly of cholera. Every minute of that awful day remains in my memory as if it were yesterday.

"Your
"P. Tchaikowsky"

Tchaikowsky's letters from Kamenka do not often speak at length or in detail of his work at hand. News is set down at hazard and includes everything from the worm scourge which has attacked Leo Davydoff's beets to an enthusiastic account of his sister Alexandra's healing power over the sick. After two weeks of abstinence the composer again began writing to Nadejda every day, in the form of a diary or bulletin. . . . *Onegin* was to have a second performance in Moscow, ordered by the Grand Duke Constantine . . . Good news had arrived from abroad concerning his compositions; in Wiesbaden and London he had had great successes. And Colonne—that same Colonne whose orchestra had given Peter Ilyich chills and fever, playing *The Tempest* to an unresponsive Paris audience—Colonne had written that he wanted more Tchaikowsky music to play, hisses or no hisses! But the best news of all, said Tchaikowsky, was the fact that his arrangement of the *Liturgy of Saint Chrysostom*—for mixed chorus—had been sung several times in the University Church at Kiev; long ago he had thought the work doomed to oblivion.

Nadejda expressed herself much pleased over all this, but would it not be well to follow up the European successes by some gesture of compliment to the conductors who had played his music—Colonne in Paris and Bülow in Germany? Why not dedicate an opera to the one and a concerto to the other? These foreigners were very susceptible to flattery. . . . Peter Ilyich, who always replied meticulously to Nadejda's questions, sometimes numbering his answers, 1, 2, 3, 4, 5— to this made no reply whatever. More than once he had told her he was incapable of toadying, of "self-advertising," he called it.

Meanwhile Antonina was again in pursuit. She had hunted up Anatol in Moscow to demand an increase in pension. Don't you do it! cried Nadejda, reiterating the old refrain. Be firm, Peter Ilyich, Be *firm!* . . . Peter sat down instantly and wrote Anatol, attempting the firmness Nadejda had advised, and succeeding only in being nervous and blustering. "One must be as flint," he wrote, "so as not to let the Reptile imagine she scares me. Believe me, in everything she does lurks a vague but undoubted desire to blackmail. And I haven't the money, not a kopek, and God knows whether it will come soon."

Nadejda, it seems, had offered to send the June allowance some time ago, to which Tchaikowsky had replied that he was in no hurry at all, and this somewhat grandiose gesture was now causing him the utmost concern. Peter Ilyich complaining about money is an unusual and somewhat disconcerting sight; it had never happened until Antonina appeared. Fortunately, his fear was momentary and Peter was soon restored to his gentle, hard-working self.

Meanwhile Nadejda von Meck down in Brailov, all unconscious of these alarums, was joyfully preparing for Peter's visit. He would come, he had said, as soon as he finished orchestrating the second act of his opera. So the widow drove to Simaki farm with her little daughter Milochka, and the two busied themselves over the cottage, hanging curtains, arranging lamps. Milochka became so excited that she went to bed that night and dreamed about Peter Ilyich. Next morning she told her mother she was determined to pay him a visit as soon as he came.

The boat-house was ready, Nadejda wrote, and the bath-house at the bottom of the garden should Peter Ilyich choose to bathe in the river. But Tchaikowsky doubted if he would enjoy the boat: "I only enjoy the kind of motion that is very personal and spontaneous, like walking," he wrote. "Where I may turn from the road and stop if I choose to lose myself in meditation or musical composition. I like to go on foot and alone. Perhaps on a wide river or lake I might enjoy boating by myself, but as I have never done it, I can't say for sure. I do know that the narrow space of a boat and the necessity to sit still are irksome to me. But I am perfectly willing to try to learn the pleasure of water sport when I come to Simaki."

On the 22nd of August, Tchaikowsky and Alexis left Kamenka. Peter was glad to go; much game hunting had been toward, this last week; Anatol was there and loved to shoot birds, but the sight of blood made Peter sick, even if it were only the blood of ducks. Also, the Davydoff children had been ill with fever and dysentery; there was nothing an uncle could do to help, and the opera was suffering in consequence of his own sympathetic distress for his sister.

The travellers arrived at Brailov in the evening. Vladislav Pahulsky met them with his best Warsaw bow, handed Peter Ilyich the keys to his house and garden and expressed himself enraptured to welcome Russia's greatest musician. It was a beautiful summer night and Tchaikowsky was enchanted with all he found. On his writing-table lay a note of welcome from his hostess, just as it had lain the night he arrived in Florence—and just as reassuring. "My dearest friend," he read. "If you need anything, I beg you to ask your servants; your usual staff will be at hand. I hope you will drive and walk in the forest and have tea served anywhere you please. There are so many of these forests that we shall not disturb each other; moreover, we can arrange beforehand who will go to which place. But because I know how particular you are about this, I shall inform you every morning where we intend to go on the day following.

"I greet you, my dear, with both my hands. . . . Loving you with all my heart.

"N. v. Meck

"P. S. On your desk you will find everything necessary for writing."

Instantly and with enthusiasm Peter Ilyich took the postscriptum hint. It was all perfect—he wrote gayly, and far surpassed his happiest imaginings. Tomorrow he would set to work orchestrating the last act of *Jeanne d'Arc,* and when it was finished he could breath freely and enjoy the consciousness of having accomplished a difficult task. "A delight," said the composer to his hostess, "that is second to none."

And now began three of the happiest weeks of Tchaikowsky's life.

It is a pleasure to read these Simaki letters, because when Peter was happy he was so very happy. No applause of multitudes, no toasts drunk nor wreaths presented upon a glittering stage, could content him as did the blissful solitude of his low-roofed farm-house. The garden was all delicious shade, deep green under boughs of ancient oak and lime trees; from his verandah the land sloped downward to a stream, and through the trees beyond one caught a glimpse of sunny fields and the village. Nadejda had placed at her guest's disposal an old man-servant named Leon, a cook and a coachman with a phaeton and four horses. Completest solitude was his. Pahulsky ran in with frequent messages, but the messages were welcome and the Polish bows were brief. Besides, Pahulsky adored music and Tchaikowsky liked to teach him and here in Simaki, gave him many lessons in musical theory.

Peter Ilyich to Nadejda Philaretovna
Simaki
August 24, 1879
at 7 P. M.

"I am sitting on the verandah enjoying the wonderful night and mentally addressing thanks to the author of my welfare. I slept wonderfully last night, and directly after morning coffee started work and didn't notice the time until they called me to lunch. After going through that indispensable ceremony with the greatest pleasure, I set to work again and kept at it until four, when I decided to take a long walk, seeing the weather had cleared. I went down through the kitchen gardens to a small birch grove, crossed a ditch and after following various paths and pushing through many hedges, found myself in a forest. I don't know what forest it was. I know only that, standing at the edge of it, I could see Mariengay and the spire of the monastery church in the distance, and to the right, the roof of the mills, the barracks and the green alley leading to Simaki.

"I did not meet *one single soul,* which for me is the greatest charm of walking, and after two hours and a half of brisk exercise I was back at my peerless dwelling! I wrote four letters and then brought my desk out to the porch to write you these lines in the wonderful fresh country air, which is something we have to do without in Kamenka.

"I have no words to tell you how well I feel here, how easy and brave. Thank you, my friend. Until tomorrow. . . ."

On that same day, Peter Ilyich wrote Modeste of his happiness, adding, however, that he was a little troubled by the proximity of Nadejda Philaretovna: "I know," he wrote, "that this is foolish, and that my solitude will not be broken into, but I am so used to thinking of Nadejda Ph. as a kind of far-away, invisible angel that the consciousness of her near and mortal presence is disturbing."

Peter Ilyich was on his guard, therefore, when Pahulsky announced that another visitor was coming:

To Nadejda Philaretovna

August 23
at 8 P. M.

"Mr. Pahulsky has told me that next time he comes he intends to bring Milochka. Now, I am fond of Milochka, I enjoy her charming face in photographs; I know she is a wonderful child, very dear and sweet. Also, I like children very much, and naturally such an offer should receive the answer, 'Yes, I shall be very glad, etc.' This is how I answered Mr. Pahulsky, but it is not what I shall say to you. . . .

"Forgive me, dear friend and laugh if you will at my queerness, but I shall not invite Milochka to visit me, and this is why: My relationship with you, exactly as it now stands, is my greatest happiness and the rock on which all my welfare rests. I do not want it to change even a little. I have become used to thinking of you as my good and invisible angel. All the charm, all the poesy of my friendship with you is based on the fact that you are so close to me, so infinitely dear to my heart, and yet in the ordinary sense of the word, we are not acquainted. And this same condition of not meeting, must extend to those most nearly related to you.

"I want to love Milochka as I have loved her until now. Should she appear in the flesh, the charm would be broken. Every member of your family is close to my heart, Milochka especially—but for God's sake, let it remain as it is. What could I reply if Milochka asked me why I do not call on her mother? I should be compelled to open our acquaintance with a *lie*—a very innocent one, but still, a lie, and I should find this hard. Forgive me, my own dear wonderful friend, for my frankness.

"Today I went again to the forest where I walked yesterday, and my pleasant sensations were all repeated. My work goes excellently. I should like to be alone a few days longer and therefore have not in-

vited Mr. Pahulsky to come again, although I like him very much and
shall be very glad to see him when I have had more solitude.

                                            "Yours,
                                              "P. Tchaikowsky

"If you have any Beethoven sonatas, will you be kind enough to send
them to me?"

Nadejda's answer was reassuring: "I understand our relationship,
my dearest Peter Ilyich," she wrote, "quite as you do. And like you, I
don't wish to change it in any way. I laughed to myself at Pahulsky's
naïveté. He really thought Milochka might go to you; she is forever
plaguing him to take her. I told her however, that it would be quite
out of the question for you to be disturbed at your work. You guessed
rightly that the child's curiosity has been roused and she is filled with
questions. One day she asked me, 'Is it true you have not even met
Peter Ilyich?' I don't remember just when I must have told her we
were not acquainted. I replied that on the contrary I knew you very
well and loved you very much. She was quite satisfied with this for an
answer. So you see, my dear friend, in this matter our feelings are the
same, and we understand one another.

"I send you the sonatas. Forgive the deplorable condition in which
you find them; my Sasha" (Nadejda's son) "has pulled them to
pieces. I am so happy that your work advances successfully.

                                            "Heartily yours,
                                              "N. von Meck."

Next day Nadejda wrote asking her guest to visit the big house. On
his former visit it had been empty, and no home looks the same that
is not lived in. Tchaikowsky replied that he would come with greatest pleasure, and would his hostess tell him what day she would go to
the forest? Not this week, please, because he is working so quickly
and well that if he keeps at it he should be through the whole orchestration by the end of the week. He will enjoy the big house more with
a heart free of musical anxiety. He has, he adds, been mushroom hunting but has not yet found enough to send her some. . . .

But if hostess and guest were content with this strange ghostly
friendship, others were not so satisfied. The widow's children were
consumed with curiosity concerning Peter Ilyich. Milochka in particular, a child of seven with her mother's black hair and her mother's

brilliant black eyes and big, generous mouth—could not bear to let romance rest in the clouds; she must needs bring it to earth, where the young know that romance belongs. So she plotted and schemed, and one day—it was the last day of August—she managed to delay dinner until very late. Dinner in the Russia of 1879 was eaten at four in the afternoon, so at four Peter Ilyich, thinking his hostess two miles away in her big dining-room, surrounded by her family, sallied forth for a drive to the mushroom forest. Alexis sat on the box with Ethim the coachman, Tchaikowsky sat in the phaeton and Leon, the old servant whom Nadejda had appointed as second valet to Tchaikowsky, rode on the footman's box behind.

The carriage rolled merrily along woodland roads, across a stream and around a field; Tchaikowsky sitting quite silent, unaware of anything save the sweet summer air and the shadowed tracery of leafy branches across the road ahead. Suddenly another carriage approached—a whole cavalcade of carriages which must pass slowly on the narrow road; Peter heard laughter and voices which evidently did not belong to peasants or servants. The first carriage drew alongside, Tchaikowsky looked up and met Nadejda face to face, her eyes level with his. He was dreadfully confused, he wrote Anatol afterward. He bowed, but Nadejda seemed even more at a loss. For one long moment a dreadful tension reigned, and then, returning his bow, Nadejda ordered her coachman to drive on.

Peter Ilyich continued his drive, saying nothing to the servants, but he was quick to write his hostess:

To Nadejda Philaretovna

August 30, at 8 P. M.

"I have just got home. For God's sake, Nadejda Philaretovna, forgive me for miscalculating the time so carelessly, and meeting you. Now I have no doubt provoked renewed questions from Milochka and new complications for you in explaining why the mysterious inhabitant of Simaki farm enjoys your hospitality but refuses to visit you at your house. Instead of walking out at four as I usually do, I left home a little earlier.

"How charming Milochka is!

"I have worked so hard that I have nearly finished the first half of the last act.

"Yours,
"P. Tchaikowsky"

As for the widow, her reaction to the meeting was not at all like Tchaikowsky's, nor did she trouble to pretend that it was:

Nadejda Philaretovna to Peter Ilyich

Brailov
Thursday

"You apologize, dear friend, because you met me, while I am delighted to have met you! I cannot tell you how comforting it was to meet like that. It convinced me of the reality of your presence in Brailov. I don't seek any close personal relationship with you, but I love to be near you passively, tacitly—to be under the same roof with you, as in the theatre in Florence, and to meet you on the road. To feel you, not as myth but as a living man whom I love sincerely and from whom I receive so much—this gives me greatest delight. To me these occasions are extraordinary good fortune.

"When first we met I did not realize who it was, as we often pass carriages and I exchange bows without inquiring as to the person. This time, looking neither at the driver nor the horses, I merely noticed a bow—which I learned later came from your Alexis. I returned it, and only when my eye fell upon Leon riding behind did I realize whom we had met, and I felt so gay and splendid that tears came to my eyes and I myself asked Milochka if she knew whom we had passed. She did not, but a long conversation arose about you. Don't think though, dear friend, that her questions or pleadings trouble me. When she asks why we don't exchange visits, I tell her it is because you are composing beautiful music and must not be disturbed. This always quiets her and she asks merely what you are composing at the moment. Our meeting reminded her how she had met you in the street at Florence—she added, 'but he did not see us.' She told me that her German governess often asks why we never go to Simaki any more, and that she has to run away to avoid telling a lie! She is well able to keep a secret. When we got home she put her arms around Pahulsky's neck and whispered that we had met you, not daring to say it aloud although no one was in the room but me.

"Yours,
"N. von Meck"

Neither of them ever mentioned this episode again; Tchaikowsky's apprehension of danger was acute, and the widow took her tone from him. Anyway the topic changed immediately: Would Nadejda please send him some books? Tolstoi and Dostoyevsky, or Dickens if she had a good Russian or French translation. He liked to read at night, and while eating his solitary meals. He must tell his hostess, the letter continues, about the delightful family of rabbits that is living under his verandah. Such a nice animal, the rabbit! And on the roof a whole family of cats with kittens. Now he need not fear his great and ancient enemies the rat and mouse, and besides, he likes cats and kittens. Everything in Simaki is heavenly, and as to his opera, the end is in sight, which makes him only the more furiously impatient to reach it.

Like most artists, Tchaikowsky craved solitude and was vociferous about it, but like most artists he was very particular about the kind of solitude he required; just any old solitude would by no means do. The surroundings must be quite perfect, not in the sense of luxury but of natural beauty; also, a companion must be within calling distance. One day at Brailov, for instance, Peter Ilyich, in search of solitude, launched himself into the forest and got lost. In some agitation he found his way into sunlight and broad field—but he had left his *pince-nez* at home, and stare though he would, all four points of the compass remained but forest and green field. So Peter did literally what he had so often done figuratively when in a bad place, he stood still and shouted for rescue. He shouted loud, until he was hoarse, and at last Ethim came running. . . .

When he got home he sat on the verandah, resting and thinking about his nearly completed orchestral suite. How had he been so unobservant as to write the first five movements in four-four rhythm? It would be intolerably monotonous. . . . The summer air was soft, the bells of the monastery carried sweetly across the fields, and suddenly Peter heard a new melody in his head—in three-four time. He hurried inside and set to work, and before two days were gone he had added a redeeming sixth movement to the suite, a *minuet* which he called (by want, he told Nadejda of a better name) *Divertimento*.

And while her guest wrote and rested and hunted the elusive mush-

room, Nadejda up at the big house gloried in his proximity and devised further means for his happiness. Taking tea on the river bank
one afternoon, watching her boys row vigorously up stream, a splendid thought occurred to her, a plan for bringing herself and Peter
Ilyich closer without violating sanctuary. Why not marry one of her
boys to a Davydoff, to any one of the Tchaikowsky nieces? It would
by no means be a step down for a von Meck to marry a Davydoff; and
as for dowry, the Davydoff name was dowry enough. Kolia was only
fourteen it was true, still a schoolboy, but Nadejda was aware that
these things can never be arranged too soon. One never knows at
what ridiculous age a boy will become infatuated and ruin himself
with the wrong marriage. No continental mother ever despised love
matches more than the widow von Meck.

Casually then, Nadejda inquired the age of Natasha, the youngest
Tchaikowsky niece. He told her and she thanked him. "Guess why
I want to know!" she challenged.

Peter Ilyich replied that he had guessed already, and that nothing
would please him better than such a match. His letter provoked a
long correspondence on the subject of marriage. Her dear friend
knew, began Nadejda, that she was a mortal foe to marriage; perhaps
he would think her present plan inconsistent with her principles? But
the point of the matter was that having preached the evils of marriage
endlessly to her four elder children and seen them go off and marry
anyway, this time she would not try to throw herself against the stream
but would swim a length ahead, and make for her children "a suitable
choice that might avoid for them the futile entanglements of passion."

Poor Nadejda! Twelve children had not diminished the strength
of her own passions; behold her then, by repeated denial seeking to
destroy that demon which was in truth the very angel of her inmost
nature. Perhaps, she suggested to Peter Ilyich, your Natasha may not
like my Kolia? Well, and what if he doesn't? Falling in love. . . .
Bah! said Nadejda: "This is the very nonsense I wish to eliminate in
marriage. Let husband and wife learn to appreciate each others' moral
qualities, and love each other in consequence."

This was not so priggish as it sounds; by moral qualities the widow meant more than virtue; she meant personality, *flair*—the things that had made her love Peter Ilyich. Only one thing troubled her. Reminding Peter Ilyich that she, as mother-in-law, had never met her son-in-law's parents, had even stayed away from her favorite son's wedding for fear of the in-laws—what, she asked, would the Davydoffs think of such a queer, ridiculously shy woman?

Tchaikowsky's reply was soothing. Surely these two children would be happy together, and as to Nadejda's shyness, let it not trouble her at all. Already, the Davydoffs knew and loved her, through him. But let us wait, dear friend, he cautioned. Let us not be in haste; after all, these are but children.

Very well, she would wait, the widow replied. But oh, Peter Ilyich, suppose she should die before the plan took effect? With characteristic despotism she proceeded to plan for that eventuality also. This time her assurance seems a little ingenuous, perhaps even a little pathetic:

"If I should not live until that day, I shall will my plan to Julia,* who upon my death will be entrusted with all my interests, affections and desires—I am convinced the matter will be in good hands. My love and friendship for you I entrust to her also, and I will you, my dearest friend, to transfer to her the relationship between us, which is so dear to me. She and I will talk it over with you further at the proper time."

Tchaikowsky was always agitated by the thought of death, not because he feared it but because he loved to work. He did not want to die while music remained in him. The moment he had Nadejda's letter, he replied to it. He was anxious, he wrote, to live a long time; it would require many years for his musical ability to reach its full peak. But the thought that he might outlive his friend was unbearable. Might he, however, while they were on the subject, make one request? If Nadejda Philaretovna should outlive him, would she take his servant Alexis? He had grown so fond of Alexis, a friend rather than a servant; he could not abandon him to the service of strangers. . .

* Nadejda's daughter.

"But let us have an end to this conversation!" said Peter Ilyich. "Let us live, my dear good friend. We shall always have time to die!"

Let us live! Again and again throughout his life Tchaikowsky said it; nervous sufferer though he was, even his deepest depressions were not those of your true melancholic; rather they appeared as the temporary exhaustion of a too-sensitive nature—compensation and counterbalance for the ecstasy he received at the other end of the wire. Peter Ilyich loved life, not as your optimist loves it, unconsciously, taking it for granted—but rather with the furious and grateful joy of the pessimist who, expecting evil and eternal darkness, discovers every morning anew the sun. Glorious surprise, bounteous gift of heaven! Seize it, Peter Ilyich, take life in your hand and hold every moment tightly, tightly; use this moment fully ere it escape forever. . . .

Thus Peter Ilyich to himself, and thus he let slip a line of it to his friend. But Nadejda was not concerned with time. Nadejda was not one who loved life for itself—heaven had vouchsafed her no such gift. Rather, she fought life, as though with characteristic imperiousness she cried to it: Life—prove yourself! You have put me here, in this black and troublesome place. . . . Now, show me what you have to offer!

But in Tchaikowsky's letter, one phrase blinded the widow to all the rest. "My dearest friend," she replied, "I cannot resist telling you of the deep ineffable gratitude inspired in me by one of your sentences, 'But the thought that I may outlive you is unbearable.' *Mon dieu,* how I thank you for those words, and how precious they are. If you could imagine how I love you! It is not only love, but worship and adoration. If I feel sad or painful or afflicted, a few kind words from you can make me forget and forgive everything. Then I know I am not alone in the world; there is a heart that feels as mine feels, a man who understands and is in sympathy with me and who speaks of me in such a kind, human way. How grateful I am, and how dear you are to me! I have read that sentence scores of times each day since it came, and from the fullness of my heart unconsciously pressed the letter to my side."

Sometimes, reading these outbursts of Nadejda's, the reader trembles, wondering if Tchaikowsky will be equal to such emotional assault. Will he flee? Will he simply pack up and leave, instructing Anatol by mail to "arrange matters" for him? Will he answer Nadejda at all?

But of course he answers, and in kind! Her letter, he vows, gave him infinite joy. He knows it is wrong for him ever to doubt her love, and yet he does doubt; he needs the assurance of her word. But when this dread comes, when he darkly knows that she is far above him and all her love undeserved, then he has but one consolation—his music. Whatever its merits or demerits, his music is real, it has been wrought in deepest sincerity; may it lift him, then, to that high place on which Nadejda stands by her very nature.

And now especially, he needs her. Again the Certain Person is on his trail. She has repudiated all their agreements, she refuses a divorce and wants more money. What will be the end of it, God only knows. . . . Furthermore, today he finished proof-reading the piano arrangement of the third act of *Jeanne* and the *Marche Slav,* and now he has no work even should he desire it.

"In spite of the pleasure of knowing I have earned the right to idleness, I prefer that other more salutary condition, when serious work absorbs one's every thought and feeling. Sometimes this is upsetting, but on the other hand it has power to lift one out of any temporary dissatisfaction, whether one's own, or due to a care for one's fellow men. No sooner am I idle than thousands of disquieting thoughts rush upon me, as though glad I was free to welcome them. The moment I ceased work this time, I was besieged by remembrances of the alarming condition of my sister's health, your frequent headaches, Anatoly's job in Petersburg and some of the annoyances of Modeste's position as tutor in Mr. Conradi's house. And Tasia" (Tchaikowsky's youngest Davydoff niece)—"and the as yet unsatisfactory management of Brailov farms that we have discussed, and the fate of my opera" (*Jeanne d'Arc*) "which will reach the stage God only knows when.

"On top of all this, fear and grief because I must soon leave Simaki grew so strong that I was on the verge of tears, and when Leon" (the old servant Nadejda had assigned to Peter Ilyich) "entered my room, I almost embraced him! In a word, my nerves, aware they are not needed for work, have relaxed. To collect myself I took a long walk to a distant forest where I have never been. It helped me greatly and now on my return I feel only my usual joy at the realization that I am still in Simaki, writing you from a distance of only two miles. These remaining days I shall enjoy the right I have earned to idleness."

And now that his orchestral suite was completed, Peter Ilyich accepted his hostess' oft-repeated invitation to visit her house. Elaborate plans were made so that they should not meet, and this time nothing miscarried. Tchaikowsky spent two hours roaming around the big house, upstairs and down.

"How I love this house!" he wrote. "Especially the rooms on the ground floor, yours and the ones I had when I was here before. I spent most of the time sitting in your room, and it would be hard to tell you how confident and happy I felt, there in a room you had just left and which was still so full of you. All the new furniture is most attractive, the cupboards and tables and the antique clock with its figures of knights. You can never guess which of all the familiar objects I like best: the embroidered bandit in my room! I myself can't imagine why that terrible man is dear to me; nothing is in fact, more inartistic than an embroidered human figure.

"I played your piano and pianino, had tea, went through Mr. Pahulsky's rooms and walked in the park. I came away in the pleasantest frame of mind, one reason was that in your album, among the cards of your closest friends I came upon my photograph—twice. It touched me to discover myself the only person in the book who is not a member of your family."

Tchaikowsky had called himself idle; as a matter of fact, when the Suite was done he kept right on working at Simaki to finish orchestrating the *Maid of Orleans;* this was accomplished the first week in September. As it was, Tchaikowsky had gone too fast with this work; conceived nine months ago in Florence, its composer had written another big work along with it—the First Orchestral Suite. The *Maid* was a four-act, six-scene opera; whether excessive haste or an unfortunate subject defeated him, something did. From the whole opera only one song survives: Jeanne's lovely aria, *Adieu forêts*

Tchaikowsky finished with *Jeanne* on a day of annual festivity for
Brailov manor-house. It was young Alexander (Sasha) von Meck's
name-day. In the afternoon Peter Ilyich saw the procession of flower-
garlanded boats float down the stream, and in the evening went again
to the summer-house by the pond to watch the fireworks and the little
regatta of lantern-strung boats. Twice, Nadejda passed close to him
where he stood hidden by trees. What pranks had Milochka been up
to?—he asked Nadejda later. Time and again he heard her name
called with much severity, not Baby, but Milochka. He had smiled
to himself, standing there; he had admired Sonia's perfect French
accent as the girl scolded her older sister for having gone off with the
boat just because she herself got to the river a minute late! Kolia,
rowing gallantly down in a decorated barge, shouted to the peasants
on the bank: "Isn't it fine?" "Isn't it splendid?" It was all Peter Ilyich
could do, he confessed, to keep from shouting back, "Yes, it's very
fine indeed!" Then Nadejda's handsome mastiff ran close to the
summer-house and Peter shrank back, fearful lest the huge creature
mistake him for a tramp; the rattle-box scared him, and the watchman scared him too, poking about with his lantern.

When Kolia heard about his invisible sympathizer on the bank, he
was immensely pleased and asked his mother to thank Peter Ilyich.
It was characteristic of the boy, said Nadejda, to want to be sure
everyone was enjoying the spectacle. Her other young son would not
have cared enough to ask for approval. As to Sonia, her mother dared
not tell her Peter Ilyich had been looking on because the girl's French
governess had wrapped her in shawls, and Sonia would die of chagrin to have had anyone see her thus. Sonia's French and German
were indeed excellent, but she spoke Russian like a foreigner; she
had an accent and could not pronounce the hard "l"—Deplorable!
—said Nadejda, and must be corrected. Had Peter Ilyich noticed how
she herself had hurried everyone? It was because she was afraid of
keeping him standing there too long; they had all been thrilled to
know he was watching.

All the time he was in Brailov, Tchaikowsky had busied himself
every few days teaching harmony to Vladislav Pahulsky. Early in

September Pahulsky's older brother appeared from Poland for a visit. Both were musicians, but Nadejda was vehement in her preference. "My Pahulsky," she wrote, "is impressionable, enthusiastic, passionate, whereas his elder brother is nothing more than a Warsaw gentleman, more like an Englishman than a Pole, always self-possessed. Vladislav may commit ten follies a day and still have more of my sympathy than his irreproachable brother; V. is a restless enthusiast, with an infinitely kind and passionate nature. Which of them do you prefer, my friend?"

Tchaikowsky's reply was tinged with caution. In Paris and Florence last winter he had spent not a little time over Vladislav Pahulsky's music, and Vladislav, as far as work was concerned, had not overtaxed himself in return:

"You ask, dear friend, which character wins my sympathy: the passionate Vladislav or his wooden brother? Certainly, the former! But frankly, here is how I feel about Vladislav: The abundance of flaming youth that he possesses and which is evident in his every word, has of course, great charm, but at the same time, it carries danger. It is imperative that he devote himself to deeds, action—not to words alone. I don't know why, but Pahulsky seems to me like one of Turgeniev's heroes—a man greatly gifted, sincere in his desire to achieve great things, and yet . . ."

Please God, went on Peter Ilyich, Nadejda would be able to influence Pahulsky to work harder, especially at counterpoint. Let Pahulsky not be angry if Nadejda should repeat this to him, let him see how much his teacher liked him and wished him well. . . .

And now into paradise, into this quiet heaven under the ancient lime trees, came disquieting news. From Petersburg, Anatol telegraphed that he had lost his job, owing to "an unpleasantness" in his department. He was most anxious, said the message, to talk with Peter. Dreadfully distressed, Tchaikowsky ordered Alexis to make ready for immediate departure. Into the carryall went the comfortable country clothes, notably the cool wash suits of heavy rough silk imported from China—so much enjoyed by Russian country gentlemen. Into the carryall went also the First Orchestral Suite and the *Maid of Orleans*, both works fully orchestrated and ready for printing press or public stage.

Good-bye and good-bye, my kindest hostess!—cried Tchaikowsky And good-bye, my incomparable, my precious friend!—replied the widow. May we meet again very, very soon. . . .

21

*Nadejda's confession. Tchaikowsky's fame
begins to spread in Europe*

Tchaikowsky went back to Petersburg, homesick for Brailov the instant he left it and feeling, here in the city, dazed and unhappy as if he had been struck, he said, butt-end on the head. As to Nadejda, down in Brailov alone, something epochal had just occurred. Jurgenson had sent her Klindworth's long-delayed piano arrangement of the Fourth Symphony—"our" symphony. Over and over she had played it and as a result had lain awake for two nights in fever and in frenzy. In this music she vowed she heard the whole story of her life; had she been condemned to die for listening, she would, she protested, have listened just the same.

So completely did the symphony disarm her that Nadejda wrote an extraordinary letter, revealing not only her emotion of the moment, but the long pent-up reality of her suffering at the time of Tchaikowsky's marriage two years ago.

Nadejda Philaretovna to Peter Ilyich
Brailov
Sept. 26, 1879
Friday at 8 A. M.
"How sorry I am, my dearest, that you feel so badly in Petersburg, but—forgive me—I am glad you are homesick for Brailov. I doubt if you could ever understand how jealous I am of you, in spite of the absence of personal contact between us. Do you know that I am jealous in the most unpardonable way, as a woman is jealous of the man she loves? Do you know that when you married it was terribly hard for me, as though something had broken in my heart? The thought that you were near that woman was bitter and unbearable. And do you know what a wicked person I am? I rejoiced when you were unhappy with her! I reproached myself for that feeling. I don't think I betrayed myself in any way, and yet I could not destroy my feelings. They are

342

something a person does not order. I hated that woman because she did not make you happy, but I would have hated her a hundred times more if you had been happy with her. I thought she had robbed me of what should be mine only, what is my right, because I love you more than anyone and value you above everything in the world. If this knowledge bothers you, forgive my involuntary confession. I have spoken out. The reason is, the symphony. But I believe it is better for you to know that I am not such an idealistic person as you think. And then, it cannot change anything in our relationship. I don't want any change. I should like to be sure that nothing will be changed as my life draws to its close, that nobody . . . But that I have no right to say. Forgive me and forget all I have said—my mind is upset.

"Forgive me, please, and realize that I feel well and that I am in need of nothing. Good-bye, dear friend; forget this letter, but do not forget your heartily loving,

"N. von Meck

"P.S. Would you mind, please, acknowledging the receipt of this letter?"

This was the first and last time that Nadejda ever asked to have a letter acknowledged. And mark this: She wanted to be sure that nothing in their relationship would change, "that nobody . . . But this I have no right to say." Did Nadejda mean that she hoped Peter Ilyich would never take another wife, that no woman would come between them again? If so—and what else could she have meant?—she must in truth have been totally ignorant of one dominant trait in her friend's nature.

Tchaikowsky answered from Grankino, on his way to Kamenka. Petersburg and Moscow had in turn proved too much for him—especially Moscow, where the instant he showed his head, friends appeared in swarms, urging him to breakfast with them, dine with them. "Oh, Moscow!" cried Peter Ilyich to his brother. "The instant one arrives, one is expected to get drunk."

Answering Nadejda's reckless confession, Tchaikowsky did the wise thing and the only thing he could have done. He ignored all that had been said about Antonina and about jealousy, and gave expression to his very honest pleasure in Nadejda's reaction toward the symphony.

To Nadejda Philaretovna

Grankino
Oct. 10, 1879

"It is impossible to say how glad I was to see your handwriting and to know we were again in communication. Jurgenson forgot to tell me that the piano arrangement of our symphony had at last been published, so your letter was the first news I had of it. I am tremendously elated that you are satisfied with the arrangement, which in truth is well and skillfully done.

"As for the music itself, I knew beforehand that you would like it; how could it have been otherwise? I wrote it with you constantly in mind. At that time, I was not nearly so intimate with you as now, but already I sensed vaguely that no one in the world could respond more keenly to the deepest and most secret gropings of my soul. No musical dedication has ever been more seriously meant. It was spoken not only on my part but on yours; the symphony was not, in truth, mine but *ours*. Forever it will remain my favorite work, as the monument of a time when upon a deep, insidiously-growing mental disease, upon a whole series of unbearable sufferings, grief and despair, suddenly, hope dawned and the sun of happiness began to shine—and that sun was embodied in the person to whom the symphony was dedicated.

"I tremble to think what might have happened if fate had not sent you to me. I owe you everything: Life, the chance to pursue freedom —that hitherto unattainable ambition, and such abundance of good fortune as had never occurred to me even in dreams.

"I read your letter with gratitude and love too strong for expression in any medium but music. May I be able some time to express it thus!

"Dear friend, may you keep well. I wish it for you more than for myself. Reading how our symphony caused you sleepless nights, I felt my heart constricted. I want my music henceforth to be a source of joy and consolation, and with all my strength I desire for you a spirit well and calm.

"Yours,
"P. Tchaikowsky"

Was ever man more elusive and yet more honest? Nadejda von Meck, fired with music and with love begotten of music, had confessed, and her confession had in it nothing ethereal, nothing other-worldly. It was the letter of a woman to a man, a woman deeply enamoured, asking nothing—except insomuch as such a declaration asks everything. Tchaikowsky's reply had not been slow in coming, nor was it cold. It glowed—but not, as had the widow's words—with fire. Behind Peter's words was not heat but light; this was incandescence; this was the whole reflection of a man who could be, to woman, never man, but spirit only. Peter Ilyich was a ghost, and his name was Music. . . .

Nadejda did not forget herself again. If music was indeed to be all the food of love, why then, she would have more nourishment and more! Why should not Colonne, who had played the *Tempest* in Paris last winter, play the Fourth Symphony, she, of course, to supply the funds? Tchaikowsky received her suggestion in Kamenka and wrote to thank her:

To Nadejda Philaretovna

Kamenka
Oct. 12, 1879

"Concerning the performance of our symphony by Colonne, first let me thank you, my dear kind friend, for your care concerning my glory! Certainly, I should like extremely to have Colonne play the symphony, although I know beforehand that it can meet with no success in France. I don't feel at all sure of what Colonne will say to your suggestion. It is considered a great opportunity to be on one of his programs, an honor that even the Parisian composers solicit in vain. It may easily be that Colonne could not dare to play a whole symphony written by a foreigner; it was an act of great civic courage in him to play my *Tempest,* which consists of only one movement. Whether or no the fact that you offer him money will be a deciding factor I cannot say, but anyway, dear friend, I warn you not to be surprised if Colonne turns down your proposition quite politely and firmly."

As soon as she had Tchaikowsky's approval, the widow, who by now had, as usual in autumn, left Brailov for the continent—"for the West"—the Russians call it, and hurried to Paris to set the musical wheels in motion. Tchaikowsky's warning had not been unwarranted. Nadejda found that the names von Meck and Tchaikowsky, which opened wide every musical door in Russia, in Paris fell on unresponsive ears.

A gentleman could elbow in where a lady could not, suggested Pahulsky, all afire for action. Suppose the three of them went to Colonne's concert next Sunday at the Chatelet? Afterward he, Pahulsky, could waylay the grand vizier at the stage door. . . .

Next Sunday the grand vizier (so Nadejda called him in her letter to Tchaikowsky) was bearded as per schedule. After some trouble Pahulsky succeeded in seeing Colonne alone and telling his story. . . . So Russia would like to have Tchaikowsky's Fourth Symphony played at the Chatelet? said Colonne dryly. . . . Not Russia, explained Pahulsky, eagerly. A lady, a great admirer of Monsieur Tchaikowsky's talent. A Madame von Meck who knew that M. Colonne appreciated the Russian maestro's compositions.

"Ah, a lady!" said Colonne, with eloquent inflection. And who, he inquired blandly, would pay the expenses of all this? Tchaikowsky's publisher? It cost money to produce a symphony.

Pahulsky was indignant. He flushed. By no means the publisher. The *lady* would pay. M. Tchaikowsky was far too famous to need any such stimulus to the sale of his works; publishers all over Europe were fighting for his name on their lists. Besides, M. Tchaikowsky was a gentleman born, with a good position in society. . . .

Mr. Colonne's tone changed. He smiled. He made an appointment to discuss the matter further with M. Pahulsky next day. And when tomorrow came, Colonne agreed to play the symphony, provided that after two rehearsals the usual committee of musicians approved the score. Suppressing a sigh of relief, Pahulsky got to his feet and bowed. M. Colonne bowed too, then darting to a table, extracted from a drawer two large photographs of himself and signed them with a flourish— One for Pahulsky and one, he explained with a smile, for Madame von Meck. Nadejda, waiting in her hotel for this news, rushed off and telegraphed Moscow for the score of the symphony. Then she wrote Tchaikowsky the whole story, half in triumph, half in derision. "M. Colonne," said the widow, "at first gave himself airs." Until, in fact, his palm had felt the flutter of green-and-white paper. Then the airs had turned to friendliness, even enthusiasm. Money, thought the widow, grimly, that could assault any pride.

The committee passed favorably upon the score when it came, and Nadejda was beside herself with delight. Tchaikowsky was in Kamenka; Nadejda kept her letter, knowing that Peter Ilyich was coming abroad very soon, and would stop in Paris. Meanwhile, in Kamenka, Peter had had depressing musical news from Moscow. His professional objectiveness—the only objectiveness he possessed—did not fail him, however, and he was able to criticize his opera *Vakoula* (written in 1874) as severely as the audience apparently had criticized it.

To Nadejda Philaretovna

Kamenka
October 24, 1879

"Yesterday I heard from brother Anatol about the performance of *Vakoula* in Petersburg. The theatre was crowded but the reception was cool, which Anatol attributed to the really awful performance. I myself, however, see that coolness as the result of my own grave mistakes. I like to think that *Jeanne d'Arc* is free from this false operatic manner—consisting of a tiresome superfluity of detail, a too-intricate harmonization and lack of proportion in orchestral effects. In *Vakoula* the listener is presented with too much spiced musical food and no repose whatever.

"Operatic style should be broad, simple and at the same time pictorial, whereas *Vakoula* was written in the style of a symphony or even of quartet music. I am surprised the opera was not a complete failure long ago, I can't see why it attracts an audience or indeed why it appears on the stage at all. The way it seems to be going, perhaps some day the public will even like it! My own reaction as a listener is that while I am conscious of its defects as an opera, still I place it in the front rank of my compositions. I wrote it with love and delight, the way I wrote *Onegin,* the Fourth Symphony and the Second Quartet.

"P. Tchaikowsky"

Had Tchaikowsky turned these operatic criticisms round the other way, he would have been nearer the mark. *Vakoula* (heard in New York in 1922 as *Oxana's Caprice*) is by far the better of the two operas, both dramatically and musically. But whether or no the composer wrote *Vakoula* with "love and delight," it does not deserve a place with *Onegin* and the Fourth Symphony—and neither does the Second

String Quartet. Peter's theory about operatic style was sound, but he did not, unfortunately, know how to practise it.

Vakoula's reception in Moscow was poor. However, only a day or two later the composer heard that Nicholas Rubinstein had played his new piano sonata superbly, and that Moscow had received it well. Tchaikowsky went to Moscow on business and then up to Petersburg to take train for Paris and Nadejda. They had planned another fortnight "together." From Petersburg at two in the morning he wrote one of the most blandly self-critical notes ever penned from gentleman to lady at that time of day:

To Nadejda Philaretovna

Petersburg
Nov. 10, 1879
Two A. M.

"My dear, kind friend,

"The journey was not unpleasant. I spent two days in Moscow proof-reading and saw all the Conservatory people, including N. G. Rubinstein who wanted me to hear how he plays my sonata." (This was the G major Sonata written in the spring of 1878.) "He plays it wonderfully; I am sorry you could not hear it. I was astonished at the amazing artistic effect he got from that rather dry and complicated piece."

This time, Tchaikowsky was right in his self-criticism. The G major Sonata is dry, now as then.

And now once more, the cold Warsaw Station at night, the long journey to Berlin and Paris. Then the Gare du Nord early on a November morning, with Pahulsky bowing eagerly from the platform, Nadejda's letter in his hand. But Pahulsky could not wait for Peter Ilyich to read the news; in the cab rattling over cobblestones to Tchaikowsky's hotel, Pahulsky related all the Colonne story. As soon as he reached his rooms, Tchaikowsky wrote Nadejda: "Thank you, dear friend, for this new proof of your sympathy with my music. You have rendered great service to the cause of spreading my music beyond Russia. I know the public will be hard upon our symphony, but its performance will excite interest, and this is what I need most just now."

Pahulsky went home and told Nadejda that Peter Ilyich had promised to write his thanks to Colonne. The widow was pleased, but she cautioned Tchaikowsky to come right out and tell Colonne that his admirers, not his publishers, were behind this project. She wanted it plain that this performance was a gesture of love, inspired by extremest enthusiasm for Tchaikowsky's talent—not a mere scheme of publishers and professional musical promoters. Would Peter Ilyich therefore, please explain to Colonne that she was the "best friend" mentioned in the dedication?

Tchaikowsky replied that he would be only too glad to do so; it was what he himself had desired. After this exchange the two were silent concerning the symphony; the performance was not to take place for over a month, and Tchaikowsky busied himself with other work. He settled down easily in Paris; by now, he and Nadejda were so used to living in the same city that they accepted the situation like any old married couple reunited. Tchaikowsky began work at once, sketching the first rough draft of a new piano concerto (his Second Piano Concerto, to be dedicated to Nicholas Rubinstein).

During this November and December in Paris, Nadejda provoked from Peter some interesting critical opinions concerning his own early works, Berlioz and the recently published *Paraphrase,* a set of twenty-four variations written by the Petersburg composers, Borodin, Cui, Liadov and Rimsky-Korsakov:

To Nadejda Philaretovna

Paris
Nov. 30, 1879

"I know the *Variations,* by Rimsky-Korsakov & Co. Of its kind, the work is certainly unusual and displays remarkable harmonic virtuosity. However, I don't like it. Even as a *tour de force* it is heavy, bulky and difficult to digest with all those tiresome thematic repetitions. As an artistic creation it is nul. It is not surprising that a few talented people should invent for their own delectation a set of variations on a trivial drawing-room theme, but it is amazing that such a work should be published and advertised. Only amateurs imagine that any piquantly conceived chord is worth printing.

"As for Liszt, he is an old hypocrite who replies to any piece submitted to his august judgment with the most exaggerated flattery. By nature he is kind; indeed he is one of the few famous artists who has never been touched by jealousy or the temptation to impede the success of his fellow-men. Wagner and—in part—Anton Rubinstein owe their success to him, and he has done a great deal for Berlioz. But he is too much the hypocrite to be trusted for sincere criticism."

To Nadejda Philaretovna

Paris,
Dec. 1, 1879

"Yesterday I heard Pasdeloup's concert. They performed two acts from Berlioz' *Siege of Troy,* both of which met with frenzied applause. The French are a queer people. Whatever appears under the name of Berlioz is received with uniform rapture. In truth the *Siege of Troy* is a weak, tedious piece, revealing the principal defects of its composer; namely, poverty of melody, over-harmonization and an imagination too rich for its owner's musical invention. Berlioz was a high-minded man who conceived beautiful things but lacked the power to fulfill his conceptions. The performance itself was mediocre, rather bad in fact, but this did not prevent the audience from going mad with enthusiasm.

"You ask, dear friend, if I wrote any early works that were never published. Indeed I did, and many of them! And how I bless the Fates that did not permit me to find an amateur who might have been willing to publish all that infantile lisping, which at the time I considered serious composition! A few of my early things have been preserved, most of them I burned. Among these, *Voyevoda,* from which the dances were saved, and *Undine.* The latter was rejected by the directors of the Petersburg theatres in 1868, at which I was much offended, but later I was thankful enough that the directors had rendered me this service. It was an atrocious opera, and I threw it in the fire without a regret."

Curiously enough, Tchaikowsky's criticism of his own work was frequently more objective as well as more just than his criticism of his contemporaries. He was quite right in recognizing that his highest powers were symphonic rather than operatic. Nevertheless the drama had for him a fascination that drew him again and again to the stage, with all its panoply of costume and color—and all the hateful wire-pulling necessary to achieve operatic production.

To Nadejda Philaretovna

Paris
Dec. 10, 1879

"You ask about *Voyevoda*, and I reply that there is no doubt about its being a very poor opera. In so saying, I take into consideration not only the intrinsic merits of the music, but all the other requirements of good opera. First, the subject itself is void of all dramatic interest and movement; secondly, I wrote it hastily and carelessly, so that the final libretto was not fit for any stage. I did not know enough to be aware of the tremendous difference between operatic and symphonic style. The composer of an opera must never for a moment forget the stage, he must realize that in the theatre more is required than melody and harmony; action must exist for the satisfaction of an audience which comes not alone to listen, but to look.

"Lastly, operatic style must correspond to the style of mural or scene painting; it must be plain, clear and colorful. Put a Meissonier painting on a theatre stage and all the charm of its delicate detail will be lost. And the same with music; small, fragile, intricate harmonies are overlooked in a theatre, where what is needed is brightly-outlined melody and clear harmonic design. Writing the *Voyevoda*, I lost sight of the stage and its requirements and busied myself tracing a thematic filigree.

"Naturally, these theatrical requirements paralyze to a great extent the composer's purely musical inspiration, and this is why symphonic or chamber music is far superior to operatic music. Writing a symphony or sonata, I am free, I feel no constraint and no false limitation. On the other hand, opera has an advantage in that it speaks to the masses in a language they can understand. Also the fact that an opera may be performed forty times in a season gives it preference over a symphony which may be heard once in ten years!

"After hearing an opera several times, a hostile listener may become friendly to the work—but what a long time it takes for the masses to appreciate a good symphony! In spite of the temptations of the operatic siren, I take far greater pleasure in composing symphony, sonata or string quartet.

"To return to *Voyevoda*, the orchestral effect is far too massive, and over-rides the voice parts. These defects were all due to inexperience. To reach perfection, a whole series of trial-and-error is necessary, therefore I am not ashamed of my failures. They served their purpose as lessons and as sign posts to further effort. You may gather from all this, dear friend, how stubbornly I refused to recognize my own faults, and how slow I was to admit the practical requirements of operatic writing. *Undine* (the opera I burned) as well as the *Oprich-nik* and *Vakoula* are none of them what they should have been. It is not an easy science for me to master, but I believe I handled the *Maid of Orleans* properly. Perhaps, however, I am once more mistaken, and if this proves so, if even the *Maid* does not come up to the requirements of operatic style, it will be plain that the people who • say I am by nature exclusively a symphonist and that I should never attempt the stage—are right. Then for once and all I shall give up trying to write opera."

Nadejda was persistent in urging Peter Ilyich to give some of his compositions to a French or German publisher and thus advertise himself abroad in a legitimate and dignified way. From the rest of Tchaikowsky's letter it will be seen that Nadejda was not the only tempter to woo him thus. His refusal and his reasons for it are proof enough of why Jurgenson, Tchaikowsky's Russian publisher, remained a lifelong friend. There is loyalty here as well as independence and the warm quality of gratitude which was, with Tchaikowsky, a never-failing trait:

"By the way, yesterday I had an offer from Furstner, a Berlin publisher, for all my future works. He asks me to name my terms, and this is not the first such offer I have had from German publishers. It is all very flattering but I refused, and this is why: Long before I enjoyed any musical reputation, Jurgenson willingly undertook to publish my things, at first free of charge and then at a very reasonable fee. Later, he began to publish anything and everything I wrote, and as you know, I write a lot. Up to now, owing to slowness of recognition where music is concerned, I have not earned him a cent, because while a few of my things sell well, others lie forever on the shelves of his warehouse. He bases all his calculations on the hope that some day my reputation will cross the frontier and my works will move in a free European market.

"So doesn't it follow that just now when my name is becoming known in Europe, it would be unfair to confine Jurgenson's profit on my works to Russia? Besides, I don't want to cater to the German prejudice against Russian music. For a long time now, the Germans have sent their own musical goods to Russia and refused to export anything therefrom. They actually prefer to pirate an edition—as they did with my short pieces and romances—rather than buy the music from a Russian publisher. Probably Jurgenson will be the first Russian publisher to have his editions ordered from abroad. I believe it is the duty of every honest Russian to refuse relentlessly any such German offers.

"So yesterday I wrote Furstner a polite but decisive refusal."

It was nearly Christmas when Tchaikowsky wrote this in Paris. Nadejda was planning to leave France immediately in order to spend the holidays at home in Brailov, and Peter Ilyich, whose nomad life was to continue for some six years before he would see fit to find himself a homestead in Russia, was well content to celebrate Christmas in Rome with Modeste and his pupil and of course, the ever-faithful Alexis. This time his farewells to Nadejda were not so ardent. He was not to be left completely alone and moreover, a heavy program of work lay ahead. Here in Paris he had finished the rough draft of the new (and second) piano concerto. His farewell letter does not omit the usual inexorable summing-up of work accomplished during the Paris visit. In Rome he hoped to rewrite the Second Symphony. His notebook, he said, was filled.

Fortunately, Nadejda was one of those rare women who are capable of feeling that a man's work is more important than any personal attachment; indeed, for her the two things were in this case, synonymous. And curiously enough, when the Fourth Symphony was finally played by Colonne, both Nadejda and the composer had left Paris. Tchaikowsky had not been to so much as a rehearsal; whether indifference or shyness kept him away, no one knew. But Colonne, emerging from the wings for the final performance before his fashionable holiday audience at the Chatelet, must surely have thought it strange that he had had no word from either Tchaikowsky or the bountiful benefactress. Oh, well, all Russians were queer, how could one expect conventional behavior from a couple of barbarian Tartars?

And as one of the barbarian Tartars had predicted, his symphony was received rather coldly. Yet the venture was well worth while; Nadejda had done her friend a service. This performance marked the beginning of Tchaikowsky's recognition in Europe. A few days later his finest string quartet, the third (E flat minor) was played in Paris, together with his B minor Serenade for violin, with orchestral accompaniment. In Berlin, Budapest and New York the brilliant, staccato B Flat Minor Piano Concerto (over which Tchaikowsky and Rubinstein had quarrelled) was performed with great success, and Leopold Damrosch wrote that New York had enjoyed the (first) orchestral suite enormously. This of course, was the suite upon which Tchaikowsky had worked so hard at intervals during the past year, and had finished upon his last visit to Brailov in August—the one to which he had with so much satisfaction added a sixth movement in slow waltz time, conceived upon the verandah of Nadejda's Simaki farm-house.

22

Rome—Russia—A present from Nadejda

TCHAIKOWSKY went down to Rome at Christmas-time, and found Rome overpowering. There were too many things in this city, he complained. He envied Nadejda the stillness of Brailov. All this *sehenswürdigkeiten*—museums, ruins! What he craved was a quiet room and plenty of blank music paper.

To Naaejda Philaretovna

Rome, Dec. 30, 1879
Tuesday

"Today I set out to remodel my Second Symphony" (C minor, written in 1872, called sometimes the *Little Russian Symphony*). "It went so well that before lunch I made a rough draft of nearly half the first movement. How I thank the fates that caused Bessel to fail in his contract and never print this score! How much seven years can mean when a man is striving for progress in his work! Is it possible that seven years hence I shall look upon what I write today as I look now at my music written in 1872? I know it is possible because perfection—the ideal—is boundless, and in seven years I shall not yet be old.

"All the music to be heard in Rome is so bad that I am confined to what I make myself, so I play a great deal alone and with my brother, who can manage piano four hands quite tolerably. Last night we became greatly enthusiastic over a very good arrangement of Beethoven's B flat major String Quartet, when suddenly we were informed that a general on the floor below wanted us to be quiet so he could go to sleep. Of course we had to comply—one of the many annoyances of hotel life."

Modeste Ilyich was an inveterate sightseer and a real lover of painting. He tried to convert his musical brother, but among all the magnificence, ancient and modern, that Modeste dragged him out to see, only one painter truly stirred and refreshed Peter Ilyich —Raphael—"that Mozart of painting," Tchaikowsky called him.

But all these other people, how disappointing! "For instance," wrote Peter Ilyich, "Julius Caesar. He does not look at all the way he does in the book. His face is bereft of grandeur or force; he seems to me like a government clerk. And Trajan—who would think, from his narrow forehead, long chin and general impression of vacancy, that he was really a great man? Why is it I feel this terrible fatigue in museums? Isn't it strange? Outdoors I can walk for hours without being tired, and the minute I get in a museum I am utterly exhausted."

Peter Ilyich was not alone in his museum sufferings; it might have comforted him to know that in the next century, scientists in laboratories, studying to vanquish that great enemy of man, fatigue, would consider "museum fatigue" important enough to have a name and a remedy of its own. But Peter could not know this, and so once more, he was in need of rescue. Oh, do not worry! the reader wants to cry. Peter Ilyich, do not feel this guilt! In all justice, you should be exempt; you of all people need not wander footsore past the Trajans. Heaven made you, Peter Ilyich, a museum piece yourself. Go home and write your music.

But even at home there was no peace. Downstairs the general persistently desired to sleep and in the daytime ambassadors' wives called, seeking the Russian lion for their dinner parties. If they asked him again, Tchaikowsky told them (but indirectly, through a friend) he would leave Rome immediately. Local musicians began appearing. "I dislike musicians most of all," he fretted. "In the old days, I should probably have forced myself to call on all of them in return; I felt it my duty then to fight my painful shyness. But I can fight it no longer; moreover, I am no longer ashamed of it. Experience has taught me it is quite useless to torment myself with the struggle."

In truth Peter Ilyich was a man of but one language. His letters from Rome remind one of the letters written from Italy by his idol, Mozart. One of Mozart's biographers complained that it was always thus with musicians—blind, single-minded folk that they were. During his visit to Italy, Mozart never mentioned the Vatican or the

Colosseum. All he talked about was the street singing, the dancers, and the opera.

"What a great work is Michael Angelo's *Moses!*" wrote Tchaikowsky. "I have stood before it again and again, and each time with profounder veneration. This is indeed the creation of a supreme genius. They tell me it has irregularities—faults of taste. Did you ever hear about old Fetis, who occupied himself looking for irregularities in Beethoven's music, and announced in triumph that he had found in the *Eroica Symphony* an inverted chord which good taste does not permit? Isn't it true that Beethoven and Michael Angelo were spiritually very close?"

It would seem that Tchaikowsky translated all esthetic emotion into musical terms. Not that he was incapable of experiencing emotion through the other arts; literature—Rousseau, Dickens, Dostoyevsky—moved him profoundly. He loved poetry, that sister art to his own. But for sheer, pure esthetic experience, for the complete losing of himself—or finding of himself—he must needs turn to music. Even when, in the presence of some great painting or sculpture, Tchaikowsky felt emotion, he could express it only in terms of comparison to music. Standing, hat in hand, before the *Moses* of Michael Angelo, man was magnified to heroism. Trumpets crashed the note of victory—where before had Peter heard this glorious, exalted symphony—Beethoven!

Tchaikowsky returned his hat to his head, his *pince-nez* to his pocket, and turning reluctantly from *Moses*, went home to his hotel. He spent a bad night; his description of it and the day following could have been written by none but a Russian pen. How strange, to the Anglo-Saxon, reads this quite simple, candid admission of a grown man's tears as catharsis.

To Nadejda Philaretovna

Rome
January 30, 1880

"I spent a terrible night, my nerves as bad as they used to be. I thought I was dying, so dreadful were my sensations. In the morning I fell into a troubled, restless sleep . . .

"Anatol's letter came just now, with the details of my father's illness and death, a very touching story. Reading, I wept copiously, and it seemed to me that those tears, shed in farewell to a good man, a man who was truly pure in heart, had a healing influence upon me. My confusion disappeared and in its place came resignation. Anatol says my father was conscious of approaching death, but that he accepted it bravely and cheerfully."

A few days later, with the revision of the Second Symphony completed, Tchaikowsky began a new composition.

To Nadejda Philaretovna

Rome
February 17, 1880

"I am still nervous and irritable, sleep badly and in general am out of order. But I have been working, and during the past few days have sketched the rough draft of an Italian capriccio based on popular melodies. I think it has a bright future; it will be effective because of the wonderful melodies I happened to pick up, partly from published collections and partly out in the streets with my own ears."

"Yours
"P. Tchaikowsky"

Peter's hotel was next door to the barracks of the Royal Cuirassiers, Italian cavalrymen; how surprised their plumed and resplendent bugler would have been had he known that a Russian barbarian in the Hotel Constanzi, listening every evening to his call, had copied it down for the opening fanfare to a piece for full orchestra! It is a brilliant piece of music, and still popular today. Like other of Tchaikowsky's works that are supposed to reproduce Italian or French scenes, the *Capriccio* is strikingly Russian. When the usual waltz breaks out—(Taneyeff had been right; there is always a waltz to Tchaikowsky)—one can see the officers dancing in their most dazzling uniforms. But they are Russian officers, and beneath the clear strains of the horns one senses, somehow, the snow falling on cold and boundless steppes. . . .

Tchaikowsky's sudden nervous depressions are unchartable. Here in Rome, for instance, he should have been content; Modeste was with him, the weather was glorious, and he was working.

"And yet," wrote Peter Ilyich, "a worm gnaws at my heart; I don't understand why, being quite well physically, I cannot sleep and feel this lassitude. *Dieu,* what an incomprehensible and complicated machine is the human organism! The closest self-examination does not explain the phenomena of our spiritual and material life. And how can one draw a line between the mental and the purely physical? Sometimes I believe myself suffering from some mysterious, purely physical illness that is responsible for my changes of mood. Lately I have thought my heart was out of order, but only last summer a doctor pronounced it in perfect condition. So the blame must rest with the nerves—but what are the nerves? Why, on the same day, without apparent reason, do they behave normally and then lose their elasticity and energy, become unreceptive to artistic impressions, incapable of work? It is all a riddle.

"As I write, I have before me a lovely bunch of violets. Already they have appeared here in quantity. Little by little, spring assumes her kingdom."

Besides the symphony revision and the *Capriccio,* Tchaikowsky worked in Rome at his Second Piano Concerto which he had conceived in Kamenka and had sketched out in Paris. It was to be dedicated to Nicholas Rubinstein—partly in gratitude for his splendid playing of the B Flat Minor Piano Concerto at the Paris Exposition and partly, perhaps, in the hope that Rubinstein would do as well by this one. But even Rubinstein's glorious playing would not be able to make the Second Concerto into something as brilliant and vital as the First.

At intervals all during his life, Tchaikowsky received orders from Jurgenson or a Grand Duke or one of the conservatories, to write some kind of a *pièce d'occasion.* He always balked, but the professional artist in him would never let him turn down a commission.

To Nadejda Philaretovna

Rome
February 8, 1880

"My dear and kind friend:

"Yesterday Davidov" (Director of the Petersburg Conservatory) "wrote informing me there is to be a big pageant of tableaux with music on March 2nd.* All the Russian composers are contributing

* Celebrating twenty-five years of Alexander II's reign.

something and I was imperatively requested to write music for the seventh tableaux. I couldn't refuse, so wired Davidov my acceptance. My tableau represents 'Montenegro receiving the Russian declaration of war.' You can imagine what an inspiration this will be! However I shall do my part, though reluctantly, and I spent all today at it. It can't possibly result in anything good, and the vexing part is that I have no idea how the other composers will treat their subjects. Something tells me they all chose what they wanted and then I was sent the left-over. However there is no time to get in touch with Petersburg, so I set to work as hard as I could. If I don't satisfy them they have no right to complain.

"Yesterday I had your letter, and am tremendously happy that you like my suite" (the First Orchestral Suite, which had just been published). "I believe, dear friend, that when you become better acquainted with the suite, you will like the *Andante* best; I wrote this with real warmth.

"P. Tchaikowsky"

Nadejda was much agitated over this commission. Was he actually going to execute it? What for? *Must* he write this horrible thing? What was the use—she implied—of her sending registered letters every quarter if Peter Ilyich was not to be freed of musical orders from outside? From first to last, this was Nadejda's reaction to Tchaikowsky's commission-writing, and it was in very essence the attitude of the amateur. Art was for art's sake; how could her adored, her heaven-dowered composer write with sincerity a piece about Montenegro receiving a declaration of anything? And if he did not write with sincerity, would it not be a prostitution, a betrayal of his art? Nadejda's jealousy was not personal pique because Tchaikowsky took money from someone else, it was jealousy for his musical honor.   •

But Peter himself was not worrying about his musical honor. Montenegro and a few boomings and bangings had nothing to do with music. It was a job, and he was a musical craftsman who had long ago learned to do a job when necessary. Before Nadejda's protest reached him, the work was already done and forgotten.

"I mailed Davidov's music long ago," he reported to Nadejda. "I wrote it in frank disgust, knowing it could not possibly result in anything good. But then I don't see how the best-intentioned composer could find anything intriguing in the subject of 'The Impression produced in Montenegro by the Russian Manifesto.' I made a great noise with drums and trombones—and that was all."

But the drums and trombones remained forever silent. That same month, an attempt was made on the Tsar's life; national celebrations became, of course, impossible. Tchaikowsky's manuscript disappeared and has never been found; the composer himself, who owed much to royal patronage, was terribly distressed at the news of attempted assassination. "Whose fault was it?" he demanded. "Is there no strength or loyalty left among those whose duty it is to guard our Emperor? The picture this conveys of the awful disorder at home has driven music and indeed all other interests from my mind."

These letters were addressed to Nadejda in Russia; she was in Brailov for Christmas, surrounded by her children and grandchildren. It was unfortunate for the widow that her generation did not yet, in tubercular cases, connect cause and effect; here in Brailov where the southern sun caressed her, Nadejda was happy and her headaches were infrequent. But always she returned North to hurl herself against the Moscow winter. That shimmering snow so beloved by Tchaikowsky was relentless to the widow; it drove her indoors where she remained for months at a time in rooms overheated by huge porcelain stoves, while day by day her strength diminished and her nervous depression increased. Then in spring—Brailov again and recovery, then Italy in autumn, with continued health until it was time for Moscow. Now, late in February of 1880, she was again on the Boulevard Rojdestvensky, again she endured agonizing three-days' pains in her head; she could not lie down, and wrote Peter Ilyich standing, she said, against a desk.

But whenever Tchaikowsky's music was played in Moscow, Nadejda, sick or well, managed to be at hand. This month she heard his old opera, *The Oprichnik,* and found it delightful. The composer had completed this opera in 1872 and the censor had straightway, after the well-known lunacy of censors, forbidden its performance, deeming the subject revolutionary—the plot centered around Ivan the Terrible and his notorious bodyguard, the *Oprichnik*. Ivan, one of the most picturesque figures in the play, had not, as we have said elsewhere, been permitted on the stage at all because Tsars were not supposed to appear on stages. Tchaikowsky was soon to have an even more insane proscription concerning *The Maid of Orleans*. Writing to Nadejda now, Peter Ilyich reviewed the *Oprichnik* episode, declaring he wished the censor would continue to forbid that opera because as a work of art it deserved nothing better than suppression! The widow, of course, cavilled at this, but went on to say that Tchaikowsky's ballet *The Swan Lake* had also been performed in Moscow; Rubinstein had had a pupils' recital and a boy of sixteen had played the piano marvelously; his name was Siloti.

But best of all, went on Nadejda, was Tchaikowsky's new orchestral suite; it had had a brilliant success both in Petersburg and Moscow. Peter Ilyich was especially pleased at this news because not two months since, Jurgenson had written that Rubinstein considered the suite much too difficult for any orchestra to play. "Either Rubinstein is mistaken," Tchaikowsky had replied, "or I must give up composing. I try my very best to write simply and easily, and the more I try, the less I succeed. It is terrible." He had asked Taneyeff to write him in detail just what Rubinstein objected to, and Taneyeff did so, an enormous letter filled with technical argument, complaining in particular of the flute and oboe passages. Tchaikowsky was indignant; he could blow a flute himself, he replied, and those passages were child's play—certainly in comparison with *Francesca* or the Fourth Symphony.

"Here," wrote Tchaikowsky, "is one explanation: Monsieur Z, the oboist, was in one of his bad humors, and Rubinstein was influenced by it. . . . So the high notes were bad for Z's lips? That is quite an idea. What a pity those precious little lips, from which Madame Z has plucked so many kisses, should be ruined forever by my two high E's! Nevertheless this will not hinder me in future if I find it necessary to spoil those precious little lips with high notes which any oboist can play quite easily, and without a special French mouthpiece too."

Nadejda, however, knew nothing of this controversy. She had merely heard the Suite under Rubinstein's baton and was stirred. Before it was published, she and Tchaikowsky agreed that to dedicate it "To my best friend," like the Fourth Symphony, would be a reckless invitation of gossip, so the dedication remained a secret between them. But hearing it played, Nadejda conceived a vigorous idea. Why not have Colonne perform it in Paris? Even if the Fourth Symphony had not taken these stubborn French by storm, it had been excellent advertising for Peter Ilyich. What more reasonable than to hammer in one impression by another before Tchaikowsky's name was forgotten in France? She was writing Colonne now, she said, suggesting that he perform the suite at the Chatelet. . . .

But this time the widow's zeal had led her astray. She had stepped upon forbidden ground, the ground of professional self-respect. Any rich amateur can stage his own opera or symphony, but this kind of bribed performance means less than nothing to a serious musician. Tchaikowsky wrote the widow what amounted to a sharp rebuke, addressing her as his dear, kind and benevolent friend, he said he could not endure the humiliation of having Colonne paid again to play his music. To do it once had been splendid; as a single generous gesture, Colonne could understand it. As far as they both knew, Colonne had not divulged the financial side of the transaction, but "one can never be sure of anything. Should the news leak out that my symphonies are being played in Paris because they are *paid for,* oh, what a *coup* for all my enemies who write for the newspapers!

"And so I take the liberty of requesting that if you are going to recommend my further works to Colonne, you do it without supporting your recommendation with any pecuniary reward. But still I thank you once and again, my dear friend, for wanting to help me."

Reading this, Nadejda was horrified. She had sinned innocently and she implored forgiveness. But on the other hand, when, she asked, had anyone been able to bribe his way into the good graces of the Parisian public? All Parisians, including Colonne, were hard as brass. Here she was, dying to hear Tchaikowsky's music played, and here was a man who could play it. And Peter Ilyich asked her to sit supinely while opportunity walked by with its hand out!

Peter Ilyich read this letter in Rome just as he was leaving for Russia; in Moscow and Petersburg his operas were in rehearsal and his presence had been demanded. Spring was nearly here and it was good to be going home. Perhaps Nadejda Philaretovna was right and he had been too straight-laced in this Colonne matter. Peter got out his pencil and scribbled a letter, asking forgiveness for his harsh words and consenting to Nadejda's plan. But nevertheless, he would trust Colonne's motives only when he should hear that the gentleman had agreed to play his music without compensation.

And now Petersburg once more, and Moscow—letters, greetings, telegrams, evening parties and morning parties and all the dizzy routine of success. Up and down Peter travelled in train and cab through the spring mud and the spring rains, met at the station by his brothers and escorted to where celebration waited. Rehearsals to attend, singers to interview (A pest on all temperamental tenors and sopranos!). And always musical proof to correct, always those fat envelopes from Jurgenson. His eyes hurt, his head ached, and he knew that nobody cared except Nadejda. Letter after letter Peter sent frantically to Moscow; and soothingly, from her boudoir the widow replied. . . . So the Grand Duke Constantin stops his carriage in the street to greet you? wrote Nadejda. Well, but that is no calamity, Peter Ilyich! His Highness begged you to go round the world with him on his battleship, and you declare it would be a prison? My friend, do not let these people harass you. Find a quiet place, and do your work. . . .

"God alone knows, and in all the world you alone understand, Nadejda Philaretovna, how burdensome these visits and attentions from aristocracy are for me."

So wrote Peter Ilyich after two entire days in full dress and white tie. Taneyeff teased him by letter, "Peter Ilyich, you are only pretending. You love glory as anyone loves it." Peter frowns, and laughs, and puts on his white tie for another dinner party. Would that Taneyeff were right! Truly, he does love glory, but the manifestations of glory are so extremely fatiguing.

In April Peter left glory behind and went out to Kamenka to assume once more the congenial role of Uncle Petia. His sister Alexandra asked his help with the music in their village church. So he and she together, with Anatol and the pretty eldest niece Tatiana, formed a vocal quartet to sing a hymn. Tchaikowsky loved to sing in church; as a schoolboy in Petersburg he had had a beautiful soprano voice and on holy days—especially on Saint Catherine's day —had been selected with two other boys to stand by the altar and sing the trio which comes at the beginning and end of the service. The whole year round, the pupils of Peter's school had prepared for this great day; the Metropolitan himself officiated, and the Holy Liturgy, thus participated in, made an indelible impression upon Peter. After service, the boys who had sung were permitted to sit at table with the Metropolitan—poetic old figure with round white cap and flowing beard. He blessed the boys and thanked them for their singing, after which they all ran home to tell their admiring families about it.

But on this spring day at Kamenka, catastrophe rather than blessing dogged Peter's heel. At home the hymn had sounded lovely; everybody said so. But in church when they stood up to perform, pretty Tatiana lost her head, forgot her notes and led them all astray. Uncle Petia, always the complete professional, kept on singing alone—but it was a mistake. The voice that at ten had been angelic was now something else. It was, in brief a typical "composer's voice"; Uncle Petia sang like a goat. Finding that no one caught up with him, he stopped, ignominiously. "Sister and Tatiana," he reported to Nadejda, "are much afflicted with this episode, but next Sunday we shall have a chance to redeem ourselves. We have undertaken to learn *The Cherubs,* by Bortniansky and the *Pater Noster* from my *Liturgy.*"

Mention of the Davydoff nieces caused Nadejda to speak again of the proposed alliance of the two families. Convinced that married life is more successful when the wife is older than the husband, would it not be wiser, asked Nadejda, to choose one of the older nieces for her Kolia?

Let Kolia choose whichever of the four girls he pleases, replied Uncle Petia, gayly. For his part, he loves them equally. And is there anything more comforting, he adds, than the sight of lovely children's faces about one? Here in Kamenka the children are everywhere; they run in and out his little garden at will, and as long as he has no responsibility toward them, they do not disturb his work. He is orchestrating the *Italian Capriccio,* also, he is reading proof —hateful task!—on the first act of the *Maid of Orleans,* in hopes it will reach the Petersburg stage next August.

This was late May. "Lilac is in full bloom," wrote Peter. "The bushes remind me constantly of Brailov, where for two years in succession I saw the lilacs in bloom. How lovely it must be there now!"

When Uncle Petia was at Kamenka, his sister and her husband often availed themselves of his presence to go away for a week. "Small anarchies occur," the composer reported to Nadejda, and although he enjoyed the children, his work suffered. During any enforced separation from music paper, Tchaikowsky's head seemed suddenly to teem with melody and musical ideas; a furious restlessness possessed him until he could transmit the ideas to paper. Lacking the regularity of long daily hours necessary for symphonic work, he would write songs and short piano pieces.

To Nadejda Philaretovna
Kamenka, June 17, 1880

". . . Yesterday I began to compose some short vocal pieces, beginning with a duet to Tolstoi's words, 'All passion spent'. Tolstoi is an inexhaustible source of musical texts; for me he is one of the most appealing of the poets. Do you know the Moscow poet Surikoff, who died of consumption this spring? He was entirely self-educated; all his life he sat behind a counter in a miserable little hardware store and sold nails and horseshoes. But his talent was genuine and his verse filled with sincere feeling; I want to use some of it for future compositions."

Three weeks later he wrote his publisher:

To P. I. Jurgenson

Kamenka
July 5, 1880

"Dear Soul,

"You seem to believe that to compose pompous pieces for the exhibition is a species of sublime delight to which I will hasten, pouring out inspiration without having an idea what it's all about—how, why, when, what, etc. I won't move a finger until I have a definite commission.

"If they want me to write something local, they must send me a text—(if it's a real commission I am ready to set to music even the advertisement of the Moscow druggist, 'Come to Tchaikowsky for your corn plasters'). If they want something instrumental they must indicate the form and· what the piece is supposed to illustrate. Meanwhile they must decide a definite price, indicating exactly who is to pay it and when I am to receive the money.

"I don't make these demands from caprice, but because I can't write these huge noisy pieces without knowing really what is wanted, also the fee and time limit. There are two kinds of inspiration: one comes from the heart freely, for some creative reason, the other comes to order. For the latter one needs a definite plot or text, a time limit and the future advent of many Great Catherines.

"You give me the choice of one or two solemn subjects as if I ought to be charmed by one of them. You blame me for delaying to reply to you on a business matter. You call it business, but business matters should be exact and clear. Suppose I had worked myself up to writing a solemn overture for the exhibition. What would have been the result? In all likelihood, the great Anton (Rubinstein) would have already an-toned one himself, and where should I have been with my little garbage?

"So I refuse to so much as think about the exhibition till you tell me exactly what they want.

"Today I shall finish correcting proof for the Fourth Act (*Maid of Orleans*), and will send it on Thursday. What a long opera it has grown to be. My poor publisher! Your warehouse will have to make room for many extra plates. . . . Well, we live in hopes. . . ."

But Kamenka, with the "small anarchies," was beginning to weigh a bit heavily on Uncle Petia. As the children grew older and their troubles assumed moral rather than physical proportions, Peter worried overmuch about them. The pretty and self-willed eldest niece Tatiana, in particular caused him real grief. Nadejda, down in Brailov, knew he was overwrought and urged him to come south and occupy her house or the farm at Simaki; she herself was going abroad again, to Switzerland.

Early in July, therefore, Tchaikowsky and Alexis set forth for Brailov. They were to arrive at ten in the evening, and on the way, Peter's imagination became all too active. It was a year since he had been in Brailov; maybe they would not even recognize him when he got off the train! Some of his misgivings he wrote afterward to Jurgenson, some to his hostess, but the real story went to Anatol Ilyich up in Petersburg.

To Anatol

Brailov
July 18, 1880

"In the train it was very hot, and I was horribly nervous. Would the horses be at the station? I was haunted by all kinds of nonsense. What if N. Ph. had given orders I should be thrown out the minute I arrived? Lately I have been insane over the idea, first, that N. Ph. has changed toward me, and then I persuade myself that her solicitude has increased. So in the train, all the time I kept looking forward to a little sealed package containing several thousands, which I need devilishly.

"I arrive pompously, walk in, ask 'Are there any letters?'—'Yes!'—I go to my study and find two letters and a little sealed box. In much agitation I tear it open, but in place of thousands I find a watch and a note requesting that I accept it as a present! It was ordered during the winter in Paris, and has only just been delivered; it must be worth several thousand francs" (ten thousand, Peter had told Jurgenson). "On one side is Jeanne d'Arc on horseback—on the other Apollo with two muses, done on black enamel with little gold stars. Very delicate, sumptuous work. *Dieu!* but Nadejda Ph. is sweet.

"Just between you and me, I should have preferred the price to the watch. N. Ph. had spoiled me so with anticipation of my wants and wishes, that somehow I expected her to know instinctively what I needed now. I was wrong though, and see now that I won't have a kopek before autumn."

What could Peter do? Nothing but sit down and write his thanks to Nadejda. There had been a letter with the watch, a short note saying that, as she had not long to live (thirteen years of life were ahead of Nadejda) she wished to leave her dearest friend a token, something he would always carry about his person so that he would be reminded of her very often.

"Do not speak of dying!" wrote Peter Ilyich. "Let us be on earth together as long as possible. Life has held much bitterness for us both, yet we have much to live for. Please God that all you say about *Jeanne d'Arc* may be true; for myself I shall be satisfied if my opera proves, if not great, at least outstanding. I shall carry the watch always, not because I need to be reminded of you—never for a moment do I forget you, nor ever shall, if I live to be a thousand—but because it is sweet to me to possess something etc. etc."

What Peter Ilyich said here is what anybody might say when suddenly presented—confronted, we might almost say—with Jeanne d'Arc in black and gold enamel, prancing across a watch costing ten thousand francs. He could not sell the watch, he told Jurgenson; it would be too shameless. So he kept it. Moreover, he became extremely proud of it, wearing it, as Nadejda had desired, "next his heart."

Nadejda was in Switzerland now; she had left Russia on the day she forwarded the watch from Moscow. She wrote as the solicitous hostess: did Peter Ilyich like her parrot and Milochka's poodle, Croquet? Had he driven her Moscow trotters? Why hadn't he mentioned the new furniture in her bedroom and sitting-room, and would he please forgive her for not clearing out all the bureau drawers? She had not realized he would be in the big house at all, but had thought he would go right down to Simaki farm-house.

Peter Ilyich replied happily to these questions. He liked everything in Brailov, and as to the big grey parrot, she fascinated him. Every morning, composer and parrot sat on the terrace and conversed for hours. The parrot could imitate anything and after repeated coaxings she actually came into Peter's hands. Poor Croquet, Milochka's poodle, was quite eclipsed; she stole up one morning and put her nose into Peter's hand for a caress, but the parrot screamed

and Croquet backed hurriedly away. Marcel, crossing the lawn with
a pot of flowers, laughed. "Marcel," said Peter Ilyich, "may I take
this parrot to Simaki with me when I move my things down there
tomorrow?" Marcel shook his head gravely. It would never do to
part the parrot from Matrena, the little parlor maid. Why, the two
of them would fall sick and die!

Tchaikowsky's month in Brailov moved now with ever-increasing
emotional tempo. He was not working hard, merely correcting proof
on *Jeanne d'Arc,* but he could get drunk upon nature and solitude
as other men upon applause. He moved into the Simaki farm-house
and in the wheat field beyond his garden one day fell on his knees
and thanked God for letting him be part of all this summer beauty,
this holy country stillness. At night he would sit by his open window hour after hour, watching the moon above the giant branches
of the oaks, breathing the flower-laden air and listening, every nerve
taut with ecstasy, to the mystic untraceable noises of the night.

One rainy day Peter Ilyich went up to the big house and wandered
about Nadejda's library of music. His resultant remarks on Glinka
prove Peter to have been not the first to puzzle over the dual personality of an artist, over the discrepancy between moral and artistic stature that seems to exist especially in musicians. . . .

"What a strange phenomenon was Glinka! Reading his memoirs,
one meets a kind man, frivolous to the point of triviality. Playing his
smaller pieces, too, one cannot believe that either words or music were
written by the creator of *Slavsia* which belongs among the greatest
artistic creations of all time. How much beauty there is in his operas
and overtures! And how strikingly original is his *Kamarinskaya,*
from which all of us—the moment we need Russian dance-tunes—
have borrowed contrapuntal and harmonic designs quite frankly! In
this one short composition, Glinka succeeded in concentrating what
smaller men could do only by dint of heroic effort.

"And then, at the peak of his talent, what does this man do but
compose such a trivial, foolish thing as the *Coronation Polonaise,*
written a year before his death! And the *Children's Polka,* which in
his memoirs he mentions with as much satisfaction as though it were

a masterpiece! Mozart, in his letters to his father revealed equal naïveté—but of quite another kind. Mozart was an inspired being, childishly innocent, mild as a dove and modest as a maid; he did not belong to this world. One can find no conceit in him, no self-applause; he never seemed to suspect the grandeur of his genius.

"Glinka, on the contrary, is filled with self-love, reciting in detail every trifling event of his life and the publication of his smallest compositions as though it all belonged to history. He was typical of the Russian nobleman of his time" (Glinka died in 1857)—"ambitious, ill-educated, filled with vanity and intolerance, and painfully sensitive to any criticism of his own music. These are the qualities one expects to find in a mediocrity. How could they belong to one who deserved with a proud, quiet modesty, to recognize his own power? I simply cannot understand it. In his memoirs Glinka tells about his bull-dog, which behaved badly, and how his servant had to clean up after it. Kukolnik, to whom Glinka entrusted the editing of the memoirs, asked in the margin, 'Why put this in?'—and Glinka pencilled beside it, 'And why not?' Isn't this characteristic of him? And yet, he wrote the *Slavsia!*"

And a day later.

July 18, 1880
Sunday

"Today I went to church at the Monastery, the Orthodox and the new Roman Catholic. In the singing of the local nuns there is one thing that irritates me extremely—their frequent abuse of the dominant seventh chord in its first position. There could be nothing less musical or less suitable to the Orthodox service than that meaningless chord, which last century Messrs. Galuppi, Sarti and Bortniansky introduced, and with which our church music has become so permeated that they cannot sing a *Kyrie* without it. This chord reminds one of a hand accordion which possesses no harmonies beyond the tonic and dominant. It ruins the naturalness of the words as sung, it dilutes and vulgarizes the whole effect. To make plain exactly what I dislike, here is a sample:—

This is how it should be sung:

"The new Roman Catholic church impressed me favorably. However, I much prefer the Orthodox liturgy to the Catholic Mass, especially the so-called Low Mass, which lacks solemnity. . . .

"Last night I went to the Vladimirsky forest. This year I have no luck mushroom hunting; I haven't found a single one. Your parrot and I are intimate friends; he comes right to me and is pleased when I invite him into my hands.

"I feel so well, so quiet and completely happy! My friend, it is you I have to thank.

"P. Tchaikowsky"

And now, into this paradise, this beneficent solitude of forest and stream where Peter Ilyich might stand before his house and watch the sun go down, appeared once more that spectre of his past mistakes, that reminder of the inexorable whip of fate—Antonina. Not in person; only a letter. She wrote that she consented to a divorce, and in the next paragraph swore to repudiate any "scurrilous and improbable papers," meaning that she would never accept adultery as grounds, thereby making divorce impossible!

Analyzed, Antonina's letter was nonsense. Why, therefore, Peter asked Nadejda, should nonsense affect him like a dose of strongest poison? "The mere sight of her handwriting on the envelope, with my address written by her, makes me actually sick, not only mentally but physically. Yesterday, for instance, I had such pain in my feet that I could scarcely move; I am ashamed to confess that the severest nausea and weakness possessed me all day."

Tchaikowsky's physical reaction to emotional strain carries an extraordinarily evident symbolism. Properly to interpret it would require the tools of a psychiatric specialist. These nocturnal tremblings of which the composer complained, these sudden pains in the feet that made movement impossible—were they symbolic of a frustrated desire to escape? The layman dare not say, but common sense makes him hazard a guess. Antonina wrote Peter Ilyich that he was a liar, that he and his cousins had been spreading slander about her around Petersburg. And on the fragrant terrace of Brailov, Peter Ilyich, the letter in his lap, sat helplessly wondering if it had been a lie and slander to tell Tolia the girl was stupid and that he hated her. . . . "If you must gossip about people's faults," went on Antonina's letter—for the life of him Peter could not leave it unread —"why don't you begin with your own terrible vices and tell about them?"

Peter drops the letter on the ground as if it burned his fingers. In a panic he gets to his feet; he must run, run away from here, to where these letters cannot reach him. But when he tries to walk he stumbles and halts, surprise and pain in his face. Why, there are knives in his feet! Every step is agony. . . .

If a man cannot run from danger there is but one alternative: to forget danger. Oblivion comes only in work. In such a state of mind, Peter could not compose music, but he could correct proof. So he finished the proof sheets of the *Maid of Orleans,* then went to Nadejda's piano and played over the first two acts before mailing them to Moscow.

To Nadejda Philaretovna

Simaki
July 30, 1889

"Either I am much mistaken or you, my dear friend, did right in having the heroine of my latest composition engraved on my watch. I don't believe the *Maid* is the best and deepest thing I have written, but it seems to me it is the piece which may make me popular. *Onegin* and some of my instrumental works are children that lie closer to my heart and personality. I wrote the *Maid* with less self-absorption than, for instance, our symphony or the Second String Quartet, but at the same time I gave the opera more care as to scenic-phonetic effects, and this in opera, is the main consideration."

In his estimate, the composer was right indeed in sensing that the *Maid of Orleans* was not so inspired as *Onegin,* but utterly wrong in prophesying that the *Maid* would be the most popular of his operas. Now, except for Jeanne's *Aria,* the *Maid* is forgotten, but Tatiana, singing by candlelight, still writes the fatal letter to Onegin while the world beyond the footlights heaves rhythmical, sympathetic sighs—a world that even as it boasts brave scorn of sentimentality, succumbs in tearful delight, a few scenes later, to the spectacle of love denied by virtuous womanhood.

Tchaikowsky was much nearer the mark in his criticism of *Carmen.* One night in Simaki, in order to rest, he said, from his own music, he played Carmen over from beginning to end. Bizet had written it five years ago.

"To me," Tchaikowsky wrote, "this is in every sense a *chef d'oevre,* one of the few pieces which, will some day mirror most vividly the musical endeavor of a whole generation. It seems to me that the era we live in differs from the preceding in one way; our composers are *searching*—and first of all, they *are* searching for pretty and piquant effects—a thing which Mozart and Beethoven and Schubert and Schumann never did. What is the so-called New Russian school, if not the cult of various spicy harmonizations, eccentric orchestral combinations and all kinds of purely exterior effects? The musical idea has become merely the excuse for new sound effects. Where they once composed and created, they now, with a few exceptions, dovetail and invent. This is a purely rational process; modern music, therefore, though very ingenious and piquant, remains cold, unwarmed by feeling.

"And suddenly appears a Frenchman in whose music these piquant and spicy passages are not the result of ingenuity but flow freely. They please the ear, but at the same time they touch and trouble. It is as though Bizet said to us: 'You are not seeking for something lofty and grandiose; you want something pretty. Well, here is a pretty opera.' And indeed, I know of no music which has better title to the quality I would call pretty—*le joli.* From beginning to end, it is charming and delightful. In it one finds a number of striking harmonies and entirely new combinations of sound, but these do not exist merely for themselves. Bizet is an artist who pays tribute to modernity, but he is warmed by true inspiration.

"And what a wonderful subject for an opera! I can't play the last scene without tears. Here is the mob at the bullfight with its coarse merriment and excitement—and to offset this, a terrible tragedy and the death of the two principals, who through fate—*fatum*—reach at length a climax and their own miserable end.

"I am convinced that in about ten years *Carmen* will have become the most popular opera in the world. But no man is a prophet in his own country; in Paris, *Carmen* did not win real success. Soon after its first performance Bizet died, though in the bloom of youth and health. Who knows, perhaps the failure of his opera killed him?"

Next day Tchaikowsky wrote again, about Massenet this time. In the *Maria Madelene,* he had thought at first he would be offended by the idea of Jesus Christ on a stage singing arias and duets; such a spectacle would of course never be permitted by the Russian censor. But as he played on, tears had moved him instead of scorn. . . . And had he told his dear friend that he was studying English? He had been at it regularly and with some success; he knew he could never learn to speak fluently. What he hoped, as a delight to his declining years, was to read Shakespeare, Dickens and Thackeray in the original.

And now it was August and Peter had no work to do. With idleness, his former contentment mounted now to almost dangerous ecstasy. Ahead of him was Kamenka, with all the family troubles awaiting. Furthermore, Kamenka, for all its romantic history, was far from romantically landscaped; the mills and township ruined both air and scenery. The contrast between this and Simaki made Tchaikowsky even more aware, during these last few days, of the beauty he must leave. This was natural enough; what surprises the reader is Tchaikowsky's own very sane criticism of his too-emotional state; he wrote his hostess that it would be really dangerous for him to indulge himself by staying longer in Brailov. One does not expect the artistic temperament thus to check and forewarn itself; who, one asks, had been responsible in Peter's youth, for this saving grain of caution? Had it been instilled by the gentle old Ilya, his father, or was it due to the training of that mother he had adored and lost in adolescence?

Nadejda by now had gone down from Interlaken to Arcachon, on the coast of France. Tchaikowsky hated to leave Simaki before hearing of her safe arrival. Was she well— Was she tired— Would he hear from her soon? "My dearest, my blessed friend," wrote Peter Ilyich, "I have been very happy here; I do not know how to thank you. I take leave now of my hostess and wish her good health. . . ."

23

Nadejda's little Parisian pianist.
Tchaikowsky's growing fame

WHILE Tchaikowsky made his farewells to Simaki, his hostess at Interlaken was writing history in her own way; she had, indeed, taken history into her house.

Nadejda to Peter Ilyich

Interlaken, July 22, 1880

". . . A young pianist from Paris, who has just finished the Conservatoire course with the *Premier Prix,* has come to stay with us. He was in M. Marmontel's class. I invited him to give the children lessons during the summer, to accompany Julia's singing and play four hands with me. The boy plays well, with virtuosity; his technique is brilliant but his playing carries no expression of himself, absolutely none. He has not lived long enough for that; he says he is twenty, but looks no more than sixteen.

"N.v.M."

This boy with the brilliant, cold technique was Claude Debussy, who was indeed to mature in time to show plenty of originality. He was destined, in fact, to be the most influential French composer of his generation, the founder of musical impressionism, the man to introduce the artistic conception of "atmosphere." Also he broke, at his convenience, the boundaries of traditional tonality and by his example gave music a wider scope.

But this was all to come much later. In Nadejda von Meck's household that summer of 1880, the young Debussy was exactly what his hostess said he was, a brilliant pianist without depth or maturity. History has proved the justice of Nadejda's criticism. Debussy, who was in fact eighteen at the time, matured, for a musician, very late; he was twenty-eight before he began to write great music. In her first mention of him to Tchaikowsky, Nadejda gave the young man no name; the next time she speaks of him he has become Monsieur Bussy, this young man who was to push open a new musical door.

Nadejda Philaretovna to Peter Ilyich

Arcachon, Aug. 18, 1880

". . . I myself have never played either Massenet's *Maria Madelena* nor Bizet's *Carmen,* but as far as I can judge from the *musicus,* Bussy, the Parisian musical world at present holds Bizet very high. Judging also from M. de Bussy as a sample, I have become convinced that one cannot draw any parallel between Parisian and Russian pianists, so incomparably higher are our own as musicians and masters of technique. And mine is *un lauréat*—received the *Premier Prix* when he was graduated this year. Now he is working for the *Prix de Rome*—all nonsense, those prizes, not worth a rap."

Arcachon, Aug. 19, 1880

"Yesterday I decided to play our Symphony with my little Frenchman and as a result I am in a terribly nervous state. I cannot play it without fire darting through my every fibre! It took twenty-four hours for me to recover. My partner did not perform the symphony well, but sightread wonderfully. It is his only—but very great—talent, he reads compositions, even yours, *à livre ouvert.* His second virtue—a reflective virtue, so to speak, is that he is delighted with your music. He is a pupil of Massenet's in theory, so of course Massenet is his hero; but yesterday he and I played your suite and he was delighted with the fugue and said, 'Among all the modern fugues I never found anything so beautiful. M. Massenet could never have equalled it.' He does not like the Germans and says, 'They have not our temperament and are too heavy, possessing no clarity of utterance.' On the whole, he is purely a product of the Paris Boulevard."

Tchaikowsky made no reply to this. He had gone up from Brailov to Kamenka and was extremely busy as Uncle Petia; the nieces were planning another fête with an operetta and he had been to Kiev to find a libretto. Furthermore, he knew that Nadejda was always taking young musicians into her house. How would young artists live were it not for the Madame von Mecks and their masculine counterparts who patronized the arts? But with Monsieur Bussy, Nadejda seemed more than usually pleased. It was unfortunate, of course, that he was a Frenchman and not a Russian, but his

facility in sightreading was truly uncanny, and he was so willing
and agreeable round the house! All during this autumn she mentioned him often by the affectionate diminutive of Bussyk.

From Switzerland, that autumn of 1880, Nadejda went to Arcachon on the east coast of France and thence to Florence, taking her
little Frenchman with her. She was to occupy the same Villa Oppenheim out among the hills, and no sooner had she arrived—at
seven on the morning of September 20th—than she partook of
some hasty breakfast and drove to the Villa Bonciani. It was a sad
pilgrimage. Nadejda, setting off eagerly down the road, was not the
first woman to meet bitter disappointment at the revisiting of an
abandoned trysting place. "That small house Bonciani," she wrote
Peter Ilyich, "so dear to me, so filled with tender reminiscence—
how happy I was when you were there and when in passing I could
sense your invisible presence and hear the sound of your fingers on
the piano! Today, driving by that cherished spot, tears came to my
eyes, and my heart constricted with a pain that became fury the instant I saw that someone else was living there. What a vile thought!
I wanted to evict this person immediately and rent the house myself
so nobody could live there. But I forebore because I am considered
queer enough already!

"By night, when the moon was up, I went again. The Villa was
all lighted from within and I could hear someone playing the piano;
I felt even sadder and more disappointed. Oh, my dearest, matchless
friend, why are you not here? If only you could see how nice it is,
the green is so fresh and the countryside so charming. . . ."

Nothing could console the widow but music. It was fortunate that
she had her little Bussyk from Paris. She sent Tchaikowsky an opera
of Ponchielli's for criticism, adding to the parcel "a little composition, one of many completed by my little pianist, Bussy. The boy is
preparing to be a composer and writes very nice little things, but it
is all an echo of his professor, Massenet. He is now writing a *trio*,
also very good, but redolent of Massenet. He reads music and accompanies a singer perfectly."

Tchaikowsky replied that he would look over the opera and Bussy's

composition with the greatest interest. Meanwhile Nadejda had enlarged her household orchestra.

Florence, Oct. 11, 1880

"Another musician has arrived at my house—Danilchenko"—(a
cellist). "He finishes at the (Moscow) Conservatory this spring and
planned to go abroad; my engagement with my little Frenchman
is drawing to a close. So, not wanting to take a new one—it is
annoying to have so many new faces in the family—I wrote to Moscow saying that if Danilchenko was going abroad, to come to me
for work. My letter reached him on the eve of his departure for Berlin, so he changed his plan and came to me in Florence. As Bussy is
still here and Danilchenko has nothing to do, they play trios every
evening. My little Frenchman has written a very nice trio. I regret
that I cannot send it to you for criticism, dear friend, because there is
not time to copy it, as he is leaving some day soon. I am sorry he is
going, because he is such a good partner for four-hand playing; he
reads music wonderfully, and as I am constantly playing new things
—new to him also—this talent is particularly valuable."

In October Nadejda received the piano arrangement of Tchaikowsky's new opera, the *Maid of Orleans*. In spite of a headache, Nadejda studied an act a day. "It was fortunate," she wrote, "that the
opera came while my little Frenchman is still here. He played it to
me perfectly. Listening, I was moved to ecstasy. I must admit, dear
friend, that I was a little fearful about this opera, and this is why:
The chief characteristic of your compositions is their Russian-ness,
and I was afraid that, unnoticed by you, this quality might creep
into a French opera and then those nasty Frenchmen would raise
a shout about it and laugh, and I am terribly sensitive to every
criticism of you, terribly jealous for your reputation."

The widow's fears were justified; the opera is a very samovar for
Russian-ness. But Nadejda, carried away as her little Frenchman proceeded with the playing of the opera, soon declared the music possessed a scope, a grandeur that over-rode all national boundaries,
all limitations of time and place. "And how good the love scenes
are!" the widow exclaimed, adding with one of her characteristic
jibes at love: "In these scenes you are always higher than the sub-

ject." Might she be permitted to give her little Frenchman a copy
of the opera, and might she have Bussyk make a four-hand arrangement of the dances from *The Swan Lake* and then have them published? Another thing, many private persons have orchestras of their
own, as witness the *Orchestre de M. Derwiss,* in Nice, and the
Helmeberger Quartet in Vienna. Why should she not have a *Trio
de Mme de Meck?* So she has had a photograph made of her trio
and is sending Peter Ilyich a copy.

Tchaikowsky enjoyed the photograph. "Bussy's face and hands,"
he wrote, "bear an indefinable resemblance to Anton Rubinstein's
in his youth God grant Bussy's fate may be as fortunate as that of
the Tsar of pianists. Please give Bussy's arrangement of my opera
to Jurgenson, no other publisher. I shall be very glad to let your
little Frenchman have the *Maid of Orleans."*

But Nadejda decided not to let Bussy carry away the opera score,
after all. "I am afraid," she wrote, "that those knavish French composers—Massenet, Delibes, Godard, etc.—will steal whole handfuls
from your opera and present them to the Parisian public as their
own. I assure you, Peter Ilyich, they steal from you constantly; the
other day when we were playing your First Symphony, four hands,
I realized it. I too noticed Bussy's resemblance to Anton Rubinstein.
I believe in his future because of his devotion to his chosen work;
it is his only interest in life. He has a very frivolous nature, quite
French, but his heart is very kind. I am sending you his arrangement of your dances from *The Swan Lake,* to give to Jurgenson for
printing. Please don't put M. de Bussy's name on them, because if
they fell into the hands of Jules Massenet, my young man might be
scolded."

Florence, Oct. 25, 1880

"My little Frenchman is leaving in a week; I have kept him an
extra fortnight. I regret his going because musically he gave me such
pleasure, and all in all, he is a boy with a good heart. But as I should
have foreseen, his friendships with our Russian tutor had a bad influence on him. That youth, for some unknown reason, set himself
up as an aristocrat, and Bussy, still quite a child, caught the con-

tagion and succeeded only in making us laugh at his airs. But the tutor left a month ago, and Bussy is his old self again."

"N.v.M."

October 26, 1880

"Now that Bussy is soon to leave, we have more music than ever. Last evening I made Bussyk, as I call him, and Danilchenko, whom we have taught Bussy to call Petrushka, play four hands. Very seriously, Bussy said to him, '*Petrushka, jouez quelque chose.*' So last evening they played Bizet's suite for orchestra, *L'Arlésienne*. It is a charming thing. Then they began to play Glinka. . . . It quite transported me to Moscow and the Hall of the Nobility, into that sea of lights, that noisy crowd in which I have always played a merely passive part. At sound of the overture—*Jota Aragonese*—music and memory made my heart beat high. Whatever we have becomes twice as dear when we are far from it."

"N.v.M."

Florence

Nov. 15, 1880

"My little Frenchman has left, and it is very annoying that I can no longer hear your piano sonata and other charming compositions, of which I adore especially the F minor Waltz, which Bussy played very well. My trios are ended too. Imagine, Peter Ilyich, the boy wept when he left. It truly touched me deeply; he has such a loving heart. He would not have gone at all, but the directors of the Conservatory were already annoyed because he had postponed his return these two weeks."

Perhaps all of Bussyk's tears were not for his kind hostess. Nadejda's daughter Sonia was fourteen now, extremely pretty with her red-gold hair and velvety brown eyes—and well aware already of the use and value of these weapons. Debussy gave her a piano lesson every day, and long before it was time for him to return to Paris, he was utterly vanquished. He was however, still master of his feelings enough to deceive Nadejda; he hoped to be invited back next year. He would be nineteen then and Sonia nearly at marriageable age. He was poor and he was nobody, but there was power within him and he knew it—and at nineteen a man will aspire to anything. Before he was halfway to Paris, Bussyk was mentally imploring Mme von Meck to let him return next summer and play duets with her.

Mme von Meck did let him return, not only next summer but the summer after; she greeted him affectionately and wrote Tchaikowsky how glad they all were to see little Bussyk. Sonia's eyes were deeper now, brown velvet under the gold of her hair, and Sonia knew more than one way to play duets. Bussyk's hands upon the piano keys were cold no longer; even the widow admitted that his *Premier Prix* virtuosity had caught flame somewhere. . . .

And then one summer's day Bussyk came to her. Perhaps the widow was not altogether surprised at his confession of love; young men were always sighing after Sonia. What truly astonished her was that the boy actually asked to marry Sonia. A von Meck and a Bussy, penniless minstrel from the Parisian boulevards! The interview was brief. The widow smiled, pressed Bussyk's hand and Bussyk found himself on the train for Paris, every kind, inexorable word of Nadejda's more bitter in his heart than if she had denounced him. Why, she had scarcely taken him seriously. . . .

Little Bussyk, as the world knows, became famous. In after years, when he had become one of the first musicians of Europe, the von Mecks still spoke of him affectionately, and with Sonia safely married would have been glad to welcome him back. But a great man can go or stay as he chooses, and Claude Debussy never revisited the scene of his defeat.

All this of course, did not take place at once. That autumn of 1880, when Bussyk in Florence first played trios for Nadejda von Meck, assuring her that nobody living could write a fugue to equal Monsieur Tchaikowsky's, Monsieur Tchaikowsky himself was in Kamenka reading proof, caring for his sister's children, struggling with nervous fatigue. "There is a republic here," wrote Uncle Petia one night—at two A. M. "Master and mistress of the house are away and chaos reigns. The children are more than usually mischievous and I tremble to think what may happen before their parents return. Yesterday Volodia fell off his horse twice and only luck kept him from being smashed to bits. Mitia, however, gives me most anxiety; he is terribly mischievous. Brother Anatol is still here. . . . Our fête with the operetta took place last week amid much excitement; afterward I went to bed with a nervous fever, as always when my routine is broken by contact with strangers."

In the night, little George, stifling with croup, woke them all with a scream. Leo Davydoff's cornstacks were destroyed by fire; his beets and winter corn devoured by worms and beetles. Tchaikowsky wrote Nadejda a whole chapter on how to get rid of beetles; dozens of panaceas were always being suggested, even professors from the Moscow University came out to Kamenka to discuss this scourge. But so far, the only effective action had been to pay the children a few kopeks to collect beetles, and then burn them in piles. Even this was rather hopeless because next day half of the creatures revived, said Uncle Petia disgustedly—and crawled up and down their own smoking pyramids.

But beetles and croup notwithstanding, Tchaikowsky's work progressed; three parts of a brand new orchestral suite were finished. (Suite Number Two, in four movements, not completed until 1883.) The *Maid of Orleans* was to be performed in Petersburg simultaneously with *Eugene Onegin* in Moscow. There was no longer any question as to who was the most popular musician in Russia; Peter Ilyich was famous and knew it. Nadejda knew it too, and in her villa among the Tuscan hills had been pondering the subject of fame. Should not Peter Ilyich's face and form, as well as his music, be perpetuated? All these Italian monuments and statues in the public parks—why, half of them were people one had never heard of! And here was Tchaikowsky, a truly great man; should he not have a statue too? Instantly, she wrote him; she herself would not like a monument even if she deserved one, but how did Peter Ilyich feel about this?

She had touched a tender spot. "Fame?" cried Peter Ilyich, in reply. "Glory? What contending feelings the word raises! I desire it, I struggle desperately for it, and yet it is hateful to me."

And how he longs for his music to be known!—the letter goes on to say. If a wider musical audience is the meaning of fame, then with all his soul he desires fame. But when he realizes that in proportion to musical fame a personal notoriety will develop, raising the curtain between himself and the world—then he wishes for ever-lasting silence instead of more music. . . . Or if not silence everlast-ing—he adds with characteristic honesty—at least a *little* silence un-til the world forgets him. . . . "This is not because I fear exposure. I can state frankly that my conscience is clear and I have nothing to be ashamed of."

Coming from a man who suffered intermittent terror lest his wife blackmail him for sexual abnormality, this is the kind of statement the biographer would prefer to omit. Yet who can condemn the dis-abled man for not naming his disability a vice? Peter Ilyich was in-deed humiliated that he was not as other men; had he not, again and again, confessed that only his music redeemed him for man-hood? But this statement was not the voice of the wrong-doer tell-ing his remorse; it was rather the voice of the cripple who in agony cries out his shame, hoping that his own voice or another's will refute him and give him leave to live on an earth so implacably re-served for normalcy.

Also, Peter Ilyich was well now, and writing music furiously. What he said to Nadejda concerning publicity was true enough at the moment; with Antonina temporarily out of the way, Peter did not dread publicity for his conscience' sake but simply because he hated to be stared at.

"There is," he wrote Nadejda, "something almost tragic in this struggle between one's desire for fame and disgust at fame's conse-quences. Sometimes I am seized with a longing to hide, to be buried alive that I may forget everything and be forgotten by these strangers. Alas! I return to the fire and burn my wings anew.

"And my wings will soon have to suffer singeing through the performance of *Jeanne d'Arc* in Petersburg. I shall have to plunge headlong into the nauseous waters of theatrical and bureaucratic tittle-tattle, to breathe the rotten atmosphere of intrigue, small but venom-ous ambition, every kind of chicanery and conceited stupidity. How-ever, either I stop writing operas or prepare to face all this. I really don't believe I shall ever write another opera, but shall keep exclusively to the domain of symphony and string quartet. When I remember what I had to endure last spring in staging *Onegin,* I feel as if I never wanted to write for the theatre again. Soliciting is really awful.

"All this time here I have been very busy correcting proof for my" (second piano) "concerto and the *Italian Capriccio.* The latter is easy enough to play."

How could Peter Ilyich know that in two years he would be deep in the writing of *Mazeppa,* a three-act opera, and still later would write one of his best creations, the opera *Pique Dame?* This man would never be finished with the theatre; the year before his death he was to write *Iolanthe.* In spite of himself, the theatre fascinated him; his very persistence proved it—because while he loved the boards, he truly hated the whole atmosphere of theatrical excitement upon which your real showman thrives.

Nadejda however, was delighted with every word Tchaikowsky said. She loved his independence of all fawning and solicitation. "Is there another man," she exclaimed, "as sincere as you? Peter Ilyich, you are nothing but your music, while your music is nothing but you, your very self."

Even posterity, with all its raising of the curtain, has not been able to make truer estimate of the man than that sentence of Nadejda's. In truth he was all music, was effective only in music, alive only in music, and conversely, his music was so personal to him, so expressive of his individuality as to be his very ghost. Nadejda von Meck was passionately, painfully in love with this ghost; its voice caused her to tremble in every limb—even the remembered sound could make her lie sleepless through successive nights. She was possessed by it, was beginning to know that this voice was, for her, life itself. . . .

And Tchaikowsky? Each time he tried to separate himself from music, to "rest" from it, he was a lost soul; to cease creating music was for him a stoppage of the very rhythm of living, as though his breath—his essential connection with life—had been cut off. He was well aware of it.

To Nadejda Philaretovna

Kamenka
Sept. 21, Tuesday

"How fickle my plans are, whenever I decide to devote a long time to rest! I had just begun to spend a series of entirely idle days, when there came over me a vague feeling of discomfort and real sickness; I could not sleep and suffered from fatigue and weakness. Today I could not resist sitting down to plan my next symphony—and immediately I became well and calm and full of courage. It proves that unless I am travelling I cannot exist for two days without work. This has its good and bad side. I am afraid of becoming a writer like, for instance, Anton Rubinstein, who feels it a kind of duty to supply the public with a new creation every day. The result is that he has put his great creative power into small change, so that most of his later compositions are only nickel instead of the pure gold he could have produced had he written more moderately.

"Lately, I have tried to plan some other interesting work to divert me from music. Alas! Nothing can divert me. There is no Russian textbook on the history of music, and it would have been well for me to busy myself writing one. But this would have meant renouncing all musical composition for about two years—too long a time. Well then, what remains? To set about translating someone else's history? Not interesting enough. To write biography? Much has already been written about the European artists. I cannot write with enthusiasm about Glinka, Dargomisky and Serov, because in proportion as I admire their music, I dislike their personalities. I wrote you about Glinka; Dargomisky was a man even more ignorant and less interesting. As for Serov, he was extraordinarily clever, a living encyclopedia of knowledge, but I knew him personally and never cared for him as a man. He was not *kind,* and this alone is sufficient to deter me from dedicating my leisure time to him. How joyfully I could have worked on Mozart's biography, but Otto Jahn has left nothing to say; his whole life was devoted to Mozart's history and personality.

"So it seems there is no way to occupy myself and satisfy my inward craving for work, except musical composition. I am already planning a symphony and a string quartet! I don't yet know which I shall choose."

A few days after writing this, Tchaikowsky was informed that the *Maid of Orleans* had been accepted by the directors of the Imperial Theatre in Petersburg, and would be performed in January. And now his troubles began. With the letter of acceptance was returned his libretto from the Board of Censors, marked with that red pencil which was the despair of opera writers in Imperial Orthodox Russia. The slightest criticism of monarchy or religion was enough to outlaw any work from the State theatres; the censorship followed no law of rationality; simply, what was sacred must not be impersonated on the stage. Across Tchaikowsky's score the censor had written: "The archbishop in this production must be called 'pilgrim,' not archbishop. All conversations concerning the Cross must be omitted, nor may any cross be permitted on the stage. . . ."

"How stupid it all is!" raged Tchaikowsky. "At the end of the opera when Jeanne is led to the stake, she asks for a cross, and one of the soldiers ties two sticks together in the form of a cross and gives it to her. The whole scene has to come out. . . . The silliest thing of all is calling the archbishop a pilgrim; it makes no sense. Who would believe that such commands issue from a state institution that supervises every printed thing in Russia, and which should therefore consist of educated men? There is nothing to do about it however, and I have had to comply."

Nadejda was furious. Those idiots! she cried. Those *bashibazouks!* Why didn't they make Jeanne herself into a pilgrim, while they were about it? To add to her indignation, Peter was at work on another commission, this time from Nicholas Rubinstein. There was to be an Exhibition in Moscow and the Chief wanted a large piece for choir and orchestra, or simply for orchestra. Either way, it had to be "big." Tchaikowsky was given three choices of subject: (1) The inauguration of the Exhibition. (2) The twenty-fifth anniversary of the Coronation of Alexander II. (3) The inauguration of the Cathedral of Christ the Saviour. . . . Loathsome, impossible themes! cried Peter Ilyich, and before his complaint was fairly silenced, had set to work. Twelve days later he wrote from Kamenka:

October 22, 1880

"Just think, dear friend!—My muse has been so kind that in a short time I have got through—before my sister's illness—two pieces:

A big solemn overture for the Exhibition, and a *Serenade* for stringed orchestra in four movements. I am busy orchestrating them both. The overture will be very showy and noisy, but it will have no artistic merit because I wrote it without warmth and without love."

This "exhibition piece" was the *Overture 1812*— Need more be said? Damnably inseparable from Tchaikowsky's name, it is fully as noisy as the composer declared; certainly, it contains little of that quality called by Peter Ilyich "love" or "warmth."

Tchaikowsky's attitude toward commission writing, as we have seen, never varied. Upon receiving an order, he complained bitterly, set eagerly to work, wrote something "noisy," as he called it, and presented it promptly to the authorities, with a sardonic grin— as sardonic, that is, as Peter's smile could be. His commission dealings can have no better illustration than a letter he was to write later to Jurgenson, upon being commissioned to arrange for chorus and string orchestra Glinka's famous *Slavsia,* from his *Life for the Tsar;* 7500 voices were to sing it at a big Imperial celebration. After finishing the job, Tchaikowsky sent it to Jurgenson with the following note:

"As far as original composition goes, there are only a few new measures in the work, so the City of Moscow, which you say is prepared to surrender me a mountain of gold, owes me only as follows:
For the simplification of the choral parts and instrumentation of
  sixteen measures, repeated three times......3 roubles
For the composition of eight measures leading into the anthem
....4 roubles
For adding four lines to the third verse, at forty kopeks per line
....1 rouble, 60 kopeks

Total   8 roubles, 60 kopeks
"These 8 roubles, 60 kopeks I present to the City of Moscow. But seriously, it is ridiculous to think of payment for such work; it would be offensive. Such things should be done without payment or not done at all."

Nadejda von Meck, of course, hated all this business even more than Peter Ilyich. He knew she hated it and, that autumn of 1880, tempered his official news with something more personal. Along with the noisy Exhibition piece for Rubinstein, Tchaikowsky had said he was orchestrating a newly composed *Serenade* for strings; the two works presented a complete contrast. "I wrote the *Serenade* on impulse," he told Nadejda. "I felt it deeply, from start to finish, and therefore I dare to believe it will not be without merit. As always, in the best places in the music, you were in my mind as I wrote."

Whatever his inspiration for the *Serenade,* it proved to be one of the loveliest things Tchaikowsky ever wrote; tender and melodious, it charms each hearer anew. Nadejda was madly happy that she had been part of the inspiration for a piece Tchaikowsky believed in; from Florence she told him so, and she did not spare paper to say it. At the end she asked: "Why, Peter Ilyich, have you never written a trio for piano and strings? Every day I regret it, because I hear so many trios and then I sigh that you have not written one."

Debussy and the Moscow 'cellist, Danilchenko, were responsible for the widow's interest in piano trios. They had only just left Florence, and the Villa Oppenheim still rang with the echo of many trios—Pahulsky of course, had played the violin parts. But this was not the first time Nadejda had thought about trios; a year ago, when Tchaikowsky was working on the *Maid of Orleans,* she had written him one summer day from Brailov of a dream she had had the night before. Such a lovely dream! She thought that Peter Ilyich had written a trio for piano, 'cello and flute, and it had been so beautiful that all next day the music had remained with her, singing like angelic voices. . . .

Tchaikowsky had answered nothing to that, but to her direct question, this autumn of 1880, he made a detailed reply.

To Nadejda Philaretovna

Kamenka
Oct. 26, 1880

"You ask why I never write trios. You will have to forgive me, my friend, but this is something quite beyond my power. There is some arrangement of my auditory organs that simply will not accept any combination of piano with single violin or 'cello. To me the different *timbres* of these instruments are at war, and I assure you it is real torment to listen to a trio or sonata with violin or 'cello. I cannot explain this physiological fact, I can only state it. Quite otherwise is the combination of piano and orchestra; here also the *timbres* cannot fuse—moreover the piano is incapable of merging with the rest; the elasticity of its make-up causes it to bound away from any other phonetic mass. *But* there are here two balancing forces; namely, the mighty, inexhaustible richness of the colorful orchestra, set against a small, plain but spirited rival who emerges victorious—provided the performer is talented.

"In this battle is much poesy and, for the composer, many tempting combinations of sound. But what could be more unnatural than to combine three such definite personalities as the violin, 'cello and piano? The merits of all three are lost. The warm, wonderfully sustained sounds of violin and 'cello lose all their value in competition with the king of instruments, while the latter tries in vain to sing as its rivals can sing! In my opinion, the piano is of value only: (1) as solo, (2) with orchestra, (3) as accompaniment, meaning as background to a picture. A trio, however, presupposes equality and similarity, and how can this ever be achieved between fiddlestick instruments and piano? It cannot. Therefore a piano trio is an artificial thing, each instrument playing, not what is natural to it but what the author has forced upon it because of difficulty in distributing the voices in accordance with his musical idea.

"I appreciate the skill and ingenuity with which such composers as Beethoven, Schumann and Mendelssohn have overcome these difficulties and I know numbers of trios with an excellent musical form, but as a form I don't like the trio and therefore cannot write for it with true feeling. I know, dear friend, that we disagree in this, and that you like trios, but in spite of the sympathy of our respective musical dispositions, after all we are still two distinct individuals and it is natural for us to differ upon fine points.

"How I should like to have pleased you by writing a trio! Indeed, I am always ready to work at anything for your pleasure. But this time my music would not have pleased you, because it would have lacked true inspiration. Even sitting here thinking about the sound of a trio, I feel a definite, disagreeable physical sensation."

Tchaikowsky was not the first artist to repudiate an idea and then be roused, by the very force of his own negation, to an interest in the thing he had condemned. To the layman who thinks a man should know what he wants to do, and then *do* it, the suggestibility of the artist seems amazing. Tell a Cowper to write a poem about the par lor sofa, or suggest a *Last Supper* to a Leonardo, and the mysterious yeast of creation begins to ferment. If these men are so great, says the layman, why don't they think of subjects by themselves? Why are they not so charged with subject matter that they simply ignore other people's ideas?

This is an esthetic question, the answer to which can be no more than speculation. Many of the greatest artists pass through periods of sterility engendered by nothing more than their own lack of confidence in themselves. Doubt assails them with cold fury of onslaught, and nothing but praise—or desperation or need for money --will vanquish it. Sometimes praise will be more efficacious even than hunger or fear, and surely, a suggested idea for execution, given by a friend, is a species of praise? Thinks the artist, "This lady would never tell me to write about a sofa unless she thought me so consummate a craftsman that I could write about anything and everything. Very likely she is wrong and I can never write again about anything, let alone a sofa, but it will not hurt to try. I can always tear the poem up. . . ."

Or, more simply, an idea from a friend may be a healthy challenge to workmanship. In the case of Tchaikowsky and the trio, for a year after he had so flatly refused the widow's suggestion, Peter did not mention the word "trio." But the ferment had begun, and the widow was later to have a surprise.

It was nearly December now, of 1880, and daily the voice of the world penetrated more insistently to Tchaikowsky in Kamenka. Theatre and concert stage called loudly for his music—and called for the composer to direct rehearsals and conduct orchestras. The time was soon to come when a deeper retreat than Kamenka would be needed; Tchaikowsky could no longer afford to play, in his rare leisure moments, the strenuous role of Uncle Petia.

24

Fame. Farewell to the Chief

TCHAIKOWSKY went up to Moscow and found himself head over ears in work. He loved to work, but this was something different. Whereas an obscure man may create symphonies alone in his room, flooded with the peace and joy of inspiration—fame requires him to sit proof-reading in a glass cage, with all the world pointing its finger.

On December 3rd, 1880, he wrote Nadejda at four in the morning:

"Next week the Musical Society will play my *Italian Capriccio. Oprichnik*"—(the opera written in 1872) "is being performed today at the Grand Theatre. . . . From all sides my music is received with sympathy. All morning I spend reading proof, and as I finish the sheets they are handed to the printer."

So moved the life of a famous musician and man of affairs. Many men would have been flattered by it; it would have suited Nicholas Rubinstein to a T. From Moscow, Tchaikowsky went up to Petersburg. The autumn fog, the damp and the darkness did not improve his spirits. At eleven in the morning, although his room had good exposure, he had to write by candlelight.

To Nadejda Philaretovna

Petersburg
November 27, 1880

"I arrived here this morning and hasten to talk with you a little, my dear, best friend. For God's sake do not be angry with me for writing you so little from Moscow. My life there was nothing but forced labor, and because of eye-strain in proof-reading, my neuralgic headaches came back and I had to leave Moscow without finishing the work I had planned. I thought it best to change my routine and see if I could get some rest. So I came to Petersburg strictly incognito, and hope to keep this except for one or two close relatives.

"In Moscow I had the strangest sensation; in spite of everything, my love for that ancient city did not decrease. On the contrary it grew stronger and stronger, but in the most painful way. It seemed to me I had been dead for a long time, that all my former life had dropped to oblivion and that I was quite another man, living in another world and another age. It would be hard to tell you how or why this sensation was so painful, but it was. I could conquer it only by excessive work or excessive libations to Bacchus, and I had wide recourse to both remedies. The result was extreme fatigue.

"There were, however, happy moments. The Directors of the Moscow Musical Society became much interested in my *Liturgy*" (Saint John Chrysostom) "and one of them—Alexiev—gave the best choir in Moscow a generous fee to study the music. As a result, my *Liturgy* was performed in the concert hall of the Conservatory last Friday. The choir sang perfectly and I experienced one of the happiest moments of my life as a composer. Everyone who was there seemed as pleased as I. The Musical Society has decided to perform it again at a special concert. So at last my *Liturgy*, which has suffered much persecution, will become known.

"And on that same evening the professors and students of the Conservatory played, as a surprise for me, the *Serenade* for strings which I just wrote in Kamenka. They played it well, and it gave me the greatest pleasure. At the moment, I consider this the best thing I have written. And have I told you, my dear, that *Eugene Onegin* will be staged at the Moscow Opera? Beviniani will see that it is well done, and this makes me very happy. . . ."

As to the *Liturgy*, when the special concert took place the hall was crowded, largely owing to the fact that the *Liturgy* had formerly been forbidden performance by the censor. As applause was prohibited for church music, it was impossible to tell which parts made the most favorable impression. Modeste Tchaikowsky reported that opinion was divided everywhere except amongst the numerous clergy and church officials present. These condemned the whole performance. Why, they asked indignantly, should M. Tchaikowsky clamber into church music? Let him stick to his waltzes, polkas and operas.

Most of all, the clergy were annoyed by the enthusiastic ovation given Peter Ilyich at the end of the concert. Again and again he was called to the stage and finally presented with a lyre made of laurel leaves. What, asked the clergy, had the blessed Liturgy to do with personal applause and laurel leaves? Bishop Ambrose wrote the newspaper *Rus* about it. This, said the Bishop, was the Liturgy of Saint John Chrysostom, and it had appeared upon the program as the *Liturgy* of P. I. Tchaikowsky! Church music is meant for church, not the concert hall, nor is a liturgy a folk legend to be used as a libretto. Applause—laurel leaves? Let the Orthodox rejoice that this time the Liturgy had fallen into the hands of a reputable musician and was well written and well performed. Let them beware of the time when the sacred Mass would be produced under the name of Rosenblum or Rosenthal, and be received with hisses and cat-calls. . . .

Tchaikowsky was genuinely hurt by this criticism. He had written the music not as a musical "piece" at all, but with deepest religious and artistic spirit, in an endeavor to purge church music of modern dilutions and cheap substitutes for the old musical modes. He was not the first man nor the last to fight a losing battle with the church—whether Catholic or Protestant—over the restoration of the ancient dignity of its music.

As to the *Italian Capriccio*, it blew its cavalry call in Moscow under Rubinstein's baton that same December, also in Petersburg under the direction of the faithful Napravnik—and received its just deserts. All these concerts required no more of Tchaikowsky than attendance at the final performance—Rubinstein especially was furious if the composer ruined the box office by refusing to be present and make his twenty bows. What really occupied Peter Ilyich this month was the operatic stage. With the *Maid of Orleans* in rehearsal in Petersburg and *Onegin* preparing for performance in Moscow, December rapidly assumed nightmare proportions. Travelling up and down between the cities, Peter watched jealous sopranos fight for the part of Jeanne d'Arc; as for *Onegin*, Moscow gave it a bad press after the first night, added to which the prima donna fell ill and the opera had to be laid aside. Never another opera! cried Peter Ilyich. Never let me put pen to paper where opera is concerned! Roars of protest, vows that he would not bear another such child—and all

the while he knew, like a mother in the midst of her worst agony
—that he would give birth again and yet again.

"Are you surprised, Nadejda Philaretovna," he wrote, "that a man
enjoying success in his career, should complain of fate? Well, my
success is not as great as it may seem, and anyway, success could
never compensate for the unbearable suffering I experience when
coming in contact with human beings, compelled forever to parade
as a spectacle, robbed of the hope of living as I wish, with no time
for reading or writing—pushed about senselessly, as in a ball room.
A month of this is ahead of me. I think of it with horror, and wonder
where I shall find strength to sustain it.

"Even the newspapers that pretended to praise *Onegin* have an
undercurrent of scorn: I lack inspiration, Tatiana's part is pale and
dry, my *Maid of Orleans* will prove thoroughly commonplace. . . .
I could stand abuse, but what is hardest to bear is that I am in everyone's sight, pointed at in the streets . . ."

In Petersburg, Napravnik performed the Second Symphony as revised by Tchaikowsky in Rome a year ago; the first movement was
completely new, and sweeping changes had been made throughout.
After the performance, the newspapers were most laudatory—but
not one critic had noticed that the symphony had been rewritten or
changed at all! No wonder Peter Ilyich grew indifferent to professional criticism. . . .

Nadejda was in Brailov now with her boys for the Christmas
season, but Tchaikowsky was travelling so busily that he seldom
heard from her. In the midst of the Bishop's protest and Petersburg
rehearsals of the *Maid of Orleans,* came a few words from Brailov
that were to Tchaikowsky, he confessed, as heavenly manna. He
needed such spiritual nourishment; everyone, including the newspapers, was prophesying failure for the *Maid;* also, Peter's enemies
seized upon the dedication to Napravnik, calling it a piece of shrewdly
managed flattery on the composer's part—a mean charge, considering that Napravnik had long been one of Tchaikowsky's best friends,
and also that toadying was one fault of which Peter was never
guilty.

When the *Maid* was performed late in February, Tchaikowsky had a great personal success—twenty-four times, he was called before the curtain. Nevertheless this ovation gave him no real pleasure; Tchaikowsky knew that the directors of the Maryinsky Theatre were hostile to the opera, and that the singers themselves were angry and dissatisfied with their parts. Next day the press tore both opera and performance to shreds and the *Maid* was crossed from the Maryinsky repertory.

Tchaikowsky shook the Petersburg dust from his feet and entrained for Italy. From Florence he wrote Nadejda a quiet happy letter and then went on to Rome, incognito, as he thought, and looking forward to rest and freedom. But no sooner had he registered at the hotel than Grand Dukes and princesses besieged his door. On Sunday morning he was compelled to lunch with royalty, which meant rushing about Rome in search of a dress suit—a difficult program on a Sunday with all the stores closed. At lunch he was shy and miserable, he told Nadejda. Some evil fate induced him to accept two more invitations and it was plain he would have to go away. "I simply have not the strength to refuse these invitations; I am pursued by a false fear of offending people." Baroness Iksul, wife of the Russian Ambassador, invited him to dinner, and Lady Hamilton. What do they want of me? he fretted. "I am not a pianist, and cannot entertain them!" But on March 14th, news came of the assassination of Alexander II, and Tchaikowsky, terribly distressed, and shocked that social festivities should continue under such circumstances, fled from Rome.

But a more personal grief awaited. In Nice, Peter found a letter from Anatol, saying that Nicholas Rubinstein was on his way from Moscow, travelling for his health. Before leaving home, Peter had known the Chief was ill and needed a rest; he and Nadejda had discussed it. The Moscow physicians were at their wits' end; Rubinstein was seriously ill—whether with liver or kidney condition they could not decide—but they knew he ought to be in bed, and bed was the last place Rubinstein would consent to occupy.

"Nicholas Grigorievitch cannot rest," wrote Tchaikowsky. "He is a perfect contrast to you and me. In proportion as we love seclusion, he loves to walk about the world and roar. He simply cannot live without excitement and rushing about; it is life to him. He dislikes reading, to walk bores him and he even has no pleasure in making music for himself—others must be there to listen. What can rest and tranquillity give such a man? Nothing but torture."

And now, in Nice, Peter Ilyich heard by telegram from Jurgenson that the Chief was in Paris, terribly ill, in danger of his life. Peter wired for news and received an answering telegram with the one word, "Hopeless," followed by a second which announced simply: "Rubinstein is dead."

Tchaikowsky left instantly for Paris, enduring on the journey, he afterward wrote Modeste, all the tortures of the damned. The full realization of his loss had not yet come; Peter was concerned now with an immediate—and what he himself called a shameful fear: dread of the sight of Rubinstein's dead body. Peter would have to go straight from the station to the hotel; Madame Tretiakoff, wife of Rubinstein's Moscow friend and patron, would open the door of Rubinstein's suite; Madame Tretiakoff had been with Nicholas at his death. . . .

But when, twelve hours later, Madame Tretiakoff opened the door to Peter Ilyich, she told him that Rubinstein's body had been taken to the church very early that morning. Poor Nicholas had suffered a frightful death; not once during the last six days and nights of his life had she left him. Those idiot Moscow doctors had designated his pains as gout, had told him to give up wine and red meat and had sent him off, poor gallant soul, on this long journey of recreation. And what had he had but tuberculosis of the intestines! All during the trip he had suffered horribly, and all during the six days here in Paris. To the end he had remained conscious, trying all the time to be brave and gay, even when he became so weak he could scarcely speak or move his hands.

Rubinstein's last gesture was made with something of his old bravado. On Wednesday, March 26th, at noon, he said he was hungry and would like some oysters. . . . The watchers round his bed looked at each other in dismay; oysters, for a man whose viscera were practically non-existent! Nevertheless, if the Chief wanted oysters, oysters he must have, and they were brought with a flourish of napkins and covered silver dishes. Rubinstein ate them, and said that they were good.

Three hours afterward, he was dead.

The funeral was held in the Russian church in Paris, the coffin being brought down to the lower chapel to rest in state. Here, for the last time, Peter Ilyich looked upon the Chief's face. The dreaded moment proved even more terrible than in anticipation; the familiar face was almost unrecognizable. Peter stood there, among the candles, the full-skirted priests, the chanting, the incense that should disguise the hideousness of man's mortality—and he was not deceived. Looking down at the bier, wave after wave of terror and grief passed over Peter Ilyich. This shrunken mask that had been a face, these grey claws crossed upon the breast. . . . Oh, above all, these colorless, motionless hands proved Nicholas Grigorievitch was no more! Whenever, in twenty years, had he seen these hands quiet? How wrong, how cruel to display thus helpless, those splendid fingers through which had moved the very river of life, those hands that had evoked magic to make the stupidest listener aware of the power and the glory that was man's inheritance. . . .

The Chief, lying dead at forty-five. Twenty years ago this man had set him, Peter, upon his feet, had said, "Here, Peter, is your job. Music is your job. Now, prove yourself a musician."

And to what end? To the end that he, Peter, might in turn lie thus, hands crossed upon his breast in candlelight while the curious filed by, pretending grief? Standing beside the body of his Chief, doubt swept over Peter Ilyich. In that moment, and indeed for days to come he lived in a painful confusion, engrossed in the desperate search to which every sensitive man is propelled by the sight of death. "I long to believe in a future life," he wrote Nadejda. "When I can say the longing has become belief, then I shall be happy."

Rubinstein's body was sent home to Russia for burial. Tchaikowsky went to the station and watched the coffin put on the train. "I am crushed with grief," he wrote Nadejda. "My God, my God, how terrible are such moments in our lives."

Anton Rubinstein, it was true, had come immediately from Spain upon news of his brother's death—but Anton's presence could not make Nicholas—alive or dead—less alone. Tchaikowsky perceived this at once, the more so as all the world knew of Nicholas' devotion to his older brother; Nicholas had always been immensely proud of Anton. When Nadejda wrote asking about Anton's reaction to his brother's death, Peter Ilyich replied that Anton's bearing had shown less sorrow than relief that his celebrated brother was out of the way at last. The whole exhibition had so shocked and depressed Tchaikowsky that he had refused to accompany Anton home to Russia for the public funeral.

Nadejda had not much comfort to give. "Poor, poor Nicholas Grigorievitch!" she wrote. "Or rather, poor we who have lost him! Now who will be able to play your music so well?"

Who indeed? Tchaikowsky might have answered; and posterity might add: That man is yet to come.

25

Good-bye to Brailov. Antonina disposed of

Tchaikowsky did not accompany the Chief on this last journey home, but he planned to return to Russia none the less. The Moscow Conservatory was without a director; whether or no Peter Ilyich accepted the position (he knew it would be offered him), duty and common decency required that he be in Moscow to help choose Rubinstein's successor. Also, Nadejda had written him vague but extremely alarming letters concerning financial losses; if she were indeed on the verge of bankruptcy, as she intimated, Peter would have to go back to teaching. She had declared, Peter wrote Modeste, that compared with the millions she had lost, his pension was nothing and she would continue it as before. But one never could tell. This, and the sad fact of Rubinstein's death brought Peter, so he said, face to face with changes that would affect his whole life.

Peter went home by the northern route that landed him in Petersburg. He wrote often to Nadejda, reminding her that now she was in trouble, it was good he need be a burden to her no longer. "I am absolutely secure now from poverty and even from financial discomfort; I have only to say the word to be admitted to either conservatory with an excellent salary. The fact that if I take up a professorship it will be done for necessity, and without any pleasure whatever, is not worth thinking of."

This last was no bid for sympathy; it was a perfectly sincere statement, answering Nadejda's anxiety lest Tchaikowsky again take up the Conservatory burden.

"Whatever you do and however you conduct yourself," she wrote, "I must tell you that *I will not give up my right to take care of you*, nor have you any right to take this from me. In Paris, after Nicholas Grigorievitch's death, you expressed beautiful religious feelings in a letter to me. Belief in God's providence, submission to His will.

Well then, are you planning to stand up now and fight Him? He has arranged things as they are. You and I are but tools in His hand. . . ."

Thus the widow von Meck, imperious as always. If being a tool in God's hand would serve her purpose, very well, she would be a tool, and incidentally, shape the mold to her liking.

Good! replied Peter Ilyich. I shall obey you . . . "Let us, as you say, trust in God. May His will be done. But don't forget, dear friend, that either conservatory would receive me with excellent salary. . . ." Arrived in Moscow, he found this indeed to be the case. Moscow without Rubinstein was a ship without a helmsman and everyone—even Rubinstein's enemies—admitted it. The heads of the Musical Society implored Tchaikowsky to accept the Directorship of the Conservatory. It required all his strength, Peter wrote Nadejda, to refuse. His own choice as Director was Taneyeff, whom later he hoped to see appointed. Such matters move slowly; meanwhile, Tchaikowsky went out to Kamenka where the children gave him a touching welcome. Their parents were away and Uncle Petia assumed charge.

"I was with them the whole day and am so tired I can write only these few lines. It made me sad to see old Madame Davydoff, my brother-in-law's mother, who is nearly blind. She is the last of the wives of the Decembrists who followed their husbands to Siberia. Last year she lost one eye and now she is losing the other through the many tears she has shed over family troubles and the Tsar's death. But such is her religious faith that she bears her misfortune calmly, fully resigned to God's will."

But this valiant old lady was not quite so resigned to blindness as her grand-nephew-in-law liked to believe. She had cataract on both eyes, which she was fully convinced came from weeping over first one Tsar's death and then the other—a typical Russian paradox, considering a Tsar had exiled her husband and herself in the first place. However, she decided to be operated on by the village doctor at Kamenka, a brilliant surgeon and confirmed drunkard whose hands, when he was sober, shook so he could not pick up an instrument

Well fortified by vodka he operated on the old lady not once but twice, and she kept her eyesight until her death. This, it might be remarked, was a tough generation.

Nadejda von Meck replied to Peter's letter in a tone quite remote from the resignation he had commended in Madame Davydoff. Things were going from bad to worse, wrote Nadejda. So much so that she feared for the proposed union of the families von Meck and Davydoff. Her money seemed to be dissolving; would Leo Davydoff want a pauper for son-in-law?—"It may seem strange to you"—so ran her letter—"for a woman to worry about money when she owns a railroad a hundred and sixty miles long, leading to one of the best seaports in Russia, also an estate of twelve thousand acres" (Brailov), "the most luxurious house in Moscow and a huge collection of diamonds and every kind of *objet d'art,* etc. But my children, although possessing all this, may very well have no money to live on, because, although every one of these properties is sound and should bring in a return if properly handled, I have no one capable of this management. Volodia cannot do it because he bears the von Meck name and everyone tries to exploit him—as they do me—in each and every matter. No one has ever tried to help us with our affairs; on the contrary, people have tried to obstruct us. The envy and wickedness of the world is incredible."

As she grew older, whenever somebody got the better of her or of her eldest son, Volodia (Vladimir), Nadejda was apt to complain bitterly of the world's wickedness and the ingratitude of man. As to Peter Ilyich, he was at present engrossed in Davydoff family troubles and had no spirit to comfort Nadejda. . . . Tatiana, his beautiful eldest niece, once gay and fairylike as her name, had got herself engaged to a gentleman of noble blood who had behaved far from nobly. Uncle Petia tried to distract her. For hours on end the two played duets on the piano or read aloud from a book in the garden. But all to no purpose. Tatiana had recourse to morphine and refused to rally. Uncle Petia wrote page after page about her to Nadejda in Moscow, but Nadejda, who never had much sympathy for love's alarums, merely replied that the girl was well rid of a bad bargain, and Peter Ilyich had better leave Kamenka if he was going to be so disturbed. . . . "I want so terribly to be useful here," wrote Peter, "but every day convinces me that I am powerless to do anything really valuable for any of them. I feel no desire to write music; I have never been this way for such a long time before. I ask myself if inspiration is gone forever, and then I recall other periods of equal flatness and hope that when my moral horizon clears, my desire to create will dawn once more. . . . Jurgenson wants me to come to Moscow and talk over some work he has for me."

Jurgenson was a sensible publisher who knew when his authors needed prodding. He and Modeste sent Tchaikowsky a box of books on the rites and ceremonials of the Russian church; Peter stumbled through them, hoping they would be of help in revising and restoring some of the ancient chants. What Jurgenson really wanted was for Tchaikowsky to edit the works of the late Bortniansky, who had arranged much music for the Church—the very composer to whose dominant sevenths Peter had taken such violent exception in a letter to Nadejda. Jurgenson forwarded the Bortniansky material to Peter, who pronounced it a mass of rubbish, advised his publisher to abandon the plan and then, after examining what he called his "finances," and finding them far from satisfactory, plunged into the job. All through July and August he worked at Bortniansky—"a loathsome task," he wrote Jurgenson, "which I shall finish because I always finish what I have begun. But one of these days I shall burst with sheer irritation."

When Nadejda von Meck heard about Bortniansky, she was furious. Must the composer of the Fourth Symphony be compelled to deaden his inspiration with such nonsense? "If you have contracted with Jurgenson to do this work, you will have to finish it, but can't you do it at intervals, spread it out and work on your own music in between?"

A check fell out of the envelope; Peter looked at it and looked back at the long letter that accompanied it. Nadejda was offended, she said, because in money difficulties Peter Ilyich had gone to

Jurgenson. "Do as you please, of course," she wrote, "but surely, you cannot refuse me this time?"

Tchaikowsky did not refuse her. He was completely worn out with this Bortniansky. What with the sheer tedium of the work and worry over Tatiana, he had been ill for two weeks with a heavy fever. Diphtheria, he called it, quite calmly, adding that everybody in Kamenka had been down with it. The minute he got out of bed he went doggedly back to Bortniansky. . . . Now he could pay a hack Moscow musician to do half the work. But he is ashamed, he tells Nadejda, to have whined; if ever again he gets into money difficulties, let his friend remember it is nobody's fault but his own, and he can very well expiate it in uncongenial work. What happens is—says Peter—he gets hold of some money and then needy people ask him for it. What can he do but give the money away? It makes the family angry; here in Kamenka they tell him he cannot afford this role of benefactor. "But I have so much money! Thanks to you, Nadejda Philaretovna, in the last four years I have attained to riches such as I never dreamed of. Not just enough, but far in excess of my needs."

One is reminded here of the time, not so long ago, when Peter Ilyich, penniless in Berlin, could not leave town because of an unpaid hotel bill, yet wrote Nadejda that his finances were in the most brilliant condition because so many people owed him money. . . . But now, in Kamenka, he implores the widow never again to give him money over and above his quarterly allowance; he is horribly afraid he may take advantage of her generosity. Indeed, when he opened her letter and saw the money, then read what she said about Bortniansky, he shed tears.

And anyway, finished Tchaikowsky with the candor he was at all times helpless to control, even though he had worked all these weeks at Bortniansky and been bored to death by it, he could not have composed anything worth while with all this Tatiana affair raging round him. So probably Bortniansky had been valuable as a nerve-steadier.

It is easy to see why the widow—so suspicious of the world where her fortune was concerned—loved to give money to Peter Ilyich. Here was a man who not only was worth supporting as an artist, but who did not seem to know the meaning of the word greed. Six thousand roubles a year was a fortune to him. Unfortunately for the widow, the rumors that had gone round Moscow in the spring concerning the von Meck properties were true; she had lost a serious amount of money. Not enough to interfere with Peter's pension, but enough so that immediate funds must be raised if Nadejda were not to lose her capital.

Ensconced in what she had called "the most luxurious house in Moscow," the widow sat at a desk that was deep in bills, financial statements. . . . Something must be sacrificed to meet these demands. This house? These paintings? Could she reduce the allowance of her grown children? Vladimir's wife, the frivolous little Liza, had just forwarded a dressmaker's bill from Paris that was nothing short of outrageous. But if it remained unpaid, Liza would not send little Volichka to his grandmother next month. . . . *Brailov!* All the time, Nadejda had known Brailov was the solution, but she had not liked to face it. Brailov had never paid as an estate; in spite of enormous outlay on the latest scientific equipment for farm and beet-sugar factory, each year had seen a deplorable financial deficit. Peter Ilyich had expressed himself distressed and puzzled over this and had offered in all seriousness to send his brother-in-law, Leo Davydoff, down from Kamenka to interview Nadejda's steward. Surely, Peter had said, Nadejda Philaretovna was being badly cheated somewhere. Kamenka, with only old-fashioned equipment, brought in more revenue.

But Nadejda had refused Leo Davydoff's help. Such an investigation would hurt her steward's feelings, she said. And now, this August of 1881, a buyer had appeared for Brailov, offering 1,440,000 roubles ($720,000). A shocking loss of course; the property was worth twice that sum. . . . So Nadejda, with a sad backward glance, sold Brailov and bought a less elaborate estate. "We shall have to forget Brailov now, my dear friend," she wrote Peter; "put it forever from our minds and imagine it as occupied by strangers. . . ."

This advice was characteristic of Nadejda, who believed that by saying she had put a thing from her mind, she had actually done so. She professed herself an atheist—presto! God was outside her mind; she could do without Him. She renounced the world, and lo! the world would have no power to plague her further. As to Brailov, she would forget it, would tell herself it belonged to strangers now and behold, its loss could cause her no pangs! Again and again the widow played this dangerous part, and again and again it recoiled upon her with the deadly spring, the powerful inevitable blow of heaven and law defied. This was the trait which, pathologically multiplied, in the end was to separate Nadejda forever from Peter Ilyich.

But when Tchaikowsky heard that Brailov was gone, he offered no comfort and no system of philosophy. He had best not tell Nadejda how he felt; let his dear friend go away somewhere, said he, and try to forget. Could she go to Italy now, in the autumn? Perhaps he could join her there. Meanwhile he went up to Moscow for the month of September, living with Anatol quite happily, as fashionable Moscow was still in the country for its summer vacation and the two could roam the streets undisturbed. Then he went again to Kamenka, where he was harried by the appearance of another young man asking for help. Peter, of course, emptied his pockets into the boy's and then wrote Jurgenson, imploring him to take the lad at once into his publishing house. "Laugh if you must," wrote Peter, "but *please* take this person off my hands. What can I do with him here?"

The patient Jurgenson complied and gave the boy a job, upon which the lad proceeded to become queerer and queerer. Truly, the duties of a publisher are manifold!

And this was not the only good turn Jurgenson did his famous client this summer of 1880. Carefully tracking Antonina (Jurgenson, apparently, had not forgotten that unpleasant interview when the conversation had turned "like a squirrel in a cage"), Jurgenson discovered something unpleasant but important. As long ago as the winter before last, Antonina had taken a lover and had had a child by him. She had placed the child in a foundlings' home, and she herself was now in Moscow, living with the child's father. There was no uncertainty about any of it. Jurgenson had been at pains to collect positive evidence. "She will leave me in peace now," wrote Peter Ilyich, a little wearily.

She would leave him in peace, truly enough, where terror of black-mail was concerned. That fear was gone, as far as Antonina had been able to evoke it—not gone forever because only death, for this man, could lay that spectre. But news of Antonina's "misconduct," as the 1880's would have called it, was the best news Peter could have had concerning his wife. A weapon was in his hands; he who had been so long the guilty party, so long defenseless, could fight Antonina on equal terms at last.

Antonina was not out of his life, however; she would always remain his responsibility and he would pay her an allowance. The mere sight of a letter in her handwriting would continue to prostrate him, make him physically ill. Jurgenson remained go-between and Tchaikowsky's valuable protector; no publisher wants his best author incapacitated by a woman, and anyway, Peter Ilyich was Jurgenson's very good friend.

Thus, except for a few harried allusions in Tchaikowsky's diary later on, we take leave of poor Antonina. She was born to be a victim, and perhaps it is the worst tragedy of the born victim that the pity they win from us is tinged rather with impatience than with liking. Her mania that the world of men was in love with her mounted until in 1896 she was put in an insane asylum in Petersburg, where she remained until her death in 1917. During the progress of her insanity, Antonina went right on having children and placing them in the foundlings' home; none of the Tchaikowskys ever knew who the father was nor did they see the children, but everyone was grateful to Antonina that she did not give them the Tchaikowsky name, as she might have done—never, of course, having divorced Peter Ilyich. The Tchaikowskys were grateful also that Antonina did not seek them out; they tried to forget her—if her name was mentioned, cold silence met the question and the conversation shifted quickly.

But now, at the end of October, Tchaikowsky, in Kamenka, was concerned over something nearer at hand. His niece Vera, whom he and Nadejda had destined as wife of Nicholas (Kolia) von Meck, had fallen in love elsewhere, Peter wrote Nadejda in Rome. Vera was engaged to marry one of the Rimsky-Korsakovs. There was no need to add that this was a distinguished name in Russia. Like everyone, Nadejda knew of the Rimsky-Korsakovs, knew that the family belonged by proud tradition to the Navy and that the composer of that name was already, by reason of his serious musicianship, a thorn in the family's side.

The Grand Duke Constantin, Korsakov's great friend, had been matchmaker, Peter Ilyich went on to explain. He had always feared that Vera would slip away from them before Kolia von Meck was out of school—but he had not given up the idea of becoming related to Nadejda Philaretovna. Might he present another candidate, Anna? Anna was only sixteen and not so beautiful as her older sisters, but agreeable and extremely clever. Would it not be as well for Kolia to go down to Kiev this winter for the Carnival, and make the acquaintance of the Davydoffs? After all, it was risky to keep on losing nieces before Kolia von Meck had even met them!

Much correspondence ensued concerning Anna's character; Nadejda was a little suspicious of her at first, because the girl was a student and had been sent away to school. For all Nadejda's independent attitude, she was anything but progressive in her ideas about women's education. But Tchaikowsky assured her that in spite of a brilliant intellect and natural aptitude for study, Anna was a charming creature.

And now the Bortniansky edition was finished, thanks to Nadejda's check earlier in the summer. Tchaikowsky started north to Petersburg; he was planning to go to Rome with Modeste. Nadejda was in Florence. At Kiev, Peter stopped off for a fortnight, becoming engrossed once more with church music as heard at the Lavra Monastery. Here the ancient chants were sung in the ancient manner, preserving the original harmonies. Tchaikowsky was much impressed, and angry with a stupid public that spurned this traditional singing, preferring the doctored and sweetened music of the more modern churches.

"It outrages me," he wrote, "and I cannot bring myself to admit that I am powerless to do anything about it. All my efforts to work for Russian church music have met with persecution. My liturgy has been forbidden by the authorities. Two months ago, when Mass was held for the soul of Nicholas Rubinstein, those in charge of the funeral asked that my liturgy might be performed. Alas! I was deprived of the pleasure of hearing my liturgy sung in church because the Moscow diocesan authorities absolutely forbade it; Bishop Ambrose called it Roman Catholic. This was the same Bishop who wrote articles last year in the magazine *Rus* about the indecency of singing my liturgy at concerts, as the Musical Society had sung it. I am helpless to fight these strange and absurd persecutions. Ranged against me are influential people who persistently keep any ray of light from penetrating that sphere of ignorance and gloom."

From Kiev, Tchaikowsky went to Italy. Nadejda was still in Florence, but the composer stopped there only for a day or two; Modeste with his young pupil wished to be in Rome, and Nadejda seemed to understand that the brothers needed some time in Rome together. Also, Nadejda was happy now in her Villa Oppenheim because her favorite grandson, Volichka, was with her. She wrote glowing descriptions of him, sending his latest photograph. During this December of 1881 the two exchanged easy conversational letters. Sarah Bernhardt had been touring Russia; they both heard that in Kiev she had had little success. Tchaikowsky's sister had not liked her at all. "Plainly," wrote Nadejda, "Bernhardt is a good actress, but not the genius they tried to make her out in Vienna."

Tchaikowsky, who usually complained about Rome because there were too many things in it, wrote now in great content.

"Rome is like Moscow," he said. "The more one knows the city, the more one loves it." At Saint Peters they had sung Palestrina *a capella*—a cheering occasion for a man who loved church music performed in its original purity. "My room is very comfortable," wrote Tchaikowsky, "and the minute I arrived I began to compose. I don't know how it will turn out, but I am writing music for the scene between Mazeppa and Maria from Pushkin's *Poltava.* If I become really fascinated by it, perhaps I shall write a whole opera on the subject!"

This from the man who not six months ago had declared he was through with opera forever. He did write the opera *Mazeppa,* completing it the following year. It was not performed until 1884, and had only a moderate success. It has since gone into complete oblivion.

Disquieting news reached the composer now from Petersburg: Napravnik had resigned his leadership of the Musical Society because he could not weather the quarrels and intrigues. He is too honest! cried Tchaikowsky. Davidov, Director of the Petersburg Conservatory, was to conduct the orchestra in Napravnik's stead. Also, from Petersburg, Leopold Auer declared he would not perform Tchaikowsky's Violin Concerto because it was too difficult, too startling in its harmonies and effects. Adolf Brodsky, a violinist who had taught for a time at the Moscow Conservatory, had courageously championed this piece ever since its appearance (Tchaikowsky had written it in the spring of 1878 when Nadejda sent him to Switzerland to recover from his marriage). Now, on December 4th, 1881, Brodsky played the concerto in Vienna at a Philharmonic concert—and fury broke over his head. Hanslick, the famous German critic, attacked it viciously, and Peter Ilyich, picking up the *Neue Freie Presse* downstairs in his hotel, came upon a savage paragraph which he repeated in a letter to Nadejda.

"All my compositions, Hanslick says, are 'uneven, coarse, savage and in bad taste.' As for the violin concerto, the beginning is tolerable, but the further it goes the worse it gets. At the end of the first movement, says he, the violin does not play but roars, shouts and bellows. The Andante begins pleasantly, but soon plunges into the atmosphere of a Russian feast, where everybody is drunk and the faces of the people are brutal and revolting. 'A critic,' Hanslick goes on to say, 'once called a picture so realistic that it stank; when hearing Tchaikowsky's concerto I realized that music also may stink.'

"Isn't this a strange criticism? I have no luck with critics. Since Laroche left Russia there isn't a person at home who has a friendly word for me on the printed page. And now in Europe my music is called 'stinking.'"

Peter Ilyich was not the man to be crushed by criticism; the very next paragraph of his letter—pausing not a moment to revile the critic—describes his newest musical venture.

"My dear, what do you think I have begun to write? You will be astonished! Maybe you will remember suggesting to me once that I write a trio for piano, violin and 'cello, and maybe you remember my answer—in which I told you plainly how I disliked that combination of instruments. And now, in spite of this antipathy, I have decided to make a trial with that kind of music. I have already written the beginning of the trio; I don't know whether it will be successful or whether I shall ever complete it. But I want to finish at least as much as I have sketched.

"I hope you will believe me when I tell you that my chief reason —or rather my sole reason—for reconciling myself to this combination of strings and piano, which I never liked, is to give you pleasure. At other times I have tried, it is true, to put my musical ideas into forms new to me. I want to overcome all technical difficulties, and to this inspiration is added now the warm encouraging knowledge that perhaps I shall please you by so doing!"

Nadejda was actually embarrassed by this. Could it be that she had forced Peter Ilyich into work uncongenial to him? Of course the music would be wonderful, but how very distressing to think of her dear friend struggling with unsympathetic material just for her sake!

Peter Ilyich replied instantly that Nadejda must not think it tiresome for him to work on the trio.

"At the beginning, it was a real effort to reconcile myself to this combination of instruments, but now the work interests and intrigues me, and again I love to think it will give you pleasure. As to the violin concerto, I was awfully touched by Brodsky's courage in making his very first Vienna appearance with a work so intrinsically difficult to play, and moreover, Russian, which the Viennese don't like. It is however very strange to me that Auer, to whom the concerto was dedicated in token of his former public championship of my music—and Davidov, my good friend, refused to play the concerto in Petersburg."

Tchaikowsky changed the dedication of the concerto after this episode, substituting the name of Adolf Brodsky. Meanwhile Nadejda, true friend that she was, searched the newspapers until she found a favorable Viennese review of Brodsky's performance. She sent it to Peter, followed next day by still another. "You see?" she wrote triumphantly. "I was right, Vienna has other men than Hanslick. Let them curse your music if they will—only let the music be performed! It will find more admirers than abusers. . . . And now I see that Damrosch played your concerto two years ago in New York. What a brave fellow! The Lord give us more such men."

So much for the violin concerto, reviled so bitterly, and now a popular part of every violinist's concert repertory. Even Auer reversed his opinion a little later and became one of the concerto's most vivid interpreters. In truth, the piece is uneven, even jerky in its effect; also, it is as Russian as Hanslick said. And this very Russian-ness, this alternation of melting Slavic melancholy with the stamping Cossack rhythms that so outraged the Viennese concert public of 1882, constitutes now the concerto's chief charm.

As for the trio in process of composition in Rome that January of 1882, it did not prove quite the matchless music Nadejda had anticipated. It was dedicated, as all the world knows, *À la mémoire d'un grand artiste* (Nicholas Rubinstein), and Tchaikowsky's fears as to its form were in some measure justified. Requiring an hour and a quarter to play—tremendous length for a piece of chamber music—it attempts too often to burst the confines of its medium and soar unsuccessfully into symphony, a lack of discipline happily not so discernible in the composer's string quartets. The second movement is a long set of variations on an andante theme in E major, intended, says Rosa Newmarch, as recollections of Rubinstein and his musical characteristics at various times of his life. The elegiac bits of the *Trio,* where one definitely feels Tchaikowsky's grief at the loss of his friend, are eminently successful and touching. But all the way through, Peter veered startlingly from the elegiac strain; lively mazurkas, gay waltzes alternate with rapidly varying rhythm until the last page, marked *"lugubre,"* recalls to us the fact that Rubinstein is in his grave.

While he was writing the *Trio,* Tchaikowsky walked about Rome, enjoying himself and hearing all the music he could.

"The other evening," he wrote Nadejda, "I attended a solemn concert in honor of Liszt's seventieth birthday. The program consisted entirely of his works, the performance was worse than mediocre. Liszt himself was there. One could not but feel emotion at sight of this genius, now an old man, so touched and moved by the ovations of the enraptured Italians. Liszt's compositions leave me cold; they show more poetic coloring than true creative power, more paint than drawing. In brief, what he writes, though dazzling, is devoid of inward structure. A complete contrast to Schumann, whose great and vigorous creative force was too big for his means of expression. An Italian celebrity, Sgambati, played. A good pianist, but cold as could be."

And now, as the New Year—1882—arrived, Tchaikowsky, from his little room, which he had said was so comfortable, wrote further that he was "filled with ideas and plans and I am much disposed toward writing music. I think, my dear friend, that I shall write better than I used to, or else it will prove that although my cartridge has grown bigger, I have no more powder. I have grown cold to my former music; all of it, without exception, seems immature, imperfect as to form, and empty. Reason tells me I exaggerate my defects, yet I cannot force myself to look on any of my music with pleasure. In brief, either my song is done, or henceforth I shall sing a better one."

26

1882-1890. The Fifth Symphony. "Do not forget . . ."

In truth, Peter's song was not done and he was to sing a better one. The Fifth and Sixth Symphonies were as yet unwritten, as were the *Nutcracker Suite, Hamlet* and the opera *Pique Dame.* Peter was forty-two now, he had definitely "arrived," he was a musical lion, the most popular musician in Russia. With Antonina in abeyance, with money worries gradually vanishing as his music began bringing in a securer income, Tchaikowsky found himself strong, healthy and surprisingly adequate to the world's demands. He came out of his neurotic shell, emerging consciously, confessing that he had resolved to show himself to the eyes of the world.

Nevertheless, the pension from Nadejda continued to arrive with quarterly regularity. Nadejda clung to her "right," as she called it, to "watch over" Peter Ilyich. The pension was to her a symbol of Peter's dependence, and the widow dispatched it eagerly, awaited eagerly the acknowledgment, which reached her now from increasing distances—from England, Bohemia, France—wherever Peter travelled on behalf of his profession. Nadejda herself lived abroad nearly all the year now, reluctantly following the sun from season to season, outlawed for increasingly longer periods from her beloved Moscow.

Brailov was gone, but when he needed retreat, Peter went down to Plesheyevo, the new von Meck country estate south of Moscow where Nadejda spent a month or two each summer. Plesheyevo was a beautiful old place, built in the eighteenth century before Russia's bad period of architecture had set in. When Nadejda bought it the house was filled with magnificent old furniture. Characteristically, Nadejda threw it all out, replacing it with the plush-and-gilt Parisian atrocities she loved. Between herself and Peter Ilyich, the technique of invisible intimacy and invisible guestdom was by now comfortably established; the widow's proximity caused Peter no alarms.

Meanwhile, music flowed unceasingly from the composer's pen. Between the years 1882–1885 he wrote the opera *Mazeppa,* which has since found oblivion; the second and third orchestral suites and the *Fantasia Concerto* for piano and orchestra, which followed soon afterward, met with instant success. The performance of the Third Orchestral Suite in Petersburg in 1885 marked a period in the composer's career; von Bülow's skillful baton rendered it Tchaikowsky's greatest triumph to date. It was followed by another triumph, when *Onegin* was performed soon afterward for Tsar Alexander III. Peter was summoned to the Imperial box, a long and friendly conversation was held, and forever after Tchaikowsky was assured of Imperial patronage—no small matter to a nineteenth-century Russian musician whose career could be made or marred by royal patronage. Tchaikowsky's music, so Russian yet so cosmopolitan and easily comprehended, comprising none of the wild dissonance, the strange distastefulness (to Imperial palates) of a Moussorgsky or a Borodin, suited the Imperial family perfectly. In truth, they adored Tchaikowsky's music and said so. The Grand Duke Constantin wrote often to Peter Ilyich, obviously eager for the friendship of Russia's first musician.

What might be called Peter's Kamenka period ended about this time, 1885. By then his sister Alexandra Davydoff was launched into the long illness which was to end in her death, the children were grown, Kamenka was a quieter and a sadder place. Anna Davydoff was by now married to Nadejda's son, Nicholas. The lovely Tatiana upon whom Uncle Petia had spent so much time and pity, was at Kamenka no longer; she had met a death as dramatic and swift as her brief young life. Peter grieved deeply and looked about for another home, one that would be his own and would be permanent. He found it in Maidanovo near Klin, a small village easily accessible to Moscow and Petersburg.

Peter's manner of settling into his new home was very characteristic. He entrusted the whole thing to Alexis, who rented the house, purchased all the furnishings, arranged them in the rooms, and when all was ready notified the master he could move in. Peter himself bought nothing except an antique English clock that would not go and two horses which he had a hard time getting rid of afterward. Alexis' taste was deplorable and the place was truly hideous, but Peter loved it, pronouncing himself pleased and proud and often speaking with obvious pleasure of "my table linen, my silver, my cook, my dog." (Alexis hated dogs, so his master dared not have more than one.) As soon as he moved in, Tchaikowsky began work on the symphonic poem, *Manfred*. He wrote Nadejda about *Manfred* and his new house and she replied with sympathy for the music and misgivings as to Peter Ilyich as landlord. She hoped he would continue renting and not be tempted to buy, as property-owning was an irksome business. The following September when Peter reported that he had not only finished *Manfred* but had completed also the first act of a new opera, *The Enchantress*, Nadejda was again in a skeptical mood. "I like your uncompromising statements regarding my opera," Tchaikowsky replied. "You have a good right to look with suspicion upon this insincere form of art." But opera, Peter went on to say, was a serious composer's only means of reaching the mass of people. When Beethoven wrote *Fidelio* he was not motivated by ambition for fame so much as a natural desire to find his way as far as possible into the real heart of humanity. Take *Manfred*, now, or any of his own symphonies, they would be heard once or twice a season and then lie upon dusty shelves for years. Symphony was no doubt a higher, purer form of art than opera, but to refrain from writing the latter, to resist the glitter and attraction of the stage, required the soul of a hero. "Only one such hero," continued Peter, "is alive today—Brahms." Both as man and artist, he wished to say that Brahms had never deviated from the highest ideals. "Unfortunately," finished Peter, "Brahms' creative gift is meagre, unworthy of his aspirations."

It was from his country home that Peter penned this regrettable remark. It was from thence indeed that he wrote most frequently during these years. He took much interest in the village of Maidanovo. Distressed over the idleness and mischief-making of the village children, he consulted the priest concerning the founding of a school. Money, said the priest, was all that was needed, a regular annual sum. Tchaikowsky promised it and after due time the priest reported that permission had arrived from the government. "I am very glad," wrote Peter, and putting on his long heavy coat and his round fur hat, tramped across white January fields to attend the formal opening of the school.

So frequent, by now, were Tchaikowsky's trips abroad, that when he found himself, happily, in his country home, he asked nothing more than to be let alone that he might write his music in peace. *Manfred* was the last composition he wrote in anything but completest solitude. Peter liked *Manfred* at first, but three years after its composition he wrote the Grand Duke Constantin that *Manfred* was a "repulsive work, and I hate it heartily, all except the first movement. In the near future, I plan to destroy the three last movements, which musically are simply trivial (especially the final movement which is impossible. So, from a piece of music that is much too long for a symphony, I shall make a symphonic poem. Then and then only I feel sure my *Manfred* will please. The first movement I wrote with delight, the rest with such effort that I was quite ill for a time afterward."

Previous to the composition of *Manfred,* Tchaikowsky had been very communicative about what he was writing, but from now on he became extremely reserved about his work, never discussed it or mentioned it to the many friends who came out from Moscow to see him. This is not to say Peter did not enjoy his friends' company; on the contrary, he often invited friends to stay with him in Maidanovo. Taneyeff, austere and scholarly soul whom Peter had succeeded in having elected head of the Moscow Conservatory, but who soon resigned to devote himself to composition—being too innocent for the Conservatory job, said Peter Ilyich. Too honest. Jurgenson, Albrecht, Kashkin, Hubert, and especially Peter's beloved brother Modeste— all these were treated most hospitably, but the unbidden guest had need to beware. Not for nothing did Peter tack a placard on his garden gate:

"Peter Ilyich Tchaikowsky. Receives Mondays and Thursdays from 3 to 5. Not at home. Please do not ring."

Peter's friends and intimates were all musicians and knew how to respect a musician's privacy and daily routine of work. And the routine was invariable: Peter rose about seven-thirty, took his tea an hour later, studied English or read seriously in philosophy or history, then went for a short walk and was ready to begin the day's work. If, during the morning tea, Tchaikowsky conversed or invited anyone to share his early walk, it meant that he would not compose that day, but would write letters, correct proof or some other easy business. But on the days when he composed, Tchaikowsky could endure no company until evening. And then he loved it, loved the geniality, the laughter and the wine that helped to free the laughter. That something stronger than wine was enjoyed, Peter's diary records with amusing candor:

Maidanovo
July 11, 1886

"They say it is harmful to abuse alcohol, and with this I willingly agree. Yet for me, a man harassed with nerves, it is simply impossible to live without the poison of alcohol, against which Micluha Maclaw protests. A man with that strange name professes himself happy that he does not know the delights of vodka and other alcoholic drinks. But how unjust, to judge others by oneself, and forbid to other people what one does not like oneself! For instance, myself—every evening I am drunk and cannot live otherwise. How would I do as one of Maclaw's colonists? And is he right? In the first stage of drunkenness I feel an absolute delight, and in that state understand infinitely more than when I avoid the Micluha Maclaw poison!!! Nor have I noticed that my health suffers from it especially. As to the rest—'*Quid licet Jovi, non licet bovi.*' And God knows which is nearer right—I or Maclaw."

Peter said he was drunk every evening; let no Western reader think this meant he was roaring drunk and carried to bed. No, Peter was a Russian and his system was inured to alcohol. Probably his digestive tract would have been better without it, but on the other hand, the relaxation of alcohol was in truth as necessary to him as air. Wine flowed at Maidanovo—but concerning the table,

witnesses declare it was anything but abundant. Tchaikowsky did
not seem to know good food from bad. After every meal he dispatched Alexis to the kitchen with enthusiastic compliments for the
cook, while often enough, the guests, still hungry, exchanged glances
indignantly. As a host, Peter was domestically quite unconscious;
tables could wabble on rickety legs, bedsprings sag, doors refuse to
close, and Peter remained quite satisfied. The only thing that could
draw a complaint from him was when, on returning from a journey,
he did not find the house exactly as he had left it. Let Alexis move
so much as a photograph—the walls were covered with them—and
Peter's blue eye narrowed ominously.

1886 saw the completion of *The Enchantress,* an opera in four
acts which failed completely when produced the following autumn
in Petersburg. Tchaikowsky was much humiliated and wrote
Jurgenson how ashamed he was to have exposed his publisher to
such a financial loss. His publisher, however, sustained the loss quite
philosophically, knowing he would soon be recompensed by new
Tchaikowsky successes. Orchestral suite number four, called *Mozartiana,* was already in the printing press. This suite was an arrangement for orchestra of some of Mozart's smaller, less known works.
In his preface to the score Tchaikowsky said he had arranged the
suite in order to bring these gems of musical literature to the attention of the public. Never did he forget his god, Mozart, "that Christ
of music," Peter called him. Even during this period of strenuous activity and achievement he took time off to remind Nadejda of his
and the world's debt to the great, the gay master of form in music.
Peter was forever conscious that a lack of form was his own worst
musical defect; he confessed it in a letter to the Grand Duke Constantin:

"All my life I have been much troubled by my inability to grasp
and manipulate form in music. I fought hard against this defect and
can say with pride that I achieved some progress, but I shall end my
days without ever having written anything that is perfect in form.
What I write has always a mountain of padding; an experienced eye
can detect the thread in my seams, and I can do nothing about it."

This letter was written in 1888, and with this date Tchaikowsky found himself at the peak of his fame, a peak which he was never to descend and one which was higher than he himself had ever dreamed of climbing. One thing that hitherto had hampered Peter greatly was his inability to conduct an orchestra. His old stage fright had hung on, vaguely and dreadfully reminiscent of the days when he had conducted with one hand to his chin so his head would not fall off. But just before the New Year of 1887, Tchaikowsky decided to try to conduct his revised opera, *Les Caprices d'Oxane,* and wrote Modeste and Nadejda von Meck about it from Moscow:

"Today, Modichka, something happened that may prove of great significance for me. I conducted my first orchestral rehearsal, and the result—unless they were only flattering me—was general astonishment, everyone having expected me to fail shamefully. I will spare you a recital of the torments I suffered when Altani, some days previously, set the hour for rehearsal. The closer the terrible day came, the more unbelievably I suffered and more than once I decided to abandon the whole business. Somehow at the last I forced myself out upon the stage, was greeted enthusiastically by the musicians, made a rather brave speech and began very bravely to brandish the stick. Now I know I can conduct, and it is even probable that I shall not be frightened on the night of the performance."

To Nadejda von Meck

Moscow
January 26, 1877

"My sweet, dear, priceless friend:

"For a week, now, I have enjoyed your hospitality. I live in your house as in Christ's bosom. I can't say enough about the care your servants show for my comfort. Unfortunately I can be at home very little as we have rehearsals daily. Every morning I take a walk, and by eleven o'clock I am seated before the orchestra at the conductor's desk. The rehearsals are over at four and I am so tired that when I get home I can only throw myself down and sleep. By evening my strength returns and I can eat something.

"Certainly, conducting is hard for me and takes a great toll of my nervous system, but I must admit it gives me real pleasure. (1) It is pleasant to know I have conquered my inborn timidity. (2) It is extremely pleasant for the author of an opera to conduct his com-

position himself, and not be forced to keep approaching the conductor with requests to change this or that. (3) Everyone who takes
part in the production shows me such sincere sympathy that 1 am
deeply touched.

"And, dear friend, in truth I am much less worried and anxious
now than when I used to have to sit passively at rehearsals. I believe
that if all continues to go well, the aftermath will be favorable rather
than unfavorable to my sick nerves."

On the day of performance, Peter woke feeling, he wrote, "really
ill," convinced that a horrible nightmare was about to be enacted.
All day he endured agonies, and when evening came could barely
walk onto the stage at the appointed time. The curtain rose, and
Peter found himself almost smothered with wreaths of flowers presented by the chorus, the orchestra and friends. This gave him, he
said, time to recover, and from then on the evening rang with applause. Peter was a bit skeptical about Moscow applause. The theatre
being at least half full of his friends he could not tell if the compliment was for his work or himself. "I shall conduct twice more," he
wrote, "and the third time should tell me for certain how much all
this noise has been worth."

The third time was a success, convincing Tchaikowsky that from
now on he could conduct without, figuratively or literally, losing his
head. The news spread, and from that evening Peter Ilyich was in
great demand as a conductor of his own works. Concert tour followed concert tour; even Paris was conquered, and as to Prague, it
went wild over *Eugene Onegin*. Tchaikowsky wrote Nadejda a bit
ruefully that he had left Prague "laden with laurels—but only laurels.
I don't know how to look after my pecuniary interests." Anton
Dvorak especially had been entranced with the opera.

Anton Dvorak to Tchaikowsky
Prague
January 14, 1889

"Dear Friend,
"When you were in Prague, I promised to write you about your
opera *Onegin*. But now I write, impelled not only by your request
but by my own feelings when 1 heard your work. I joyfully con-

fess the great and deep impression your opera made upon me. I always expect work of genuine artistic value from you, and I do not hesitate to say that not one of your compositions has pleased me so much as *Onegin.*

"That beautiful composition, so rich in warmth and poetry, shows mastery in every detail; in short, this is music that calls out to us, and that enters so deeply into our soul we can never forget. Listening and watching, I felt myself transported to another world.

"I congratulate you—and all of us—on the existence of such a composition. God grant you may leave many more such to the world.

"In sincere greeting,

"Your devoted friend,
"Anton Dvorak."

In between all these triumphs and activities, Peter Ilyich had moved again—or rather, Alexis had moved for him—while the composer was down in Tiflis visiting his brother Anatol, the brother whose duties as a district attorney had taken him to this southernmost border of Russia. Peter's new country home was not far from the old one, in the village of Frolovskoe. It was an extremely simple, unpretentious little place, built like a bungalow, with a little terrace containing a pond. In the middle of the pond, to Peter's vast delight, was an islet. From Frolovskoe, on his return from Tiflis, Peter wrote enthusiastically to tell Nadejda he was planting a garden. He went at it with a furious delight that was equalled only by his horticultural ignorance. On these cold June nights he would not sleep, he said, for fear the frost would kill his seedlings.

To Nadejda Philaretovna

Frolovskoe
June 10, 1888

"I shall work very hard now for a while. I want terribly to prove not only to others but to myself that I am not yet played out. Very often, doubt seizes me and I ask myself, Isn't it time to stop writing music, haven't I overstrained my imagination, hasn't the wellspring itself dried up? This must happen sometime if I live on for ten or twenty years, and how do I know that the time is not arrived when I should lay down my arms. . . . I don't remember if I told you I have decided to write a symphony. When I began it, composition came hard, but now it looks as if inspiration had come. . . . We shall see."

This was to be the Fifth Symphony. It was completed in two months, the composer maintaining, during his work, quite strict silence concerning his progress. The first performance took place in Petersburg under the composer's baton a couple of months after the score was completed, and fell rather flat. Considering the Fifth is now Tchaikowsky's best, or second-best loved work (many persons prefer it to the *Pathètique*) the indifference with which it met must be attributed to poor performance. Also, even though Tchaikowsky succeeded in staying on the podium without accident, he was anything but an inspired conductor. His modesty stood hopelessly in his way and time after time, works that later became famous met with failure or indifference when conducted by himself. Concerning the Fifth Symphony, Peter wrote Nadejda von Meck in December, 1888:

"Having played my symphony twice in Petersburg and once in Prague, I have come to the conclusion that it is a failure. There is something repellent in it, some over-exaggerated color, some insincerity or fabrication which the public instinctively recognizes. It was clear to me that the applause and ovations referred not to this but to other works of mine, and that the symphony itself will never please the public. All this causes a deep dissatisfaction with myself. It is possible that I have, as people say, written myself out, and that nothing remains but for me to repeat and imitate myself. Yesterday evening I glanced over the Fourth Symphony, *our* symphony. How superior to this one, how much better it is! Yes, this is a very, very sad fact."

Few people today would admit that Tchaikowsky's Fourth was superior to his Fifth Symphony, and no one at all would declare that the man was played out who was to write the *Nutcracker Suite,* the *Hamlet Overture,* and the Sixth Symphony. Perhaps such periods of profound dissatisfaction are necessary to the artist; Peter himself suspected as much. Anyway, in the midst of this attack of melancholy, Tchaikowsky set to work to compose one of his gayest, most popular works, the ballet, *Sleeping Beauty,* written from sketches he had made one summer at Kamenka for a little holiday play staged by his

Davydoff nieces. This was the ballet that was destined to be a favorite with two Tsars in turn. Peter worked at it easily, with an enthusiasm he had not felt in composing, he declared, since the days of *Eugene Onegin*. He did it in six weeks, at Maidanovo, and in the midst of it he had a pleasant surprise. At Christmas, Alexis brought to his study a tiny Christmas tree, all decorated, and with it a complete edition of Mozart, with Jurgenson's card enclosed.

And now, in January, 1889, Tchaikowsky embarked on another concert tour. From Berlin to London the plaudits rang and Peter should have been content. Yet strangely enough, it was now that his peace of mind, the healthy objectivity he had possessed for the past five years, began to crumble. Perhaps crumble is too strong a word. Peter remained well and active; but in every letter we find a note of doubt and bitterness—the old note, and somehow, endearing. This furious travelling, this rushing from city to city in pursuit of fame: what was it for, his heart asked him? Would he not do better to stay at home and write his music? In the midst of rehearsals and concerts he was "doing nothing," he wrote Nadejda. "I say doing nothing because my real mission is to compose, and all this other activity is incidental and useless and will only shorten my days."

Leipzig, Berlin, Hamburg, Prague, Paris, Dresden, Geneva, London. . . . Brilliant public successes, accompanied by devastating homesickness and gloom. And all the while, when he had a few days' respite, he wrote music. The opera *Pique Dame,* second only to *Onegin* in charm and still very popular. Truly, Tchaikowsky's operas cast a spell. Intellectually, one is conscious that this is not the greatest music, yet from the curtain's rising one sits entranced, transported, as Dvorak truly said, to another world. What an uprush of sheer delight in *Pique Dame* where the duet of ladies implores the handsome shepherd to heed their pleadings, while the shepherd, whose gentle pipes trill through the ladies' song, strolls unheeding away!

Pique Dame was finished in the spring of 1890. Peter went to Italy for a rest and took with him the opera score in order to make the piano arrangement. The moment he returned to his country home at Frolovskoe, he wrote Nadejda that he had commenced a new work, a sextet for strings.

"Knowing your great love for chamber music, I rejoice that you will surely hear my sextet. You won't have to go to a concert because it will be quite easy to arrange a good performance at home. I do hope this music will please you. . . . I wrote it with the greatest pleasure and enthusiasm, and no effort whatever."

In truth, Nadejda Philaretovna was by now in need of music that could be heard easily, and at home. During these years while Peter had been so active, so outward-going, while he had been saying *Yes* to life, Nadejda had been saying *No*. Tuberculosis, that her strong constitution had resisted for so long, was laying now its wasting hand upon her. Daily, yearly she sank backward, downward along the path of illness and decay. Quite early in the eighties, Modeste Tchaikowsky had written his brother that he had met Nadejda Philaretovna in Rome one day, out walking; the letter had exclaimed upon her altered appearance: "How old she has become, and how queerly she dresses!" Nevertheless, Modeste had been so pleased to see her that involuntarily, in the midst of the fashionable throng, he had shouted her name.

The "queer" costume was not to be blamed upon illness; rather, it was a symptom of the lady's imperiousness; she did as she chose and she dressed as she chose. Disliking fashion and modernity, when Nadejda favored a style of dress she clung to it; with all the world in summer muslins, Nadejda Philaretovna sailed serenely through the streets in stiff black silk. Her high-handedness, her lavish manner of living, continued unabated; when she was abroad and wished to hear the music of her adored Peter Ilyich, she simply went to Paris and commanded Colonne to teach his renowned orchestra to play it, and Colonne, well fortified by crackling French banknotes, complied. Not one soul did the widow invite to share these performances—except young Vladimir von Meck, her favorite grandson. Alone in a box above the darkened empty theatre the two sat happily, sharing a secret joy. . . .

Writing to Peter Ilyich, Nadejda seldom mentioned her illness except as explanation for occasional lapses in her correspondence. We do not know exactly what form her tuberculosis took; she mentions her cough, her frequent "colds," her dread of snow and dampness. Also the painful migraine attacks arrived with increasing frequency, followed by several days of prostration during which the victim could not sit up to write. Peter always grieved for Nadejda's suffering, but, himself accustomed to indifferent health, was not alarmed by his friend's condition; never once had she spoken the word *consumption*. Therefore he had no warning of what was to come that autumn of 1890. How was Peter to know that all these years, while he had been climbing steadily upward to artistic maturity and achievement, Nadejda von Meck had been sinking, turning ever inward upon herself? The fever and disease that her body had for so long withstood was now to attack, not her mind—that remained sane—but her spirit. From Peter she had concealed only too well her increasing fear and depression; these are not the things that woman tells to man, particularly a woman who stands in the guise of mentor and adored saint. Peter thought he was secure in this friendship; indeed, he would have called this friendship the one secure spot in a life that he had himself described as having "no haven." "You are the only person in the world," he had written Nadejda, "who can make me deeply, profoundly happy. I am infinitely grateful, and hope only that what inspires your feeling for me will never end or alter, because such a loss would be unendurable."

And even while Peter wrote these words, the ground under friendship's feet was slowly cracking, weakening—due, tragically enough, to no diminution of love on the part of either friend. *Fatum,* that Peter believed in and feared, was sounding the note so familiar to him, yet which came, this time, with such sudden shock.

In September, 1890, Peter went down to Tiflis to conduct a concert of his works, staying, as usual, with Anatol. Peter loved the Caucasus. Tiflis was in the mountains, on the River Kura, and it was more Persian than Russian; the brothers roamed the strange foreign streets and walked the fertile valleys beyond the town, Peter never ceasing to marvel at the luxuriance of the verdure, the profusion of flowers and the glorious heat of the sun. And here, in the midst of beauty, came a letter that put happiness from Peter's mind. Nadejda's fortune, she wrote, was on the edge of collapse and she could send Peter Ilyich no more money ever, from now on. It was not this statement that frightened Peter so much as the tone of the letter which was curt and strange and unlike any words Nadejda had written him during all their long intimacy together. The whole letter was tinged with inexplicable, ominous finality. . . . As for the money, this was not the first time Nadejda had cried wolf, wolf! —but always, afterward, she had made amends by forwarding an extra, totally uncalled-for check or a handsome present like the 10,-000 franc watch. Only last summer, she had sent a generous sum over and above Peter's pension, had insisted upon his accepting it and had declared that even if she were losing money in Moscow through someone's mismanagement, Peter's six thousand roubles a year were nothing to her.

But this time, somehow, her statement about money losses carried conviction. How, wondered Peter, could ruin have come so swiftly? The von Meck fortune was too public an affair to dissolve thus secretly and suddenly; there had been no such rumors around Moscow, and Moscow always seemed to know von Meck family business as soon as the von Mecks knew it. Perhaps illness had depressed Nadejda, perhaps she was having one of her migraines and exaggerated her troubles. Also, when people lost their money they often lost their friends with it. Rich people especially seemed to think friendship depended upon money, and Nadejda was an avowed skeptic where human nature was concerned. Only to Peter Ilyich had her skepticism never applied. How many times had she not assured him that among mankind he was the only soul she could trust?

Peter read the letter and re-read it, and, profoundly troubled, took up his pen:

To Nadejda Philaretovna

Tiflis
October 4, 1890

"Sweet, dear friend of mine:

"Your letter just came; what you have to say grieves me deeply—

not for myself, but for you. I say this with utmost sincerity. Certainly it would be false to pretend that such a radical change in my budget will not affect my material welfare, but it will affect it far less than you probably think. In the last few years my income has markedly increased, and there is no reason to doubt it will continue so to increase, and rapidly. So if among your many troubles you are troubled also a little about me, I pray you be assured that I have not felt even the smallest passing grief at the idea of this material loss. Believe me, this is absolutely the truth; I am no master of those phrases intended to deceive. Therefore, the point is, not that for a while I shall have to curtail expenses, but that you, with your habitual large scale of living, will have to endure privation. This to me is a terribly offensive and vexing thought.

"I cast about to find someone to blame for all this (plainly, you yourself are not the guilty party), but I can never know who the real culprit is. Also, I realize such indignation on my part is useless and altogether futile, as I have no right to pry into your family matters. Rather than press you thus, I think it better that I ask Vladislav Pahulsky to write me at his convenience how you plan to settle down, where you will live and to what extent you will suffer privation. I can't imagine you without wealth.

"The last words of your letter (Do not forget, and think of me sometimes) offended me a little, but I tell myself you could not really have meant them. Is it possible you think me capable of remembering you only when I use your money? Could I forget for one second all you have done for me, all that I owe you? Without exaggeration I can say that you saved me, that I would surely have gone mad and perished had you not come forward with your friendship and sympathy. With the money you gave me as safety anchor, you rallied my expiring forces and gave me back my ambition to continue on the road of music. No, my dear friend, be assured I shall remember you and bless you to my last breath. It makes me happy to know that now, when you can no longer share your wealth with me, I can let myself go and express the whole strength of my warm and unlimited gratitude. Probably you yourself do not realize the extent of what you have done for me. If so, you could never have said what you did—that now you are poor you hope I will think of you 'sometimes.' Never for one moment have I forgotten you, nor will forget you, because every thought I have concerning myself, concerns you also.

"I kiss your hands with all the warmth my heart contains, beseeching you to realize, once and for all, that no one has greater sympathy for you, no one feels himself more truly part of your troubles or shares them more than I.

"Some other time I will write about myself and what I have been doing.

"Forgive this hasty scrawl. I am too upset to write clearly."

Peter had said he no longer needed Nadejda's money, and it was true that his own earnings had greatly increased during the past few years. But, characteristically, he had taken on a whole list of pensioners. Modeste alone received two thousand roubles a year and Peter supported his servant Alexis' wife and family, besides countless young musicians who appealed to him for help and were never refused. At the moment, therefore, his funds were low, and for Peter the present, *le moment qui passe,* always represented eternity. From Tiflis he wrote Jurgenson that he would have to start life anew on an entirely different scale; he would have to go to Petersburg and look about, actually beg for a salaried position in the Conservatory— the thing he had avoided and scorned a dozen times in the past years.

On his way north from Tiflis, Peter stopped in Moscow, and the first thing he learned was that there was nothing wrong whatever with the von Meck fortune. The railroad was as good as it had ever been and so were the other properties. Nothing had been sold, nothing confiscated. Bewilderment was followed by profound depression: Nadejda then had never really loved him. He had been her hired man, her toy; she had sent him money lightly, as the caprice of a rich woman and he had never truly earned his pension by the music he wrote. She had tired of him now and of his music; and to rid herself of him she had invented the flimsy excuse of financial ruin—an excuse that she well knew circumstance would soon disprove.

Truly this was the bitterest blow that Fate had dealt to Peter; he would not accept it, he told himself, arguing in his friend's behalf even as the facts arrayed themselves against her. He would not accept the fact of her cruelty, her light abandonment of this long friendship—until he gave her more time. Perhaps she would ever

yet reply to his letter from Tiflis; after all, very little time had passed
since he had written, and Nadejda was probably getting ready for
her autumnal migration to Italy or France. Peter shook his head and
went about his business, fortunately unaware that six months would
pass before a word of news would come—and that when it came, it
would be bitter news.

Externally his life moved rapidly and brilliantly during the six
months. Petersburg went wild over the first performance of *Pique
Dame,* and Tchaikowsky's empty pockets were filled beyond any
need of a salaried job. In Kiev the opera had even greater success;
but Tchaikowsky, depressed and skeptical of applause, wrote to no
one and told Modeste that *Pique Dame* was a failure. He accepted
several big commissions and went out to Frolovskoe to work on them.
First, the *Hamlet Overture,* prepared for a benefit entertainment
for Lucien Guitry (father of Sascha Guitry). "I am very tired," he
wrote Modeste in January, 1891. "My uncertainty as to the future
weighs on me. My brain is empty; I have not the least pleasure in
work. *Hamlet* oppresses me terribly."

Nevertheless *Hamlet* was written, and the world is still grateful
for the professional conscientiousness that would not let Tchaikowsky leave a piece of work unfinished. No sooner was it done than the
Imperial Opera in Petersburg commissioned an opera and a ballet.
King René's Daughter was chosen for the opera, and for the ballet,
the *Nutcracker* legend. *King René's Daughter* became eventually.
the one-act opera, *Iolanthe;* Modeste prepared the libretto and was
a long while doing it.

Meanwhile, Peter received an offer to go to America on a concert
tour. On the way thither he was asked to stop off in Paris and conduct a whole concert of his works played by no other orchestra than
Colonne's own, at the famous *Concerts Populaires* series. All these
offers were accepted, and in March, 1891, with the completed first
act of the *Nutcracker* ballet in his pocket, and with grief still heavy
at his heart over Nadejda Philaretovna's continued silence, Peter set
forth on his travels.

27

New York. Nadejda accepts a strange guilt

THE Paris concert was a decided success and Tchaikowsky should have rejoiced that at last he had taken so difficult and scornful a musical citadel. But he seemed totally indifferent to triumph, and the instant the concert was over, fled to Rouen to wait for sailing time and to work on his ballet. The day before he embarked for New York, he picked up a newspaper and read the news of his sister Alexandra's death in Russia, the sister he loved best and whose house at Kamenka had for so long been home to him. It was too late now to cancel the American contract and, numb with grief and the bewilderment which always beset him on a long journey, Tchaikowsky boarded the *Bretagne* for what he thought would be strange, unfriendly shores.

Peter remained in America about a month, giving six orchestral concerts, four in New York, one in Baltimore, one in Philadelphia—and had, in spite of himself, a good time. He visited Washington and Niagara Falls and professed himself duly, though vaguely, impressed with both. He found himself, as he wrote Modeste, "much more important here than in Russia," and kept a diary, part of which has been translated into English by Rosa Newmarch.* The diary is an amazingly naive document. The bathtubs of New York and the tremendous buildings on Broadway—actually thirteen stories high, some of them!—impressed Peter profoundly, as did the hospitality of the Americans, their frankness and ingenuousness. Accustomed when abroad to look behind every overture of friendship for some reason, some *arrière pensèe.* Peter found to his amazement that here was no *arrière pensèe;* these people came to his hotel door and asked if there was anything they could do for him, anything he needed— and when he said no, and waited for them to ask him a favor, they

* *Life and Letters of P. I. Tchaikowsky.* The Bodley Head, London, 1906.

merely said, "Have a drink?"—and paid for the drinks, and laughed, and shook his hand and went away. It was, Peter wrote Modeste, unbelievable, and if he had not been so hideously homesick he would have fallen quite in love with these people. One of them at whose house he dined, a Mr. Carnegie, who owned thirty million dollars (in his next letter Peter called it forty million)—this singular, warm-hearted character who had once been a telegraph boy, adored Moscow and looked just like the dramatist Ostrovsky. At the dinner party Mr. Carnegie had whacked Peter on the back, called him the un-crowned king of music, hugged him heartily (without kissing, Peter added. Men did not kiss in America). This Mr. Carnegie had given a pantomime representation of Peter on the conductor's box which had been simply wonderful and had made everyone roar with laughter.

The Americans ate so much, said Peter. And so extravagantly. Why, at Mr. Hyde's, in the middle of dinner, ices were served in live roses. . . . Everywhere, his music met with enthusiasm, but it was disconcerting the way the newspapers commented more on his personal appearance and characteristics than on his music. Why did they do this? They said he was "stout, with greying hair, well built, an interesting-looking man of about sixty. . . ." And here he was just turned fifty! They said he was timid on the stage and responded to applause with short, sharp bows, and that only with baton in hand did he regain his assurance. Everybody in this strange cordial country seemed to want his autograph. On Sundays one could not buy a drink without plotting; some remnant of English Puritanism caused them to close all the cafés. Negro faces were everywhere; the porters on the trains were Negroes and were such kind, nice men! On the train to Baltimore when he had been so dead tired the Negro had made his bed for him and helped him into it and waked him next morning in time to get off. Before one big dinner party in Peter's honor, the host had turned suddenly solemn and closed his eyes and said the Lord's Prayer! The steamer was awful, going and coming, rolled and plunged and Peter was sure he would perish; the fog horn emitted "terrible roars like a colossal, enraged tiger." Nerve-racking in the extreme, wrote Peter. The passengers discovered his identity and tried to make him play the piano. A mademoiselle sang Italian songs all evening in an excruciating voice, but nobody was rude to her. How strange! Somebody stole 460 francs from his stateroom. . . .

Nothing mattered, however, except that the steamer should get quickly back to Hamburg. Until it did, Tchaikowsky would be in a daze, as he had been since the moment he left Russia. And when finally he felt German ground beneath his feet, the composer fled swiftly eastward to Petersburg and thence to his country home. Before sailing for New York, disgusted with Frolovskoe since his landlord had cut the forest down, Peter had ordered Alexis to move back to the old house at Maidanovo. So it was at Maidanovo he settled again in June of 1891, working hard at the *Nutcracker* ballet and the opera, *Iolanthe*. Still no letter came from Nadejda von Meck, and after a few days Peter went to Moscow. Here at last he found an envelope postmarked Plesheyevo—but it was not from Nadejda It was from Vladislav Pahulsky, and it was short and polite and noncommittal; it was, in fact, more damning than no letter at all. Pahulsky, it will be remembered, was the Polish violinist—more gentleman, perhaps, than violinist—who had lived for so long in Nadejda's house and who by now was married to Nadejda's daughter, Julia.

Tchaikowsky wrote an instant reply.

To V. Pahulsky

Moscow
June 18, 1891

"Your letter has just come. You say that Mme Nadejda Philaretovna is ill, weak and so nervously upset she can no longer write me as before. Truly, not for anything in the world would I be the cause of adding to her suffering. What hurts, troubles, and, I may say, offends me deeply, is not the fact that she does not write, but that she has lost all interest in me. If she wished to hear from me without writing, it would be quite feasible; you and Julia Karlovna could be constant intermediaries. Yet not once has she requested either of you to find out how I am living or how my life is going. I tried, through you, to re-establish a correspondence with N. Ph., but your every letter put off politely my attempts to preserve even for a little, the shadow of what had been. Surely you know that last September, N. Ph. informed me she was ruined financially and could render me no more material aid. You probably saw my reply. What I urgently desired was that my relationship with N. Ph. should not change, now that I no longer received money from her. Unfortunately, that seems to be impossible because N. Ph. has evidently become quite cold to me. As a result, I stopped writing to N. Ph., and every connection between us was severed as soon as the money ceased coming. This is terribly humiliating; it makes the realization that I accepted a pension from her an unbearable worry and torment.

"This autumn while I was in the country I re-read all N. Ph.'s letters. Not illness nor anxiety nor financial troubles could, I thought while reading, alter the feelings expressed in those letters. Yet those feelings have changed. Perhaps it is because I never met N. Ph. that I always idealized her. In such a person, half-divine, I could not imagine such a treason; it seemed to me the earth would fall to pieces under my feet sooner than that N. Ph.'s feelings toward me would alter. But it has happened, and all my faith in people, all my trust in the world has turned upside down. My peace is gone and whatever happiness fate intended for me is poisoned.

"Without meaning to, N. Ph. has surely behaved very cruelly toward me. Never before have I felt such humiliation or suffered such a blow to my pride. And the hardest part of all is that because of N. Ph.'s weak physical condition, I dare not risk grieving or disturbing her by telling her how all this troubles me.

"Therefore it is impossible for me to speak out frankly—the only thing that could give me relief. But enough of this. Perhaps I shall regret writing, but I could no longer resist the impulse to pour out somehow, somewhere this bitterness that has accumulated in my heart. Of course, not a word of it to N. Ph.

"If she asks about me, tell her I returned safely from America and have settled in Maidanovo to work. My health is good.

"Do not answer this letter."

Pahulsky did answer it. He returned Peter's letter, repeating what he had said before: that Nadejda Philaretovna was sick, physically and mentally. Severely ill, and her apparent indifference came from illness and nothing else. In her heart she still loved her old friends, said Pahulsky, but he dared not, in her present condition, show her Peter's letter.

This was the end for Peter Ilyich; it was his last attempt to re-
establish communication. His best friend was gone, lost to him forever. What he had considered an ideal relationship had been then,
he wrote Jurgenson, nothing more than a "commonplace, meaningless farce, which fills me with humiliation and disgust." Phrases of
Nadejda's early letters leaped tauntingly to his memory: "You are
life itself to me," she had written from Brailov. "I wandered today
through the rooms you have just left, sat in the chair at your writing
table and felt your dear presence. Peter Ilyich, my best of friends,
how can I express my gratitude for what you are?"

Those were not words inspired by caprice. But if love such as that
could fail without a reason, what then, in the world of human beings,
remained for a man to believe in? The anger and indignation that
for a time had upheld him, now deserted Peter Ilyich; a deep hurt
remained, a wound from which he was never to recover. He was not
a young man, to recoil easily from such a blow—a blow not only to
his self-esteem but to his belief in human nature. He was fifty-one
and he was tired, too tired to make new friends or to wish for them.

This was June of 1891. Scarcely more than two years of life remained to Peter Ilyich.

And Nadejda von Meck—did she know what she was doing, what
pain she was causing? Peter was aware that his friend was very ill,
but he knew also that illness alone was not sufficient cause for her
sudden cruelty. What he did not know and was never to discover was
that something outside of her illness, outside of herself, had caused
Nadejda's change of heart. Something had risen to break, once and
for all, that proud fierce spirit, something which had nothing to do
with Peter Ilyich. Yet it was upon Peter, ironically enough, that the
widow let the consequences fall.

From time to time, in these pages, mention has been made of
Nadejda's eldest son, the handsome, brilliant, lavish, Vladimir, who
once defied the House of Rothschild with twelve manufactured
secretaries. Vladimir's life had continued as recklessly as it had begun and now, in 1890, he fell mortally ill of a slow disease against

which medicine had then no weapon. Day by day, herself fevered, coughing, Nadejda watched her son, this charming, invincible creature, decay before her eyes, mind as well as body.

Nadejda watched, and there came an hour when she could accept this thing no longer. Here was no opportunity for courage or for pride; here was only the indignity of slow decay. Here was nothing to fight, and Nadejda, who had confessed that resignation had no part in her nature—Nadejda had to fight or perish. So she groped for an enemy, for something she could come to grips with, something she could withstand and battle every waking moment.

She found it in a sense of her own guilt. She had neglected her son, the widow told herself. All these years, these thirteen years, she, a mother, had been interested in but one thing, but one person—and that person had been far outside the province of motherhood: *Peter Ilyich Tchaikowsky.* Daily, nightly Peter Ilyich had occupied her mind; his music, his letters, her replies to his letters. Plans for him to "visit" her, plans for his comfort and protection, plans for Colonne's orchestra to play his music. Oh, a thousand delightful, intimate plans that had seemed so innocent, but which she knew now had been sinful. In secret she had had this joy; she had told no one but Julia and Julia's husband. Vladimir had not known. She had thrust her son from her and had set up a secret idol in his place, and thereby she had destroyed her son. . . .

Sitting alone in the garden at Plesheyevo, gazing into the hot summer sunshine, the picture of her guilt rose sharp before the widow's eyes, fierce and sure as the devils that had beset the saints of old. Fiercer even and surer, for Nadejda, still an atheist, lacked all trust in divine forgiveness. She could suffer punishment, but she could never achieve the reward of punishment. She would hasten now to punishment, hasten to put from her this evil thing that she had cherished as holy and had called by the name of love—or art, or music. This thing that had caused her to deceive those closest to her, to sit for hours alone with her pen and writing paper, to snatch whole weeks in Florence, Paris, Rome—weeks that should have been devoted to her son.

Impossible to tell all or any of this to Peter Ilyich. Impossible to attempt any explanation whatever, or indeed, to confide in anyone except, perhaps, Julia. But she would not tell even Julia until later, much later, when she had safely put this wickedness from her.

Nadejda rose and went into the house. Slowly, her hand on the banister, she made her way upstairs to her writing desk. Unfaltering, her pen went down the page. Only at the end, it weakened. "Do not forget," wrote Nadejda to her once beloved friend. "Do not forget, and think of me sometimes."

This was the letter addressed to Tchaikowsky at Tiflis in September, 1890. After it, Nadejda von Meck lived nearly four years. She died far from home, in Wiesbaden, January 13, only three months after Tchaikowsky himself had died in Petersburg. She was buried in Moscow, the city she loved, in the cemetery of Saint Alexis Monastery, by the side of her husband, that valiant knight, Karl George Otto von Meck.

Thus ended one of the strangest intimacies in all history, and its end was as inexplicable as its course. Nadejda's final letter was, on the face of it, as utterly cruel as Peter said it was: to refuse a man's friendship the instant she ceased sending him money, to refuse, in other words, to admit him on terms of equality, was the apotheosis of arrogance; it was outright denial not only of everything Nadejda had herself promised and written, but of the most elemental structure of friendship itself. A dream was shattered—how real and warm a dream! Peter saw himself as pauper to princess, a shabby musician who had been kept by a rich woman. Yet Peter was a gentleman; he was no nameless adventurer, but was born to the same stratum of society as Nadejda—and was far better educated. It is to his credit that these last words are ours, not Peter's; to no one did he speak or write such words of pride or bitterness; his chagrin was all for himself, and what bitterness he felt was not toward his old friend but toward the world and human nature. "My faith in people, all my trust in the world is turned upside down."

Homely phrases, but sincere, carried deep in Peter's consciousness until he drew his last breath. On his death-bed, delirious, Peter was to call again and again upon the name of Nadejda Philaretovna.

Perhaps the sharpness of this blow to friendship, the unbearable heaviness of it, was due mostly to its total unexpectedness. During thirteen years there had been no hint, late or early, of distrust or estrangement on the widow's part. On the contrary, Nadejda had set Peter very obviously on a pedestal of her own making; she had stood below and looked up to him, a creature incomparably higher than herself. Had she not confessed again and again her pride in being permitted to foster genius, to be humbly, indirectly instrumental in the creation of music that would belong to the whole world? Never was relationship more seemingly selfless on a woman's part; Nadejda gave and gave and in return asked for—what? For nothing except that the man to whom she gave should continue to live as his best self, should continue on the road he desired most to tread, continue to be what his whole spirit and every beat of the blood along his veins told him to be—a good composer.

From the beginning, no one can doubt the sincerity of the widow's attachment. Even her most high-flown letters carry conviction. If pizzicato ran "like an electric current" through all her nerves, if, hearing the Fourth Symphony she could "gladly have died listening," if a word from Peter could make her day turn from "despair to happiness"—if the widow said these things, she meant them. Peter knew she meant them. And we, inhabitants of another century and another clime that does not speak in words so extravagant—we, too, know Nadejda meant what she said.

No more than Peter Ilyich, can we condemn Nadejda for her denial of truth and of friendship. She was a sick woman. While we have no record that her mind was actually affected, while the word insanity has not come down to us attached to her name, we know that toward the end she suffered from what her daughter called "a terrible nervous affliction"—and devoted daughters have a right to choose their words. Nadejda Philaretovna, an autocrat, a woman to whom wealth had given a tremendous power over all her surroundings and who for twenty years had exercised this power as though it were her divine right, was visited suddenly by a guest to

whom divine right meant nothing. Nadejda could not command
this grim visitor, could not buy him off. Her every weapon was
powerless. Small wonder, then, that she took refuge in delusion.

One of the most interesting things about the correspondence between Nadejda and Peter Ilyich is the way one's judgment alters,
during the years, toward the two. At first one is inclined to admire
Nadejda Philaretovna, even while smiling at her extravagant, ecstatic
manner of conducting a correspondence. And one is inclined to
blame Peter Ilyich a little—even, at times, to suspect him of self-
interest. But this is only during the Antonina period, when Peter was
ill and distraught and terrified, a man ready to clutch at any straw
of escape. Little by little, as Peter regains his strength and comes into
his kingdom, as he attains his stature, is set upon his spiritual—and
physical—feet, we learn to respect him and to love him. And little
by little, while we never lose respect for Nadejda Philaretovna, we
begin to understand why, among all the persons of her household,
no one loved her except Julia and the tender, gentle-natured young
grandson, Vladimir II.

This was a woman too proud, too fiercely independent, to merit
love. Toward Peter her generosity was real and it was admirable.
She gave all, asked nothing. But against all others the widow protected herself. Wrapped in the armor of wealth and solitude she
drew into herself, grew downward and inward.

The truth is, perhaps, that at the time we meet the two, Peter was
at his lowest, Nadejda at her highest. And Peter's foot, once it felt
solid ground beneath it, climbed steadily, faithfully, persistently upward. The widow, on the other hand, already forty-five when we
meet her, carrying within her the germ of disease, fought a valiant
fight, but slipped ever downward, toward fear and defeat. Dowered,
like Peter Ilyich, with over-emotionality, over-intensity, Nadejda
did not say, "This is a curse, let me tear it from me." No, she indulged her nature; we never see her laugh, as did Peter, at her own
wild orgies of self-dramatization. "After my usual habit," wrote Peter
one day from San Remo, when his brother had been late in arriving

from Russia, "I invented a whole drama of horror, and enacted it.
I leaped the first train for Genoa, expecting to find the travellers
dead or surely dying. And I found Modeste's pupil in bed, sleeping
off a cold. . . ."

Peter Ilyich, in short, was not what the world calls a "strong
character," yet he possessed one strength Nadejda never had. He
knew his weakness and fought it, and for this quality of courage,
of honesty toward himself, the gods rewarded him by granting the
one gift he desired above all others—the privilege of conscious
growth.

28

1891-1893. The Sixth Symphony. Death of Peter Ilyich

Nᴀᴅᴇᴊᴅᴀ was gone, for Peter Ilyich, farther from him now than if she had been really dead. He had thought he could not live without her. "I know well," he had written one day, "that I shall never lose your support in what I do. I do not believe I could write another line of music if I did not know that no matter what the world thinks, my friend will hear my music and will understand what I have tried to say."

And now he had lost, not only Nadejda's present support, but even the memory of it. He could not look back fondly, could not say, as bereaved lovers are permitted to say, "Here on this spot my friend told me all her love. Here in her handwriting lies proof of her trust in me." No, that was only illusion, he knew now. Best put it from him entirely and forever. . . .

But Peter was no Nadejda von Meck, to put things from him by sheer strength of will. He would live and he would remember; again and again he would call upon his friend and she would not answer. Music . . . ? But of course he would write music! More than ever now, Peter had need of music. Furiously rang the voices in his head and furiously he hurried, writing them down. Peter was an artist: put him on the rack and he would have written music; put him on a feather bed and he would have risen uneasily in a little time, his conscience heavy within him because his pen had been idle.

That summer of 1891, after Peter's return from America, and after Pahulsky had returned his letter, Peter lived on at Maidanovo, completing *Iolanthe* and the *Nutcracker* suite—this latter being, as the world now knows, one of the most brilliant bits of orchestration the composer produced. In Paris, while waiting for his ship to New York, Tchaikowsky had found a new instrument, the *celesta*, which he now described to Jurgenson as a cross between a piano and a glockenspiel. He urged Jurgenson to buy one and have it ready for the first performance of the *Nutcracker* ballet. Let the instrument be sent from Paris secretly; should Rimsky-Korsakov or Glazounov hear of it they would seize upon it and make use of it first, spoiling the fun.

Jurgenson, that enterprising man of business, accomplished all expeditiously. In the *Nutcracker* suite the celesta, now so popular, had its first and extremely successful introduction as an orchestral instrument.

The suite, however, was not performed for many months. Meanwhile at Maidanovo, toward the end of that summer of 1891, something unfortunate happened, a seemingly trivial incident which under the circumstances, depressed Peter very much. The watch that Nadejda had had made for him in Paris, the black-and-gold 10,000-franc Jeanne d'Arc watch, was stolen. Peter had grown very fond of this watch and proud of it. For years he had worn it as Nadejda had desired him to wear it, over his heart, a constant reminder of his friend. He scarcely let it out of his sight for cleaning and repairs And now, when any link with Nadejda was doubly precious, Peter went for a walk one afternoon and, by a combination of small accidents, left the watch in his room. Although Alexis was in the house taking his afternoon siesta, a thief must have entered, for when Peter returned, the watch was gone. The police could not find it, but they found the thief and brought him to Tchaikowsky. The man promised to tell where the watch was if they would leave him alone with Peter Ilyich. The two went into the next room, where the thief, in the dramatic manner that seems to accompany even the most trivial Russian incident, went down on his knees and implored forgiveness. Gazing upon him, Peter Ilyich in agitated tones forgave all. Whereupon the man announced that he had never stolen the watch and could not possibly tell anybody where it was. So was broken one more link with Nadejda von Meck.

This autumn Peter Ilyich made his will, and no sooner was it signed than he realized he was almost penniless because he had given away all his money. To crown his irritation he received an offer of a return trip to America at only one-half the fee of the first tour. To Modeste he expressed himself humiliated, and his cabled reply to the agent in New York read merely, "Non. Tchaikowsky."

Pique Dame was given in Prague and Kiev that winter, as well as in Moscow; *Onegin* was performed in Hamburg. Tchaikowsky travelled about, conducting these and other performances of his works, and suffering from a really terrible homesickness. It was to his nephew Bob Davydoff that he wrote his troubles now; Bob was the son of Peter's beloved sister Alexandra, and after Alexandra's death Tchaikowsky and the boy became increasingly intimate. Tchaikowsky wrote Bob from all over Europe and finally dedicated the Sixth Symphony to him. Unfortunately, Bob was a weak reed to lean upon. With none of the inward grace of youth and all of its irresponsibility, he was an example of the Tchaikowskys at their worst. Boasting the Tchaikowsky charm and none of the Tchaikowsky loyalty, his insincerity would have been detected by anyone less ingenuous than his Uncle Peter. Bob took from his uncle all he could get; he was a drug addict who was eventually—long after his uncle's death—to end as a suicide in Tchaikowsky's house at Klin.

Behold Peter Ilyich, therefore, that winter of 1892-1893, travelling about Europe as though pursued and sending frantic letters home to Bob—letters which seemed to give the writer no comfort. Gone were the days when Peter could write his nightmare to Nadejda and, sure of her warm, strong protection, see the nightmare dwindle even as his pen described it. Sometimes, on these European tours, he became so depressed he cancelled his concerts on the spot and fled home to Maidanovo. Even Maidanovo proved unsatisfactory, and the composer moved again, in the spring of 1892. This time the house was in the town of Klin, the last estate on the road to Frolovskoe, and like Tchaikowsky's other houses, was in no way distinguished or attractive—typical of the Russian architecture—or lack of architecture—of the 1860's. It was, however, the best house in the village. The first floor was low, made of brick, the second of wood, with higher ceilings; Tchaikowsky slept upstairs and his servant, after the Russian custom, on the first floor. This was Tchaikowsky's last home and the house that was afterward to become the Tchaikowsky museum. There was a big garden round it, whose boundaries adjoined the estate of Taneyeff's brother, an extraordinary man, not at all musical but a great admirer of Tchaikowsky.

The summer after moving into his Klin house, Tchaikowsky suffered from a return of a physical ailment called in the 1890's catarrh of the stomach, and which seemed to be a kind of nervous colitis. Peter had had it at intervals for the last twenty years, sometimes with extreme severity. Once, staying in a Petersburg hotel during the rehearsals for *Pique Dame,* he had sent for Modeste and declared he would not live through the night. The doctors always prescribed the water cure, but Peter hated Vichy. Now, however, in the summer of 1892, he agreed to try it because Bob Davydoff was also in need of a cure. So the two set off together. Peter hated it, even in Bob's company, and cut short his visit to return in July and busy himself with the mountains of proof-reading that had lately become an obsession with him. The older he grew, the more Tchaikowsky hated any mistake of print, however small. He wrote Bob at this time that even in his dreams, sharps and flats rose up before his eyes and refused to do as they were ordered. But the work was interrupted by another concert tour and yet another. Some demon seemed to be driving Peter Ilyich before the public, in spite of his very real desire to remain at home in peace. Honors fell upon him in showers. He was elected a member of the Academie Française, and the University of Cambridge invited him to come to England and receive the degree of Doctor of Music. More concert tours all over Europe, and from all over Europe, letters flying home to say that Peter Ilyich had "nothing to write about but fits of weeping." He was even surprised, he confessed, that this extraordinary homesickness did not drive him mad. Once, in a railway carriage, he was taken so ill he became delirious. He got out at a nearby station, dosed himself with his usual remedies and was, as usual, well the next day.

Peter himself did not know why, considering all this suffering, he continued to travel. "It seemed," wrote Modeste afterward, "that my brother had ceased to belong to himself; some irresistible force had taken possession of him and drove him blindly forward and outward. And that 'something' was not a simple deference to public demand. By now he had learned how to refuse artistic engagements or commissions that did not appeal to him. Nor was it the old restlessness and desire to be on the move, because the old places that he had loved so much had become impossible for him. Kamenka and Verbovka were no more now than the ruins of his sister's memory; even Italy had lost its charm. Paris, now that he was so famous, only frightened him. Simaki and Brailov belonged to strangers. The only thing that took him voluntarily from the seclusion of Klin was the desire to go to Petersburg to see his relatives.

"Nor does vanity explain my brother's persistent wandering on these concert tours. Although he possessed, in common with all artists, the desire for recognition, we know that in reality these ovations gave him more anxiety than pleasure, and the longing to be present at any great success of his works was spoiled by the torment of feeling himself under the eyes of the crowd. As for the money earned on these tours, it was less than negligible; always, Peter Ilyich returned home poorer than he set out.

"No, this mysterious force that drove him was a deep, inexplicable anxiety, a mood of despair that sought forgetfulness in distraction anywhere and everywhere. I cannot explain it as a premonition of death; there is no foundation for such a presumption. Nor have I the right to speculate too deeply concerning my brother's psychological condition during these last years; but I must remark upon the fact that such a period of despondency and bewilderment preceded every decisive change in his life. Before deciding upon a musical career in the early sixties, just before his marriage in Moscow, in 1885 directly before he made up his mind definitely to emerge from solitude and show himself in the eyes of the world—then as now, during this last winter of his life, one had the conviction that things could not go on longer as they were, that a change was coming, that something old and finished would shortly give place to something new and unknown."

And now, in February, 1893, seven months before Tchaikowsky

was to drink the fatal glass of unboiled water, now in the midst of depression and darkness, a light broke and, as always with Tchaikowsky, the light came from within. He began to compose the Sixth Symphony, and the work, says Modeste, "was like an act of exorcism, by which Peter Ilyich cast out all the black spirits that had possessed him for so long."

The first mention of the symphony is found in a letter to Anatol, under date of February 22, 1893. Next day, writing to Bob Davydoff, the composer said:

"I want to tell you how contented I feel about my work. You know I destroyed a partly composed, partly orchestrated symphony I wrote last autumn. It was the right thing to do, because there was little good in the thing—an empty play of sound without real inspiration. On the way to Paris last December the idea for a new symphony came to me, this time a symphony with a program, but a program that will remain an enigma to all. Let them guess for themselves; the symphony will be called merely 'Programmatic Symphony' (6). But the program is indeed permeated with subjectiveness, so much so that not once but often, while composing it in my mind during my journey, I shed tears. As soon as I got home I began to write out the sketches, and it went so quickly and eagerly that in less than four days the first movement was done and all the rest clearly outlined in my head. Half of the third movement is ready. Its form will contain much that is new; for instance, the finale will not be a noisy *allegro,* but, on the contrary, a quite long *adagio.* You cannot imagine the joy it gives me to know my day is not yet done, and that I am still capable of work. Of course I may be mistaken, but it doesn't seem so. Please don't tell anyone except Modeste."

This letter is the chief evidence of those persons who think Tchaikowsky committed suicide, who think that seven months later he drank intentionally that glass of raw water. The program of the Sixth Symphony, say they, was *death,* and no wonder the composer refused to reveal it. This is a theory that on the face of it is too ridiculous to need refutation. Concerning the letter above and its mention of tears—surely no one who knows Peter Ilyich, no one, indeed, who is even a little familiar with the artistic temperament—will consider tears shed in the act of artistic creation as anything but happy

tears, tears of triumph over the painful, ecstatic labor of giving
birth. . . .

His day was not yet done, wrote Peter to his nephew, he was yet
capable of work. Sitting in the big, ugly, cluttered room at Klin over
his sheets of lined music paper, Peter was once more filled with that
furious, mad energy he had once described to Nadejda as the greatest joy life had to offer. Once more, driven by that inner consciousness of the immense value of time, the immense privilege that is
man's if he but rouse himself to use it, Peter, bent over his work
table, forgot the hours themselves in a realization of life that rose far
above any ticking of the clock.

His mood was not, however, one of unremitting inspiration. The
symphony progressed, after those first sketches, more slowly. During the spring Tchaikowsky had a letter from Jurgenson saying his
presses were for the moment idle, and he would publish as many
songs and piano pieces as Peter could compose. A month remained
before he must travel to England to receive his Cambridge degree,
and Peter made up his mind to write one piece a day for thirty days;
the fifteenth day found him three pieces ahead of schedule. He wrote
Jurgenson that he could not, however, deliver these pieces at his old
fee of 100 roubles, but would have to ask more "in consequence," so
the letter read, "of the number of paying propositions made to me
lately (I swear it is true)."

Once more we see Tchaikowsky, the workman, settling to his
tools with the true workman's pleasure in his craft—and this even
in the midst of a far deeper inspiration. It had not been so long ago
that he had written the Grand Duke Constantin, "Most of my fellow-
workers do not like composing to order; but as for me, I never feel
more inspired than when I am asked to write something or other,
with a fixed time limit that means somebody at the other end is impatiently awaiting my work." Apropos of this commission of Jurgenson's in the spring of 1893, Tchaikowsky wrote Bob Davydoff:

"I continue to bake musical pancakes. Today the tenth has been
tossed. The remarkable thing is that the further I go with this business, the easier and pleasanter it becomes. In the beginning it was

very hard, and the first two pieces were the fruits of much effort of will, but now I scarcely have time to get one idea in shape before another follows, and so on the whole day long. So if I could stay a whole year in the country, and if my publisher were willing to print all that mountain of notation and pay for it, I could, working *à la Leiken,* make thirty-six thousand, five hundred roubles. Not a bad idea."

About the middle of May Tchaikowsky threw down this ardent craftsman's pen and went to England for the Cambridge honors. In London he conducted the Philharmonic in a performance of his Fourth Symphony—"our symphony," to which Nadejda Philaretovna was by now as sadly deaf as she was deaf to all the world of reality and health and beauty. The symphony had a truly brilliant success in London, eclipsing even the famous Saint-Saens, who followed on the program with a symphony of his own. But Tchaikowsky, writing home to Bob Davydoff, merely inquired if it was not strange that of his own free will he had chosen to undergo "this torture?" He could neither sleep nor eat, he wrote; what fiend could have suggested this trip to him? Yesterday he had resolved to throw over the whole thing and turn tail; but he would be "ashamed to come home now with nothing to show for it. . . . I suffer not only from distress that cannot be said in words (there is a place in my new symphony where I think I have expressed these feelings quite well)—but from an extreme distaste for strangers, from some indefinable fear and from the devil knows what. Physically this fear has expression in pains through the lower abdomen and in an aching and weakness in my legs. Well, this is certainly the last time in my life I shall permit such a business, or at least, not except for big money and then not for longer than three days at a stretch. Two more weeks, I have to sit here, and it might as well be for eternity, it looms so long."

The dreaded day arrived, and Peter Ilyich went out to Cambridge to receive his degree in company with the other musicians to be so honored: Saint-Saens, Boito, Max Bruch and Grieg. The festivities began on the twelfth of June, a composition of each musician was performed, Tchaikowsky's being the beautiful *Francesca Overture-*

Fantasia. Professors and lords and maharajahs did him honor; a grand dinner followed with toasts drunk and compliments flying high. Next morning the future doctors of music donned huge robes of scarlet and white silk; on their heads—empty now of melody and by their own report filled with astonishment—were placed velvet caps with gold tassels. Thus they walked through town, under what Saint-Saens described as a tropical sun, led by the maharajah in a gold turban and diamond necklace, and cheered all the way by enthusiastic spectators. Arrived upon the platform, Tchaikowsky, who by now was having quite a good time in consequence of having discovered a Cambridge professor and his wife who could speak Russian, stood up and listened to a Latin oration in his honor and received his degree. After a garden party and a dinner in London, he was free to go home, and home he went, via Moscow and a visit to Bob at Grankino.

To Bob Davydoff

Nicholas Tchaikowsky's
Estate in the Government
of Kursk
July 31st, 1893

"I spent two very pleasant days in Moscow after I left you. Tell Modia that the day after he left I was very ill, and they said it was from drinking too much cold water at dinner and supper. Castor oil soon cured me and I left next day. It is so nice here. For the next two days I must write letters, and then I can start again on my symphony."

To Modeste

Klin
August 3, 1893

"I am up to my neck in the symphony. The further I get with the orchestration, the more difficult it becomes. Twenty years ago I would have pushed at it, unthinking, with all the strength of my shoulders and it would have come out well. Now I have become a coward, with no faith in myself. For two whole days I have sat stewing over two pages; they won't work out as I wish. Yet it progresses.

"My house, thanks to Alexey's efforts, has a very coquettish appearance. Everything is neat, the garden is a mass of flowers, the paths are trimmed and we have new fences with gates. I am well served as regards food. And yet, except during working hours, I am bored, and wish myself elsewhere. . . . Still, I have noticed before that after long trips and much society, I am tired like this. Probably it will soon pass. . . ."

To Bob Davydoff

Klin

August 15, 1893

"The symphony that I planned to dedicate to you—I have since changed my mind—is progressing." (Tchaikowsky had not changed his mind, and was merely teasing his nephew.) "I am very pleased with its contents, but not quite so pleased with the orchestration. Time after time, things don't work out the way I want. It will be neither unusual nor surprising if the symphony meets with lack of appreciation and abuse. It won't be my first such experience. But I can say positively that I consider it the best of all my works to date; especially, I know it is the most sincere. I love it as I never loved any of my musical children.

"My life just now lacks all variety; sometimes the evenings bore me but I have no right to complain because the important thing now is the symphony and I can work nowhere so well as at home. My great amusement here is my godson (Alexey's son), to me a wonderfully attractive child."

To Taneyeff

Klin

August 24, 1893

"I have finished the symphony. There remains only to add the instrumental signs and tempo marks. Regarding the former, I want to ask Konius' advice, who will come here shortly for the purpose. He will bring a violin and his youngest brother Leo. I need the latter to play through the piano arrangement which I have just finished making. When you come to Moscow—I ask this very earnestly—will you play over the symphony with Konius and determine all the doubtful places that I can't decide without you? I did not so much as dare to ask you to make the piano arrangement because it would have been the greatest impudence on my part. You have no time for such work now. But I do earnestly beseech

you to play it over. What a disgusting business, these piano arrangements! One has to drive oneself to it.

"Take care of yourself. God grant your work goes well.

"Yours,

"P. Tchaikowsky."

On the same August day, Tchaikowsky wrote Jurgenson:

"Dear Friend,

"I have finished the orchestration of the new symphony. Now for
about a week I shall busy myself putting in the signs and generally
looking it over. I made the four-hand arrangement myself and must
play it through, which I shall do when the youngest Konius gets
here. As soon as we have gone through it together, I can send it to
you, providing you want to publish my symphony. As regards the
score and parts, I cannot promise to finish them before the first performance, which will be in Petersburg on October 28th.

"On my word of honor, never in my life have I been so satisfied
with myself, so proud, so happy to know that I have made, in truest
fact, a good thing."

Thus the summer wore away. In September, Tchaikowsky went
to visit his brother Anatol at Mikhailovskoe, and wrote happily to
Modeste about the beauty and quiet of the country. Early in October
he returned to Klin and busied himself with orchestrating a piano
concerto he had made out of parts of the symphony he had written
the previous May—the symphony he had written Bob Davydoff about,
and had called uninspired. This was afterward published as a piano
concerto (Number Three), for piano and orchestra, Opus 75. Early
in October he heard of the death of an old friend, Zverev, for whom a
memorial service was to be held in Moscow next week. Two friends
came out from Moscow the day before to accompany Peter back to
town, and on the 19th of October therefore, late in the afernoon, the
three boarded the train for Moscow, a two-hour ride. As the train
passed the village of Frolovskoe, Peter pointed to the belfry tower and
to the quiet, pretty churchyard below. "There," he said, "is where I
shall be buried, and passing by, travellers will point out my grave."

He repeated to Taneyeff next day at Zverev's memorial service
this wish to be buried in Frolovskoe, but he said it in no morbid

mood; it was a natural remark at such a time, in the presence of death. During these days, it is the testimony of all who saw Peter Ilyich that his mood was in no way depressed. On the contrary, he seemed cheerful, filled with faith in himself and in the future. He had brought the new piano concerto with him to Moscow and showed it eagerly to Taneyeff. That honest person, who often called a spade worse than a spade, pronounced the concerto a virtuoso piece, and no real music. There was, as usual, truth in Taneyeff's criticism, but it did not seem to depress Tchaikowsky, nor did he destroy the concerto as he sometimes did with music Taneyeff condemned. Merely, he decided not to publish it. (It was published after the composer's death, and Taneyeff was the first to perform it in public.)

The morning after the memorial service for Zverev, Tchaikowsky went to the Moscow Conservatory to hear a Mozart vocal quartet with piano accompaniment that Tchaikowsky had lately arranged from the Mozart Piano Fantasia (Number Four). It was well sung by some of the Conservatory students and Peter was pleased; he adored that simple melody, he said, and wondered wherein lay its potent fascination. That evening he dined with friends. Kashkin in his memoirs tells how the conversation turned on the sad facts of Zverev's and Albrecht's recent deaths, and how few of the old circle were left. Who would be the next to go? "Peter," said Kashkin, "you will outlive us all." Peter denied this prophecy, but declared he had never felt so well and so happy as at the present moment. The friends sat together until it was time for Peter to take the midnight train for Petersburg. His Sixth Symphony was to be performed in a week's time and he was going up to conduct the rehearsals. Concerning the first three movements of the symphony, the composer professed himself, to Kashkin, well satisfied, but concerning the last movement, the long *Adagio lamentoso,* he was still doubtful, and if in performance it did not work out well, he would perhaps destroy it, he said, and write a new one.

Peter rose to go to the station; no one offered to go with him, as it was known that he did not like to be seen off on trains. He and Kashkin made an appointment to meet in Moscow two weeks later for supper after a concert of the Musical Society. Then they said good-bye, and neither of them dreamed it was forever.

Next morning in Petersburg Modeste and Bob Davydoff met the composer at the station and took him to the apartment they were sharing that autumn. Peter was delighted with their new living arrangements and his spirits were excellent, especially while his presence in town was not known and his time could be his own. Only one thing worried him, said Modeste. At rehearsals, the new symphony seemed to make no impression on the orchestra players and this caused the composer anxiety as well as chagrin; he knew the performance could be ruined by indifference on the part of the musicians. Also, any apparent coldness on the part of the orchestra, a yawn, a bored look, paralyzed Peter Ilyich; he lost all sense of the music's structure, all sense of shading and nuance and hurried through the rehearsal so as to free the musicians from their irksome task of playing his music. And this was usually repeated at the concert itself, resulting, of course, in a performance that lacked all strength and precision and rendered his work insipid and lacking in color. Modeste says this was the case with the Fifth Symphony and with *Hamlet,* both of which did not attain recognition until conducted by someone other than the composer.

But in spite of the orchestra's coolness, Peter did not lose faith in the intrinsic excellence of his new symphony. With other works, his friends had seen him easily elated or depressed by the most casual criticism; this time he remained firm, reiterating his conviction that the Sixth Symphony was the best thing he had ever written or ever would write. On the 28th of October the concert took place and was flatly received, because, Modeste says, of being flatly played. "The symphony was applauded and the composer called before the curtain, but the enthusiasm was no greater than had been shown for other works of Tchaikowsky's. Certainly the symphony did not make the deep impression it made when conducted by Napravnik on November 18th" (alas, too late for the composer to enjoy!). The newspapers were as lukewarm as the public, the critics finding the symphony lacking in originality. "As far as inspiration is con-

cerned," wrote one of them, "this music stands far below Tchaikowsky's other symphonies."

Modeste attributed all this to bad performance, arising from lack
of sympathy between conductor and players. But Rimsky-Korsakov,
in his memoirs, disagreed with Modeste's judgment, declaring that
although the symphony was splendidly played by Napravnik, it had
gone very well at the author's hands, too. The public had not fath-
omed it the first time, and had not paid enough attention to it;
precisely as several years earlier it had failed to give due attention to
Tchaikowsky's Fifth Symphony.

The day after the concert, Modeste found his brother up and
dressed early, sitting at the tea table with the score of the symphony
in his hands. He was trying to think of a name for it before sending
it to Jurgenson for publication. Somehow, merely *Number 6* did not
seem sufficient, yet his first idea of "Programmatic Symphony" would
not do. "How," Peter asked his brother over his glass of tea, "can it
be called Programmatic when I refuse to give it a program?" Modeste
suggested the word "tragic," but Peter shook his head and Modeste
went out of the room, leaving his brother frowning indecisively.
Suddenly Modeste reappeared at the door. "Pathetique!" he called
out. "Perfect, Modia!" cried Peter. "Bravo! *Pathètique.*" And he wrote
the word on the score and mailed it to Moscow.

But the composer must have felt a bit doubtful, for next morning
he wrote Jurgenson:

> Petersburg
> October 30, 1893
>
> "Please, my dear, put the following on the title page of the sym-
> phony,
>
> " 'To Vladimir Lvovitch Davydoff
> No. 6
> Comp. P. Tch.'
>
> "I hope it isn't too late.
>
> "Something queer is happening with this symphony; we can't say
> it has displeased the public, but it has perplexed them. As for me, I
> am prouder of it than of anything I have written. But we can talk
> it all over soon, because I shall be in Moscow next Saturday."

Next evening Peter Ilyich went to hear Anton Rubinstein's opera, *The Maccabees*. The day following, he was quite well, even gay and bright, records Modeste. That night he dined at Vera Butakov's. Vera was a Davydoff, a sister of Leo Davydoff, Tchaikowsky's brother-in-law, and she was a very old friend of Peter's. Years ago, indeed, Vera, who was older than Peter Ilyich, had embarrassed him greatly by falling in love with him. Peter, much irritated, had fled rapidly. But the breach was soon healed. Vera married an admiral in the Russian army and moved in court circles. It was at Vera's house that Tchaikowsky had met the Grand Duke Constantin, and it was to Vera that Tchaikowsky owed much of the Imperial patronage that had served his music so well.

So Peter dined gayly at Vera Butakov's that November night of 1893. Afterward he went to the theatre and during intermission paid a back-stage visit to the actor, Varlamoff. The conversation turned upon spiritualism; Varlamoff, with sly humor, poked fun at these ghost-raisers. Peter laughed heartily. No use, he agreed, in running after death. "Time enough, before we need meet that ugly snub-nosed one. We can all wait awhile, and as for me, I know I have a long time to live."

After the theatre, Peter had supper with friends at the Restaurant Leiner, eating macaroni and drinking his favorite white wine and soda water. At two in the morning they all walked home, Peter quite well and serene.

Next day was Thursday, November 2nd. Modeste, coming to the sitting-room for morning tea, was surprised to find his brother not there and went to Peter's room. Peter was in bed. "I've had a bad night, Modia," he said. "But its nothing. Just the old complaint."

Modeste offered to fetch the usual remedy, castor oil, but Peter shook his head. He had to call on Napravnik later in the morning to talk business, and later on he did go out. In half an hour he returned, feeling out of sorts, and Modeste suggested calling a doctor. Not an important, fancy doctor, said Modeste pleadingly as Peter shook his head. Just their old friend, Vasili Bertenson, to look him over?

Peter refused. He would take Hunyadi water, he said. What good could a doctor do? Hadn't the two of them seen him this way scores of times? It was nothing but the usual infernal nervous dysentery. "Go on about your business, Modia," said Peter. And Modia went.

Peter wrote some letters until lunch time, when Mulbach arrived to talk business. The three sat together; Peter did not eat, but seemed in no way indisposed. He would take no wine or coffee, he said; it might be bad for what ailed him. Peter got up, and pouring himself a glass of water from the tap in the next room, brought it back and drank it before anyone noticed what he was doing.

He set his glass down. "Petia," cried Modeste. "That water wasn't boiled. What crazy folly! Its November and you're in Petersburg."

Peter shrugged. He had never feared cholera, he said. Oh, yes, he knew one shouldn't touch fruit or raw water in cholera season, but a man couldn't go tiptoeing round in fear of death. Now, about this contract to play the First Suite in Prague; did Mulbach think . . .

Peter's face changed suddenly; he got up from the table, went to his room and was ill. Modeste left him on his bed and went back to Mulbach. Next time Modeste looked into the bedroom, his brother was asleep. Good, thought Modeste. All Peter needs is rest, and Modeste went out with Mulbach. Returning at five he found his brother feverish and suffering from cramps; this time Peter's protest was not heeded and Vasili Bertenson was sent for. "This is a very sick man," said Vasili, and prescribed hot applications on the stomach and feet. Complete rest. Vasili was an easy-going man and an old friend of Peter's; he knew what a high-strung fellow this was.

The word cholera was not mentioned. Nor was it, records Modeste, so much as thought of.

Uneasily, Modeste, as the evening wore on, heard his brother groan in the next room, heard him get up again and again, but always, when Modeste came in, Peter refused help. Modeste called his servant and bade him fetch Vasili's brother, the famous Leo Bertenson, doctor to royalty and all of fashionable Petersburg. By the time Leo came, Peter was screaming aloud, not from abdominal pain but from a horrible constriction in the chest. "The dry cholera!" whis-

pered Modeste to himself, his face stiff with horror. "Peter will suffocate; in a few hours he will be dead. Oh, impossible." . . . Only the
figment of imagination; Peter had often been as sick as this. . . .

Bertenson sent the specimens out for analysis. Waiting, Modeste
saw his brother stiffen in the first convulsion, watched him slowly
relax, sweating. . . . "Modia," whispered Peter, "Is it cholera?"

"No," said Modeste. "No, Petia . . ."

At eleven that same evening the messenger returned from the hospital, bringing a male nurse with him. Modeste, watching Bertenson's face as he read the report, needed no further word. The glass
of raw water had not been responsible; Peter had probably had the
germs of cholera in him when he came to Petersburg; he might have
picked them up on the journey. But the raw cold drink, and especially the bitter Hunyadi, had quickly intensified the irritation.

And now, swift action to fight this ancient enemy. White aprons,
carbolic soap, antiseptic powders, sulphuric acid for Peter to take,
quinine, nitre. . . . Peter turned, half sat up as he saw the men
enter the dim room in their white hospital aprons. When he was
fourteen, his mother had died of cholera. White aprons, and this
sickish pungent odor of carbolic. . . . "Here she is then, the cholera!" exclaimed Peter, and a moment later screamed aloud in
pain. . . .

And now the ranks of watchers must be augmented: cholera needs
constant nursing, and nursing which is horribly dangerous as well
as unpleasant. This ancient enemy of man that came from the East
to lay waste to Asia, and that even now can take its toll of eighty
deaths out of every hundred stricken—this is a scourge transmitted
with terrifying swiftness. One touch of a polluted garment is enough.
Peter worried constantly over the care expended on him, thanked
his attendants for the smallest service, begged them to go and rest.
A small army of men surrounded the sickbed. Nicholas Tchaikowsky, the eldest brother, was sent for; the only woman in attendance
was the wife of Modeste's servant. Bob Davydoff was there, young
and blond and beautiful in his smart uniform of the Preobashensky
Guards—Russia's crack regiment, the Tsar's own bodyguard. Erect,

booted above the knee, his fair hair wild, his young face lined with
ill-concealed horror, Bob heard his name spoken and sprang to the
bedside. Peter put out his hand. "Bob," he said, and smiled. "Bob . . .
I am afraid, after seeing this mess, you will lose all respect for me?"

Bob shook his head wildly and turned away. The sick man was
in the living-room now, his small iron bed had been rolled out from
the tiny bedroom. Even the living-room was dark most of the day,
nearly always a light burned. That Thursday night it began to rain,
a raw wind blew from the northwest; outside, horses slipped on the
cobblestones. How Peter had hated these Petersburg Novembers,
and how he had complained to Nadejda Philaretovna about them!
. . . During the night his suffering increased and the convulsions
were followed by helpless weakness. "It seems to be death," Peter told
his brother. "Good-bye, Modia."

But unhappily it was not death. All night the watchers took turns
massaging the patient after his convulsions. By five next morning
the constriction in his chest had ceased but another suffering came
to take its place: the unappeasable, tormenting cholera thirst. Peter
called for water, begged for it, bargained with the doctors for it, and
when they offered it on a spoon, refused it in disgust. At nine on
Friday morning Leo Bertenson went away. Peter was easier for a
time, the blueness of his face yielded to a healthier pallor, but cholera
spots appeared around his mouth and his lips were dry and black.
When the spots disappeared, the watchers breathed more freely,
and on Bertenson's returning toward noon, Peter thanked him.
"You have rescued me from the claws of death," he said. "I am much
better." He held this improvement until nightfall and the watchers
were sent off to bed.

But on Saturday the patient woke much depressed. "Leave me,"
he told the doctors. "You can't help me. I shall not recover." And
from now on he continued depressed though quite conscious, ceased
his little jokes with Bob, his bargaining for water, and submitted
passively to treatment.

And now arrived the most dangerous symptom of cholera: inac-
tivity of the kidneys. The doctors put much hope in a hot bath that

was to be administered in the evening, but when they heard the word *bath,* Modeste and Nicholas Tchaikowsky looked at each other and winced: their mother had died when put into this cholera bath. "Will you consent to the bath, Petia?" they asked. "With pleasure," replied Peter wearily. "But when you put me in it I shall certainly die as my mother died before me."

That evening Peter was too violently ill for the bath to be attempted. "You are wasting all this kindness and patience," he told Leo Bertenson again. "I tell you I cannot be cured." He slept now, restlessly, moving his head and lips. Over and over he repeated the name of Nadejda Philaretovna, reproaching her indignantly one moment and the next, smiling quietly, as though listening to a reply. When he woke, consciousness returned slowly so that it was some moments before he recognized his servant and good friend Alexis, who had come up from Moscow on the night train. "I am glad you came, Alexey," said Peter, and smiled. At two that afternoon Leo Bertenson ordered the last extreme measure to be tried: the bath. Peter was asleep, but they carried him to the tub across the room; when he felt the water he roused, pronounced it pleasant but asked to be put back to bed; he was so weak, he said.

From now on, Peter sank rapidly; perspiration was profuse, the pulse weakened, the patient roused to consciousness only for brief intervals. All hope was abandoned, the priest was sent for and read aloud the prayers for the dying without, apparently, reaching the sick man's consciousness. Modeste, dry-eyed, numb with exhaustion, moved about the room, polite as always, but seeming not to comprehend when spoken to. This was more to him than brother, this wasted, suffering figure on the bed. Modeste looked down at Peter's blackened lips, at the fingers shrivelled with cholera. This man had been Modeste's life. Modeste had lived in this stronger life, had moved in its shadow. . . .

On the bed-table, Modeste saw the fat night-candle flutter under its glass hood; windows shook with a hard wind from off the Baltic. . . . How interminable the hours, yet how all-too-quick! Not long now, Bertenson had said. Not very much longer. Bob was asleep in his chair, poor boy, in his dressing-gown with the white apron over it. . . . That dressing-gown would have to be burned. . . . Modeste looked at his watch. It was Monday morning. A little after three. . . .

There was a slight sound from the bed and Modeste leaped to his feet. Bob woke, too, and got up quickly; Alexis was already there, by his master's side. Peter's face cleared, his eyes opened; he looked in turn at the three men standing by him, then looked upward, in his eyes a clear light which remained for some moments, until without a sigh or a struggle, Peter Ilyich breathed his last.

Contrary to all the rules of cholera hygiene, usually strictly enforced by the city officials, Peter's body lay in state in his brother's apartment. Mourners came by the hundreds, filing through the room, kissing the dead man's hands and face—and the legend goes that not one of these mourners caught the infection. Then, with the coffin closed, the body was taken to Kazan Cathedral for funeral service. Peter's wish to lie in Frolovskoe churchyard was not realized and he was buried in Petersburg in the Alexander Nevsky Lavra Cemetery. The shock of his sudden death roused the country, and when, not two weeks later, Napravnik played the Sixth Symphony in Petersburg, interest had mounted to furor. People listened avidly to this music which rumor said the author had written as his own requiem. Their biographical curiosity was never satisfied; music is not one of gossip's servants. Nevertheless this curiosity served Peter Ilyich well in sharpening the ears of the world to what the composer himself had been convinced was his best work.

Peter had willed his royalties to Bob Davydoff; the Klin house was not Peter's to bequeath, but the furniture was left to Alexis, who with such devotion and consummate lack of taste had assembled these dreadful chairs and tables and clocks and carpets. Alexis bought the house and began immediately to collect everything he could find pertaining to or belonging to his dead master. When, in 1897, he sold the house to Modeste Tchaikowsky and Bob Davydoff, the two continued Alexis' plan of making the house into a Tchaikowsky

museum. Well for Peter that he could not know the fate of those
dear ones who lived on in his house; there Bob, the charming, spoiled
child of fortune, shot himself; there Modeste, in 1916, knew that he
was to die of cancer. . . .

But the Tchaikowsky brothers were not easy to kill. Modeste died,
but Hippolyte Tchaikowsky lived on at Klin, old Hippolyte the
Admiral, despoiled of his cherished uniforms by a new world that
considered epaulets a crime and good manners a nonsense. The
revolutionary government let Hippolyte keep his position as assistant curator of the Tchaikowsky museum. Seriously, with his straight
old back, his military bows, Hippolyte received museum visitors,
showed them Peter's big black piano, showed them the glass case
wherein lay the *Pathètique* score, traced with the delicate, precise
strokes of his brother's penmanship; seriously bowed them out again
into a world so wildly new that even had he been set down in its
streets, Hippolyte would have failed to recognize it as the world he
and Petia had lived in. . . .

Surely, it was well for Peter Ilyich that he died when he did, died
in the very fulness of his time, before a world changed, before an era
faded. Imperial thrones were yet secure when Peter passed away.
Peter had truly loved his Tsar in the old-fashioned way. When
Peter died, anarchy and communism were but theories. Gentlemen
still sent pressed violets in letters to ladies, and ladies, when they
could afford it, responded with slim enamel watches across which
Apollo pranced in diamonds. . . .

Surely, Peter Ilyich would not have been happy in a world that
found the waltz a thing to ridicule, a world which with proud de-
fiance put the word sex in place of the word romance. A world that
for a time indeed, considered Tchaikowsky—even dead—as out-
moded, ridiculous as the waltz-time he had loved. When he died,
Peter Ilyich was but fifty-three, still young, as composers go. Yet
somehow, the world does not mourn him as a man cut down in his
prime. The world does not, sighing, say as it says of Mozart, of
Keats, of Schubert, "Oh, had this man lived longer, what still more
glorious gifts he might have had for us!" No; there is about the

Sixth Symphony something strangely final, something that tells us: This man's cup was full; he had reached his zenith, he had attained that which so often he had told his "best friend" he longed to attain: he had perfected his talent to the limit of his ability, he had fulfilled his urgent duty toward that gift which the gods had given him. . . .

God rest him, then, as the Russians would say. God rest the soul of Peter Ilyich, who worked hard, who sinned and suffered for his sins—who was an artist, and true to himself.

Chronological List of Tchaikowsky's Compositions

1865–1866

String Quartet in B major and *Overture in F major,* performed by Petersburg Conservatory pupils at a concert at the Michael Palace. Tchaikowsky conducted.

Began music for Schiller's *Ode to Happiness* for chorus and orchestra, written on command of his teacher, Anton Rubinstein, for a Conservatory festival the last day of December, 1865. All three of these works are in manuscript, never published.

Began to write *Symphony No. 1.*

1866–1867

Op. 15. *Festival Overture* upon the Danish anthem.

Op. 13. *Symphony No. 1, in G minor. Winter Day Dreams.* First performed in Moscow, February, 1868; conducted by N. Rubinstein.

Op. 1. *Russian Scherzo* and *Impromptu.* The *Scherzo* is built on the theme of the first movement of the *B major Quartet.* These two pieces and the *First Symphony* were dedicated to N. Rubinstein.

Op. 2. *Souvenir de Hapsal.* Three pieces for piano. Dedicated to Vera Davydoff.

Tchaikowsky also began work on the opera *Voyevoda.*

1867–1868

The Voyevoda. Full-length opera after Ostrovsky's play. Score destroyed by the composer in the seventies. The *Dances of the Maids* and the *Entr'acte* were published as Op. 3 by Jurgenson.

1868–1869

Op. 77. Symphonic poem, *Fatum.* First performed in Moscow, February, 1869; conducted by N. Rubinstein. Dedicated to Balakirev. In the seventies Tchaikowsky destroyed the score but the orchestral parts were preserved and from them the whole was reconstructed and published by Beliayev in 1896. Hence the late opus number.

Op. 4. *Valse Caprice* for piano. Dedicated to Anton Door.

Op. 5. *Romance* for piano. Dedicated to Désirée Artôt.

Twenty-five Russian folksongs arranged for piano, four hands.

Recitative and chorus for Auber's opera, *Le Domino Noir*. The manuscript has been lost.

Undine. Opera in three acts. Libretto by Count Solloub, which Modeste T. says is so ridiculous one wonders that Tchaikowsky could have thought of treating it seriously as an opera. The composer destroyed the score in 1873. All that remains is *Undine's* aria, afterward used in *Sniegourochka*, and a march in the last act which afterward became the *Andantino Marziale* of the *Second Symphony*. Kashkin says that an *Adagio* in the ballet, *The Swan Lake*, also came from *Undine*.

1869–1870

Twenty-five Russian folksongs for piano, four hands. Finished September, 1869. Published by Jurgenson with twenty-five of the previous season.

Romeo and Juliet. *Overture-Fantasia* for orchestra based on Shakespeare's tragedy. Completely revised in the summer of 1870. Dedicated to Balakirev. First performed in Moscow, March, 1870. Conducted by N. Rubinstein.

Arrangement for piano, four hands, of Anton Rubinstein's overture, *Ivan the Terrible*.

Op. 6. Six songs.

Chorus of Insects from the unfinished opera, *Mandragora*. The score of this work has been lost; the piano arrangement was published by Jurgenson. In 1898 Glazounov orchestrated it. Manuscript.

Op. 7. *Valse Scherzo (A major)* for piano. Dedicated to Alexander Davydoff.

1870–1871

Op. 9. Three pianoforte pieces.

Song, *"So schnell vergessen."*

Nature and Love. Trio for two sopranos and alto, with chorus and piano accompaniment. Dedicated to Mme Valsek, and written for this lady's pupils. Published posthumously.

Op. 11. *Quartet No. 1 (D major)*, for strings. Dedicated to Rachinsky. First performed March, 1871. The *Andante* is based on the Russian folksong, "Vania sat on the sofa and smoked a pipe"; Tchaikowsky heard it sung by a carpenter under his window at Kamenka while he was working on the score of *Undine* in the summer of 1869.

Manual of Harmony, written during the summer of 1870 while the composer was writing the opera, *Oprichnik*.

1871–1872

ʻOp. 10. Two pieces for piano, dedicated to V. Shilovsky. Middle section of the second piece is a popular song the composer heard in Nice.

Cantata for chorus, orchestra and tenor solo. Composed for the opening of the Polytechnic Institute. First performed in May, 1872, K. Davidov conducting.

The Oprichnik. Opera in four acts. Dedicated to the Grand Duke Constantin. The composer used for this many compositions he had put aside. The censor forbade the figure of *Ivan the Terrible* to appear on the stage, but in spite of this the opera was more effective than *Voyevoda* and *Undine*.

This summer Tchaikowsky also sketched the *Second Symphony*.

1872–1873

Op. 17. *Symphony No. 2 (C minor)*. Dedicated to the Moscow Musical Society. First performed in Moscow in 1873, under N. Rubinstein. Later drastically revised.

Op. 16. Six songs, published by Bessel.

Op. 12. Music for Ostrovsky's *Sniegourochka*. First performed in Moscow at the Opera House in May, 1873. Several numbers in this work are taken from *Undine*.

Perpetuum Mobile, from Weber's sonata, arranged by Tchaikowsky for the left hand. Dedicated to Mme Zograf.

Also the rough sketches for the symphonic fantasia, *The Tempest*.

Seventeen newspaper and magazine articles concerning the season's musical events in Moscow.

1873–1874

Op. 18. *The Tempest*. Symphonic fantasia for full orchestra, after Shakespeare's tragedy. Dedicated to V. Stasoff. First performed in December, 1873, in Moscow under N. Rubinstein.

Op. 21. Six pianoforte pieces upon one theme. Dedicated to Anton Rubinstein.

Op. 22. *Quartet No. 2 (F major)* for strings. Dedicated to the Grand Duke Constantin. First performed soon after composition in 1874 at N. Rubinstein's house. Probably the composer noticed defects at this performance because he worked on it several weeks longer. First public performance, March, 1874.

Op. 14. *Vakoula the Smith*. Opera in three acts and seven scenes. Libretto by Polonsky, taken from Gogol's *Christmas Night*. Dedicated

to the memory of the Grand Duchess Helena Pavlovna. Later changed to
the opera *Cherevichki*. Still later called *Les Caprices d'Oxane*.

Nine newspaper articles on musical subjects.

1874–1875

Op. 25. Six songs.

Op. 23. *Concerto* for pianoforte and orchestra (*B flat minor*). Dedicated to Hans von Bülow. Besides the Ukrainian peasant air used for the principal theme of the *Allegro*, Tchaikowsky used the chansonette, *"Il faut s'amuser, danser et rire,"* which Anatol and Modeste used to sing in remembrance of a charming singer they admired.

Op. 26. *Serenade* for violin, with orchestral accompaniment (*B minor*). Dedicated to Leopold Auer.

Op. 27. Six songs, dedicated to Princess Tserteleff (Lavroskaya).

Op. 28. Six songs.

Op. 29. *Symphony No. 3* (*D major*) in five movements. First performed in Moscow in November, 1875.

In August, Tchaikowsky began to write the ballet, *The Swan Lake*.

Also fifteen articles on musical subjects, one in defense of Anton Rubinstein who had been accused of writing too much and too quickly —a criticism which had also been made of Tchaikowsky himself.

1875–1876

Op. 30. *Quartet No. 3* (*E flat minor*) for strings. Dedicated to the memory of F. Laub. First performed in March, 1875.

Op. 20. *The Swan Lake*. Ballet in four acts. First performed in the Opera House, Moscow, March, 1877.

Op. 37. *The Seasons*. Twelve pieces for piano. Commissioned monthly by a musical magazine.

Translation into Russian of Mozart's opera, *Figaro*, requested by N. Rubinstein for a performance by the Conservatory students.

After this season, the composer wrote no more newspaper and magazine articles. His last article concerned Wagner's Trilogy, and was never finished.

1876–1877

Op. 31. *Marche Slav* for full orchestra. First performed in Moscow, November, 1876, conducted by N. Rubinstein.

Op. 32. *Francesca da Rimini*. Symphonic fantasy for full orchestra, based on Dante's poem. Dedicated to Taneyeff. First performed in Moscow in February, 1877, under N. Rubinstein.

Op. 33. *Variations on a Rococo Theme,* for violoncello and orchestra. Dedicated to G. Fitzhagen. Composed December, 1876.

Op. 34. *Valse Scherzo,* for violin and orchestra. Dedicated to Joseph Kotek. Composed in January, 1877. Besides these, the sketches for the *Fourth Symphony* were made, and for two-thirds of *Eugene Onegin.*

1877–1878

Op. 36. *Symphony No. 4 (F minor)* dedicated "To my best friend." First performed in Moscow, February 10; conducted by N. Rubinstein.

Op. 24. *Eugene Onegin.* Lyric scenes, in three acts and seven scenes. Text from Pushkin arranged by the composer himself, with the help of C. Shilovsky. First performed in Moscow in May, 1879, by the pupils of the Moscow Conservatory.

Op. 38. Six songs, dedicated to Anatol Tchaikowsky. Four of them written to words of A. Tolstoi: (1) *Don Juan's Serenade,* (2) *Das war im ersten Lenzesstrahl,* (3) *Im irregenden Tanze,* (4) *Ach wenn du könntest,* (5) *Aus dem Jenseits* (Lermontov) and (6) *Pimpinella*—Florentine song.

Op. 40. Twelve pianoforte pieces, dedicated to Modeste Tchaikowsky. Of these, *No. 12* was written first, in Florence. The middle section of it is a Venetian song that Tchaikowsky had heard sung in Venice under his window. *No. 10* had been written in 1876 as a number for the ballet, *The Swan Lake.*

Op. 37. *Sonata* for pianoforte *(G major).* Dedicated to Klindworth. First performed in Moscow, October, 1879, by N. Rubinstein.

Op. 35. *Concerto* for violin and orchestra. First dedicated to L. Auer, afterward to A. Brodsky. Begun at Clarens in March, 1878. The *Andante* as played by Kotek did not please the composer and in two days he wrote a new one. First performed by A. Brodsky in Vienna in 1879.

Op. 42. *"Souvenir d'un lieu cher,"* three pieces for violin and piano. (1) *Meditation,* (2) *Scherzo,* (3) *Melodie. No. 1,* composed in Clarens, was the original *Andante* for the Violin Concerto. The others were written at Brailov in May.

Op. 41. *Liturgy of St. John Chrysostom,* for four-part mixed chorus. Begun in May, 1878, at Kamenka, and finished at Brailov.

Op. 39. *Kinderalbum,* 24 pieces for pianoforte (*à la* Schumann). Dedicated to Vladimir (Bob) Davydoff.

Skobelieff March. Tchaikowsky signed this work by the pen name of Synopov. It was written on Jurgenson's commission. Besides these, in August, 1878, Tchaikowsky wrote most of the *First Orchestral Suite.*

1878-1879

Op. 43 *Suite No. 1* for full orchestra, in six movements. Dedicated secretly to N. Ph. von Meck. First performed in Moscow, November, 1879, under N. Rubinstein.

The Maid of Orleans. Opera in four acts and six scenes, dedicated to Napravnik. Libretto arranged by Tchaikowsky from Jukovsky's Russian translation of Schiller's *Maid of Orleans,* with some ideas borrowed from Barbier and Mermet. The day before his fatal illness, Tchaikowsky professed an ardent desire to rewrite this libretto, using only Schiller's tragedy, in the realization that in discarding Schiller's conception of the last act, he had greatly weakened the libretto.

1879-1880

Op. 44. *Second Concerto* for pianoforte and orchestra. Dedicated to N. Rubinstein. First performed by Taneyeff in Moscow, May, 1882.

Revision of *Op. 17, The Second Symphony,* only the *Introduction* and *Andante* remaining unchanged.

Op. 45. *Italian Capriccio,* for full orchestra. Dedicated to K. Davidov (the Petersburg musician).

Music for a *"tableau vivant."* "Montenegro when war was declared," etc. Score was lost and never recovered.

Op. 46. Six vocal duets, dedicated to Tatiana Davydoff.

Op. 47. Seven songs, dedicated to Panayeff.

Also, a revision of the *Romeo and Juliet Overture.*

1880-1881

Op. 48. *Serenade* for string orchestra, in four movements. Dedicated to C. Albrecht. First planned as symphony or quartet. Writing to Jurgenson, Tchaikowsky said: "I have accidentally written a *Serenade.*" First performed in Moscow in January, 1882, conducted by Erdmannsdörfer.

Op. 49. *1812.* Overture for full orchestra, composed for the consecration of the Cathedral of Christ the Saviour.

Besides these works, Tchaikowsky made some experiments in harmonizing the Vesper Service and sketched out the opera *Mazeppa.*

1881-1882

Op. 50. *Trio* for piano, violin and violoncello. Dedicated *"À la memoire d'un grand artiste"* (N. G. Rubinstein). Performed privately in Moscow by Taneyeff, Grimaly and Fitzhagen on the anniversary of

Rubinstein's death. Revised somewhat by Tchaikowsky. First public performance in Moscow, October, 1882.

Op. 52. Seventeen sacred numbers for church choir based on the ancient church singing.

Edition of Bortniansky's works.

More sketches for *Mazeppa* and completion of two acts.

1882–1883

Op. 51. Six pieces for pianoforte.

Verses on Glinka's *Slavsia* theme, ending with Russian National Anthem, written for orchestra and huge chorus at time of coronation of Alexander III. Never published.

Coronation March, for orchestra. Composed under commission from the City of Moscow and conducted by Taneyeff at Sokolniki at a coronation festival in May, 1882.

Moscow, cantata for chorus, soloists and orchestra. Composed on commission for coronation festivities. Conducted by Napravnik in May, 1883.

Mazeppa. Opera in three acts and six scenes. Subject from Pushkin's poem, *Poltava,* arranged by Tchaikowsky and Burenin. First performed in Moscow, February, 1884, at the Imperial Theatre.

Besides these works, Tchaikowsky began his *Second Orchestral Suite.* By August the greater part of it was sketched.

1883 to January, 1885

Op. 52. *Suite No. 2* for full orchestra, first performed in Moscow, in February, 1887.

Op. 54. *Sixteen Children's Songs,* with piano accompaniment.

Op. 55. *Suite No. 3* in four movements, for full orchestra. Dedicated to Erdmannsdörfer. First performed in Petersburg under Hans von Bülow's baton, June, 1885.

Op. 56. *Fantasia Concerto,* for piano and orchestra, in two movements. Originally dedicated to Esipova, afterward to Sophie Menter. First performed in Moscow, February, 1885, by Taneyeff.

Impromptu Capriccio for piano. Dedicated to Sophie Jurgenson.

Elegy for string orchestra, written in memory of I. Samarin.

Three Songs for the Cherubims (church anthems).

Op. 57. Six songs.

Besides these works, Tchaikowsky began the revision of his opera, *Vakoula the Smith.*

From January to September, 1885

Opera *Vakoula the Smith* rewritten as *Cherevichki* (later *Les Caprices d'Oxane*). Addition of many new numbers.

Hymn to Saint Cyril, an old Slavonic melody arranged for church choir.

Sacred Songs. Five church hymns.

Ecossaise, for the sixth scene of *Onegin.* Composed and orchestrated in one day at Maidanovo.

Op. 58. *Manfred.* Symphonic poem in four scenes for full orchestra, after Byron's poem. Dedicated to M. Balakirev. First performed in Moscow, March, 1886. Conducted by Erdmannsdörfer.

1885–1886

Words and music of a chorus in honor of the fiftieth anniversary of the School of Laws. Never published.

School of Laws March for full orchestra.

The Domovoi (Spirit of the House), for Ostrovsky's comedy, *Voyevoda.* Not published.

Op. 59. *Dumka,* Russian village scene for piano. Dedicated to Marmontel, Director of the Paris Conservatoire.

Besides these unimportant works Tchaikowsky worked all this season on his opera, *The Enchantress,* finishing the rough sketches in August, 1886.

September, 1886, to January, 1888

Op. 60. Twelve songs. Dedicated to Her Majesty the Empress Maria Feodorovna. Written during three summer weeks at Maidanovo.

The Enchantress. Opera in four acts. Libretto by Shpajinsky.

Op. 61. *Mozartiana.* Suite No. 4, in four movements. First performed in Moscow, November, 1887, conducted by the composer.

Op. 62. *Pezzo Capriccioso,* for violoncello, with orchestral or piano accompaniment. First performed in Moscow, November, 1889, by Brandukoff, with the composer conducting.

Op. 63. Six songs. Dedicated to the Grand Duke Constantin.

Chorus for men's voices, *a capella.* Dedicated to the student choir of the Moscow University.

1888. January to September

Op. 64. *Symphony No. 5 (E minor)* for full orchestra. Dedicated to Ave-Lallemont of Hamburg. First performed in Petersburg, November 1888, and conducted by the composer.

Op. 65. Six songs to French words. Dedicated to Désirée Artôt.

The Nightingale, chorus for mixed voices *a capella*. Dedicated to the choir of the Petersburg Imperial Opera.

Besides these, Tchaikowsky made rough sketches for the *Overture-Fantasia, Hamlet.*

1888–1889

Orchestration of an overture by Laroche. Not published.

Op. 67. *Hamlet,* Overture-Fantasia, for full orchestra. Dedicated to Edward Grieg. Written for Tchaikowsky's friend, Lucien Guitry, the actor who had promised to play Hamlet if Tchaikowsky would write incidental music for it. Tchaikowsky had intended to write something brief, for a small orchestra, but became enthusiastic and wrote the full overture. The overture was first performed in November, 1888, in Petersburg, Tchaikowsky conducting.

Valse Scherzo, for piano. Written on commission for a musical journal.

Op. 66. *Sleeping Beauty*. Ballet in three acts with prologue. Dedicated to Vsevolojsky. First performed in Petersburg at the Marinsky Theatre, January, 1890.

1889–1890

Impromptu, for piano. Dedicated to Anton Rubinstein.

Welcome to Anton Rubinstein, chorus *a capella*. Both works performed in Petersburg, November, 1889, at a festival in honor of Rubinstein.

Pique Dame (*Queen of Spades*). Opera in three acts and seven scenes. Libretto by Modeste Tchaikowsky, with the composer's help. Subject from Pushkin's novel. First performed in Petersburg, Marinsky Theatre, December, 1890.

Besides the above, Tchaikowsky sketched his string sextet.

1890–1891

Op. 67. Music for Shakespeare's *Hamlet*. Medley of numbers taken from others of the composer's work, arranged for Lucien Guitry's benefit, February, 1891.

Three choruses *a capella*. Dedicated to Melnikoff's Free Choral Class.

Besides these, *The Nutcracker* ballet and the opera *Iolanthe* were roughly sketched.

1891–1892

Op. 78. *Voyevoda,* symphonic ballad for full orchestra, after Pushkin's theme. First performed in Moscow at Siloti's concert, conducted by Tchaikowsky. Next day the composer destroyed the score. The instrumental parts were, however, preserved by Siloti, and after Tchaikowsky's death the score was reconstructed and published by Beliayeff.

Op. 69. *Iolanthe.* Lyrical opera in one act. The subject is taken from Hertz' drama, *King René's Daughter.* Libretto by Modeste Tchaikowsky. First performed in November, 1892, at the Marinsky Theatre in Petersburg.

Op. 70. *Souvenir de Florence.* String sextet in four movements. Dedicated to the Petersburg Chamber Music Society. First performed by this society in Petersburg, November, 1892.

Op. 71. *The Nutcracker.* Fairy ballet in two acts and three scenes. Subject taken from Dumas' *Casse Noisette* which in turn was taken from Hoffman's tale. First performed, with *Iolanthe,* in December, 1892.

Besides these works, Tchaikowsky sketched two movements of the symphony which later became the *Third Piano Concerto.* Also an *Andante* and *Finale,* for piano and orchestra, which he never finished.

1892–1893

Military March, for band, dedicated to the 98th Infantry Regiment. Written on request of Tchaikowsky's first cousin, Andrew P. Tchaikowsky, colonel of this regiment.

Op. 72. Eighteen pieces for piano. Written in fifteen days at Klin.

Op. 73. Six songs to Rathaus' words. Dedicated to Figner.

Night. Vocal quartet with piano accompaniment. Words by Tchaikowsky. The music is based on Mozart's pianoforte *Fantasia No. 4.* Napravnik was Peter's guest at Maidanovo and played the piano to him frequently, to Peter's great delight. Especially the Mozart *Fantasy* pleased Peter so much that he decided to make a quartet from it.

Op. 74. *Symphony No. 6 (B minor).* Dedicated to Vladimir (Bob) Davydoff. First performed October 28th, in Petersburg, the composer conducting.

Op. 75. *Concerto No. 3* for piano and orchestra. Dedicated to Louis Diemer. This was rewritten from the symphony Tchaikowsky had composed the year before. First performed by Taneyeff in Petersburg.

Posthumous publications

Momento Lirico. Piano piece, not quite completed.

Duet, *Romeo and Juliet.* Only the voice parts had been sketched in; Taneyeff made the accompaniment from Tchaikowsky's symphonic fantasy of the same name.

Andante and Finale, for piano and orchestra. Arranged by Tchaikowsky from sketches of the symphony written in 1892. First performed by Taneyeff at Beliayeff's first Russian symphony concert in February, 1896. Taneyeff, therefore, was the first to play in public every one of Tchaikowsky's works for piano, except the *B flat minor Concerto,* which was first played by Kross.

Index

477